THE GREAT LIBERATION

THE GREAT LIBERATION

(MAHANIRVANA TANTRA)

BY

ARTHUR AVALON

GYAN

Published by

Gyan Publishing House
5, Ansari Road
Daryaganj, New Delhi-110002
Phone: 011-47034999, 9811692060
E-mail: books@gyanbooks.com

Distribution Network
gyanbooks.com
India, USA, Canada, UK, Australia

ISBN: 978-93-6280-154-8 (PB)
First Published, 1913

2nd Impression 2024

Printed at: Gyan Press, Delhi.

THE GREAT LIBERATION
Author: ARTHUR AVALON

THE GREAT LIBERATION

THE GREAT LIBERATION

(MAHĀNIRVĀNA TANTRA)

SANSKRIT TEXT WITH TRANSLATION AND COMMENTARY

BY

ARTHUR AVALON

(Third Edition)

PUBLISHERS:

GANESH & Co., (MADRAS) LTD., MADRAS—17

1953

PREFACE

THE Indian Tantras, which are numerous, constitute the Scripture (*Shāstra*) of the Kaliyuga, and as such are a voluminous source of present and practical orthodox "Hinduism". The Tantra Shāstra is, in fact, whatever be its historical origin, a development of the *Karmakāndā* (using that term in the general sense of ritual section of the scripture), promulgated to meet the needs of that age. Shiva says: "For the benefit of men of the Kali age, men bereft of energy and dependent for existence on the food they eat, the Kaula doctrine, O auspicious one! is given" (Ch. IX, verse 12). To the Tantras we must therefore look if we would understand aright both ritual, *yoga*, and *sādhanā* of all kinds as they exist to-day, as also the general principles of which these practices are but the objective expression.

Yet of all the forms of Indian Shāstra, the Tantra is that which is least known and understood, a circumstance in part due to the difficulties of its subject-matter and to the fact that the key to much of its terminology and method rests with the initiate. The present translation is, in fact, the first published in Europe of any Indian Tantra. An inaccurate version rendered in imperfect English was published in Calcutta by a Bengali editor some twelve years ago, preceded by an Introduction which displayed insufficient knowledge in respect of what it somewhat quaintly described as "the mystical and superficially technical passages" of this Tantra. A desire to attempt to do it greater justice has in part prompted its selection as the first for publication. Another reason for such selection is that this Tantra has been the subject of Indian Commentary and Bengali translation. This Tantra is, further, one which is well known and esteemed, though perhaps more highly so amongst that portion of the Indian public which favours "reformed Hinduism" than amongst some Shākta Tāntrikas, to whom, as I have been told, certain of its provisions appear to display unnecessary timidity. The former admire it on account of its noble exposition of the worship of the Supreme Brahman, and in the belief that certain of its passages absolutely discountenance the orthodox ritual. Nothing can be more mistaken than such belief, even though it be the fact that "for him who has faith in the root, of what use are the branches and leaves". This anyone will discover who reads the text. It is true that, as Ch. VII, verse 94, says: "In the purified heart, knowledge of Brahman grows," and *Brahmajnāne samutpanne krityākrityang na vidyate.* (When Brahman knowledge has arisen there is no longer distinction of what should or should not be done.) But the statement assumes the attainment of *Brahmajnāna*, and this, the Shāstra says, can be attained, not by Vedantic discussions nor mere prayer, after the manner of Protestant systems of Christian worship, but by the *Sādhanā* which is its main subject-matter. I have referred to Protestant systems, for the Catholic Church possesses an elaborate ritual and a *sādhanā* of its own which is in many points strikingly analogous to the Hindu system. The section of Tāntrikas to whom I have referred are, I believe, also in error. For the design of this Tantra appears to be, whilst conserving commonly-recognised Tāntrik principles, to secure that, as has sometimes proved to be the case, they are not abused. Pārvatī says (Ch. I, verse 67): "I fear, O Lord! that even that which Thou hast ordained for the good of men will, through them, turn out for evil."

Hitāya yāni karmāni kathitāni tvayā prabho
Manye tāni mahādeva viparītāni mānave.

It is significant, in connection with these observations, to note that this particular Tantra was chosen as the subject of commentary by Shrīmad Hariharānanda Bhāratī, the Guru of the celebrated Hindu "reformer," Rājā Ram Mohun Roy. As to this see Chapter V of "*Shakti and Shakta*".

The Tantra has been assigned by one of my informants to the division known as Vish*n*ukrāntā and the eclectic Vilāsa Sampradāya. According to the Mahāsiddhasāra it belongs to Rathakrāntā. It was first published by the Ādi-Brāhma-Samāja in 1798 Shakābda (A.D. 1876), and was printed in Bengali characters, with the notes of the Kulāvadhūta Shrīmad Hariharānanda Bhārati under the editorship of Ānandachandra Vidyāvāgīsha. The preface to this edition stated that three MSS. were consulted; one belonging to the library of the Samāja; the second supplied by Durgādāsa Chaudhurī, and the third taken from the library of Rājā Ram Mohun Roy. This text appears to be the basis of subsequent publications. It was again printed in 1888 by Shrī K*r*ish*n*a Gopāla Bhakta, since when there have been several editions with Bengali translations, including that of Shrī Prasanna Kumāra Shāstrī. The late Pandit Jīvānanda Vidyāsāgara published an edition in Devanāgara character, with the notes of Hariharānanda; and the Venkateshvara Press at Bombay have issued another in similar character with a Hindī translation.

The translation published is that of the first part only. It is commonly thought (and was so stated by the author of the Calcutta edition in English to which I have referred) that the second portion is lost. This is, however, not so, though copies of the complete Tantra are rare enough. The full text exists in manuscript, and I hope that an opportunity may some day be given of publishing a translation of it. I came across a complete manuscript some two years ago in the possession of a Nepalese Pandit. The exact date of the MSS. I forget. It was about Shakābdā 1,300 or say some 500 years old. He would, however, only permit me to make a copy of his manuscript on the condition that the *Shatkarma* Mantras were not published. For, as he said, virtue not being a condition precedent for the acquisition of *siddhi* in, that is, power to work, such Mantras, their publication might enable the evilly disposed to harm others, a crime which, he added, was, in his own country, where the Tantra Shāstra was current punishable by the civil power. I was unable to persuade him even with the observation that the mere publication of the Mantra without knowledge of what is called the *Prayoga* (which cannot be learned of books) would in any case be ineffectual. I could not give an undertaking which would have involved the publication of a mutilated text, and the reader must therefore for the present be content with a translation of the first part of the Tantra, which is generally known, and has, as stated, been several times printed. The incident has further value than the direct purpose for which I have told it. There are some to whom "the Tantra," is "nothing but black magic," and all its followers are "black magicians". This is of course absurd. In this connection I cannot avoid interposing the observation that certain practices are described in Tantra which, though they are alleged to have the results described therein, yet exist "for delusion." The true attitude of the higher Tāntrika is illustrated by the action of the

Paṇḍit who, if he disappointed my expectations, at any rate by his refusal afforded an answer to these too general allegations.

The second portion of the manuscript in his possession contained over double the number of Shlokas to be found in the first part here published.

The edition which has been used for the translation is that (now out of print) edited and published at Calcutta by Shrī *Krishna* Gopāla Bhakta in Chaitra 1295 Bengali era (April, 1888), with Commentary of Shrīmad Hariharānanda Bhāratī, and with additional notes by the learned and lately deceased Pandit Jaganmohana Tarkālaṁkāra. A new edition of the same work has been published with further notes by the latter's son, Pandit Jnānendranātha Tantraratna since deceased.

This valuable Commentary alone is not, however, suitable for the general reader, for it assumes a certain amount of knowledge on his part which he does not possess. I have accordingly, whilst availing myself of its aid, written my own commentary. For the first edition I also wrote an Introduction explaining certain matters and terms referred to or presupposed by the text which, as they required a somewhat more extended treatment, could not be conveniently dealt with in the footnotes. Some of the matters there explained were, though common and fundamental, seldom accurately defined. Nothing, therefore, was lost by a re-statement of them with an intention to serve such accuracy. Other matters were of a special character, either not generally known or misunderstood. The Introduction, however, did not profess to be an exhaustive treatment of that with which it dealt. On the contrary, it was but an extended note written to help some way towards a better understanding of the text by the ordinary reader. Since however the date of the first edition I have published a number of works on the Shāstra both of a popular and technical nature. These more fully deal with the matters treated of in the former Introduction which is therefore no longer needed.[1] To the reader who would understand this work I would recommend the books "*Shakti and Shākta*" where in a popular manner the author has explained the doctrine and ritual of the Shākta Tantras of which the present volume is one; "*The Garland of Letters*" (Var*n*amālā) dealing with "Sound" (Shabda) and the technique of Mantra which forms so important a part of the Tantrashāstra that its other and common name is Mantra-Shāstra; and the "*Serpent Power*," which has as its subject Yoga and in particular that portion of it which is done by the arousing of Ku*nd*alinī Shakti famous in all Tantras. The reader who desires to come into the closest contact with the Indian spirit in these matters will find what he wants in the two volumes "*Principles of Tantra*"[2] under which title I have published a trans lation of the Tantratattva by Pandit Shivachandra Vidyār*n*ava. Other works on the Tantrashāstra which I have published will be found in the advertisements at the end of this book. Further ritual detail is given in the English Introductions to my series of "Tantrik Texts". There are, however, some matters in the *Shāstra* or its accompanying oral tradition which the reader must, and if disposed thereto will, find out for himself. This, too, is implied by the saying in this Tantra that it is by merit acquired in previous births that the mind inclines to Kaula doctrine (Chapter VII, verse 99). However this may be, no one will understand the *Shāstra* who starts his inquiry with a mind burdened with the current prejudices agaist it, whatever be the truth some

[1] Since published as "Introduction to Tantra Shastra" 2nd Edn. 1952.

[2] Now published in one volume 2nd Edn. 1952.

of them may possess by reason of actual abuse of Shâstric principles. I have taken advantage of the present edition which supersedes the last to correct mistakes and to improve the translation generally. Working in a new field it is difficult to escape error.

The Sanskrit text[1] is in preparation and when ready will form Vol. XIII of the series of Tantrik Texts issued with the aid of Indian Pandits under my general editorship.

In conclusion, I wish to thank my Indian friends for the aid they have given me in the preparation of this and other kindred works, and to whom I am indebted for much information gathered during many pleasant hours which we have spent together in the study of a subject of common interest to them and myself. The Tantras generally are written in comparatively simple Sanskrit. For their rendering, however, a working knowledge of their terminology and ritual is required, which can be only fully found in those to whom it is familiar through race, upbringing, and environment, and in whom there is still some regard for their ancient inheritance. As for others, they must learn to see through the Indian eye of knowledge until their own have been trained to its lines of vision. In this way we shall be in the future spared some of the erroneous presentments of Indian beliefs common in the past and even now too current.

Fagernes Valdres ARTHUR AVALON
17th August, 1927

[1] Now Included in this volume.

CONTENTS

CHAPTER I

THE LIBERATION OF BEINGS

CHAPTER II

THE WORSHIP OF BRAHMAN

CHAPTER III

THE WORSHIP OF BRAHMAN (*Contd.*)

CHAPTER IV

THE WORSHIP OF SHAKTI

CHAPTER V

MANTRAS AND PURIFICATION

CHAPTER VI

MANTRAS AND RITES

CHAPTER VII

HYMN AND AMULET

CHAPTER VIII

CASTES AND ĀSHRAMAS

CHAPTER IX

THE TEN SACRAMENTS

CHAPTER X

RITES AND INITIATION

CHAPTER XI

EXPIATORY ACTS

CHAPTER XII

THE ETERNAL DHARMA

CHAPTER XIII

INSTALLATION OF THE DEVATĀ

CHAPTER XIV

CONSECRATION AND AVADHŪTAS

THE GREAT LIBERATION

(MAHĀNIRVĀNA TANTRA)[1]

CHAPTER I

THE LIBERATION OF BEINGS

THE enchanting summit of the Lord of Mountains,[2] resplendent with all its various jewels, clad with many a tree and many a creeper, melodious with the song of many a bird, scented with the fragrance of all the season's flowers, most beautiful, fanned by soft, cool, and perfumed breezes, shadowed by the still shade of stately trees;[3] where cool groves resound with the sweet-voiced songs of troops of

[1] Bhāratī says that Sadāshiva of limitless power (Ameyashakti) after having framed the Six Āmnāyas (see Woodroffe's "Shakti and Shakta") was moved by the Mother, the Ādishakti, to reveal this Tantra which is mighty and the Bridge across the Ocean of Kula (Kulavārirāshi). When the Kali age, the uprooter of all acts of merit and the instigator of endless hateful sins, commenced then Pārvatī, the Mother, became anxious for the salvation of men who are averse to meditation upon the Supreme (Paramātmā) and other religious practices and on the other hand are addicted to sinful acts. She therefore questioned Shiva who abides on Mount Kailāsa concerning the means whereby they may be saved.

[2] Mount Kailāsa, the Paradise of Shiva. Esoterically, the Sahasrāra Padma (see Tripurā-sāra, cited in Bhāskararāya's Commentary on Lalitā-sahasra-nāma, v. 17). The Kulārnava says that there is Kailāsa where His worshippers are gathered. The first few lines on this page are somewhat freely rendered.

[3] Literally; covered by the shadows of great trees, the shadows of which are motionless: that is, the trees are so great and so close to one another that there is perpetual shade.

Apsarā,[1] and in the forest depths flocks of Kokila[2] maddened with passion sing; where (Spring)[3] Lord of the Seasons with his followers ever abides—(the Lord of Mountains, (Kailāsa); peopled by troops of[4] Siddha,[5] Chāraṇa,[6] Gandharva,[7] and Gāṇapatya[8] (1-5). It was there that Pārvatī,[9] finding Shiva, Her gracious Lord, in mood serene, with obeisance bent low and for the benefit of all the worlds questioned Him, the Silent Deva,[10] Lord of all things movable and immovable,[11] the ever Beneficent[12] and ever

---

[1] Beautiful and voluptuous Deva-yoni (*vide post*) of Indra's heaven, wives of the Gandharvas, produced at the churning of the ocean.

[2] Or Koel, the black or Indian cuckoo (*Cuculus Indicus*).

[3] Vasanta, whose followers are the Koel bird (*supra*), the vernal breeze, the black bee, etc. (see Raghuvamsha of Kālidāsa, chap. ix, verses 24 *et seq.*).

[4] Hence the Mountain Kailāsa—the residence of Shiva—is called Gaṇa-parvata (frequented by troops of Spirits), because peopled and surrounded by enormous hosts of attendant Spirits and Deva-yoni begotten by the Deva (Devas eva yoniḥ—nidāna-bhūtaḥ—yasya), who are, according to the definition of the Amara-kosha, Vidyādhara, Apsarā, Yaksha, Rākshasa, Gandharva, Kinnara, Pishācha, Guhyaka, Siddha, and Bhūta.

[5] Beneficent Deva-yoni of great purity, possessing the eight magical powers (Siddhi), inhabiting, according to some, the Bhuvar-loka. To them (according to the Gāyatrī Tantra, chap. x) Gaṇesha first preached the Tantras after he himself had received them from the mouth of Shiva.

[6] Celestial dancers, singers, and bards or panegyrists of the Devas.

[7] Deva-yoni, who, according to the Vishṇu Purāṇa, were sons of Brahmā, "born imbibing melody"; celestial musicians and choristers, who play and sing at the banquets of the Devas, belonging, together with the Apsarās—their wives—to Indra's heaven.

[8] The Vināyakas. Aspects and followers of Gaṇesha, one of whose names is Gaṇa-pati.

[9] Spouse, or Shakti, of Shiva, so called as being the Daughter of Parvata, the Mountain (Himavat, Himālaya, that which has, or is, the abode of snow). Hence She is called Giri-jā, Giri-sutā, Haimavatī.

[10] Because then observing the vow of silence (Mauna-vrata). Deva = luminous One. Devam = Dīptimantam (Bhāratī).

[11] The organic and inorganic world. He is Charācharajagadguru, that is, the Father (Pitā) of all that move and are motionless.

[12] Sadāshiva the Ever Gracious One from whom all that is good and auspicious issues.

Blissful One,[1] the nectar of Whose mercy abounds as a great ocean, Whose body is Pure Sattva Guna,[2] He Who is white as camphor and the Jasmine flower,[3] the Omnipresent One, Whose raiment is space[4] itself, Lord of the poor and the beloved and loving Master of all Yogīs,[5]

---

[1] Sadānanda: He who is All-bliss and who is the delight of the good (Sat).

[2] Shuddha-sattva-maya—that is, whose body is predominently composed of the first of the three Gunas or qualities in things, Sattva, Rajas, and Tamas. And so Shiva is stated to be Sāttvika. The Gunas are never disassociated. Rajas and Tamas are always operating in relation to Sattva but here Sattva is predominant (Sattva-pradhāna). In the experience of Parameshvara during cosmic life all is presented (this is Sattva). Sattva goes on (this is the effective force of Rajas which merely keeps Sattva going on *as such*). Hence Sattva is not strained or pierced by Rajas. Tamas operates as a tendency only but not as an effective force because nothing is veiled or suppressed in Īshvara Experience. He is Sarvajna and Sarvavit. Still everything may be veiled during Laya or Cosmic Sushupti, so that there is a tendency to veiling. Here, Shiva is referred to as the Supreme Lord, in His Sattva aspect, called Sadāshiva, the Cause of Release, the Conferrer of Blessing (Anugrahada), the ever Blissful One (*vide post*), and (later) Jnānamaya. Shiva, in His Sāttvika quality, is also called *Mrida* (Happiness) in the Mahimnah-stava. He has other aspects (see *post*).

[3] Kunda (*Jasminum multiflorum* or *pubescens*). Similar descriptions of the Deva to that which follows are found in almost all the Tantras, as in Shāradā-tilaka (chap. xviii). The Nibandha Tantra describes Him as of a vermilion colour (Sindūra-varna): "I salute Isha, gem-crowned, Whose head-ornament is the shining beauty of the Moon, with smiling lotus-face, from Whose forehead an eye looks forth; Whose body is beautified by bright ornament; Who, holding a trident and *Tangka*, places the palm of His hand on the high and rounded breast of His Beloved (Spouse), Who Herself places one hand on His left thigh and holds a red night-lotus (Kuvalaya) in the other." The night lotus, "the wife of the moon," is also generally white.

[4] Exoterically, he is represented naked as the Yogīs are. In the esoteric sense he is Digambara, or "clothed with space," in the sense that He is Omnipresent. The infinity of space or the points of the compass clothe Him.

[5] Ascetic followers of, and adepts in, the Yoga doctrine. Shiva, by his great austerities, is the Lord and Exemplar of all ascetics. He is Yogīndra. Yoga is Paramātmachintana (Bhāratī). Yogi-vallabha which is rendered "beloved of Yogīs" may also mean "He whose loved ones are the Yogīs".

Whose coiled and matted hair[1] is wet with the spray of Gaṅgā[2] and (of Whose naked body) ashes are the adornment[3] only; the passionless One[4] Whose neck is garlanded with snakes and skulls of men, the three-eyed One,[5] Lord of the three worlds,[6] with one hand wielding the trident and with the other bestowing blessings[7]; easily appeased, Whose very substance is unconditioned Knowledge;[8] the Bestower of eternal Liberation,[9] unconditioned,[10] from whom

---

[1] Jaṭā, as worn by ascetics in serpentine coils (Jaṭājūṭa).

[2] Hence He is called Gaṅgā-dhara. When the Ganges descended from heaven He intercepted it by His head, so that the earth might not be crushed by the weight of the falling stream. It is said that the Ganges was first held in the water-jar (Kamaṇḍalu) of Brahmā, then in the hair of Shiva, and lastly in the body of Jahnu, whence it is called the Jāhnavī (see Shangkarāchārya's Gaṅgāshṭakam in "Hymns to the Goddess").

[3] Vibhūti-bhūshita, which Bhāratī translates as in text, but, as pointed out (ed. Bhakta), Vibhūti may here also refer to the eight Siddhis which Shiva possesses, *viz.*, Aṇimā, Laghimā, Prāpti, Prākāmya, Mahimā, Īshitva, Vashitva, Kāmāvasāyitā. Vibhūti is also halo or aura.

[4] Shānta (the tranquil) and Atīta (the transcendent), are aspects of Shiva. In man Shānta is he who has controlled his Antaḥkaraṇa. As Shruti says: "This fire is verily Rudra Himself; of Him there are two bodies, one fierce and the other gentle" (Taittirīya saṁhitā, 5-7-3).

[5] Tri-lochana: one eye (symbolically the inner eye of wisdom) being in the forehead. From this eye flashed the light which consumed the body of the Deva of Love—Kāma-deva—and at the expiration of a Kalpa, the Devas. According to Arrian, the Indian Bacchus (Bhaga, or Shiva) was called Thriambus, possibly a corruption of Tryambaka, "three-eyed". The Devī is called Tryambakī, because She is the Mother of the Three—Brahmā, Vishṇu, and Rudra. And this also is the esoteric meaning of Tryambaka as applied to Shiva, the "Father of the Three" (see the Mṛityunjaya-mantra, chap. v, 210).

[6] Tri-loka, *i.e.* The heavenly, earthly and nether worlds.

[7] Trishūla-vara-dhāriṇam which Bhāratī says may also mean "He who carries the excellent Trishūla" (trident).

[8] Jnāna-maya, that is who is, Samvit itself. Jnāna is here, according to Hariharānanda, experience of the true nature of all that is (Tattvataḥ samasta-padārthāvabodhaḥ).

[9] Kaivalya-phala-dāyaka: the giver of the fruit of Sādhanā and Yoga which is Kaivalya or Videha-mukti the bodiless Liberation or Nirvāṇa of the Advaitins.

[10] Nirvikalpaḥ=Nirgato vikalpo vividhā kalpanā yasmāt; that is He who is free of all Kalpanā the dual experience in which there is "this" and "that".

comes no fear,[1] Changeless, Stainless,[2] One without defect,[3] the Benefactor of all, and the Deva of all Devas[4] (6-10).

Shrī Pārvatī said :

O Deva of the Devas, Lord of the world, Jewel of Mercy, my Husband, Thou art my Lord, on Thee I am ever dependent and to Thee I am ever obedient. Nor can I say ought without Thy word. If Thou hast affection for me, I crave to lay before Thee that which passes in my mind. Who else but Thee, O Great Lord,[5] in the three worlds is able to solve these doubts of mine, Thou Who knowest all and all the Scriptures (11-13).

Shrī Sadāshiva[6] said :

What is that Thou sayest, O Thou Great Wise One[7] and Beloved of My heart, I will tell Thee anything, be it ever so bound in mystery, even that which should not be spoken of before Ganesha[8] and Skanda[9] Commander of the

---

[1] Nirātangka. There is no need to fear Him.

[2] Niranjana (Anjana=Collyrium), which, however, Hariharānanda Bhāratī translates as "incomprehensible to the ignorant". The Shabda-kalpa-druma gives the definition as Nirgatam anjanam iva ajnānam yatra (one in whom no ignorance like a black stain exists): "the perfect Knower".

[3] Nirāmaya. He is Health itself.

[4] Devadeva=Devesha: that is He rules over the Devas, Indra and others.

[5] Maheshvara, or Great Lord, and Supreme Person.

[6] It is Shiva, "the Ever-Auspicious," and Mahāshūnya who here speaks, voluntarily assuming form for the benefit of His devotees (see also verse 8 of Ānanda-laharī of Shangkarāchāryya, and verses 42-48 of Sureshvarāchārya's Mānasollāsa, and Bhāskararāya, Commentary on Lalitā-sahasra-nāma, v. 174).

[7] Mahā-prājne.

[8] and [9] Both sons of Shiva, the first being the elephant-headed Deva (for Dhyāna, see Mantra-mahodadhi, chap. ii), who—according to the Gāyatrī Tantra (chap. x)—wrote down the Tantras at the dictation of Shiva; and the second Kumāra, or Kārttikeya, the War God and Leader of the celestial army, who was begotten by Shiva at the request of the Devas to destroy the Demon Tādakāsura, and so called because brought up by the six celestial Krittikās. In begetting

Hosts of Heaven. What is there in all the three worlds which should be concealed from Thee? For Thou, O Devi, art My very Self. There is no difference between Me and Thee.[1] Thou too art omnipresent. What is it then that Thou knowest not that Thou questionest like unto one who knoweth nothing (14-16).

The pure [2] Pārvatī, gladdened at hearing the words of the Deva, bending low made obeisance and thus questioned Shangkara [3] (17).

Kārttikeya Pārvatī was unable to retain Shiva's seed, which was then thrown into Fire (hence called Kaumāra-teja*h*, see ch. vi, 148 notes), Who, unable to keep it, threw it into Gamgā, who in turn threw it into a reed-forest, where Kārttikeya was born. Hence he is called "Reed-born" (Shara-janmā); and because he shamed Kāma-deva by his beauty, he is called Kumāra (see Matsya Purā*n*a). The reason why these two are referred to is to show the greatness of the mystery revealed. Beloved and powerful as they are they yet know it not.

[1] Mama rūpā'si devi tvam na bhedo'sti tvayā mama: for in their ultimate ground both Shiva and Shakti are one. The former is the static aspect of the Supreme Consciousness (Samvid) and the latter its kinetic aspect as Creative Power. Power (Shakti) and Possessor of power (Shakti-mān) are one. It is a commonplace of the Shākta Tantras that there is no Shiva without Shakti nor Shakti without Shiva. In the Sanat-kumāra Sam., speaking of devotion to Pārvatī, it is said: "Janārdana (Vish*n*u) is thus in the form of Devī as well as in His own form, for the husband and wife, being one, the only One is worshipped as two." Rūpa is form and function. Rūpyate rūpakriyāvishish*t*ā vidhīyate, iti, rūpā. They are one in the ground and one in the manifestation. Some read Matsvarūpā for *M*ama rūpā, that is, my self.

[2] Sādhvī, fem. of Sādhu, good, virtuous, pure. The Devī-bhāgavata Purā*n*a says: "Thou art praised as Sādhvī (the virtuous One) on account of unequalled fidelity (to Thy Lord)." Also Lalitā-sahasra-nāma, v. 48, where the Commentator Bhāskararāya cites the Āchārya (Saundaryya-laharī), 96: "How many poets share the wife of Brahmā? Cannot every one by means of wealth become the lord of Shrī (wife of Vish*n*u)? But, O Virtuous One (Sādhvī)! First among faithful women, Thy breasts are untouched save by Mahā-deva, and not even by the paste of Kuruvaka" (made of the leaves of the red amaranth, and used to redden the cheeks, breasts, palms, and soles of Indian women).

[3] Shiva the "Blissgiver" is as Hara the creator; as Shangkara protector, and as Rudra, destroyer.

Shrī Ādyā[1] said:

O Bhagavan![2] Lord of all, Greatest among those who are versed in Dharma,[3] Thou in former ages in Thy mercy[4] didst through Brahmā[5] reveal the four Vedas[6] which are the propagators of all Dharma[7] and which ordain the rules of life for all the varying castes[8] of men and for the different stages[9] of their lives (18-19). In the First Age,[10] men

[1] Pārvatī, so called as being the Ādyā, or Primordial Shakti, or Power of the Deva symbolised as Her Spouse.

[2] Bhagavan—that is, one possessed of the six Aishvaryyas: Shrī (auspiciousness), Vīryya (power), Jnāna (wisdom), Vairāgya (dispassion), Kīrti (glory), and Māhātmya (greatness). See Wilson's *Vishnu Purāna*, vol. v, p. 212. All these are in the Devī, Who is hence called Bhagavatī (see Devī-bhāgavata Purāna, Shakti-rahasya, Bhāskararāya, *loc. cit* v. 65).

[3] Law of Form and rule of right living.

[4] Appeal is made to the pity of the Lord so that as he had liberated the men of the Satya and Tretā and Dvāpara ages (Yuga) by the teachings of Shruti, Smriti and Purāna so He may save the men of the Kali age by revealing this Tantra.

[5] Brahmāntaryāminā, that is, He as the Supreme Brahman inspired Brahmā. The Sacred Scripture of the Hindus was communicated by the Supreme to, and revealed by, Brahmā, called in the Shrīmad bhāgavata "the Primeval Poet". The Shrīmadbhāgavata says: "Let the sage be pleased with Me, Who am the remembrancer of the sublime Shruti unto the mind of Aja (Brahmā), Who sent Brahmā, from Whose mouth issued the Word (Sarasvatī)" (Book II, chap. iv, verse 22). In the text Shiva is thus spoken of as the Supreme. The Veda is Brahman. Brahmā was not its Author, but Revealer (Brihannīla Tantra, chap. iv). It came out of Brahman as His breathing (Yāmala Tantra).

[6] *Rigveda*, Yajurveda, Sāmaveda, and Atharvaveda, which are breathed forth by Brahman (Brihadāranyaka Upanishad, chap. xi, 1, 4, v. 10). These are known as Shruti.

[7] Sarvadharmopabrimhitāh.

[8] Varna.

[9] Āshrama.

[10] Krita, or Satya Yuga. This and the following verses deal with the characteristics of the different Yugas, or Ages.

by the practice of Yoga[1] and Yajna[2] prescribed by Thee were virtuous and pleasing to Devas and Pitris[3] (20). By the study of the Vedas, by Dhyāna and Tapas,[4] and the conquest of the senses, by acts of mercy[5] and charity[6] men were of exceeding power[7] and courage,[8] industry[9] and prowess,[10] adherents of the true Dharma,[11] good[12] and truthful,[13] and, mortals though they were, they were yet like Devas and went to the abode of the Devas (21, 22). Kings then were faithful to their engagements and were ever concerned

---

[1] Yoga is defined in c[illegible] e 123, as the union of the individual and the Supreme [illegible] ianor aikyam). *Cf.* Patanjali—Yogah chitta-vritti-nirodl[illegible] idātilaka, ch. xxv.

[2] In a particular sens[illegible] l in a general sense worship.

[3] Mean the human A[illegible] erally up to the seventh generation, to whom Pinda and water are offered, and whose food is Svadhā; and then the lunar Ancestors of the human race. From Brahmā, the first Pitā, issued Marīchi, Atri, Angiras, Pulastya, Pulaha, Kratu, Prachetas, the mental sons, and thence the Agnishvāttāh, Saumyāh, Havishmantah, Ushmapāh, Ājyapāh.

[4] Meditation and austerities. The term Tapas is also used in a very wide sense such as here observance of the Chāndrāyāna and other rites which involve mortification of the body for self-discipline and worship generally. It is of three kinds, bodily (Sharīra), by speech (Vāchika), and in mind (Mānasa). Each of these again may be Sāttvika, Rājasika or Tāmasika. Dhyāna is meditation on the supreme Spirit (Paramātma-chintana).

[5] Dayā: that is the desire to relieve the distress of others without being moved thereto by hope of reward.

[6] Dāna is gift to the deserving of money and other things honestly acquired by the giver, that is, they were not covetous.

[7] Mahābalāh. Amara defines Bala = Sthaulya-sāmarthya-sainyeshu, that is, material or physical power or soldiery.

[8] Mahāvīryyāh or valour of which Medinī says: Vīryyam prabhāvo shukre cha tejah-sāmarthyayorapi.

[9] Mahāsattvaparākramāh: Sattva = Vyavasāya or industry.

[10] Parākrama = Shauryya, might or prowess.

[11] Satyadharmaparāh.

[12] Sādhavah which Bhāratī says = Svasvadharmavartinah, that is, they followed their respective Dharmas.

[13] Satyasangkalpāh.

with the protection of their people, upon whose wives they were wont to look as if upon their mothers, and whose children they regarded as their very own (23). The people, too, did then look upon a neighbour's property as if it were mere lumps of clay, and, with devotion to their Dharma,[1] kept to the path of righteousness (24). There were then no liars, none who were selfish, thievish, malicious, foolish, none who were evil-minded, envious, wrathful, gluttonous, or lustful, but all were good of heart and of ever blissful mind. Land then yielded in plenty all kinds of grain, clouds showered seasonable rains, cows gave abundant milk, and trees were weighted with fruits (25-27). No untimely death there was, nor famine nor sickness. Men were ever cheerful, prosperous and healthy, and endowed with all qualities of beauty and brilliance. Women were chaste and devoted to their husbands. Brāhma*n*as, Ks*h*atriyas, Vaishyas, and Shūdras[2] kept to and followed the Dharma[3] of their respective castes in their worship and attained the final Liberation (28-29).

After the K*r*ita[4] Age had passed away, Thou didst in the Tretā Age[5] perceive Dharma to be in disorder, and that men were no longer able by Vedic rites to accomplish their desires. For men, through their anxiety and perplexity, were unable to perform these rites in which much trouble had to be overcome, and for which much preparation had to be made.[6] In constant distress of mind they were

[1] Satyadharmaparā*h*.

[2] The four var*n*as, or castes.

[3] See p. 7, n. 3. They used to worship Parameshvara according to their respective Dharmas or in other practices suited to each of these castes.

[4] The First, or Satya Yuga.

[5] The Second Age.

[6] *E.g.*, Austerities which accompany the singing of the Sāmaveda and the Soma-yajna—the K*r*ichchhra-prāyashchitta, the Ati-k*r*ichchhra-prāyashchitta, and the K*r*ichchhra, and the like.

neither able to perform nor yet were willing to abandon the rites (30-32).

Having observed this, Thou didst make known on earth the Smriti Scripture[1] which explains the meaning of the Vedas, and thus delivered from sin, which is cause of all pain, sorrow, and sickness, men too feeble for the practice of Tapas[2] and the study of the Vedas. For men in this terrible ocean of the world,[3] who is there but Thee to be their Cherisher, Protector, Saviour, their fatherly Benefactor, and Lord? (33-34).

Then, in the Dvāpara Age,[4] when men abandoned the good works prescribed in the Smritis, and were deprived of one half of Dharma[5] and were afflicted by ills of mind and body, they were yet again saved by Thee, through the instructions of the Saṁhitās[6] and other religious lore (35-36).[7]

---

[1] Such as the Dharmashāstra of Manu and other books on family and social duty prescribing for Pravritti-Dharma as the Upanishads reveal Nivritti-Dharma. Each of the four ages has its special Shāstra, differing presentments of the Truth revealed by Shruti: in Satya Yuga, Shruti; in Treta, Smriti; in Dvāpara, Purāna; in Kaliyuga the Āgama or Tantra Shāstra. See Tārā-pradīpa, ch. I, and Introduction to "Principles of Tantra".

[2] *Ibid.* and *ante* p. 8, n. 4.

[3] Ghora-sangsāra-sāgara—that is, the world is an ocean, in the waters of which are things of terror and evil, causing sorrow and pain. For a safe crossing there is need of the guidance of the Lord, and so in the Stotra in chap. iii, verse 63, He is called the "Vessel of Safety in the Ocean of Being".

[4] The Third, or Dvāpara Yuga.

[5] That is, had but one-half of the religious merit of the First Age.

[6] The term literally means collection and varies as Tarkālangkāra says according to the age to which it is applied. Thus in Tretā it means Manu and other Smritis, in Dvāpara the Purānas and in Kali the Āgamas, Nigamas and 64 Tantras for each of the Krāntās.

[7] The Purānas and the like.

Now the sinful Kali Age[1] is upon them, when Dharma[2] is destroyed, an Age full of evil customs and deceit. Men pursue evil ways. The Vedas have lost their power, the Sm*r*itis are forgotten, and many of the Purā*n*as,[3] which contain stories[4] of the past, and show the many ways (which lead to Liberation), will, O Lord! be destroyed. Men will become averse from religious rites, without restraint, maddened with pride, ever given over to sinful acts, lustful, gluttonous, cruel, heartless, harsh of speech, deceitful, short-lived, poverty-stricken, harassed by sickness and sorrow, ugly, feeble, low, stupid, mean, and addicted to mean habits, companions of the base, thievish, calumnious, malicious, quarrelsome, depraved, cowards, and ever-ailing,[5] devoid of all sense of shame and sin, shameless seducers of others' wives.[6] Vipras will live like the

---

[1] The Fourth, or worst of the Ages. It is for this age that the Tantra Shāstra is prescribed. So it is said in the Kulārnava Tantra.

K*r*ite shrutyudito dharmas tretāyāng sm*r*iti-sambhava*h*.

Dvāpare tu purānokta*h* kalāvāgamasammata*h*.

In the Satya or K*r*ita Age Dharma is as taught in Shruti. In Tretā Sm*r*iti is followed. The Dharma of the Dvāpara Age is as spoken of in the Purā*n*as and in the Kali Age it is as approved in the Āgama. That is these are the respective Scriptures for the Ages, differing presentments of the means for attainment of the one Truth which all Ages seek.

[2] See *ante*, p. 7, n. 3.

[3] Sacred Books of the Hindus.

[4] Itihāsa (histories).

[5] In Shrīmad-bhāgavata (chap. i, verse 10) it is said: "Verily, O Righteousness, in the Kali Age men are generally short-lived, indolent, of short understanding, unfortunate, and afflicted." On which Vishvanātha Chakravartin's gloss is: "Men in this age are generally short-lived, yet, if they live a little longer, they care not to know about the Supreme Being. Where persons are somewhat active in this respect, yet they are very short of understanding, and therefore unable to understand the nature of the Supreme Being. Even if they be intelligent and endeavour to understand such things, they are unfortunate, and fail to secure the company of righteous men; and even if they do they are subject to disease, pain, and sorrow" (ed. Mahendranāth Chatterjee, p. 84).

[6] That is devoid of the sense of the depravity in so doing Pā*sh*a*nd*a: followers of Non-Vaidik sects.

Shūdras,[1] and whilst neglecting their own Sandhyā[2] will yet officiate at the sacrifices of the low.[3] They will be greedy, given over to wicked and sinful acts, liars, hypocrites, ignorant, deceitful, mere hangers-on of others, the sellers of their daughters,[4] degraded,[5] averse to all Tapas and Vrata.[6] They will be false in doctrine and practice, and yet think themselves wise. They will be without faith or devotion,[7] and will do Japa[8] and Pūjā[8] with no other end than to dupe the people. They will eat unclean food and follow evil customs, they will serve and eat the food of the Shūdras, be dependent on others[9] and lust after low women,[10] and will be wicked and ready to barter for money even their own wives to the low. In short, the only sign that they are Brāhmanas will be the thread[11] they wear. Observing no rule in eating or drinking or in

[1] The lowest caste. Vipras are Brāhma*n*as. (*Veda-pāthād bhaved viprah.*)

[2] Sandhyā-vandana, for Sandhyā is also a Devī. The prayers said thrice daily by the Brāhma*n*a.

[3] A-yājya-yājaka. Ayājya is a person for whom by reason of his habits in life religious rites cannot be performed, and incompetent to employ a Brāhma*n*a. A superior Brāhma*n*a will not perform sacrifices in their houses. Degraded (Patita) Brāhma*n*as do so.

[4] That is, demanding money for giving their daughters (or sons) in marriage.

[5] Vrātya: one fallen from his Dharma. One who is ignorant of the Gāyatrī and has not been invested with the sacred thread before completion of this sixteenth year.

[6] A part of the ritual called Naimittika Karma.

[7] Shraddhā-bhakti-parāngmukha, that is, devoid of belief in the Vedas.

[8] Recitation of Mantra and worship.

[9] Bh*r*itakā*h* = Bhara*n*āyatta-jīvanā*h*, *i.e.*, dependent on others for their support.

[10] B*r*ish*a*lī-rati-kāmukā*h*: a B*r*ish*a*lī is a low Shūdra woman, with usually strong animal passions.

[11] That is, the Yajna-sūtra, or sacrificial thread. Brāhma*n*ya-chihnam etāvat kevalam sūtra-dhāra*n*am.

other matters, scoffing at the Dharma Scriptures, no thought of pious speech ever so much as entering their minds, they will be but bent upon the injury of the good (37-50).

By Thee also have been spoken for the good and Liberation of men the Tantras, a mass of Āgamas and Nigamas,[1] which bestow both Enjoyment and Liberation,[2] containing Mantras[3] and Yantras[4] and rules as to the Sādhana[5] of both Devīs and Devas. By Thee, too, have been described many forms of Nyāsa,[6] such as those called *Srishti*, Sthiti (and Samhāra).[7] By Thee, again, have been

[1] See Introduction to Author's "Principles of Tantra". The Āgama is that form of Tantra in which Shiva is the Guru and the Devī the Shis*h*ya (disciple), whilst in the Nigama the converse is the case. Ga*n*esha wrote down both these and gave them to the Siddhas. Sometimes the two terms are used in the same sense.

[2] Tantrā*n*i bhukti-mukti-karā*n*i. Bhoga, as enjoyment, is of five kinds: pleasant sound (Shabda), pleasure of touch (Sparsha), the sight of beautiful things (Rūpa), the pleasure arising from the faculties of taste (Rasa), and smell (Gandha). The Tantra gives both Enjoyment and Liberation.

[3] See "Shakti and Shākta".

[4] Diagrams used for worship, as to which see *ibid.* Kaulāvalī Tantra says:

"Yantram mantra-mayam proktam, mantrātmā devataiva hi,
Dehātmanor yathā bhedo, yantra-devatayos tathā.

(The substance of Yantra is Mantra; the Devatā is Mantra. The distinction between Yantra and Devatā is of that between the body and the Ātmā or Self). As to the great Shrī Yantra of which the Yoginī-h*ri*daya says (Ch. I): "When the Supreme Shakti of Her own will assumes the form of the Universe and sees Her own becoming then the Shrīchakra (Yantra) comes into being." See Introduction to Tantrarāja in my Tantrik Texts.

[5] Ritual worship, etc., see as to all the above "Shakti and Shākta," and "Garland of Letters".

[6] A rite, as to which see *Ibid.*

[7] Antar-māt*ri*kā-nyāsa, which consists in mentally placing the Māt*ri*kās in the six Chakras, is called Sthiti (existence, maintenance) Nyāsa. Bāhya-māt*ri*kā-nyāsa is of two kinds—the external placing by voice and hand of the letters of the alphabet from A to K*sh*a, which is called *Srishti* (creation) Nyāsa; and the placing of letters in the reverse order from K*sh*a to A, is called Saṁhāra (dissolution) Māt*ri*kā.

described the various seated positions[1] (of Yoga), such as that of the "tied"[2] and "loosened" lotus;[3] the Pashu, Vīra, and Divya classes of men,[4] (the knowledge of which, leads to the attainment of Siddhi in the Mantras of the Devatās[5] (51-52). And yet again it is Thou Who hast made known in a thousand ways rites relating to the worship with woman,[6] and the rites which are done with the use of skulls,[7] a

---

[1] Āsanas are positions in Yoga practice, as to which see Arthur Avalon's "Serpent Power".

[2] Baddha-padmāsana.

[3] Mukta-padmāsana.

[4] This refers to the three characteristic dispositions of men—Pashu-bhāva, Vīra-bhāva, Divya-bhāva—as to which see "Shakti and Shākta". "Tarkālangkāra refers the reader to Kaulāvalī (p. 84) Hara-tattvadīdhiti (p. 864) and Prā*n*ato*shi*n*ī* (p. 544, 2nd Ed.), also to Kaulīkārchanadīpikā. The Bhāvachū*d*āma*n*i and Sarvollāsa give these distinctions in greater detail.

[5] Devatā-mantrasiddhidā*h*, that is, grant Siddhi or mastery in the Mantras of the Devatās. All men cannot worship alike, all men cannot realise the supreme experience by one and the same process. So different aspects of Divinity (I*sh*t*a*devatā) and forms of worship are prescribed by the Gurus to men of different temperaments. Thus the Kulār*n*ava Tantra says that the Guru must ascertain what the disciple is qualified for before he initiates him.

[6] Latā-sādhana, the fifth Tattva. Latā, which literally means a creeper, is a Tāntrika term for woman, who is thus thought of embracing man as the creeper clings to a tree. And so the Yoga-Vāshi*sh*t*h*a describes (Nirvā*n*a Prakara*n*a, chap. xviii): Gaurī, the half of the body (Ardhāṁgī) of Shiva, "embracing Him as the Mādhavī creeper clasps the young Āmra-tree with Her bosom like a cluster of blossom, and her eyes resembling the lines of black bees fluttering in the summer sky." In "Shakuntalā" the Mādhavī is described as married to the Sahakāra (mango-tree).

Tarkālangkāra says that Latāsādhana is that Sādhana in which the Sādhaka is assisted by his Shakti. Rules relating to it are given in the Kaulāvalī, p. 29, Prā*n*ato*shi*n*ī*, p. 618, 2nd edition. Gandharva Tantra, p. 60. The Yoga method is different in Shivasaṁhitā, p. 75, also Ha*th*apradīpika and Yoga Chintāma*n*i.

[7] Mu*n*d*a*-sādhana, one of the Tāntrika Āsanas.

Mu*n*d*ā*sana is of differing kinds. The Sādhaka sits in manner enjoined over the head of a Cha*n*d*ā*la, or on the heads of a Cha*n*d*ā*la, a jackal or a monkey or on the heads of a jackal, a monkey, a snake and two Cha*n*d*ā*las or on a hundred human heads. All these heads are put inside a raised mud platform on which the Sādhaka sits.

corpse,[1] or when seated on a funeral pyre[2] (53). By Thee, too, have been forbidden both Pashu-bhāva and Divya-bhāva.[3] If in this Age the Pashu-bhāva cannot exist, how can there be Divya-bhāva? (54). For the Pashu must with his own hand[4] collect leaves, flowers, fruits, and water, and should not look at a Shūdra[5] or even think of a woman[6] (55). On the other hand, the Divya is all but a Deva, ever pure of heart, and to whom all opposites are alike,[7] free from attachment to worldly things,[8] the same to all creatures[9] and forgiving (56). How can men with the taint of this Age upon them, who are ever of restless mind, prone to sleep and sloth, attain to purity of

[1] Shavāsana. This is another Tāntrika Āsana.

In Shavāsana in the Mantra method the Sādhaka sits on the corpse of a Chandāla and does japa of his Mantra (see Kaulāvalī, p. 62). In the Yoga method the Sādhaka lies on his back and practises Yoga according to the instructions of his Guru. See the account given in the Gheranda Sanghitā, Hathapradīpikā.

[2] Chitāroha, a Tāntrika Āsana.

In Chitāroha or Chitāsādhana the Sādhaka sits on an extinguished but not purified pyre and does Japa of his Mantra in manner enjoined (see Kaulāvalī, p. 48).

[3] Pashu-bhāva-divya-bhāvau svayam eva nivāritau. As to these dispositions, see "Shakti and Shākta". For the apparent meaning of this passage, *vide* Introduction by A. Avalon to vol. vi, Tāntrik Texts.

[4] In Smārta worship, or that prescribed by Smriti, the worshipper (or his wife) must with his own hand collect the materials for his worship, and with his own hand cook his food, which he dedicates to the Deity. The meaning of the text is that in this Age this is impossible or difficult.

[5] The follower of Smriti (Pashu) should not at worship see the face of a Shūdra, or think of woman for his mind is weak.

[6] As to the "Pancha-tattva" in which woman is worshipped, see "Shakti and Shākta".

[7] Dvandvātīta, beyond all contraries. He to whom heat and cold, pain and pleasure, etc., are the same.

[8] Vītarāga = free from both love and hate. He is not atttracted or repelled by anything.

[9] Sarvabhūte samah—nothing worldly is pleasing or displeasing to him. He is the same to all men and animals.

disposition?[1] (57). O Shangkara[2] by Thee, too, have been spoken the rites of Vīra-sādhana,[3] wherein are used the Panchatattva[4]—namely, wine,[5] meat,[6] fish,[7] parched grain[8] and sexual union of man and woman[9] (58-59). But since the men of the Kali Age are full of greed, lust and gluttony, they will on that account neglect Sādhana[10] and will fall into sin, and having drunk much wine for the sake of the pleasure of the senses, will become mad with intoxication, and bereft of all notion of right and wrong[11] (60-61). Some men will

---

[1] Having in the preceding verses described the characteristics of the Pashu and Divya Bhāvas, He now proceeds to show that they do not avail for the lazy and evil men of the Kaliyuga.

[2] One of the nāmes of Shiva. The meaning of which is "the beneficent one". Shaṁ=Kalyāṇam=Good: Karoti=does. He who does good.

[3] Sādhana of Vīra-bhāva, practised by Vāmāchārīs and some Kaulas. See "Shakti and Shākta".

[4] Next described (see *Ibid.*).

[5] Madya. This Tantra substitutes in certain cases Madhu-traya (see Chap. viii, vv. 172-178).

[6] Māngsa (*vide Ibid.*).

[7] Matsya (*vide Ibid.*).

[8] Mudrā, which has been spoken of as follows: Devānām moda-dā mudrā, tasmāt tāng yatnatashcharet; ("That which gives pleasure to the Devas is Mudrā. Therefore should it be done with care,") and see chap. ii of Nirvāṇa Tantra.

[9] Maithuna, vv. 172 and 173 of chapter viii, however, state that, owing to the limited intelligence and lust of the men of the Kali Age, they cannot recognise women to be manifestations of Shakti or Divine Power and for them, therefore, the worship of the feet only of the Devī is prescribed, just as Madhu-traya is substituted in lieu of wine. In the Sāttvika Sādhana, this and the preceding terms have another and esoteric meaning (see "Shakti and Shākta"). There is Kishorī-Sādhana amongst Vaishṇavas.

[10] See *Ibid.*

[11] Kali-jā mānavā lubdhāḥ shishnodara-parāyaṇāḥ:
Lobhāt tatra patishyanti, na karishyanti sādhanam.
Indriyāṇām sukhārthāya pītvā cha bahulam madhu,
Bhavishyanti madonmattā hitāhita-vivarjitāḥ.

That is, owing to the lusts of men of this Age, the latter are likely to partake of the Pancha-tattva (wine, meat, etc.) rather for the mere

violate the wives of others, some will become robbers, and others sinful men, in the indiscriminating rage of lust, will go (whoever she be)[1] with any woman (62). Excessive drinking and the like will disease many and deprive them of strength and sense. Disordered by madness, they will meet death, falling into lakes, pits, or in impenetrable forests, or from hills or house-tops (63-64). While some will be as mute as corpses, others will be for ever on the chatter,[2] and yet others will quarrel with their kinsmen and elders. They will be evil-doers, cruel, and the destroyers of Dharma[3] (65-66). I fear, O Lord! that even that which Thou hast ordained for the good of men will through them turn out for evil[4] (67). O Lord of the World! who will practise Yoga[5] or the many kinds of Nyāsa,[6] who will sing the hymns and draw the Yantra[7] and make Purashcharaṇa[8]? (68). Under the influences of the Kali Age man will of his

---

gratification of the senses than in the manner and for the object for which they were prescribed. As to drinking see Ch. XI. vv. 105-122 *post*.

[1] Indicative of incest. Na karishhyanti te mattāh pāpā yonivichāraṇam.

[2] Tarkālangkāra here quotes the following verse from the Kulārṇava (ch. xi).

> Parihāsam pralāpancha vitaṇḍām bahu-bhāshaṇam.
> Audāsīnyam bhayam krodham chakramadhye vivarjayet.

When traced in the Chakra or circle of worship just, purposeless talk, recrimination, gamility, indifference and anger should be avoided.

[3] Dharmamārgavilopakāh; that is destroyers of the true meaning of the injunctions of Dharma.

[4] Hitāya yāni karmāṇi kathitāni tvayā Prabho!
Manye tāni mahādeva viparītāni mānave.

In the event a true prophecy.

[5] Yoga (see A. Avalon's "Serpent Power").

[6] Nyāsa (see "Shakti and Shākta").

[7] Diagrams (see *Ibid.*).

[8] Purashcharaṇa is the repetition, a specific number of times and under specific conditions, of Mantras (see "Shakti and Shākta" by Woodroffe and "Purashcharyārṇava" by the King of Nepal).

2

nature become indeed wicked and bound to all manner of sin (69). Say, O Lord of all the distressed![1] in Thy mercy how without great pains men may obtain longevity, health, and energy, increase of strength and courage, learning, intelligence, and happiness; and how they may become great in strength and valour, pure of heart, obedient to parents, devoted to their wives,[2] mindful of the good of their neighbour, reverent to the Devas and to their Gurus,[3] cherishers of their children and kinsmen (70-72), possessing the knowledge of the Brahman,[4] learned in the lore of, and ever medidating on, the Brahman. Say, O Lord! for the good of the world,[5] what men should or should not do according to their different castes[6] and stages of life.[7] For who but Thee is their Protector in all the three worlds[9]? (73-74).

End of the First Chapter,[8] of the Mahānirvāna Tantra which is the most excellent of all Tantras and wherein is set forth the essence of all Dharma, entitled "Questions" relating to the Liberation of Beings".

---

[1] Dinesha, an epithet of Shiva.

[2] Svadāraniratā*h*.

[3] Spiritual teachers.

[4] The Supreme.

[5] Lokayātrāyā*h* siddhyartham, that is, for the accomplishment of the world-harmony which is the realisation of the Dharma of each being.

[6] Var*n*a.

[7] Āshrama.

[8] Ullāsa a term which means that which arises or appears; that which is revealed. Ullāsa also indicates joy.

[9] The questions of the Devī begin at v. 18 and go on to the end of the Chapter, that is 57 verses in all.

CHAPTER II

THE WORSHIP OF BRAHMAN

HAVING heard the words of the Devī, Shangkara,[1] Bestower of happiness on the world,[2] great Ocean of Mercy, thus truly spoke.[3]

Sadāshiva [1] said:

O Exalted and Holy One![4] Benefactress of the universe, well has it been asked by Thee. By none has such an auspicious question been asked aforetime (1-2). Worthy of all honour art Thou, Who knoweth, what is right, O Benefactress of all born in this age![5] O Gentle One! what Thou hast said is verily true. O Parameshvari, Thou art Omniscient. Thou knowest the past, present, and future,[6] and Dharma. What Thou hast said about Dharma of the past, present, and future, is without doubt true[7] according to the injunctions[8] and appropriate.[9] O Sureshvarī![10] men, whether they be of the twice born[11] or other castes, afflicted

---

[1] Shiva (see note to v. 58, ch. I.)

[2] Loka-shangkara*h*=Janānāng kalyā*n*asya utpādaka*h*.

[3] Tattvena kathayāmāsa. He spoke of the essentials concerning which he was asked. Here He commences to answer the Devi's questions relating to the saving of creatures.

[4] Mahā-bhāge.

[5] Kali Yuga.

[6] Tri-kāla.

[7] Yathātattva.

[8] Yathānyāya.

[9] Yathāyogya.

[10] Sureshvarī, feminine of Sureshvara, Lord of the Suras or Devas.

[11] Referring here to the Brāhma*n*as, Ks*h*atriyas, and Vaishyas, who are spiritually reborn on being invested with the sacred thread.

as they are by this sinful Age,[1] and unable to distinguish the pure from the impure, cannot gain purity by the Vedic rituals, or the success of their desired ends or by the Samhitās[2] and Smritis[3] (3-6). Verily, verily, and yet again verily, I say unto you, O beloved, that in this Age[4] there is no way to Liberation but that proclaimed by the Āgama[5] (7). I, O Blissful One,[6] have already foretold in the Vedas,[7] Smritis,[8] and Purānas,[9] that in this Age the wise shall worship the Devas according to the method enjoined in the Āgama (8). Verily, verily, and beyond all doubt, I say to you that there is no Liberation for him who in this Age, goes counter to such scripture and follows another (9). There is no Lord but I in this world, and I alone am He Who is spoken of in the Vedas, Purānas, and Smritis and Samhitās[10] (10). All these teach that My abode is the Purifier of all

---

[1] Kalikalmashadīnānām. As to which Bhāratī says: those who are rendered wretched as a result of sins which are concomitants of the Kali Age.

[2] Here Purānas (*vide* Ch. I, vv. 30-33).

[3] v. ante, p. 10, n. 1.

[4] Kali Yuga.

[5] That is, the Tantra Shāstras (see Introduction to "Principles of Tantra"). Tarkālangkāra quotes as from the Uttara Tantra the following verse, which also occurs in the Kularnava.

Sarvāchārat paribhrashtah kulāchārang samāshrayat
Kulāchārātparibhrashto rauravang narakang brajet.

(Let him who is fallen from all other Āchāras seek shelter in Kulāchāra but he who is fallen from Kulāchāra goes to the Raurava Hell.)

[6] Shivā, feminine of Shiva.

[7] As to the assent of other Shāstras to the authority of the Tantras, see "Principles of Tantra"; the Atharva Veda, the Prashna, Kālikā, Tārā, Nārāyana, Shiva, Nrisimha-tāpanī, Gopālatāpanī Upanishads, and other works.

[8] See notes under ch. I, 34-36.

[9] The "Principles of Tantra" *loc. cit.*, refers to Kālikā Purāna, Skanda Purāna, Bhāgavata Purāna, and others.

[10] Here collections of Shāstras other than those named. See p. 10, n. 1. "He who is spoken of" (Pratipādyo'smi) that I am proved, shown, established in all these scriptures.

the worlds,[1] and they who are averse to My doctrine are unbelievers and sinners, as great as those who slay a Brāhmana (11). Therefore, O Devi! the worship of him who heeds not My precepts is fruitless, and, moreover, such an one goes to hell[2] (12). The fool who would follow other doctrine heedless of Mine is as great a sinner as the slayer of a Brāhmana or of a woman, or a parricide; have no doubt of that (13).

In this Age[3] the Mantras[4] of the Tantras are efficacious,[5] yield immediate fruit, and are auspicious for Japa,[6] Yajna,[7] and all such practices and ceremonies (14).[8] The Vedic rites and Mantras which were efficacious in the First Age[9] have ceased to be so in this. They are now as powerless as snakes, the poison-fangs of which are drawn. They were fruitful in the Satya and other ages but in the Kali Age they are as if dead (15). The whole heap of other Mantras have no more power than the organs of sense of some image in a wall. To worship with the aid of other Mantras is as fruitless as it is to cohabit with a barren woman. Nothing is gained and the labour is lost (16-17). He who in this

[1] Matpadang lokapāvanam. Pada says Bhāratī = Sthāna = place. That is He is the source of all purity.

[2] Naraka, the region of Yama, the Judge of men and Ruler of the Hells, in which the wicked suffer (Vishnu Purāna, 207, 286).

[3] Kali Yuga.

[4] See Woodroffe's "Garland of Letters".

[5] Siddha.

[6] Recitation of Mantras. See "Shakti and Shākta".

[7] Sacrificial rites.

[8] He here says that in the Kali Age the Mantras given in the Vedas (Shrauta-jātīya), are not of efficacy and it is the Mantras given in the Tantras which are efficacious to quickly give the desired object (Bhāratī).

[9] Satya Yuga.

Age[1] seeks salvation by ways prescribed by others is like a thirsty fool who digs a well on the bank of the Jāhnavī[2] (18),

---

[1] Kali Yuga. See as to these verses Preface.

On this Tarkālangkāra observes as follows: What is the reason why the Vaidik Mantras were formerly fruitful but are no longer so. As a fact the prescribed fruit may be gained by the doing of Vedic rites and following the Vaidika āchāra as also by doing the rites approved in the Smṛitis, Purāṇas, Shaivāchāra, Vaishṇavāchāra, Dakshiṇāchāra, Vāmachāra, Siddhāntachāra and Kaulāchāra. The Uttara Tantra gives the relative excellence of Vedāchāra, Vaishṇavāchāra, Shaivāchāra, Dakshiṇāchāra, Vāmāchāra, Siddhāntāchāra and Kaulāchāra the highest beyond which there is nothing higher. (Each of these Āchāras is more excellent than that which precedes them—see also Kulārṇava, Ch. II, vv. 7, 8.) Of these Āchāras the first three are included in Pashubhāva. Dakshiṇāchāra is mid-way between Pashu and Vīra. Vāma and Siddhānta are in Vīrabhāva and Kulāchāra, though it is in Vīrāchāra, in its highest stage attains to Divyabhāva. The reason why the Pashubhāva is forbidden in this Tantra is that in the Kali age no one can fully observe the rules of Vedāchāra, Vaishṇavāchāra and Shaivāchāra. If this is not done then the Vaidika, Smārta, and Paurāṇik Mantras, rules and sacrifices cannot bear any fruit. Who in the present day is able to observe Vedāchāra? Who after his investiture with the sacred thread lives in the family of the Guru rigidly observing the continent life (Brahmacharyya) and who returning therefrom between the ages of 24 and 30 takes a wife and enters the life of a householder? Who again on his attaining the age of 50 years enters the stage of Vānaprastha? Do the Brāhmaṇas of the present day maintain themselves by what they earn by teaching or the performance of sacrifices: If (as is patent) the men of the present age are not observant of the injunctions (Shāsana) of the Vedas then how can they hope that the Vaidika rules will do them good? As a fact it is impossible to observe Pashubhāva. Thus no one can carry out the injunction which says that the Pashu should collect for himself leaves, flowers, fruits and water and should not look on a Shūdra or think of a woman. It is difficult to come across a pure Pashu who is not fallen by association with the wicked—with those who are fallen by keeping the company of Mlechchhas, wine-drinking and other bad habits. On this account Shiva has said that there is no Pashubhāva in the Kali age. If there is no Pashubhāva there are no rites of Pashubhāva. Therefore under present circumstances no fruit can be gained by the use of Vaidik Mantras and the like which are appropriate for Pashubhāva only. It is on this account that Shiva revealed the Āgamas for the salvation of men who have fallen from their Āchāra. At present there is no path to Liberation outside the Āgama.

[2] Gaṁgā, Ganges; so called as coming from out of the thigh of the sage Jahnu.

and he who, knowing My Dharma, craves for any other is as one who with nectar in his house yet longs for the poisonous juice of the Ākanda plant[1] (19). No other path is there to salvation and happiness in this life or in that to come like unto that shown by the Tantras which give both happiness and Liberation[2] (20). From my mouth have issued the several Tantras with their sacred legends and practices both for Siddhas and Sādhakas[3] (21). At times, O My Beloved! by reason of the great number of men of the Pashu[4] disposition, as also of the diversity of the qualifications[5] of men, it has in some places been said that the Dharma spoken of in the Kulāchāra[6] Scriptures should be kept secret (22). And in some places again I have, O Beloved! revealed some Tantras with the object of inclining the minds of men thereto.[7] Various are the Deva and Devīs who have been spoken of as also Bhairavas,[8] Vetālas[9]

[1] This exudes a white juice like milk but poisonous.

[2] Nānya*h* panthā mukti-hetur ihāmutra sukhāptaye.

[3] Or, as it might be said analogically, "for adept and novice".

[4] See "Shakti and Shākta".

[5] Adhikāri-vibhedena. Adhikāra means competency, qualification to perform a particular act or worship. Thus that boy is entitled (Adhikārī) to the Upanayana ceremony whose Chū*d*ākara*n*a (tonsure) ceremony has been performed.

[6] The Tāntrika division of worshippers of that name, who follow the way (Āchāra) of Kula: see Woodroffe's "Shakti and Shākta".

[7] Jīva-prav*ri*tti-kārī*n*i kānichit kathitānyapi—that is, to create some desire in their minds so that they may be inclined towards it. On this Bhāratī says: In the preceding verse He has enjoined secrecy in respect of some practices. In this He says that He has also revealed some Tantras to induce men towards these practices without disclosing their difficulties. In verses 23-24 he further develops the topic of the difference in Adhikāra.

[8] Manifestation of Shiva (see following notes).

[9] The monkey-faced son of Shiva, born of Gaurī after She had entered into the body of Rā*n*ī Tārāvatī, wife of Rājā Chandra-shekhara. There were two sons born, one Bhairava and another Vetāla. See his history as given by the Muni Aurvva to Rājā Sāgara in chap. xlv of the Kālikā Purā*n*a.

Vatukas,[1] Nāyikās[2] and forms of worship such as Shāktas,[3] Shaivas,[4] Vaishnavas,[5] Sauras,[6] Gānapatyas,[7] and others. In them too, are described various Mantras[8] and Yantras[9] which aid men in the attainment of Siddhi,[10] and which, though they demand great effort, yet yield the desired fruit (23-25). As and when questions were asked of me by any one, so O Beloved, did I give as reply which was appropriate and of benefit to him[11] (26).

None before has ever questioned Me as Thou hast done for the advantage of all mankind—nay, for the benefit of all that breathes, and that, too, in such detail and with reference to the needs of the present age.[12] Therefore, out of My affection for Thee, O Pārvatī! I will speak to Thee of the supreme Essence of essences (27-28). O Deveshi! I will state before Thee the very

[1] One of the terrific manifestations of Shiva, known as Bhairava, whose Vāhana is a dog. There are others, such as Kāla Bhairava, Nakuleshvara Bhairava.

[2] Nāyikās are forms of Shakti, eight in number—Ugrachandā, Prachandā, Chandogrā, Chanda-nāyikā, Ati-chandā, Chāmundā, Chandā, and Chandavatī.

[3] Worshippers of the Devī, as the Shakti or Divine energy.

[4] Worshippers of Shiva.

[5] Worshippers of Vishnu, of which the four chief sects are the Nimbārka, Rāmānuja, Vallabhāchārī, and Mādhavachārī.

[6] Worshippers of the Sun.

[7] Worshippers of Ganesha formerly, but hardly now, a distinct sect. The worship of the Deva is popular in the Mahratta country, and all Hindus invoke this Deva before commencing any work or devotion.

[8] See Woodroffe's "Shakti and Shākti" or "Garland of Letters".

[9] *Ibid.*

[10] Success, accomplishment, realisation (*Ibid.*).

[11] All these worships lead to the same goal—the Brahman. But, as men vary, so do the forms of worship. Some natures attain spirituality in one way, others in another. For the same reasons, the means such as Yantra, Mantra and Upāsanā vary.

[12] Yugadharmānusārena. As to Dharma, special duties exist in each Yuga with reference to its varying circumstances.

essence distilled from the Vedas and Āgamas,[1] and in particular from the Tantras (29). As men versed in the Tantras are to other men, as the Jāhnavī[2] is to other rivers, as I am to all other Devas, so is this (Mahānirvāna) Tantra to all other Āgamas[3] (30).

O Auspicious One! of what avail are the Vedas, the Purānas, or the Shāstras, since he who has the knowledge of this great Tantra is Lord of all Siddhi?[4] (31). Since I have been moved by Thee for the good of the world, I will speak to Thee of that which will lead to the benefit of the universe (32).

O Parameshvarī! should good be done to the universe, the Lord of the universe[5] is pleased, since He is its Self, and it depends on Him (33). He is One. He ever is. He is the Truth. He is the Supreme Unity without a second. He is Ever-full and Self-manifest.[6] He is Eternal

---

[1] *Vide* "Shakti and Shākta."

[2] Ganges, Gangā. See p. 22, n. 2.

[3] Yathā mareshu tantra-Jnāh saritām Jāhnavī yathā,
Yathāham tridiveshānām āgamānām idam tathā.

Verses 30 and 31, speak of the excellence of this Tantra as each Tantra and in fact each Shāstra does of its own.

[4] Siddhi (*vide* p. 4, n. 3). The Tantra is thus the cream of all previous doctrine extracted for the use of the men of this Age, who may thus, without the learning of the other Shāstras, acquire knowledge of the Brahman.

[5] Vishvesha. That is the Director of all including Shiva himself. (Vishveshām asmadādīnām sarveshām niyantā). Now why should doing good to all be pleasing to Him? The answer is that the Vishva (the universe or all) is in Him. Now how is it that you say that He is Vishvatmā or Soul of the Universe. The answer is that the Vishva has its support on Him.

[6] "Without a second"—that is, every creature is one of a class but the Supreme stands apart, and is unlike any other thing, and there is none other like Him. "Ever-full" (Sadā-pūrna), entire, whole, undivided. "Self-manifest" (Sva-prakāsha), self-lustre. He has not to depend on anything else for His manifestation, such as the Sun, Moon or other Energy. "He is the Truth," and all else is relative to Him unreal.

Consciousness and Bliss[1] (34). He is without change,[2] self-existent,[3] and ever the same,[4] serene,[5] above all attributes.[6] He beholds[7] and is the Witness[8] of all that is, Omnipresent,[9] the Self of everything that is.[10] He, the Eternal and Omnipresent, is hidden and pervades all things.[11] Though Himself devoid of senses, He is the Illuminator of

[1] Bhāratī says that v. 34 establishes that the Paramātmā is alone Sat and all else Asat. It alone should be meditated upon and worshipped, since It is Reality, the pleasing subject of meditation and the Cause of Liberation. The Lord is Sadrūpa, Sat, Being itself (Svabhāva), the one true Reality (Ekah Satyah). From this it is to be inferred that all else is Asat. The Text proceeds to prove this reality stating that He is Advaita which is Sajātīya-vijātīya-shūnya, that is, free of both intrinsic and extrinsic distinctions (see n. 4) and therefore Parātpara (Parāt Brahmāder api parah, shreshthah), that is, higher than the High such as Brahmā and the rest. He is self-manifesting (Svaprakāsha) and not manifested as objects are by Sun, Moon or other Lights. Cf. Na tatra Sūryo bhāti, na chandratārakām, etc. He is Sadāpūrna, the eternally existing whole, Sarvadā akhanda and the eternal Chit (Jnāna) and Ānanda.

[2] Nir-vikāra. He is free of Vikāra which means deviation from the primary character (Prakriti) of any thing. Prakriter anyathābhāvah vikārah tadrahitah.

[3] Nir-ādhāra. That which supports itself and is supported by nothing.

[4] Nir-vishesha=Svagatabhedarahita. Bheda or difference and distinction which marks finitized being is of three kinds, *viz.*, intrinsic or Svagata such as the distinction which exists between the leaves and branches of the same tree and extrinsic which is Sajātīya such as the distinction which exists between one kind of tree and another and Vijātīya the distinction which exists between trees and things which are not trees. The Brahman is free of all Bheda.

[5] Nir-ākula.

[6] Gunātīta. The Supreme Being is, in Its ultimate Nir-guna aspect, without attribute, though, when It unfolds Itself by Shakti, It appears as One possessing attributes. The Supreme is but One and the Same, but by reason of the various beings which It pervades, It appears differently according to the characters of such being, and enjoys their attributes (Shrīmad-bhāgavata, chap. ii, verses 30-32). He is beyond the Gunas, pleasure and pain, etc.

[7] Sarva-drik.

[8] Sarva-sākshī=witness of all Karma both good and evil.

[9] Vibhu or in whom all the Powers (Aishvarya) are.

[10] Sarvvātmā=Sarvasvarūpa: the Reality of all.

[11] Gūdhah sarveshu bhūteshu. Sarvavyāpī Sanātanah.

all the senses and their powers [1] (35-36). The Cause of all the three worlds, He is yet beyond them and the mind of men. Ineffable and Omniscient, He knows the universe, yet none know Him [2] (37). He sways this incomprehensible universe, and all that has movement and is motionless in the three worlds depends on Him; and depending on His reality the world of forms appears as true.[3] We too have come from Him as our Cause [4] (38-39). He, the one Supreme Lord,[5] is the Cause of all beings, the Manifestation of Whose creative Energy in the three worlds is called Brahmā (40). By His will Vi*sh*n*u protects and I dissolve. Indra and all other Guardian Devas of the world depend on Him and hold rule in their respective regions under His command. Thou His supreme Prak*r*iti [6] art adored in all the three worlds (41-42). Each one does his work by the power of Him who dwells within and directs. None is ever independent of Him (43). Through fear of Him [7] the Wind blows, the Sun gives heat, the Clouds shower seasonable rain, and the Trees in the forest flower (44).

It is He who destroys Time at the Great Dissolution, of whom even Fear and Death itself are afraid.[8] He is

---

[1] Sarvendriya-vivarjita*h* sarvendriya-gu*n*ābhāsa*h*; or it may be translated, "Yet all the senses tell of Him."

[2] Tam na jānāti kashchana. The All-knowing Paramātmā knows all but no one knows Him.

[3] Tat-satyatām upāshritya sadvad bhāti p*r*ithak p*r*ithak: that is the reality of Brahman gives the appearance of reality to the different forms seen in the world such as earth, water and the like. Their apparent reality is really His.

[4] Tenaiva hetu-bhūtena vayang jātā*h*. The "We" refers to Shiva Himself considered as an emanation and others.

[5] Īshvara, God as Creator and Ruler of the universe.

[6] See Woodroffe's "Shakti and Shākta". His Power as material cause of the universe.

[7] That is, in obedience to Him, through fear of disobedience (see Sixth Vallī, Ka*th*opani*sh*ad).

[8] That is, who is not affected by time, fear and death.

Bhagavān,[1] Who is indicated by the words *Yat Tat*[2] in the Vedānta[3] (45). O Adored of the Devas! all the Devas and Devīs—nay, the whole universe, from Brahmā to a blade of grass—are His forms[4] (46). If He be pleased, the Universe is pleased. If aught be done to gratify Him, then the gratification of All is caused (47). As the pouring of water at the root of a tree satisfies the wants of the leaves and branches, so by worshipping Him all the Deathless Ones[5] are satisfied (48). Just as, O Virtuous One! all the beautiful Devīs[6] are pleased when Thou art worshipped and when men meditate on and make Japa and pray to Thee (49). As all rivers must go to the ocean, so, O Pārvati! all acts of worship must reach Him as the ultimate goal[7] (50). Whoever be the worshipper, and whoever be the Devatā whom he reverentially worships for some desired end, all that is given to him through the Deva he so worships comes from Him as the Supreme (51). Oh, what use is it to say more

---

[1] See note under ch. I, 18.

[2] The "That," which all in their essence are, or the Supreme—the One, that is—*Tat Sat*. The *Vishvatman* is without a name, nor is it known how It should be called other than by the designation of "That" in the neuter gender. Though the unconditioned Brahman and the apparently conditioned appear as different (by attributes), yet They are the same, and designated by Tat, the relation between them being Tādātmya (sameness). The Devī is Chidākāsha-svarūpi*n*ī (Lalitā, verse 80), non-separable from Chit, and denoted by Tat (Tat-pada-laksh*h*yārthā).

[3] Shruti and Darshana (see Introduction to "Principles of Tantra").

[4] Tanmayam—Paramātmasvarupam, ultimately these forms are Him, see the Ka*th*a Upanis*h*ad (ii, 2).

[5] Amaras—that is, the Devas.

[6] That is, the other Devīs.

[7] The same thought is contained in the Bhagavad-Gītā, where the Supreme Lord says that "All worship, to whomsoever directed, reaches Him". It has been pointed out (Max Müller, "India, what It can teach us," p. 252) that a similar idea is to be found in the Prophet Malachi (i, 14), where the worship of strange gods is accepted as a tribute which in reality falls to Yahweh.

before Thee, O My Beloved? There is none other but Him, to meditate upon, to worship, to pray to, for the attainment of Liberation with such delight or ease (52). Need there is none to trouble, to fast, to torture one's body, to follow rules and customs, to make large offerings; need there is none to be heedful as to time[1] nor as to Nyāsa[2] or Mudrā;[3] wherefore, O Kuleshāni![4] who will strive to seek shelter elsewhere than with Him? (53-54).

End of the Second Chapter, entitled "Introduction to the Worship of Brahman".

[1] Dik-kāla-vichāra. In ordinary worship, the time of the day, the position of the planets, the direction of the worshipper's face, have to be regarded, but not so here.

[2] A ritual as to which see "Shakti and Shākta," by Woodroffe.

[3] *Ibid.* Cf. Hymn in Mahākāla Saṁhitā.

[4] Feminine of Kuleshāna, a name of Shiva as Lord of the Kaulas whose way of life is Kulāchāra which is Advaita Vedānta. See Chapters VII, v. 98; X, v. 212.

CHAPTER III

THE WORSHIP OF BRAHMAN—(*Contd.*)

Shrī Devī said:

O Deva of the Devas, great Deva, Guru of B*ri*haspati[1] himself, Thou hast revealed all Scriptures,[2] Mantra, and Sādhana,[3] thereof; Thou hast also spoken of the Supreme Brahman who is higher than the highest and the Supreme Lord by worship of Whom mortals attain both Happiness and Liberation. O Lord! how shall we please that Supreme Spirit, how O Deva! may we realise Him? What is the Dhyāna of and the observances[4] relating to the Supreme Lord the Supreme Self? It is My desire, O Lord! to hear of the truth of all these from Thee. Speak, O Lord, in Thy mercy (1-4).

Shrī Sadāshiva said:

Listen, then, O Beloved of My life! to the most secret and supreme Truth, the mystery whereof, O propitious One, has nowhere yet been revealed.

Because of My affection for Thee I shall speak to Thee of that Supreme Brahman, Who is Being-Consciousness in the form of the universe and Who is dearer to Me than life itself. O Maheshvari! the unchanging eternal, conscious world-pervading[5] Brahman may be known in

---

[1] Spiritual preceptor or director of B*ri*haspati, the Deva-guru, that is, the Guru of the Devas.

[2] Shāstras.

[3] See Woodroffe's "Shakti and Shākta" and "Serpent Power".

[4] Vidhāna.

[5] That is in Its Svarūpa or by Its Laksh*ana* that is attributes. Sachchidvishvamayam: Sat = Sadāsthāyi = which ever is (that is without becoming or change in past, present or future). Chit = Chaitanya = pure Consciousness. Vishva = Ashes*h*ang jagat = the limitless universe: Vishvamaya = who pervades it.

Its real Self[1] or by Its external signs[2] (5-6). That Which is without difference[3], pure being[4] and beyond both mind and speech,[5] Which truly is in the three worlds of appearance[6], is the Brahman according to Its real nature (7). That Brahman is known in ecstasy[7] by those who look upon

---

[1] Tatsvarūpa = Svarūpalaksh*a*n*a* of Brahman.

[2] Laksh*a*n*a* = Ta*t*asthalaksh*a*n*a*. Laksh*a*n*a* is that of which anything is seen or known (Laksh*y*ate anena, iti, laksh*a*n*a*. This is the apparent as distinct from the real nature: God as manifest in the universe as contrasted with the nature of God as He is in Himself.

[3] Nirvishesh*a* = Svagatabhedabhinna. (See ch. II, 34 and notes.)

[4] Sattāmātra = Kevalaparamārthasattvarūpa. The Supreme is pure Being.

[5] Avāngmanasagochara: that is, incomprehensible by mind and inexpressible in speech.

[6] Asattrilokīsadbhānam. The Brahman in Its Svarūpa is the Sat which ever is in the existing changeful Asat or universe. Hariharānanda says that Asat is the appearance as true of that which is not so (*asatyā mithyābhūtāyāh trilokyāh sadbhānam sadvaj-jnānam*). The Svarūpa is the real in that it is the whole (Pūr*n*a) and not the subject of change.

[7] Samādhiyoga: Samādhi = Chittaikāgryam = the state of one-pointedness of the Chitta. Yoga = undivided devotion to the Lord together with full knowledge: or Samādhi = Parameshvara: Samādhīyate chittam asmin: Into whom the Mind or Chitta is placed. Yoga = Samyagdarshana or complete knowledge.

Tarkālangkāra says that Laya-yoga is called Samādhi Yoga. In the six Āmnāyas six different Yogas are spoken of. In Pūrvāmnāya it is Sāngkhya-yoga; in Dakshi*n*āmnāya it is Ekātma-yoga; in Pashchimāmnāya it is Unmanī-yoga; and in the sixth or hidden (Gupta) Āmnāya it is Sahajāvasthā. The aim of all the six Āmnāya Yogas is dissolution (Laya) in the Brahman. So it has been said that all the Yogas above mentioned denote Ātmā (Ekātma-vāchaka). Shangkarāchāryya in his Yoga-tārāvalī says: "Sadāshiva has spoken of 120,000 kinds of Laya. That through Nāda is one of these and important (Nādānusandhāna-samādhi). Patanjali defines Yoga to be 'Chitta-v*r*itti-nirodha*h*,' that is, stoppage of mental modifications." The commentator says that the Chitta (mind) has five states, *viz.*, Ksh*i*pta, Mū*dh*a, Viksh*i*pta, Ekāgra and Samādhi: The first is due to the action of Rajogu*n*a. The mind is restless roaming in all the directions. This state is antagonistic to Yoga. The Mū*dh*a state is due to the action of Tamogu*n*a. In this state wicked acts prompted by lust, anger and the like appear right. This also is antagonistic to Yoga. The Viksh*i*pta state is due to the action of Sattva-gu*n*a. Now the mind inclines towards the delights of Heaven and other pure forms of enjoyment. This also

all things alike,[1] who are above all contraries,[2] devoid of all wandering thought,[3] free of all ignorance regarding body and self[4] (8). That same Brahman is known from His external signs, from Whom the whole universe has sprung, in Whom when so sprung It exists, and into Whom all things return[5] (9). That which is known by yoga-experience may also be perceived from these external signs.[6] For those who would

---

conflicts with Yoga practice. Ekāgra is that state in which the mind is withdrawn from all other objects than that on which it is centred. This is helpful in Yoga practice. When the mind is thus made one-pointed (Ekāgra) Samādhi comes of itself. At that time the mind leaves hold of all external objects and becomes dissolved in the supreme Brahman which is supreme Bliss.

[1] To whom friend and foe are one and the same.

[2] Dvandvātīta—that is, above, or unaffected by, the contraries, pain and pleasure, heat and cold, etc.

[3] Nirvikalpa = Nānāvidhakalpanā-shūnya. The mind is poised in the equilibrium of consciousness not thinking now of this now of that.

[4] Dehātmādhyāsa-varjita. Freed of the notion which leads one to believe the body to be the Self. That is, those who have freed themselves of the false notion (Adhyāsa) that the body is Ātmā or the Self. The Brahma-svarūpa is known to Paramahangsas alone. Only those know it who are Yogīs to whom friend and foe are one, who are affected neither by pleasure nor pain, whose mind is in poise; free from now this thought now that, who are devoid of the false notion that the body is Ātmā. This they achieve by concentration of mind and that complete and direct vision (Samyag-darshana) which arises from undivided devotion to the Lord.

[5] This is paralleled by the second Sūtra of the Vedānta-Sūtra, "Janmādyasya yata*h*," from which the birth, etc., of it (this world). Cf. Kāmakalāvilāsa. Cf. Taittirīya Up., 3—1—1.

[6] That is, the same Brahman, who may be known in Its inner nature by the real or direct knowledge (Sva-rūpa-jnāna) of Self, may also be apprehended through the senses from Its manifestation in the created world. He here establishes the identity of Brahman in both its Svarūpa and Ta*t*astha aspects. And so Shiva says, that which is knowable by Svarūpa-Buddhi is also knowable through its external manifestations. Sādhanā is for those who are seeking the latter. For those qualified to seek the Svarūpa Brahman are beyond the stage of Sādhanā through which at one time or one birth or another they must have passed. Tarkālangkāra says: Although the Svarūpa Brahman known by Yogīs in Samādhi is one and the same as that which is known by external signs yet there is a difference of essential

know Him through these external signs, for them Sādhana[1] is enjoined (10).

Attend to me, Thou, O dearest One! while I speak to Thee of such Sādhana.[2] And firstly, O Ādya! I tell Thee of the Mantroddhāra[3] of the Supreme Brahman (11). Utter first the Pra*n*ava,[4] then the words "Being" and "Consciousness,"[5] and after the word "One"[6] say "Brahman".

MANTRA

Oṁ Sachchidekam Brahma[7] (12)

This is the Mantra. These words, when combined according to the rules of Sandhi, form a Mantra of seven letters.[8] If the Pra*n*ava be omitted, it becomes a Mantra

---

characteristics. The first is pure Consciousness (Anupahita-Chaitanya) without creative activity (Kart*ri*tva). Such Brahman is neither Creator, Protector nor Destroyer. The second is the Turīya Brahman with (Upahita) Mūla-prak*ri*ti. Through this union there issued from the latter Brahmā, Vi*sh*nu, Shiva, Sāvitrī, Lak*sh*mī and Bhagavatī who in accordance with their respective Gu*n*as create, protect or withdraw the worlds. It is Brahman in this second aspect who is spoken of as the Creator, Protector, and Dissolver of the universe.

[1] See Woodroffe's "Shakti and Shākta".

[2] That is Sādhanā of the Ta*t*asthalak*sh*a*n*a Brahman.

[3] Mantroddhāra, Mantra+uddhāra. In the Māt*ri*kas the Mantra lies scattered. Mantroddhāra is the formation of the Mantra by selection of the Māt*ri*kas.

[4] That is, the sacred Mantra Oṁ, from which all Devas, Vedas, the Sun, Moon, and Stars, and all things, have come, and to which they return (Prā*n*ato*sh*i*n*ī, p. 19). See Woodroffe's "Garland of Letters".

[5] Sat-Chit—that is, absolute Being and absolute Consciousness (as to the meaning of which term see "Shakti and Shākta") and which with absolute Bliss (Ānanda) is the Brahman.

[6] Ekam.

[7] "Oṁ, the One Being Consciousness Brahman."

[8] Sandhi is the rule of Sanskrit grammar by which final and initial syllables of words coalesce. Thus the words Oṁ Sat Chit

of six letters only (13). This is the most excellent of all the Mantras, and the one which immediately bestows Dharma,[1] Aatha,[2] Kāma,[3] and Moksha.[4] In the use

---

Ekam Brahma become the following seven letters, Oṁ-Sach-chid-ekam-Brahma, neither vowels, which, according to the Tantras, are Shaktis of the Consonants, nor Visarga, which they call Kīlaka, being regarded as separate letters.

[1] Rectitude, religious merit.

[2] Wealth, worldly prosperity.

[3] Desire and its fulfilment.

[4] Liberation.

The Chaturvarga as they are called are the four aims of man and are Dharma, Artha, Kāma, Moksha. The first is both Law, natural, ethical, social and so forth and the Merit acquired by the observance thereof. It is meritorious action whereby man gains happiness in this world (since obedience to Law leads to that) and in heaven and is the groundwork of all further advance. Man should seek to know and observe Dharma and to live righteously. Artha is the means by which this righteous life may be maintained such as in the material sense money, lands, goods, food, drink and so forth. These means must be righteously obtained. Kāma is desire and its fulfilment. This must be a righteous desire for that which is not such is contrary to Law (Adharma). These three are known as the Trivarga. A man may renounce the world, but if he does not do so, he must seek his happiness by meritorious acts and desires and the means by which they may be achieved. Indeed it is said that all these should be equally cultivated and the man who is addicted to one only is unworthy: Dharmārthakāmāh samam eva sevyāh: Yoga hyekasaktah sa jano jaghanyah. Thus the house-holder who is always engaged in ritual worship to the neglect of his worldly affairs is to be condemned. The fourth which with the other three constitutes the Chaturvarga is Moksha or Liberation, the final end to which all sentient being trends. This is beyond the Heaven-world which is a transitory state. For Moksha is permanent. What is the nature of this final end is the subject of discussion. According to the views of this Tantra which is written from the Advaita standpoint it is the union in one identity of the individual (Jīvātmā) and supreme Spirit (Paramātmā) by the dispelling of that ignorance which supposes them to be different. The Trivarga constitute the path of enjoyment. Moksha according to some views is to be obtained by renunciation. According to Shākta teaching there is given to its followers both Enjoyment and Liberation. The world itself is the seat of Liberation (Mokshāyate hi sangsārah, as the Kulārnava Tantra says). Worship is of the supreme Yoni, the Cause of all, Which in Its Svarūpa is Moksha and in Its manifestation the field of enjoyment. That field gives Moksha also when the unity of both are known and action is according to Dharma and the injunctions of the Shāstra. Hai yoni namas te'stu namas te'stu yoga-moksha pradāyini (Shri-yoni-stava-rāja-kavacha).

of this Mantra[1] there is no need to consider whether it be efficacious[2] or not, or friendly or inimical,[3] for no such considerations affect it (14). Nor at initiation into this Mantra is it necessary to make calculations as to the phases of the Moon, the propitious junction of the stars, or as to the Signs of the Zodiac. Nor are there any rules as to whether the Mantra is suitable or not.[4] Nor is there need of the ten Sangskāras.[5] This Mantra is in every way efficacious in initiation. There is no necessity for considering anything else (15). Should one have obtained, through merit acquired in previous births, an excellent Guru, from whose lips this Mantra is received, then life indeed becomes fruitful (16), and the worshipper, receiving in his hands Dharma, Artha, Kāma, and Moksha,[6] rejoices both in this world and the next (17).

---

[1] As is shown by what follows.

[2] Siddha.

[3] As in the case of other Mantras (Ari, enemy, inimical; Mitra, friend, friendly). Some letters and groups of letters are friendly, and some inimical to others (see Tantrasāra, p. 25). See next note.

[4] Kula, Akula. Before initiation it is usual to ascertain whether the Mantra is Sva-kula or A-kula—that is, whether the Mantra is suitable to the disciple or not. For the procedure to be taken in order to ascertain this, see Kulārnava Tantra, Tantrasāra, p. 25; and see verse 88, chap. vii, *post*. To ascertain the suitability of a Mantra for a particular disciple various methods are adopted. To ascertain the friendly or inimical character of a particular Mantra for any particular disciple figures of Chakras such as A-ka-tha-ha and the like are drawn. The A-ka-tha-ha is a square with sixteen "Houses" in which the letters of the alphabet are grouped in a particular way. Another Chakra is drawn to ascertain whether a Mantra is Svakula or Akula. By the *Rini*dhanī Chākra it is ascertained whether a particular Mantra is in the position of a debtor (*Rinī*) or creditor (Dhanī). The former is acceptable.

[5] What is here referred to are the Sangskāras of the Mantra, not the ordinary Sangskāras of the worshipper. The ten Mantra-sangskāras are—(1) Janana, (2) Jīvana, (3) Tādana, (4) Bodhana, (5) Abhisheka, (6) Vimalīkarana, (7) Āpyāyana, (8) Tarpana, (9) Dīpana, and (10) Gupti. (Gautamīya Tantra, cited in Tantrasāra, p. 90.)

[6] Chatur-varga: See p. 34, n. 4, (Tri-vargo dharma-kāmārthaish chatur-vargah sa-mokshakaih.)

He whose ears this great jewel of Mantra reaches is indeed blest, for he has attained the desired end, being virtuous and pious, and is as one who has bathed in all the sacred places, been initiated in all Yajnas,[1] versed in all Scriptures, and honoured in all the worlds (18-19). Happy is the father and happy the mother of such an one—yea, and yet more than this, his family is hallowed, and the gladdened spirits of the Pitris[2] rejoice with the Devas, and in the excess of their joy[3] sing (20): "In our family is born the most excellent of our race, one initiate in the Brahma-mantra. What need have we now of Pinda[4] offered at Gayā,[5] or of Shrāddha,[6] Tarpana,[7] pilgrimage at holy places[8] (21); of what use are alms, Japa,[9] Homa,[10] or multiplicity of Sādhanā,[11] since now we have obtained

[1] Sacrifices and worship generally.

[2] Forefathers.

[3] Pulakānchita-vigraha—literally, the hairs of whose body stand erect (from sensation of joy). This sensation, whether arising from joy or voluptuousness, is a Bhāva of the Alangkāra-shāstra.

[4] Pinda is cake made of rice, curd, honey, and various kinds of fruits, Tila seed, Tulasī leaf, offered on Kusha grass to the ancestors (Pitri).

[5] A non-sectarian Tīrtha, or place of pilgrimage, where Hindus resort to offer at the shrine of Vishnu-pāda, Pinda cakes and water to the spirits of their departed ancestors.

[6] The religious ceremonies performed for the dead for the first time, on the eleventh day for Brāhmanas, thirteenth day for Kshatriyas, sixteenth day for Vaishyas, and for Shūdras on the thirty-first day after death, and repeated annually.

[7] The offering of water and til-seed to the Pitris. This is the Tarpanam referred to in the text.

[8] Tīrtha, places of pilgrimage.

[9] Recitation of Mantras (*vide* Shakti and Shākta).

[10] The Homa, or Fire Sacrifice, is one of the five Yajnas prescribed by the Shāstras. Clarified butter and other substances are poured into the sacred fire as an offering to the Devas, accompanied by Mantras, beginning with Oṁ and ending with Svāhā. It is performed on special occasions, such as the investiture of the sacred thread, marriage, initiation, etc.

[11] Ritual and practice generally. See Woodroffe's "Shakti and Shākta". Or it may be translated "Homa with its multiple rituals".

imperishable satisfaction by the Sādhanā of this good son?" (22).

Listen, O Devī! Adored of the world, whilst I tell You the very truth, that for the worshippers of the Supreme Brahman there is no need for other religious observances (23). At the very moment of initiation into this Mantra the disciple is Brahman,[1] and for such an one, O Devī! what is there to attain in the three worlds? (24). Against him what can adverse planets or Vetālas, Che*t*akas, Pishāchas, Guhyakas, Bhūtas,[2] the Māt*r*ikas, *D*ākinīs, and other Spirits avail?[3] The very sight of him will drive them to flight with averted faces (25). Guarded by the Brahmamantra, clad with the splendour of Brahman, he is as it were another Sun. What should he fear, then, from any

---

[1] Brahma-maya—literally, becomes Brahman, or the embodiment of Brahman.

[2] These and the following are dark, or unclean, or fearful spirits. Vetāla is a spirit attendant on Shiva (Demon presiding over corpses). In the Kālikā Purā*n*a (chap. xlv) the Muni Aurva describes Vetāla and Bhairava as sons of Shiva by Gaurī, who had entered the body of Rā*n*ī Tārāvatī, wife of Rājā Chandra-shekhara. Che*t*aka, according to Hemachandra, are Deva-yoni who serve in Heaven. Pishāchas are unclean Deva-yonis. Guhyakas are Deva-yonis, attendants of Kuvera, Deva of Wealth, described in the Kāshī-kha*nd*a. Bhūtas are ghosts of all kinds, against which protective Mantras are used. A sample may be found in the Garu*d*a Purā*n*a, chap. cxcix.

[3] There are two kinds of Māt*r*ikā, the beneficent eight Shaktis—Brahmā*n*ī, Kaumārī, Vārāhī, Vaish*n*avī, Māheshvarī, Māhendrī, Aindrī, and Yamī—and the *D*ākinī Māt*r*ikās, of terrific aspect and destructive disposition, such as Mukta-keshī, Smitānanā, Lola-jihvā, and others. The Yoginī Tantra (Eighth Pa*t*ala) gives an account of the origin of the latter. At the dissolution, when nothing was left in Shiva but the five elements, He asked His Shakti to find Him a place for them, His own creation having been destroyed. Shakti said that the creation was Hers, and not His, for without Her, Shiva is but Shava (corpse). Shiva then went away in anger, and, going westward, created out of the ashes of His body a demon of huge form. He then returned to Shakti, and took Her with Him to the demon. The latter, on seeing Shakti, was overcome by his lust for Her, and begged of Her to save his life by the gratification of his desire. Shakti assented if he could defeat Her in battle. It was then that Shakti threw out from Herself the terrific Māt*r*ikās, who are those referred to in the text.

planet (26). They flee, frightened like elephants at the sight of a lion, and perish like moths in a flame (27). No sin can touch, and none but one as wicked as a suicide can harm him who is purified by truth, of pure mind[1] a benefactor of all beings, a faithful believer in Brahman (28). The wicked and sinful who seek to harm him who is initiate in the knowledge of the Supreme Brahman do but harm themselves, for are they not indeed in essence inseparate from the ever-lasting One?[2] (29). For he is the holy sage and well-wisher, working for the happiness of all, and, O Devī! should it be possible to harm such an one who can go in peace? (30). For him, however, who has no knowledge of the meaning of, nor of the awakening of the Mantra,[3] it is fruitless, even though it were inwardly uttered ten million times (31).

Listen, then, O My Beloved! while I tell Thee of the meaning and awakening of Mantra. By the letter A is meant the Protector of the world[4]; the letter U denotes Him who dissolvess it[5]; and M stands for its Creator[6] (32).

---

[1] Shuddha = Nirmalāntaḥkaraṇa = with pure inner instrument.

[2] That is, men, though phenomenally different, are in their ultimate and inner ground of being, one. Therefore, a man who seeks to harm a Brahmopāsaka Sādhu harms himself.

[3] Mantra-Chaitanya is Chaitanya Shakti, and is the name for the Jnāna of the presiding Deva (Adhishṭhātṛī-devatā) of the Mantra. The "awakening" of the Mantra is in the consciousness of the Sādhaka. See "Garland of Letters" and "Shakti and Shākta," by Sir J. Woodroffe.

[4] Vishṇu, and so also the commentator on Shankarāchārya, Ānandalahari says:

> Akāro Harirityāhurukāro Hara uchyate,
> Makāro Brahmaṇaḥ saṁjnā jāyate praṇavastu vai.

[5] Shiva.

[6] Brahmā, the creative Manifestation of the Supreme Brahman. The three letters A, U, M are the component parts of the Praṇava, which by the rules of Sandhi become "Oṁ". This explanation is at variance with the Rudra-yāmala Tantra, which says that A is the letter of Brahmā, U that of Vishṇu, and M that of Shiva. But the three are

The meaning of *Sat* is eternal changeless Being; of *Chit*, Consciousness; and of *Ekam*, One without a second. Brahman is so called because It is everywhere.[1] Now, O Devī! I have given You the meaning of the Mantra, which grants the fulfilment of desires. The awakening of the Mantra[2] is the knowledge of Him, Who is the pervading Devatā of the Mantra, and such knowledge, O Supreme

---

one—Ekā mūrtistrayo devā brahma-vishnu-maheshvarāh. The latter is perhaps the better interpretation.

Tarkālangkāra says Oṁ is formed by the union A, U, M, of which the first is Vishnu, the second is Maheshvara and the third Brahmā. By the Prānava these are knowu. The Goraksha-Saṁhitā says: "Ichchhā, Kriyā, Jnāna are Gaurī, Brāhmī, Vaishnavī. The threefold Shakti is immanent in (abides in) the world. Beyond these is the Shakti (according to another reading the Light—Jyotih) Oṁ." From the Pranava which is the Svarūpa of the Ādyā Shakti, these three Shaktis have emanated for the purpose of Creation, Maintenance and Dissolution. These three Shaktis are Ichchhā, Kriyā, Jnāna. Ichchhā is Gaurī (Mahākālī). She, united with Maheshvara and associated with Tamo-Guna, dissolves. Kriyā Shakti is Brāhmī (Mahāsarasvatī). She, united with Brahmā and associated with Rajo-Guna, creates. Jnāna Shakti is Vaishnavī. She, united with Vishnu and associated with Sattva-Guna, maintains. Here Chaitanya associated with Mūlaprakriti or Ādyā Shakti is the object of worship. It is Ādyā Shakti who divides Herself according to the three Gunas and becomes Ichchhā, Kriyā, and Jnāna Shaktis. And Chaitanya associated (Upahita) with Ādyā Shakti divides according to Gunas into Brahmā, Vishnu, Maheshvara. Brahmā united with Sāvitrī creates, Vishnu united with Mahā-Lakshmī maintains and Maheshvara united with Gaurī dissolves the Universe. The Shaktis Ichchhā, Kriyā, Jnāna are but aspects of the Ādyā Shakti, as Brahmā, Vishnu and Maheshvara are but aspects of the Turīya Brahman associated with (Upahita) Ādyā Shakti. The Pranava therefore is expressive of Brahman as united with (Upahita) Mūlaprakriti which is the state of equilibrium (Sāmyāvasthā) of the Gunas. He is spoken of as Creator, Maintainer, Dissolver. Were Brahman not united with Prakriti then there would be no activity (Kartritva) in Him and no Chaitanya in Prakriti. By mutually entering into one another Prakriti acquires the Chaitanya of Brahman, and Brahman Kārtritva of Prakriti. When separated they may both be called Jada. The meaning of the Mantra here is that the Pranava signifies the Chaitanya-maya-brahman united with Ādyā Shakti.

[1] Brihattvād Brahma gīyate *lit.* Brahman is so called because of Its greatness (Brihattva).

[2] Mantra Chaitanya *(vide ante).*

Lady! yields the fruit of worship to the worshipper (33-35). O Devī! the presiding Devatā of the Mantra is the omnipresent,[1] eternal,[2] inscrutable,[3] formless, stainless,[4] and ineffable Brahman (36). When introduced by the Bīja[5] of Sarasvatī,[6] Māyā,[7] or Kamalā,[8] instead of the Mantra Oṁ,[9] it bestows various kinds of learning, or Siddhi in Māyā,[10] or prosperity in every quarter (37). The Mantra may be varied either by the prefixing or omitting of Oṁ, or by the placing of it before each word or every two words of the Mantra (38). Sadāshiva is the *Rishi*[11] of this Mantra.

---

[1] Sarvavyāpi = Sakala-padārthavyāpanashīla = That which spreads out or makes manifest all objects.

[2] Sanātanam = Prāgabhāvadhvaṁsarahitam, *i.e.*, of which there was no absence in the past and of which there is no dissolution.

[3] Avitarkyam = *a*nūhanīyam, that is, about whom nothing can be said.

[4] Niranjanam = Manashchaks*h*urādyavis*h*ayabhūtam (Bhāratī): That which is beyound the scope of the mind (Manas) the eye (Chaks*h*u*h*) and others senses.

[5] The "seed" Mantra, see Woodroffe's "Garland of Letters".

[6] The Bīja of Sarasvatī—Devī of vāk (speech)—is Aing.

[7] Shakti of Brahma, whose Bīja is Hrīng.

[8] Laks*h*mī—Devī of wealth, consort of Vis*h*n*u*—whose Bīja is Shrīng.

[9] That is, the Pra*n*ava (Ong-kāra) is dropped, and the Bīja of any of the Devīs named is substituted.

[10] Bhārati reads it as "various kinds of learning, Māyā or prosperity in all quarters".

Thus the Mantra Aing Sach Chid Ekam Brahma bestows Learning. Hrīng Sach Chid Ekam Brahma bestows Siddhi in Māyā which according to Tarkālangkāra means actually Nirvā*n*a-mukti and Shrīng Sach Chid Ekam Brahma bestows Prosperity. This verse as Bhāratī says indicates the various ways in which the Mantra Oṁ Sach Chid Ekam Brahma may be practised. It may be recited as a whole with or without the Pra*n*ava or it may be broken up into as many parts as there are words in it. Each again of these words may be used with or without the Pra*n*ava or any two of them and so on. Tarkālangkāra adds that the Mantra may be varied by substituting each of the three Bījas above-named when the Mantra becomes a Vidyā. Eighty-five different forms of Mantra may thus be obtained.

[11] That is, the inspired Teacher by whom it was originally "seen," or "to whom it was revealed".

The verse is called Anu*sh*tup,[1] and its presiding Devatā is the Supreme Brahman, Who is without attribute[2] and Who abides in all things. It avails for the attainment of Dharma, Artha, Kāma, and Mok*sh*a[3] (39).

Now listen, dear One, whilst I speak to You of Karanyāsa[4] and Aṁga-nyāsa[5] (40). O great Queen and adored of the Devas, the Sādhaka should with great care and with observance of injunctions concerning Nyāsa place the words *Oṁ, Sat, Chit, Ekam, Brahma,* on his thumb, threatening finger,[6] middle, nameless,[7] and little fingers respectively, followed respectively by the words Namah, Svāhā, Va*sh*at, Hung, and Vau*sh*at[8]; and he should next say Oṁ

[1] A form of metre; that in which this Tantra is written.

[2] Nir-gu*n*a.

[3] Bhāratī says the Viniyoga or employment of this Mantra is for acquirement of Chaturvarga and after the introductory Mantra detailing the Sādhaka's Sankalpa runs. "Obeisance to Sadāshiva *Rishi* on the head. Obeisance to Chhanda*h* anu*sh*tup on the mouth. Obeisance to the Nirgu*n*a Parabrahman the Inner Director of all beings on the heart. The Viniyoga of this is for the attainment of Dharma, Artha, Kāma, Mok*sh*a. Shirasi Sadāshivāya *Rish*aye Nama*h*. Mukhe Ānu*sh*tup-chhandase Nama*h* H*r*idi Sarvāntaryāminirgu*n*a-parabrahmane Nama*h* Dharmārthakāmamoksh*ā*ptaye viniyoga*h*. The above is called *Rishyā*di-Nyāsa. It is followed by Karanyāsa (vv. 41, 42), Aṁganyāsa (v. 43) and spoken of in the following verses.

[4] The ceremonial touching of the fingers (see *ante*, p. 25, "Shakti and Shākta"). Karanyāsa is done with the following Mantras Oṁ aṁgu*sh*th*ā*bhyāng Nama*h*. Sat tarjanībhyāng Svāhā Chit madhyamābhyāng Va*sh*at. Ekam Anāmikābhyang Hum. Brahma Kani*shth*ābhyāng Vau*sh*at. Oṁ Sachchidekam Brahma Karatala-p*r*i*shth*ābhyāng Pha*t*.

[5] The ceremonial touching of various parts of the body (Aṁganyāsa) is as follows: Oṁ H*r*idayāya Nama*h*, Sat Shirasi Svāhā, Chit Shikhāyai Va*sh*at Ekam Kavachāya Hum. Brahma Netratrayāya Vau*sh*at. Oṁ Sachchidekam Brahma Karatalap*r*i*shth*ābhyāng Pha*t*.

[6] *i.e.*, the first, or index finger.

[7] *i.e.*, the fourth, or ring finger.

[8] Nama*h* is a Mantra, used in worshipping a Devatā. So "Nama*h* Shivāya" means "Salutation to Shiva". So also are the other Mantras mentioned. Svāhā is the Consort or Shakti of the Fire-Lord, Agni. The Liṁga Purā*n*a says that Svāhā is the Consort of Shiva in

Sachchidekam Brahma over the palm and back of the hand, followed by the Mantra Phat (41, 42).

The Sâdhaka should in the like manner, perform Amganyâsa[1] commencing with the heart and ending with the hands (43).

After this, whilst reciting the Mantra Om or the Mûlamantra,[2] Prânâyâma[3] should be performed thus: He should close the left nostril with the middle and the fourth finger, and then inhale through the right nostril, meanwhile

---

the form of Fire. In the Lalitâ-sahasra-nâma, verse 110, the Devî is addressed as Svâhâ and Svadhâ. The former Mantra is used in particular in the worship of Fire, and the latter in the oblation of water to Deva and Pitri. Different interpretations of Svâhâ are given in the Prapanchasâra, Taittirîya-Shruti, Sâmaveda-Brâhmana, and Yâska's Nirukta, for which see Bhâskararâya's Commentary on the Lalitâ verse 110.

[1] *Vide ante* and Author's "Shakti and Shâkta".

[2] Here it is "Om Sach-chid-ekam Brahma". In Shakti worship it may be the fifteen-syllabled Mantra (Pancha-dashî)—"Hrîng Shrîng, Krîng Âdyâ Kâlikâ Parameshvarî Svâhâ." Devî is Herself the Mûla-Mantra (Mûla-mantrâtmikâ) (Lalitâ-sahasra-nâma, verse 86).

[3] The description follows.

On Prânâyâma Tarkâlangkâra says that the ordinary procedure is to close the right nostril with the right thumb. Air is then drawn in by the left nostril. Whilst this is being done repeat sixteen times the Mantra or its first letter, the Pranava or the Mâyâ Bîja. This is Pûraka. Then close left nostril also with the little and fourth fingers of the same hand (by this both nostrils are closed) and do Kumbhaka (retention of breath) doing Japa of the Mantra 64 times in manner aforesaid during such Kumbhaka. Then remove the thumb from the right nostril and exhale through it doing Japa 32 times. This is Rechaka (exhalation). This is the first Prânâyâma. The process is now reversed. Inhalation is done through the right nostril the left nostril being closed with the thumb of the left hand. This is the second Prânâyâma. Then a return is made to the first Prânâyâma which is the third Prânâyâma. A complete Prânâyâma consists of these three. A man who is short of breath and unable to do it as above may practise it doing Japa of the Mantra a fourth of the abovementioned numbers (that is, 4, 16, 8 instead of 16, 64, 32). He who is unable to do even this may practise Prânâyâma doing Japa for a fourth of the last mentioned period, (that is, 1, 4, 2). The rule relating to Prânâyâma with the Brahma Mantra differs in that the right hand is alone used and the Japa is 8, 32 and 16 for Pûraka, Kumbhaka and Rechaka respectively.

making Japa[1] of the Pra*n*ava or the Mūla-mantra eight times.[2] Then, closing the right nostril with the thumb and shutting also the mouth,[3] make Japa of the mantra thirty-two times. After that gently exhale the breath through the right nostril, doing Japa of the Mantra the while sixteen times.[4] In the same way he should next perform these three acts first with the right nostril, and then repeat the same process with the left nostril. O adored of the Devas! I have now told Thee of the method of Prā*n*āyāma to be observed in the use of the Brahma-Mantra (44-48). The Sādhaka should then meditate on the Supreme Brahman for the accomplishment of his desire as follows (49).

MEDITATION[5]

In the lotus of my heart I contemplate the Divine Consciousness,[6] the Brahman without

[1] Recitation of Mantra; see "Shakti and Shākta".

[2] This is Pūraka.

[3] This is Kumbhaka.

[4] This is Rechaka.

[5] Dhyāna.

[6] Chaitanya = Chetanam (Bhāratī), also He who is Shabdabrahma as Pra*n*ava (Tarkālangkāra).

Tarkālangkāra says: Brahman should be meditated upon in the Lotus of eight Petals in the heart as it were the flame of a lamp undisturbed by any breeze. How can He who is everywhere the same and undivided Consciousness (Chinmaya) be the subject of meditation in the limited form of a flame? Again the one Brahman reflected in Māyā appears as the various Jīvas, Devas, men, beasts, insects and so forth. If the Brahman be without distinction (Nirveshe*sh*a) why are there such differences as Deva, worm and so forth? The Devas who are Ānandamaya are the reflection (Ābhāsa) just as are the worms and moths. Then why are these differences perceived in the Nirveshe*sh*a Brahman? It is not unnatural to ask such questions. Brahman is omnipresent and the same everywhere. As the rays of the sun fall evenly in every part of the city of Calcutta so the lustre (Ābhāsa) of the Brahman rests on all things everywhere in the same manner. In this there is no difference. In Māyā are the three Gu*n*as and nothing else. Sattva by reason of its purity is capable of receiving and reflecting the

distinctions,[1] in whom are all powers[2] Knowable by Hari, Hara, and Vidhi,[3] whom Yogīs[4] approach in meditation,

---

Light. Tamas by reason of its impurity is unable to do so. In Rajas there are present partially the capacities of both. The rays of the sun fall on the earth, on whitewashed buildings, on polished articles of furniture, on swords, mirrors and gems but shows more powerfully on the whitewashed houses than on the earth, on the polish than on the house, on the sword than on the polish, on the gem (sunstone) than on the mirror. Consciousness (Chaitanya) resting on (Upahita) Mūlaprakriti which is the Brahman is like the sun and our Buddhi is like the sunstone (Sūryakāntamani), our senses are like the mirror, the body like the sword, the five Mahābhūtas, insects and the like are like the earth. Each of these according to its degree of purity is capable of receiving the Light of Chidānanda in greater or less degree. In this way all things are in the Brahman which is Chaitanya but it receives it according to its purity and receptivity. When the rays of the sun fall upon the sunstone it acquires like the sun the powers of burning. When the Light of Chaitanya falls on Buddhi the Buddhi is awake and works. Chaitanya united with it (Upahita) in this way is called Vijnānamaya Purusha. It is this Purusha which does everything. It is He Who by the instrumentality of the senses sees and hears and so forth. His acting through the senses (Indriyas) is called Jāgradavasthā. When the senses are dissolved in the Vijnānamaya Purusha and the latter is in the Purītat Nādī which is as it were the sheath in which the heart Lotus is, that state is called Svapnāvasthā. When the Vijnānamaya Purusha is in the state of sameness (Tādātmyasambandha) then the state is Sushupti. The Dhyāna of Brahman detached from Māyā cannot however be had by this method because in that case no form or attribute is apprehended. By Samādhi (yoga) alone can the Brahman (attributeless) be directly realised (Sākshātkāra). Brahman united with Māyā is thought of as lustrous (Tejomaya) because of such union. Although Itself undetached It can by reason of Māyā be thought of as detached. In this sense It dwells in the heart of every creature as it were separate and individualised. By meditating on It is accomplished meditation on the collectivity of things (Samashti). The Dhyāna of Brahman should be done as above described or according to the rules of the Kulārnava Tantra. There can be no worship of the detached Brahman. The latter can be realised by the power of Yoga alone.

[1] Nirvishesham = in whom there are no distinctions, that is devoid of Svagata, Svajātīya, and Vijātīya Bheda (Tarkālangkāra). The first being illustrated by the branches, leaves, flowers and fruit of one tree, the second by the difference between things of the same class such as a mango tree and a Bilva tree and the third the difference between things not of the same class such as a tree and a rock.

[2] Nirīham = Nirākāmksham = prāpta-samastaishvaryyam ityarthah. He who desires and is in need of nothing since in Him are all powers.

[3] *i.e.*, Vishnu, Shiva and Brahmā.

[4] Adepts in Yoga.

Him Who destroys the fear of birth and death,[1] Who is Being,[2] Consciousness[2] the Root of all the three worlds (50).

Having thus contemplated the Supreme Brahman, the Sādhaka should in a devout spirit, in order to attain union[3] with Brahman, worship with offerings of his mind[4] (51). For perfume let him offer to the Supreme Spirit the essence of the Earth,[5] for flowers the Ether, for incense the essence of the Air, for light the essence of Fire, and for food[6] the essence of Water[7] (52). After mentally repeating the great Mantra[8] and offering the fruit of it to the Supreme Brahman, the excellent disciple should commence external worship (53). Meditating with closed eyes on the Eternal Brahman, the worshipper should with reverence offer to the Supreme whatever be at hand, such as perfumes, flowers, clothes, jewels, food, and drink, after having purified them with the following (54, 55).

MANTRA

The vessel of offering is the Brahman and so is the offering therein. It is offered by Brahman into the Fire which is Brahman. To Brahman he will attain whose

[1] When He is known, the fear of death passes.

[2] Sachchitsvarūpam=He who ever is (Sadāsthāyī) and Jnāna. Sat=who ever is (Bhāratī). *Cf.* Chhā 6—21. Sat eva idam agra āsīt and Asat eva idam agra āsīt.

[3] Brahma-Sāyujya, a form of secondary Liberation (others being Sālokya and Sārūpya) in which the Sādhaka is united into Brahman. The fourth or hightest is Nirvāṇa (Tarkālangkāra).

[4] As to these, see Chap. V, verses 41, 142-152.

[5] Mahī-tattva.

[6] Naivedya, offering of the eatables.

[7] The five elements—(1) Kshiti, (2) Ap, (3) Tejas, (4) Marut, and (5) Vyoma—are offered in the mental worship with the object of purifying the gross body of the Sādhaka.

[8] *Viz.*, Oṁ Sachchidekam Brahma.

mind is fixed on the Brahman by the performance of the rites which are Brahman[1] (56).

Then, opening the eyes, and inwardly and with all his power making Japa with the Mūla-mantra,[2] the worshipper should offer the Japa to Brahman[3] and then recite the hymn that follows and the Kavacha[4]-mantra (57). Hear, O Maheshvarī! the Hymn to Brahman, the Supreme Spirit, by the hearing whereof the disciple attains union with[5] the Brahman (58).

Stotra

Oṁ! I bow to Thee, the eternal Refuge of all:
I bow to Thee, the pure Consciousness who art in the form of the universe.[6]
I bow to Thee Who art One without distinction[7] and Who grants Liberation.

---

[1] This passage occurs in the Bhagavad-Gītā, chap. iv, verse 24. The Ṭāntrikas sometimes purify wine with this Mantra, called Sangshodhana (purifying), the Arpa*n*a being the Pātra, the Havi*h* being the wine, the Fire being the digestive fire, the sacrificer the Sādhaka, and the Brahma-karma the rites of the Chakra. The Da*n*dins also use it before taking food. By the Mantra the Sādhaka is taught to recognise the unity of all.

[2] Here "Oṁ Sachchidekam Brahma". By 'fruit' is meant the merit of the repetition, etc.

[3] So in the Bhagavad-Gītā K*ri*sh*n*a tells Arjuna that, whatever he does, he is to offer it to Him. Water is offered in the palm of the hand or in the Sruk. The Mantra of offering is Brahmārpa*n*amastu "Be it for Brahman".

[4] Kavacha, the protective Mantra, which is worn, contained in a metal case round the neck as an amulet. Kavacha means an armour, coat of mail.

[5] Sāyujya, one of secondary states of Liberation, namely, Sālokya, Sārūpya, Sāmīpya, and Sāyujya.

[6] Vishvarūpātmakāya. Vishvarūpātmaka = Vishvarūpa ātmā yasya.

[7] Advaitatattvāya = Sajātīya-vijātīyātmagat-bheda-rahitatattvāya, that is, One in whom there are no distinctions (Bhāratī) as to which see p. 44, n. 1.

I bow to Thee, the Brahman[1] Whose nature it is to be outspread as the universe[2] (but Who art Thyself) beyond all Gu*n*as.[3] (59).

Thou art the only[4] Refuge and Object of adoration.

Thou alone art in the form of the whole universe and art its Cause.[5]

Thou alone art Creator, Preserver, Destroyer of the world.

Thou art the sole immutable Supreme, Who art unchanging Consciousness[6] (60);

Dread of the dreadful, Terror of the terrible.

Refuge of all beings, Purificator of all purificators.

Thou alone rulest the high-placed ones,[7]

Supreme over the supreme, Protector of the Protectors (61).

O Supreme Lord[8] Who art manifest as the Form of all, yet Thyself Unmanifest[9]

Who art everywhere,[10] Who art Imperceptible by the senses, yet the very Truth.

---

[1] Brahma*n*e, that is to the very great (Atib*ri*hat) (Bhāratī).

[2] Vyāpine = Sakalavastuvyāpana-shīlāya (Bhāratī) translated as in the text.

[3] Nirgu*n*āya = Sattvādigu*n*arahitāya.

[4] Ekam which may be read as one or the chief (Mukhya). He is the object of adoration (Vare*n*yam) of those who are in fear of the pain of the circle of repeated births, and deaths (Janma-m*ri*tyu-du*h*khādi-bhīrubhirupāsanīyam).

[5] He is both Upādāna-kāra*n*a—that is, material cause, and Nimitta-kāra*n*a or efficient cause. The Universe is within and is a form of, the Lord. See Pu*n*yānanda's Commentary on v. 1 of Kāmakalāvilāsa.

[6] Nirvikalpa, a difficult word to translate in English but is the state opposed to limited experience in which there is sense of difference (Bheda-buddhi) resulting in duality and plurality of thoughts, man now thinking of this now of that. There is nothing of all this but unchanging Consciousness. Nirvikalpa = Nānāvidhakalpanā-shūnya.

[7] Devas, Brahmā, and others.

[8] Paresha as He is Lord over Brahmā and others.

[9] Sarvarūpa aprakāshin. Another reading is, Sarvva-rūpāvinashin, "in the form of all things and imperishable".

[10] Anirdeshya = incapable of location; Shabdena nirdesh*t*um ashakya (Bhāratī).

Incomprehensible, Imperishable, All-pervading, Hidden and Formless.[1]
Lord and Light of the Universe! save us from harm[2] (62).
On that One alone we meditate, that One is the sole object of our Japa.
To that One alone the Witness[3] of the Universe we bow.
Refuge we seek with the One Who is our sole Eternal Support,
The Self-dependent[4] Lord, the Vessel of safety in the Ocean of existence (63).

This is the five-jewelled[5] Hymn to Brahman the Supreme Spirit. He who pure in mind and body[6] recites this hymn is united with the Brahman[7] (64). It should be said daily in the evening, and particularly on the day of the Moon.[8] The wise man should read and explain it to such of his kinsmen as believe in Brahman[9] (65). I have spoken to You, O Devi! of the bejewelled hymn of the Great Lord, O Graceful One! listen now to the Kavacha of the name Jagan-mangala[10] by the wearing and reading whereof one becomes a knower of the Brahman (66).

---

[1] Vyāpakāvyakta-tattva. Avyakta tattva is that which is devoid of form (Avyaktatattva rupādi-rahitatvāt).

[2] Apāya: Bhārati says this means any fall from devotion, understanding (Buddhi) and the like.

[3] The Atman is not affected by pain or pleasure, but is a spectator only.

[4] Nirālamba or without support.

[5] Pancha-ratna. The hymn is composed of five verses, each of which is regarded as a jewel.

[6] Prayata = Pavitra.

[7] Brahma-sāyujya, *ante*, p. 45, n. 3.

[8] Somavāra, *i.e.*, Monday.

[9] Tarkālangkāra says (p. 66): "I have heard that Raja Ram Mohan Roy under instructions from Hariharānanda Bhārātī used to do worship of the Brahman every day in a lonely place and with the object of explaining Its Svarūpa once a week to devout friends and relatives established the Brāhma-Samāja."

[10] World-beneficent. That is the Kavacha or protective Mantra of that name.

MANTRA[1]

May the Supreme Spirit[2] protect the head,
May the Supreme Lord[3] protect the heart,
May the Protector of the world[4] protect the throat,
May the All-pervading, All-seeing[5] Lord protect the face (67),
May the Spirit of the Universe[6] protect my hands,
May He who is Consciousness Itself[7] protect the feet,
May the Eternal and Supreme Brahman protect my body in all its parts always (68).

The *Rishi*[8] of this world-beneficent amulet is Sadāshiva; the verse is Anu*sht*up[9], its presiding Devatā is the Supreme Brahman, and the object of its use is the attainment of Dharma, Artha, Kāma, and Mok*sh*a[10] (69). He who recites this protective Mantra[11] of Brahman after doing *Rishi*-nyāsa[12] attains knowledge of Brahman, and is one

---

[1] The one Brahman is here invoked by different names in order to protect different parts of the body. Supreme Self or Spirit or Paramātmā is thought of as in the Sahasrāra Padma in the head, Supreme Lord or Parameshvara is object of meditation in the heart. Protector of the world or Jagatpātā, the Vi*sh*nu aspect, is invoked to protect the throat so that the Sādhaka my utter the sacred names and Mantras of his I*sht*adevatā.

[2] Paramātmā. [3] Parameshvara. [4] Jagat-pātā.

[5] Vibhu; Sarva-d*ri*k. As knower of all and of all generals the Lord is Sarvajna as knower of particulars He is Sarvavit.

[6] Vishvātmā. [7] Chin-maya.

[8] By whom it was "seen". The name of the Mantra is Shri-Jaganmaṁgala.

[9] A form of metre.

[10] See *ante*, under v. 14. [11] Kavacha.

[12] *Rishi*nyāsa is done with this Mantra: Asya Shrījaganmaṁgalanāmaka-kavachasya Sadāshiva *rish*ir anu*sht*up chhanda*h* Parabrahma devatā dharmārtha-kāmamok*sh*āvāptaye Shrījaganmaṁgalākhya kavachapā*th*e viniyoga*h*. Shirasi Sadāshivāya *rish*aye nama*h*. Mukhe anu*sht*up-chhandase nama*h*. H*ri*di Parabrahmane devatāyai nama*h*,

directly with the Brahman[1] (70). If written on birch-bark and encased in a golden ball, it be worn round the neck or on the right arm, its wearer attains all kinds of powers[2] (71). I have now revealed to Thee the Kavacha of the Supreme Brahman. It should be given to the disciple who is worthy of favour, who is both devoted to the Guru and possessed of understanding[3] (72). The excellent Sādhaka[4] shall after reciting the Hymn and the Kavacha with reverence, bow to the Supreme (73).

THE SALUTATION

Oṁ

I bow to the Supreme Brahman.
I bow to the Supreme Spirit.
I bow to Him Who is above all attributes.[5]
I bow to the eternal Being again and again (74).

Obeisance to the Supreme Lord may be by body or mind or by word as the Sādhaka wishes; but the one thing needful is purity of disposition[6] (75). After worshipping in the manner of which I have spoken, the wise man should with his friends and kinsmen partake of the Holy food[7] consecrated to Brahman the Supreme Spirit (76). In the worship of the Supreme Lord there is no need to

---

[1] Sakshāt Brahma-mayo bhavet.

[2] Siddhi.

[3] Dhīmate. The word Dhīmān (the root Dhī is from Dhyai to think and meditate) denotes both understanding and meditative nature.

[4] Worshipper.

[5] Nirguna—*i.e.*, the Unconditioned Brahman.

[6] Vāchikam kāyikam vāpi mānasang vā yathāmati,
Ārādhane pareshasya bhāva-shuddhir vidhīyate.

Bhāvashuddhi is inner purity.

[7] Mahā-prasāda, *i.e.*, consecrated offering.

invoke Him to be present or to desire Him to depart.[1] It[2] may be done always and in all places (77). It is of no account whether the worshipper has or has not bathed, or whether he be fasting or have taken food.[3] But the Supreme Spirit should ever be worshipped with a pure heart (78). After purification by the Brahma-Mantra,[4] whatever food or drink is offered to the Supreme Lord becomes itself purifying (79). The touch of inferior castes may pollute the water of Gaṁgā and the Shālagrāma,[5] and other images and emblems but nothing which has been consecrated to the Brahman can be so polluted[6] (80). After having dedicated it to Brahman with this Mantra, the Sādhaka with his people may eat of anything, whether cooked or uncooked (81). In the partaking of this food no rule as to caste or time need be observed. No one should hesitate to take the leavings from the plate of another, whether such another be pure or impure[7] (82).

---

[1] As is done in the ordinary worship of any other Devatā. At commencement of worship of the image (Pratimā), or the Ghata, the Āvāhana Mantra and Mudrā is said and shown, thus invoking the presence of the Devatā, and at close there are Visarjana (dismissal) Mantra and Mudrā. In the case of Apratishthita (uninstalled) Devatā, the image is also thrown away.

[2] Brahmasādhanā.

[3] Asnāto vā krita-snāno bhukto vāpi bubhukshitah,
Pūjayet Paramātmānam sadā nirmmala-mānasah.

Bathing is necessary in other worships, as also fasting, but the worship of the Brahman for those competent is simply in spirit and in truth. It is not, however, everyone who is competent for the Brahma-Mantra. It is only for the Brahma-jnānī (see verse 132, *post*).

[4] Which according to Bhāratī is Oṁ Sachchidekam Brahma. According to Tarkālangkāra it is Brahmārpanam, etc., v. 56, *ante*.

[5] Shilā. Nārāyana-shilā, or Shālagrāma, the black fossil ammonite found in the Gandaka River in Nepāl, worshipped as an Emblem of Vishnu.

[6] Here there is no question of touchable or untouchable :. Parabrahmārpite dravye sprishtāsprishtang na vidyate.

[7] Ceremonially by bathing, etc., or by caste. Usually leavings (Uchchhishta) are unclean.

Whenever and whatsoever the place may be, howsoever it may have been obtained, eat without scruple or inquiry the food dedicated to the Brahman (83). Such food, O Devī! even the Devas do not easily get, and it purifies even if brought by a Chandāla,[1] or if it be taken from the mouth of a dog (84). As to that which the partaking of such food effects in men and like creatures, what, O Adored of the Devas! shall We say of it? It is deemed excellent even by the Devas. Without a doubt the partaking of this Holy Food, be it but once only, frees the greatest of sinners[2] and all sinners of their sins (85-86). The mortal who eats of it acquires such merit as can only otherwise be earned by bathing and giving of alms at thirty-five millions of holy places (87). By the eating of it ten million times greater merit is gained than by the Horse-sacrifice,[3] or indeed by any other sacrifice whatever (88). Its excellence cannot be described by ten thousand million tongues and a thousand million mouths (89). Wherever the Sādhaka may be, and though he be a Chandāla,[4] he attains to union with the Brahman the very moment he partakes of the nectar[5] dedicated to Him (90). Even Brāhmanas versed in the Vedānta should take food prepared by low-caste men if it be dedicated to the Brahman[6] (91). No distinction of caste

---

[1] One of the lowest and most uncleanly castes.

[2] The five great sins (Mahā-pātaka) are: Killing a Brāhmana or woman (Brahma-hatyā, Strī-hatyā), drinking of wine (Surā-pāna, except in Vīrāchāra and under the conditions prescribed by it), theft, cohabiting with wife of Guru or person regarded as Guru—*e.g.*, uncle and aunt, etc.—(Gurvamganā-gama), and association with people guilty of these sins.

[3] Ashva-medha of the Veda (see the "Horse Hymns" in the *Rig-Veda*, Wilson, ii, 112, 121; also Yajur Veda Mādhyandinī Shākhā, chap. xxii).

[4] Kīkasha, see note 1 above.

[5] Amrita.

[6] Brahmane bhāvitam = Brahmane arpitam (Bhāratī).

should be observed in eating food dedicated to the Supreme Spirit. He who thinks it impure becomes a great sinner (92). It would be more tolerable, O Beloved! to commit a hundred sins or to kill a Brāhma*n*a than to despise food dedicated to the Supreme Brahman (93). Those fools who reject food and drink made holy by the great Mantra cause the fall of their ancestors into the lower regions, and they themselves go headlong into the Hell of blind darkness,[1] where they remain until the Dissolution of things. No Liberation is there for such as despise food dedicated to Brahman (94-95). By the Sādhana[2] of this great Mantra, all acts of the Sādhaka become meritorious;[3] in slumber merit is acquired.[4] In this Sādhana any Āchāra which is to the liking of the Sādhaka may be followed[5] (96). For such what need is there of Vedic practices, or of those of the Tantras? For him who is devoted to Brahman and who has realised that all is Brahman the rule to be followed is his own inclination[6] (97). For them there is neither merit nor demerit in the performance or non-performance of the customary rites. In the Sādhana of this Brahma

---

[1] Andha-tāmisra, one of the Hells.

[2] See Woodroffe's "Shakti and Shākta".

[3] Even if otherwise not so (Bhāratī).

[4] Sus*h*upti*h* suk*r*itāyate. The meaning is that the Sādhaka acquires merit even when in a state of insensibility to the outer world. He is continually acquiring merit. Even his sleep is an act of merit.

[5] The Sādhaka is not restricted to any Āchāra such as Veda, Vais*h*-*n*ava, Shaiva, etc. (Tarkālangkāra).

[6] Ordinarily as regards Svechchhāchāra, a man who does whatever he wants to, is greatly blameworthy, as all his actions should be ruled by the Shāstras, and not by his wishes. To superior men greater liberty is given. But neither this nor following verses must be taken literally as Vidhi-vāda, but as Stuti-vāda, in praise of the Mahā-mantra, unless it be understood that for such a worshipper who has acquired so great a degree of perfection his desires and actions are naturally (in conformity with his nature) good. For if he has truly realised that all is Brahman and has acquired a divine nature his acts will be such.

Mantra he meets neither obstacle nor failure[1] (98). By the Sādhana[2] of this Dharma, O Great Devī! man must be truthful, conqueror of the passions, devoted to the good of his fellow-men, unaffected by what may happen, pure of purpose, free of envy and guile, merciful and pure of mind, devoted to the service and seeking the pleasure of his parents, a listener ever to things divine,[3] a meditator ever on the Brahman. His mind is ever turned to the search for Brahman. With strength of determination holding his mind in close control, he is ever conscious of the nearness of Brahman (99-101). He who is initiated in the Brahma Mantra will not lie or think to harm, and will shun to go with the wives of others (102). At the commencement of all that is done, let him say, "Tat Sat[4]"; and before eating or drinking aught let him say, "Be this dedicated to Brahman" (103). For the knower of Brahman, duty consists in action for the well-being of the world. This is the eternal Dharma[5] (104).

I will now, O Shāmbhavi[6]! speak to Thee of the duties relating to Sandhyā[7] in the practice of the Brahma-Mantra, whereby men acquire that real Wealth which comes to them in the form of Brahman (105). Wheresoever

---

[1] That is, the great Mantra is so efficacious that even if its user omits any rite enjoined by the Shāstras, and so commits Pratyavāya, it becomes no obstacle to him.

[2] See Woodroffe's "Shakti and Shākta".

[3] Brahma-shrotā, that is a willing listener to discourse on divine knowledge.

[4] Tat Sat, or "That Being or One which is," the Unity, which is the source of all diversity.

[5] Yenopāyena martyānāṁ loka-yātrā prasiddhyati,
Tadeva kāryam Brahma-jnair idang dharmang sanātanām.
Lokayātrā=Lokanirvāha. That is the ordered course of things in the world.

[6] Feminine of Shambhu, or Shiva. See "Shakti and Shākta". Shambhu=well being. Shiva=good auspicious.

[7] The daily rite of that name.

he may be, and in whatsoever posture,[1] the excellent and well-intentioned Sādhaka shall, at morning, noon, and eventide, meditate upon the Brahman in the manner prescribed. Then, O Devī! let him make Japa of the Gāyatrī[2] one hundred and eight times. Offering the Japa to the Devatā,[3] let him make obeisance in the way of which I have spoken (106-107). I have now told Thee of the Sandhyā to be used by him in the Sādhana[4] of the Brahma-Mantra, and by which the worshipper shall become pure of heart (106-108). Listen to Me now, Thou Who art figured with grace, to the Gāyatrī,[5] which destroys all sin.

Say "Parameshvara" in the dative singular,[6] then "Vidmahe,"[7] and, Dear One, after the word "Paratattvāya"[8] say "Dhīmahi,"[9] adding, O Devī! the words, "Tanno Brahma prachodayāt."[10]

MANTRA

"May we know the Supreme Lord; let us contemplate the Supreme Reality, and may that Brahman direct us."[11]

This is the auspicious Brahma-Gāyatrī which confers Dharma, Artha, Kāma, and Moksha[12] (100-111).

---

[1] Āsana.

[2] Gāyatrī Mantra. See Woodroffe's "Shakti and Shākta" where this great Mantra is explained.

[3] Whose Japa is made; in this case the Brahman.

[4] See "Shakti and Shākta".

[5] Mantra (see "Shakti and Shākta").

[6] *i.e.*, Parameshvarāya, "to the Supreme Lord".

[7] "May we know."

[8] "The Supreme Essence."

[9] "Let us contemplate."

[10] "May that Brahman direct us."

[11] That is, towards the attainment of Dharma, Artha, Kāmā, and Moksha. This is the Brahma-Gāyatrī, not the ordinary Vaidika Gāyatrī. *Cf.* also chap. ix, verse 220.

[12] The Chatur-varga.

Everything which is done, be it worship or sacrifice, bathing, drinking, or eating, should be accompanied by the recitation of the Brahma-Mantra (112). When arising at the middle of the fourth quarter of the night, and after bowing to the Preceptor who gave initiation in the Brahma-Mantra,[1] let it be recited with all recollection. Then obeisance should be made to the Brahman as aforesaid, after meditating upon Him. This is the enjoined morning rite[2] (113). For Purashcharaṇa,[3] O Beautiful One! Japa of the Mantra should be done thirty-two thousand times; oblation[4] three thousand and two hundred times; the presenting of or offering water to the Devatā,[5] three hundred and twenty times; sprinkling before worship[6] thirty-two times; and four Brāhmaṇas[7] should be feasted (114-115). In this Purashcharaṇa[8] no rule need be observed touching food or as regards what should be accepted or rejected. Nor need an auspicious time nor place for performance be selected (116). Whether he be fasting

---

[1] That is, Oṁ Sachchidekam Brahma.

[2] Prātaḥ-kṛitya (of the Brahman worshipper).

[3] The Japa of Mantras as vowed for a particular number of times by the worshipper.

[4] Havana—*i.e.*, the Homa sacrifice.

[5] Tarpaṇa.

[6] Sechana = Abhisheka (with water). Sechanam = Mārjanam (Bhāratī).

[7] According to note of Jaganmohana Tarkālangkāra; that is, roughly 1/10th of the last number.

[8] That is, Brahma-Purashcharaṇa. In the Purashcharaṇa of other Mantras there is a multiplicity of ritual. Some of these are dispensed with. Tarkālangkāra says that although in Purashcharaṇa of the Brahma-mantra there is no need for Kīlaka (concluding Mantra) and Kūrmachakra (arrangement of letters in compartments of a figure representing a tortoise) and the like, yet it is necessary to have a Vedī or altar. This should measure one cubit each way. On it a jar should be placed in manner enjoined and full Pūja should be done in the beginning and end and ordinary daily Pūjā during such time as the Purashcharaṇa lasts.

or have taken food, whether with or without bathing, let the Sādhaka, as he be so inclined, make Sādhana [1] with this most excellent Mantra (117). Without trouble or pain, without Hymn,[2] Amulet,[3] Nyāsa,[4] Mudrā,[5] or Setu,[6] or Kullukā [7], without the worship of Gaṇesha as the Thief,[8] and the like yet surely and shortly the most Supreme Brahman is met face to face (118-119).

In the Sādhana of this great Mantra no other Sangkalpa [9] is necessary than the inclination of the mind thereto. In it what is enjoined is purity of disposition. The worshipper of Brahman, Oh Devī! should see Brahman in everything (120). In the Sādhana of this Mantra no evil or demerit follows from any omission therefrom. This

---

[1] See "Shakti and Shākta".

[2] Stotra.

[3] Kavacha.

[4] See *ante*, p. 18, n. 7.

[5] Mudrā, derived from mud=to please; the disposing in different ways of various parts of the hands and the body. There are different kinds for different Devatās and for different purposes. See "Shakti and Shākta".

[6] Setu, which literally means a dam, is ordinarily the Mantra Oṁ, recited in the heart at the commencement and end of Japa, though the Setu may vary with the Devatā worshipped (see Shāktānandataraṁgiṇī, chap. x) to prevent the fruits thereof escaping as a dam does in the case of water.

[7] Kullukā is the doing of Japa of a particular Mantra over the head before and after the Japa of the Mantra of any particular Devatā, see Prāṇatoshiṇī, 2nd Ed., p. 247.

[8] Chaura-Gaṇesha, one of the Tāmasik manifestations of Gaṇesha. In this form he robs the worshipper of the fruits of his devotions. He is therefore placated before worship. But this, as the text points out, is unnecessary for the worshipper of Brahman, whom Chaura-Gaṇesha cannot harm.

[9] Other ceremonies must be preceded by Shangkalpa or resolve, the rule being: Manasā sangkalpayet: Vāchā abhilapet: Karmaṇā chopapādayet. (Let there be resolve in mind, the expression of that resolve by word, and the carrying out of that expressed resolve by act.) This is not necessary in Brahman worship. The Sangkalpa fixes the attention and directs and strengthens the will.

Sādhanā of the great Mantra is the rectification of it (121). In this terrible and sinful Kali Age[1] devoid of Tapas[2] and so difficult to traverse, the very seed of Liberation is the Sādhanā of the Brahma-Mantra (122). In various Tantras and Āgamas I have prescribed differing modes of Sādhana, but these, O Great Devī! are beyond the powers of the feeble men of this Age[3] (123). For these, O Beloved! are short-lived, without enterprise, their life dependent on food,[4] covetous, eager to gain wealth, restless in mind, so unsettled in their intellect that it is without rest even in its attempts at Yoga.[5] Incapable, too, are they of suffering and impatient of the austerities of Yoga. For the happiness and Liberation of such have been ordained the Way of Brahman (124-125). O Devi! verily and verily I say to Thee that in this Age there is no other way to happiness and Liberation than that by initiation in Brahma-Mantra; I again say to Thee there is no other way (126). The rule in all the Tantras is that, that which is prescribed for the morning[6] should be done in the morning, Sandhyā[7] thrice daily, and worship[8] at midday, but, O Auspicious One! in the worship of Supreme Brahman[9] there is no other rule but

---

[1] Kali Yuga.

[2] Devotion and the like, see p. 8, n. 4.

[3] This verse anticipates the question "Thou hast revealed various Sādanas which are the seeds of Liberation in many Āgamas, Tantras and the like. Why then dost Thou say that in the Kali Age Sādhanā of the Brahma-Mantra is the seed of Liberation".

[4] Kalau anna-gata-prā*ṇāh*. In the Kali Age, life is dependent on food; whereas in the Dvāpara, Tretā, and Satya Ages life was centred in the blood, bones, and marrow respectively.

[5] Samādhi.

[6] Prāta*h*-K*ri*tya=Morning duty, bathing, etc. (see verse 118, *ante*).

[7] Tri-sandhyā is the usual expression.

[8] Pūjā—*i.e.*, worship of the Deva with offerings and ceremonies.

[9] Parabrahmopāsana. Upāsana or worship is derived from *upa* (near) and *as* (to be) that is coming near to God.

the inclination of the worshipper (127). Since in Brahma-worship rules are but servants and the prohibitions are of no account who will seek shelter in any other? (128). If the disciple can obtain a Guru who is a knower of Brahman, placid and of steady mind, let him clasp his lotus-like feet, and supplicate him in a devout spirit as follows (129):

Supplication to the Guru

O merciful one! Lord of the distressed! to thee I have come for protection; cast then the shadows of thy lotus-like feet over my head, O thou whose wealth is fame[1] (130).

Having thus prayed to and worshipped his Guru with all his powers, let the disciple remain before him in silence with folded hands (131). The Guru will then carefully and in manner enjoined examine the signs and qualities of the disciple,[2] kindly call the latter to him, and give to the good disciple[3] the great Mantra (132). Let the wise Guru[4] sitting on a seat, with his face to the East or to the North, place his disciple on his left, and gaze with compassion upon him (133). The Guru, after doing *Rishi*-nyāsa,[5] will then place his hand on his disciple's head, and for the Siddhi[6] of the latter do Japa[7] of the Mantra one hundred and eight times (134).

---

[1] Yasho-dhana, *i.e.*, whose sole wealth is his good name.

[2] The Guru examines the disciple to see whether he is suited to receive the Mantra, and this is done by watching his demeanour and character, etc. This has been given in detail in the Kulārnava Tantra, Shārada Tilaka and other works.

[3] Sat-shishya. The Mantra is given to the Sat-shishya, and no otherwise.

[4] Jnānī = Brahma-jnānavān.

[5] See Woodroffe's "Shakti and Shākta".

[6] Ishta-siddhi = fulfilment of disciple's desire.

[7] See *Ibid.*

The excellent Guru, gem of kindness, should next whisper the Mantra seven times into the right ear of the disciple if he be a Brāhma*n*a, or into the left ear if he be of another caste (135). O Kālikā[1]! I have now described the manner in which instructions in Brahma-Mantra should be given. For this there is no need of Pūjā, and his Sangkalpa[2] should be mental only (136). The Guru should then raise the disciple, now become his son, who is lying prostrate at his lotus-feet, and say with affection the following (137).

Reply of the Guru

Rise, my son, thou art liberated: Be ever devoted to the knowledge of Brahman.[3] Conquer thy passions: May thou be truthful, and have strength and health always (138).

Let the excellent disciple on rising make an offering[4] of his own self, money or a fruit, as he may afford. Remaining obedient to his preceptor's commands, he may then roam the world like a Deva (139). Immediately upon his initiation into this Mantra he becomes united with the Brahman[5]. What need, then, O Deveshi! for such an one to practise various kinds of Sādhana[6]? O Dearest One! I have now briefly told You of the initiation into the

---

[1] Kālī.

[2] See *ante*, notes under v. 120.

In ordinary worship, Sangkalpa must be performed with Dūrvvā grass, flower, rice, sandal-paste, Harītakī, Tila-seed, which, at the conclusion of the Sangkalpa-Mantra, are poured into the Ku*nd*a.

[3] *i.e.*, Devote thyself to acquire knowledge of the Brahman.

[4] Dak*sh*i*n*ā. This is an offering so that the Dīk*sh*ā (initiation) may turn one *Dakshinā* (Auspicious).

[5] Tadātmā tanmayo bhavet. The word tānmaya = Brahmamaya.

[6] See "Shakti and Shākta".

Brahma-Mantra (140). For such initiation the merciful mood of the Guru is alone necessary (141). The worshipper of the Divine Power,[1] of Shiva,[2] of the Sun,[3] of Vishnu,[4] Ganesha,[5] Brāhmanas versed in the Vedas[6] and all other castes may be initiated (142).

It is by the grace of this Mantra, O Devī! that I have become the Deva of Devas, have conquered Death, and have become the Guru of the whole world. By it I have done whatever I will, casting from Me ignorance and doubt (143). Brahmā,[7] the Brahmarshis,[8] the Devas,[9] the Devarshis[10] first did Sādhanā of this Mantra having received it from Me. The Munis[11] obtained it from the Devarshis and the Rājarshis[12] from the Munis. All these.

---

[1] Shāktas=worshippers of Shakti. [2] Shaivas.

[3] Sauras. [4] Vaishnavas. [5] Gānapatyas.

[6] Vipras. The stages in the life of a Brāhmana are, Shūdra by birth, Dvi-ja (=twice born) after the Upanayana ceremony, Vipra when he is versed in Vedic knowledge, and Brāhmana when he has the knowledge of the Brahman. In the true sense anyone who knows the Brahman is Brāhmana, as the case of Vishvāmitra illustrates. Bhāratī says that v. 142 states that all persons be they Brāhmanas or of inferior caste initiated or otherwise have competency (Adhikāra) for initiation into the Brahma-Mantra.

[7] Of the Tri-mūrti.

[8] Brahmarshis: *Rishis* or Seers mind-born sons of Brahmā such as Bhrigu.

[9] Such as Indra and others.

[10] *Rishis* who are devas such as Nārada.

[11] Munis, Vyāsa, and others. "He whose heart is not distressed in adversity, in whom all joy in prosperity is lost, from whom passion, fear, and wrath have passed away, he is called a Muni fixed in meditation" (Bhagavad-Gītā, chap. ii, verse 56). A more specific definition is 'Mananāt munir uchyate' (a Muni is so called on account of his Manana—that is, of his thought, reasoning, and independent investigation, which follows on hearing, or Shravana, and which is itself followed by Nididhyāsana, or profound contemplation on the conclusion —Siddhānta—arrived at after Shravana and Manana).

[12] Rājarshis: Kings who became *Rishis* such as Janaka, Rituparna and others.

O beloved, by Sādhanā of this Mantra attained union with Brahman by the Mercy of the Paramātmā (144-145).

In the initiation with this Brahma-Mantra, O Great Devī! there are no restrictions. The Guru may without hesitation give his disciple his own Mantra, a father may initiate his sons, a brother his brothers, a husband his wife, a maternal uncle his nephews, a maternal grandfather his grandsons[1] (146-147). Such fault as elsewhere there is in other forms of initiation, in the giving of one's own Mantra, by a father or other near relative, does not exist in the case of this great and powerful Mantra (148). He who has heard it, however it may be, from the lips of one initiate in the knowledge of Brahman,[2] is purified, and attains the state of Brahman, and is affected neither by virtue nor sin (149). The householders of the Brāhmaṇa and other castes who pray with the Brahma-Mantra should be honoured and worshipped as being the greatest of their respective classes (150).

Brāhmaṇas at once become like those who have conquered their passions,[3] and lower castes become equal to Brāhmaṇas: therefore let all worship those initiate in the

[1] This Tantra therefore relaxes in the case of the Brahma-Mantra the rules laid down in others. Thus in the Gaṇesha-vimarshinī it is said: Initiation (Dīkshā) by the father, maternal grandfather, Yatis and Sannyāsīs who have passed out of all Āshramas does not bring good (Na kalyāṇadāyikā). Initiation by the uterine brother, husband and maternal uncle is also prohibited. The Yoginī Tantra forbids initiation by father—at any rate, as regards Shakti-Mantra—maternal uncle, and younger brother. Siddhas are exempted from the prohibition. Similarly, the Rudra-yāmala Tantra, which also prohibits initiation of daughter by father, states that the husband should not initiate his wife unless he be himself Mantra-siddha in which case he may initiate her, not as *putrikā* but as his own Shakti. The Bhairavī Tantra also permits initiation by the Guru in his own Mantra. No restrictions apply in the case of the Brahma-Mantra.

[2] Brahma-jnānī.

[3] Yatis = Paribrājakas or those who have conquered their desires and are detached from the world.

Brahma-Mantra, and thus knowers of Brahman[1] (151). They who insult them incur the sin of slaying Brāhmaṇas, and go to a terrible Hell, where they remain as long as the Sun and Stars endure (152). To revile and calumniate a worshipper of the Supreme Brahman is a sin ten million times worse than that of killing a woman or bringing about an abortion (153). As men by initiation in the Brahma-Mantra become freed of all sins, so, O Devī! also may they be freed by the worship of Thee (154).

End of Third Chapter, entitled "Instruction regarding the worship of the Supreme Brahman".

[1] Brahmajna.

CHAPTER IV

THE WORSHIP OF SHAKTI

HAVING listened with attention to that which has been said concerning the worship of the Supreme Brahman, the Supreme Īshvarī[1] greatly pleased again thus questions Shangkara (1).

Shrī Devī said:

O Lord of the Universe and my Lord![2] I am bathed with contentment in the nectar of Thy words concerning the excellent worship of the Brahman, which lead to the well-being of the world and to Brahman,[3] and give light,[4] intelligence,[5] strength, prosperity[6] and happiness (2-3). Thou hast said, O Ocean of Mercy! that as union with the Brahman[7] is attainable through worship of Him, so it may be attained by Sādhanā of Me[8] (4). I wish to

---

[1] Feminine of Lord and Ruler (Īshvara): Our Lady.

[2] Nātha.

[3] Brahmapada.

[4] Tejas, which also connotes brilliance and energy.

[5] Buddhi.

[6] Aishvaryya, which also connotes dominion and extraodinary power, such as the eight Siddhis or Vibhutis.

[7] Brahma-sāyujya = Brahmatva (Bhāratī).

[8] Tarkālangkāra says: The object of worship in Brahmasādhanā and Ādyāshaktisādhanā is one and the same. For by Brahman is meant Turīya Brahman united with Mūlaprakriti and by Ādyāshakti is meant Mūlaprakriti as united with Turīya Brahman. It is She who is worshipped under the different names of Māyā, Mahāmāyā, Kālī, Mahākālī and so forth. Brahman and Māyā are not separate entities. Could they be separated then Brahman bereft of activity (Kartritva) would be inert (Jadapadārtha) and Shakti without consciousness (Chaitanya) would also be so. The relation between Brahman and Shakti is non-separateness (Avinābhāva); that is, there can be no Brahman without

know, O Lord! of this excellent worship of Myself, which as Thou sayest is the cause of union of the worshipper with the Brahman (5). What are its rites, and by what means may it be accomplished? What is its Mantra, and what the form of its meditation [1] and mode of worship? [2] (6). O Shambhu [3]! who but Thee, Lord among Physicians of earthly ills, [4] is fit to speak of it, from its beginning to its end, and in all its detail agreeable as it is to Me and beneficent to all humanity? (7).

Hearing the words of the Devī, the Deva of Devas, Husband of Pārvatī, [5] was delighted, and spoke to Her thus: (8).

Shrī Sadāshiva said:

Listen, O Thou of high fortune and destiny, to the reasons why Thou shouldst be worshipped, and how thereby the individual becomes united with the Brahman [6] (9). Thou art the very Parā Prakṛiti [7] of Brahman the

Shakti or Shakti without Brahman. Worship of Brahman is directed towards Brahman as united with Shakti and worship of Shakti is directed towards Shakti as united with Brahman. Therefore the worship of Brahman and worship of Shakti are one and the same. That being so the fruit to be gained by Brahmasādhanā is the same as that to be gained by Shakti-sādhanā.

[1] Dhyāna.

[2] Pūjā.

[3] A name of Shiva; from Sham (happiness, bliss, beatitude), and bhū (to be). He Who is and grants happiness.

[4] Bhavavyādhi. This means both the ill of existence itself and ills flowing therefrom. The ill of existence to those on the Nivṛitti path is repeated birth and death. From this root other ills follow.

[5] Daughter of Parvata, the mountain Himālaya. A name of the Devī.

[6] Here is given the reason why the Sādhanā of the Parameshvarī leads to Brahmasāyujya, namely, that Her Svarūpa is that of the Brahman since they are essentially one.

[7] The Parā (Supreme) Prakṛiti and Paramātmā or Supreme Consciousness are united as one.

Paramâtmâ,[1] and from Thee has sprung the whole Universe —O Shivâ—its Mother[2] (10). O gracious One! whatever there is in this world, of things which have and are without motion, from Mahat[3] to an atom, owes its origin to

[1] Paramâtmâ. Bhâratî explains the word as follows: Parama= He Who is possessed of the Supreme Mâyâ or Shakti; and Âtmâ=He Who pervades all things. Âtmâ comes from the root *At*+man. *At*= to spread. He who spreads is He who pervades all things (A*t*ati sarvang vyâpnoti, iti, Âtmâ). The Âtmâ which is this is the Paramâtmâ (Parameshchâsau âtmâ cheti Paramâtmâ).

[2] On this verse Tarkâlangkâra comments as follows: Paramâtmâ and Parabrahman=Turîya Brahman beyond the three Purus*h*as, *viz.*, the Vishva, Virâ*t* and Jâgrat state, the Taijasa, Hira*n*yagarbha and Svapna state, and the Avyâk*ri*ta, Prâjna and Sus*h*upti state (Avasthâ) of which states the Purus*h*as are Abhimânî. Here Sadâshiva is describing Pârvatî who is an Angsha of Mûlaprak*ri*ti inseparable from it. Turîya Brahman and Mûlaprak*ri*ti are in direct immediate connection (Sâks*h*ât-sambandha, *i.e.*, nothing intervenes—they are one immediately). The Sâmyâvasthâ of the three Gu*n*as when at rest (Nidrâsthâna) or the Nirgu*n*a state=Mûlaprak*ri*ti. On Ks*h*obha or disturbance of equilibrium of the Gu*n*as there arises from the Tâmasik part of Mûlaprak*ri*ti Maheshvara and Mahâkâlî; from the Râjasik part Brahmâ and Mahâsarasvatî, and from the Sâttvik part Mahâvis*h*nu and Mahâlaks*h*mî. These are not in direct connection with Parabrahma but only mediately so (Paramparâsambandha) through the medium of the Gu*n*as. In Pralaya all Gu*n*as are dissolved in Mûlaprak*ri*ti when nothing else exists and as a consequence the eternal connection between Brahman and Mûlaprak*ri*ti is established. At the time of Ks*h*obha of the Gu*n*as, the latter appear separately and Prak*ri*ti takes on two aspects—the pure (Vishuddha) and non-pure (Malina). The first is Parâ Prak*ri*ti, Vidyâ, or Mâyâ and the second is Aparâ Prak*ri*ti, Avidyâ or Ajnâna. The Chaitanya to which is ascribed (Upahita) Parâprak*ri*ti is the omnipotent, omniscient Îshvara or Shiva, and the Chaitanya to which Aparâprak*ri*ti is ascribed is Ajnâna, Jîva. And so the Panchadashî says (I, 15-17) "Prak*ri*ti which is Sattva Rajas Tama Gu*n*a is of two kinds, being according to the purity or non-purity of Sattva (Prakâshâtmaka) gu*n*a, Mâyâ or Avidyâ. The Chidâtmâ reflected on Mâyâ and controlling Her is the Omniscient Îshvara. The Chidâtmâ reflected on Avidyâ and subservient to it by reason of her diversity (Vaichitrya) becomes many as Jîvas.

[3] Mahadâdi, the Tattva Mahat, and the others of the Sâṁkhya Philosophy. This word does not, as is sometimes supposed, mean "great" (Mahat), but is derived from the Vedic "Mahas," or "Maghas," which means "Jyoti*h*," or "Light". (Sâṁkhya darshana by Umesha Chandra Batavyâla.) Tarkâlangkâra says: From Prak*ri*ti originated Mahat-Tattva: from Mahat Ahangkâra: from Ahangkâra the

and is dependent on Thee (11). Thou art the Origin of all the manifestations[1]; Thou art the birth-place of even Us[2]; Thou knowest the whole world, yet none know Thee (12).

Thou art Kālī, Tārinī,[3] Durgā, *Shodashī*, Bhuvaneshvarī, Dhūmāvatī. Thou art Bagalā, Bhairavī, and Chhinnamastaka.[4] Thou art Anna-pūrnā,[5] Vāgdevī,[6] Kamalālayā.[7] Thou art in the form of all the Shaktis[8] and Thou pervadest the bodies of all the Devas (13-14). Thou art both subtle[9] and gross, manifested and veiled, though in Thyself formless, yet Thou hast form. Who can understand

eleven Indriyas and the five Tanmātras and from the latter the five Mahābhūtas. These are the 24 Tattvas of the Sāngkhya Darshana. Combination of substance (Yaugika *srishti*) does not produce any new Tattvas. In the case of the earth and jar and gold and ornament there is no difference in substance. The process according to Tantra is extremely wonderful so much so that the knowing of it produces Divyajnāna. It is not possible however to explain it in a short compass. The Nyāya and Sāngkhya are not so subtle as this. The philosophers differ but the Tantrik doctrine conflicts with none. He who desires to know it and get thereby a glimpse of the Brahman should get instruction in the Uttara Āmnāya from a good Guru; he will then gain the highest end of man.

[1] That is, primarily the Dasha-Mahāvidyā. The Devī as Kālī, Tārā, Chhinnamastā, Dhūmāvatī, *Shodashī*, Bhuvaneshvarī, Bagalā, Kamalā, Mātangī, Bhairavī.

[2] Brahmā, Vishnu, and Shiva. These are forms of and subordinate to the Great Mother assumed for the purpose of creation and so forth.

[3] Tārinī is Tārā; Durgā is another manifestation of the same Devī.

[4] See A. and Ellen Avalon's "Hymns to the Goddess".

[5] The Devī as Dispenser of food; an aspect addressed by Shangkarāchārya as the Devī bountiful.

[6] Devī of speech, wisdom, knowledge, science, art, eloquence, music—that is, Sarasvatī, Shakti of Brahmā.

[7] Lakshmī, spouse of Vishnu, "Who lives in the lotus".

[8] The energy or active power of a Deva, worshipped as His wife under various names. Each Deva necessarily has His Shakti. See Woodroffe's "Shakti and Shākta" and "Garland of Letters".

[9] Sūkshmā; subtle as the Paramānu and therefore Avyaktā. As gross She is Vyaktā.

Thee?[1] (15). For the helping of the worshipper, the good of the world, and the destruction of the Dānavas,[2] Thou dost assume various forms[3] (16). Thou art four-armed, two-armed, six-armed, and eight-armed, and holdest various missiles and weapons for the protection of the Universe[4] (17). In various Tantras I have spoken of the Sādhanā of different Mantras[5] and Yantras,[6] and the like appropriate to the respective different forms assumed by Thee as also to the three different disposition of men[7] (18). In this Kali Age there is no Pashu-bhāva: Divya-bhāva is difficult of attainment, but the practices relating to Vīra-sādhana[8] yield visible fruit (19).

[1] Bhagavatī as Mūlaprakriti is subtile (Sūkshmā), unmanifest (Avyaktā), and formless (Nirākārā). As Shakti appearing (Āvirbhūtā) from out of Mūlaprakriti; as the threefold Nāda or Mahat-Tattva issuing from Shakti; as the threefold Bindu or the three Ahangkāras (Sāttvika, Rājasika, Tāmasika or Vaikārika, Taijasa, Bhūtādika) issuing from the threefold Nāda; as Shabdajnāna, Sparshajnāna, Rūpajnāna, Gandhajnāna (of the Apanchīkrita Tanmātras) issuing from Sāttvika Ahangkāra; as Shabdashakti. Sparsha-shakti, etc., (of the same) issuing from Rājasika Ahangkāra; as the Apanchīkrita Tanmātras issuing from Tāmasika Ahangkāra; as the Bhūtas and their compounds which make up clay and so forth—She is Vyaktā, Sthūlā and Sākārā (Tarkālangkāra). According to Rāghava Bhatta (Shāradā Tilaka, I, 19, 20) the Devas issue from Vaikārika Ahangkāra, the Indriyas from the Rājasika and the Tanmātras from Bhūtādika. Nirākārā and the other first mentioned terms are apparently used in a relative sense.

[2] A class of Asuras, sons of Danu, daughter of Daksha, and Kashyapa. There are sixty-one, of which eighteen are principal.

[3] Here the question "If I am in reality formless (Nirākārā) then why do I assume different forms?" is anticipated and answered.

[4] Gives some of the forms assumed by the Devī.

[5] See Woodroffe's "Shakti and Shākta" and "Garland of Letters".

[6] Diagrams (see *ibid.*).

[7] That is, the Pashu, Vīra, and Divya dispositions (see *ibid.*).

[8] The worship suited to men in whom the passionate Guna (Rajas) prevails. See as to this passage Introduction to Vol. VI, "Tāntrik Texts". Tarkālangkāra's note is that as in the Kaliyuga Vīrabhāva alone exists, the rules of Vīrasādhana alone yield immediate fruit and should be practised.

In this Kali Age, O Devī! success is achieved by Kaulika worship[1] alone, and therefore should it be performed with every care (20). By it, O Devī! is acquired knowledge of Brahman, and the mortal who has gained it, is of a surety whilst living[2] freed from future births and exonerated from the performance of all religious rites (21). According to human knowledge the same thing appears to be pure and same impure,[3] but when Brahma-jnāna has been acquired there is nothing either pure or impure (22). For to him who knows that the Brahman is in all things and eternal, what is there that can be impure? (23). Thou art in the form of all, and above all Thou art the Mother of all. If Thou art pleased, O Queen of the Devas! then all are pleased[4] (24).

Before the Beginning of things Thou didst exist in the form of Tamas which is beyond both speech and mind, and of Thee by the creative desire of the Supreme Brahman was the entire Universe born[5] (25). This Universe, from

[1] Kulāchāra.

[2] Jīvanmukta.

[3] For him who is endowed with Brahma-jnāna, who sees the Brahman in everything, there is no distinction.

Jnānena medhyam akhilam amedhyang jnānato bhavet,
Brahma-jnāne samutpanne medhyāmedhyang na vidyate.

[4] The Devī exists in the form of all things (Sarvarūpinī) and is the true nature of all things (Sarvasvarūpā). As Mūlaprakriti She is the Mother (Jananī) of all. She is Vishva Virāt, Taijasa Hiranyagarbha, Avyākrita Prājna and Avyakta. She is the Root of the whole universe. As by watering the roots, the branches, leaves, flowers and fruits of a tree are nourished, in the same way if She is pleased then Brahmā, Vishnu and others are all pleased (Tarkālangkāra).

[5] The Maitrī Upanishad (v. 52) says: Tamo vā idam agra āsīt: tatpare syāt: tatparenaritang: vishamatvam prayāti: etad vai rajas: tadrajah khalvīritang vishamatvam prayāti; etad vai sattvasya rūpam: tat sattvam eva īritang rasah.

Verily this was at first Tamas alone. It abode in the Supreme. Then being set in motion by the Supreme it passes into inequality (loss of equilibrium). This is Rajas. This Rajas being moved passes into inequality. Then is the form of (or condition which is) Sattva.

Mahat[1] down to the gross elements,[2] has been created by Thee, since Brahman, Cause of all causes, is but the efficient Cause[3] (26). It is Pure Being, Changeless, Omnipresent, Pure Consciousness unattached to,[4] yet existing in all things (27). It acts not, neither does It enjoy. It moves not, neither is It motionless. It is true Being[5] and

---

This Sattva being set in motion there is Rasa (Rasa = Chidânanda-prakâsha). On this Tarkâlangkâra says that the word Tamas here means Mûlaprakriti: that is at the time of Pralaya (Dissolution) Tamo Guna retracts (Samhâra) the whole world. Then Sattva Guna as manifested is merged in Rajas and Rajas in Tamas which alone remains and then merges in Mûlaprakriti. By this I understand him to mean that Rajas works to suppress Sattva which becomes latent to bring into full action Tamas when all manifestation ceases. Then before the beginning of the next "Creation" or Production (*Srishti*) there is a stir (*Kshobha*) in the Gunas of Prakriti. Tamo Guna appears first: then Rajas: then Sattva. In the Shâradâ this Tamas has been called Shakti: *Cf.* "Eternal Shiva is Nirguna and Saguna. The first is He who is Prakritor anyah or the other of Prakriti," that is, "He and She are one but here He is considered as other than Her. (Râghava Bhatta says Prakriteh is used in the genitive not ablative case). Saguna is He who is with Kalâ (that is, Mûlaprakriti). From Paramashiva who is Sachchidânanda and Sakala issued Shakti, from Shakti issued Nâda and from Nâda Bindu". Here the Paramashiva who is united with Kalâ or Mûlaprakriti Shakti is Tamo Guna. Some also call it Mûla Ajnâna. By Nâda is meant Mahat-tattva which is threefold according to the Gunas. These three Nâdas are Avyakta Maheshvara, Avyakta Brahmâ and Avyakta Vishnu.

[1] Mahat-Tattva. This is the cosmic stuff of experience. See note to v. 11, *ante*.

[2] Earth, Water, Fire, Air, and Ether.

[3] Nimitta—that is, Instrumental or Efficient Cause, as opposed to Upâdâna or Material Cause. Prakriti is the latter, whilst Purusha is the former. Prakriti cannot move without the Purusha. The proximity of the latter affects the Rajoh guna or stirring passionate quality in Prakriti, and with this stirring the Evolution of matter commences. Under the influence of the gaze of Purusha, Prakriti commences the world-dance.

[4] Nirlipta, as a drop of water on the lotus-leaf. The creator unlike the creature is not affected by His Mâyâ.

[5] Satyam: that is, as Hariharânanda says, Yathârthasvarûpam; that is, as It is in Itself, the true, that is, lasting Reality.

Consciousness, without beginning or end, Ineffable and Incomprehensible (28).[1]

Thou the Supreme Yoginī[2] dost, moved by His mere desire,[3] create, protect, and withdraw this world with all that moves and is motionless therein (29). Mahākāla,[4] the Dissolver of the Universe, is Thy form. At the Dissolution of things, it is Kāla Who will devour all (30), and by reason of this[5] He is called Mahākāla, and since Thou devourest Mahākāla Himself, it is Thou who art the Supreme Primordial Kālikā (31).[6]

Because Thou devourest Kāla, Thou art Kālī, because Thou art the Origin of and devourest all things Thou art called the Ādyā Kālī[7] (32). Resuming after dissolution Thine own nature, dark and formless,[8] ineffable and inconceivable Thou alone remainest as the One (33). Though having a form, yet art Thou formless; though Thyself without

---

[1] Paramabrahma is not creator and has no activity. Prakriti like iron moved by the magnet (Purusha) creates, upholds and dissolves by the mere presence of Parama Brahma. The proximity of the spring season is the mere efficient (Nimitta mātra) of the blossoming of the leaves and flowers on the trees. In the same way the Supreme Brahman is the mere efficient in creation and so forth, the three Gunas being the material cause (Upādānakārana)--Tarkālangkāra.

[2] Mahā-yoginī. Mahā-yoginī is a title of Shiva. Yoginī is derived from Yoga Shabda with the suffix *nin*. Here Yoga means the collectivity of all that is. Yoginī is She who shines therein (see commentary to v. 2, ch. IV, Yoginīhridaya). That commentary says that Yoginī is Tripurasundarī who is Svasamvit. Her redness is Her Vimarsha.

[3] Ichchhā.

[4] A Tāmasik form of Shiva as He who dissolves all, under which He is represented as of a black colour of terrific aspect. The term comes from Mahā = Great, and Kala = to swallow.

[5] Kalanāt sarvā-bhūtānām = by reason of His devouring all gross or material existence.

[6] Ādyā Kālikā.

[7] Primeval Kālī. Mūlaprakriti united with Turīya Brahman is worshipped as Ādyā Kālī (Tarkālangkāra).

[8] Her Svarūpa is Tamorūpa.

beginning, multiform by the power of Māyā,[1] Thou art the Beginning of all, Creatrix, Protectress, and Destructress that Thou art (34). Hence it is, O Gentle One! that I have said to Thee that whatsoever fruit is attained by the initiate in the Brahma-Mantra, the same may be had by the Sādhanā of Thee (35).

According to the differences in place, time, and capacity of the worshippers I have, O Devī! spoken of Sādhanā suited to the mode of life governing them and their dispositions[2] (36). Where men perform that worship which they are competent[3] to perform, there they participate in the fruits of worship, and being freed from sin will cross the Ocean of Being (37). By merit acquired in many previous births the mind inclines to Kaula doctrine, and he whose soul is purified by such worship himself becomes Shiva[4] (38). Where there is abundance of enjoyment, of

---

[1] By and of which the universe is created.

[2] All men are not to follow the same form of Sādhanā; as men differ in their character and ability so does the Sādhanā. It is useless to prescribe a high vedāntik Sādhanā for an ignorant and untrained intellect, what is prescribed for it is what it can understand and carry out. There are therefore differences in Āchāra, that is, the Rules governing conduct, way of life such as Veda, Vaish*n*ava and Shaiva Achāras. There are also differences of disposition (Bhāva) namely Pashu, Vira and Divya. Thus no Pashu is competent for Gupta-Sādhanā or the secret ritual, the form of Sādhanā must be determined after reference to all the circumstances of the particular case. This is the doctrine of Adhikāra or competency. See note below.

[3] Ye yatrādhik*r*itā martyās te tatra phala-bhāgina*h*. Thus a Vaish*n*ava should not follow Shaiva practice, and only a Kaulika Tāntrika is privileged to perform its rites. By *Yatra*, Bhāratī says, is meant either secret or overt worship. Man's mode of worship, it is said, should be according to his *Adhikāra*, or competency, and it is only if he worships within his *Adhikāra* that he will enjoy the fruit of his worship, and thereby be freed from his sins and attain Liberation. As to Adhikāra see "Alleged Conflict of Shāstras" by Arthur Avalon, p. 288 "Shakti and Shākta", 4th Edn., based on Bhāskararāya's commentary on the Nityā*shod*ashika Tantra.

[4] Bahu-janmārjitai*h* pu*n*yai*h* kulāchāre matir bhavet,
Kulāchāre*n*a pūtātmā sāksh*ā*ch chhivamayo bhavet.

what use is it to speak of Yoga,[1] and where there is Yoga there is no enjoyment, but the Kaula[2] enjoys both[3] (39).

If one honours but one person versed in the knowledge of the essence of Kula doctrine,[4] then all the Devas and Devis are worshipped—there is no doubt of that (40). The merit gained by honouring a Kaulika is ten million times that which is acquired by giving away the world with all its gold (41). A Cha*nd*âla versed in the knowledge of Kaulika doctrine excels a Brâhma*n*a, and a Brâhma*n*a who is wanting in such knowledge is beneath even a Cha*nd*âla[5] (42).

---

[1] See A. Avalon's "Serpent Power".

[2] Kaula Tântrika. See for his Āchāra the Tantrasāra.

[3] Yatrāsti bhoga-bāhulyang tatra yogasya kā kathā
Yoge'pi bhogavirahah Kaulastūbhayam ashnute.

This is a fundamental principle of the Tantrik method. The Kaula thus enjoys both Bhoga and Yoga, the worship being with enjoyment. Yoga is the union of Prā*n*a and Apāna, of seed and ovum, of "Sun" and "Moon," of Nāda and Bindu, of Jīvātmā and Paramātmā. So also the Rudra-yāmala and the Maṁgala-rāja-stava say: "Where there is worldly enjoyment there is no Liberation; where there is Liberation, there is no worldly enjoyment. But in the case of excellent devotees of Shrīsundarī both Liberation and Enjoyment are in the hollow of their hands."

[4] He who acquires divine knowledge (Brahma-tattva) becomes no longer subject to change; the bond which holds him to worldly things is cut. The Kula-tattva-jna is one versed in the knowledge of Kula. Kula means Brahma sanātanam, as the Kulār*n*ava Tantra states: "Na kulang kulamityāhu*h* kulang Brahma sanātanam"—*i.e.*, by Kula is not meant family dignity, but the Sanātana Brahman. It is also said: "Kulang Ku*nd*alinīshaktir Akulang tu Maheshvara*h*." Ku*nd*alī is Kula, the Maheshvara is Akula, She is Shakti and He who has mastered knowledge concerning Ku*nd*alinī is Brahma tattvajna and Brahman Itself in so far as he is a realiser. For Brahman is Chaitanya united with Shakti and Ku*nd*alinī is Shakti united with Chaitanya. To the understanding they are one and the same. It is only to limited knowledge that they appear to be two and separate.

[5] One of the degraded castes engaged in work on the cremation-ground, bone-collecting, and the like. Their touch is pollution.

I know of no Dharma superior to that of the Kaulas, by adherence to which man attains Divine Experience[1] (43). I am telling Thee the truth, O Devī! Lay it to the heart and ponder over it. There is no doctrine superior to the Kaulika doctrine, the most excellent of all (44). This is the most excellent path kept hidden by reason of the crowd of Pashus,[2] but when the Kali Age advances this pathway will be revealed (45).

Verily and verily I say unto you that when the Kali Age reaches the fullness of its strength there will be no Pashus, and all men on earth will be followers of the Kaulika doctrine (46). O beauteous One![3] know that when Vedic and Purā*n*ic initiations cease then the Kali Age has become strong (47). O Shivā! O Peaceful One! when virtue and vice are no longer judged by the Vedic rules, then know that the Kali Age has become strong (48).

O Sovereign Mistress of Kaula doctrine! when the Heavenly Stream[4] is at some places broken, and at others diverted from its course, then know that the Kali Age

---

[1] Kaula-dharmāt paro dharmo nāsti jnāne tu māmake,
Yasyānu*sh*t*h*āna-mātre*n*a Brahma-jnānī naro bhavet.

The second line gives the reason for the assertion made in the first. He has divine experience (Brahmajnāna).

[2] Men of the animal disposition in whom Tamas Gu*n*a prevails. See A. Avalon's "Shakti and Shākta". A man who is Pāsha-baddha that is bound by the eight fetters (Pāsha) that is Kula, Shīla, Mo*h*a, Lajjā, Gh*r*i*n*ā, Dayā, Var*n*a, Bhaya and devoid of true knowledge of the Real (Tattva-jnāna) is a Pashu. The latter is of three kinds: best (Uttama), middling (Madhyama) and low or worst (Adhama). The first are those who faithfully follow Vedāchara, Vai*sh*n*a*vāchāra, and Shaivāchāra and are not hostile to any Devatā. The last are those who are hostile to the Devas and act as they please in neglect of the injunctions of Dharma Shāstra. The second class are between these two. Kulamārga is kept hidden by reason of the great number of these three classes of Pashu.

[3] *Lit.* one with beautiful hips. Vv. 46-55 give the signs (Lak*sh*a*n*a) of the prevalence of Kali Yuga.

[4] The Ganges—Gaṁgā.

has become strong (49). O wise One! when kings of the Mlechchha race[1] become excessively covetous, then know that the Kali Age has become strong (50). When women become difficult of control, heartless and quarrelsome, and disparagators of their husbands, then know that the Kali Age has become strong (51). When men become subject to women and slaves of lust, oppressors of their friends and Gurus,[2] then know that the Kali Age has become strong (52). When the fertility of the earth has gone and yields a poor harvest, when the clouds yield scanty rain, and trees give meagre fruit, then know that the Kali Age has become strong (53). When brothers, kinsmen, and companions, prompted by the desire for some trifle, will strike one another, then know that the Kali Age has become strong (54). Even when the open partaking of flesh and liquor will pass without condemnation and punishment, yet secret drinking will still prevail, then know that the Kali Age has become strong[3] (55).

As in the Satya, Tretā, and Dvāpara Ages wine and the like[4] could be taken (openly), so they may be taken in the Kali Age in accordance with the Kaulika Dharma[5] (56). The Kali Age cannot harm those who are purified by truth, who have conquered their passions and senses, who are

---

[1] Mlechchha is a term applied to all non-Aryan peoples, such as the English, the term Ārya, according to Hindu notions, being confined to the people of Āryāvarta.

[2] Guru includes, besides spiritual teachers, others who are deserving of respect. Thus mother and father are called Mahāguru, and the husband is the Mahāguru of the wife.

[3] This eating and drinking is the eating and drinking of non-Kaulas (see next verse), for the sake of animal appetite only.

[4] Madyādi: that is wine, meat and the like. Hariharānanda Bhāratī says that in the first three Ages wine and the like were taken openly (Prakāshata*h*).

[5] Tāntrika doctrine of the Kaulas, or Kulāchāra. As to Kula see note to verse 40, *ante*.

open in their ways, without deceit, are compassionate and follow the Kaula[1] doctrine (57). The Kali Age cannot harm those who are devoted to the service of their Guru, to the lotus of their mothers' feet, and to their own wives (58). The Kali Age cannot harm those who are vowed to and grounded in Truth, adherents of the true Dharma,[2] and faithful to the performance of Kaulika rites and duties (59). The Kali Age cannot harm those who give to the truthful Kaulika Yogī the elements of worship,[3] which have been previously purified by Kaulika rites (60).

The Kali Age cannot harm those who are free of malice, envy, hypocrisy, and hatred, and who are firm in the faith of Kaulika[4] Dharma (61). The Kali Age cannot harm those who keep the company of Kaulikas, or live with Kaulika devotees,[5] or serve the Kaulikas (62). The Kali Age cannot harm those Kaulikas who, whatever they may appear outwardly to be,[6] yet remain firm in

---

[1] Tāntrika doctrine of the Kaulas, or Kulāchāra.

[2] Law of conduct.

[3] Tattva: meat, fish, wine, parched food, and woman after purification by the Tāntrika ritual (Shodhana).

[4] *Vide ante.*

[5] Sādhus, such as practise Shmashānasādhana (worship in the cremation-ground), Shavasādhana (worship seated on a corpse), Latāsādhanā, etc., are called Kulasādhus.

[6] Nānā-vesha-dharā*h*—literally, having different dress or sectarian marks, etc. This is often understood to mean and may mean that the Vāmāchārīs' open professions are different from, and help to conceal their adherence to, the secret doctrine. But another inner meaning is said to be, not that the Kaula is enjoined to practise hypocrisy, but that a man may be a Shākta at heart, whatever his apparent sect may be. Thus there are Gossains who are known to be Vaish*n*avas, but who are in fact Shākteyas. *Cf.* Nityā Tantra, chap. iii; also Niruttara Tantra, chap. i; also Tantra-sāra, Kulāchāra-Prakara*n*a, which says: "Shāktas in their heart and outwardly Shaivas, and in assemblies as Vaish*n*avas, the Kaulas go about in this world in different guises." The reference is made to "assemblies," because Vaish*n*avas worship in assemblies, that is congregational worship.

their adherence to Kaula[1] Āchāra, and worship Thee according to its doctrine (63). The Kali Age cannot harm those who perform their ablutions, charities, penances, pilgrimages, devotions,[2] and offerings of water[3] according to the rules of Kulāchāra[4] (64).

The Kali Age cannot harm those who perform the ten purificatory ceremonies,[5] such as the blessing of the womb,[6] obsequial ceremonies of their fathers,[7] and other rites according to Kaulika ritual (65). The Kali Age cannot harm those who respect the Kula-tattva, Kula-dravya[8] and Kula-yogī[9] (66).

The Kali Age is but the slave of those who are free of all crookedness and falsehood, men of candour, devoted to the good of others, who follow Kaulika ways (67). In spite of its many blemishes, the Kali Age possesses one

---

[1] *Vide ante.*

[2] Vrata.

[3] Tarpana.

[4] *Vide ante.*

[5] Sangskāra (see *post*, verses 88-90, and Chapter IX).

[6] The Jīvaseka or Garbhādhāna ceremony, from Garbha (womb) and Ādhāna (placing upon), the placing of seed in the womb described in Chapter IX, verse 107.

[7] Shrāddha (see note, Ch. III, 2).

[8] The Tattva is ordinarily used in the sense of Pancha-makāra, as in verse 60, but the commentator Bhāratī says that Kula-dravya here refers to these, and that in this context Kula-tattva are five kinds of Tāntrika "flowers"—*viz.*, (1) Vajra-pushpa, (2) Svayambhu-kusuma, (3) Kunda-pushpa, (4) Gola-pushpa, (5) Sārva-kālika-pushpa. The word "flower" is (as in English) used symbolically for the *Ritu*, as to which see Chapter V, verse 174, where the meaning of (2), (3), (4), is given. Sārva-kālika-pushpa, which literally means "the flower of all seasons," is of any kind—that is, is not, as in (2), (3), (4), confined to the *Ritu* which first appears and of any particular woman. According to Kulachūdāmani No. (1) is used in drawing on a plate of gold the Yantra of Tārā.

[9] Kulamārgī.

great merit, that from the mere resolve[1] of a Kaulika if sincere, desired result ensues (68). In the other Ages, O Devī! effort of will produced both religious merit and demerit, but in the Kali Age men by intention acquire merit only, and not demerit[2] (69). The slaves of the Kali Age, on the other hand, are those who know not Kulāchāra,[3] and who are ever untruthful and the persecutors of others (70). They too are the slaves of the Kali Age who have no faith in Kulāchāra,[3] who lust after others' wives, and oppress the faithful followers of Kaulika[3] doctrine (71).

In speaking of the customs of the different Ages, I have, O Gentle One! O Pārvatī! briefly recounted to please Thee the signs of the dominance of the Kali Age (72). When the Kali Age is made manifest, all Dharma[4] is enfeebled and Truth alone remains; therefore should one be truthful[5] (73). O Thou Virtuous One! know this for certain, that whatsoever man does with Truth[6] that bears,[7] fruit (74). There is no Dharma higher

---

[1] Sangkalpa.

[2] Apare tu yuge devi puṇyam pāpancha mānasam.
Nṛiṇām āsīt kalau puṇyang kevalang na tu dush-kṛitam.

The Shloka is Stuti-vāda, or honorific speech and means that in former Ages men's intentions had result in good or evil as they wished, but in the present Age, whilst good intentions are quickly realised, from bad intentions evil is slow to result; for the Kali Age, though a degraded Age, is also a favoured one. The child himself may be a weakling, but the greater its infirmities the greater the Mother's help and favours.

[3] *Vide ante.* See Kulārṇava.

[4] Sarve dharmāḥ, all observances prescribed for the maintenance of the individual and community.

[5] Tasmāt satyamayo bhavet; that is, should become one with Truth, realise it in all his being. Bhāratī says that in this and the following verse Mahādeva desires to say that when Kali Yuga is dominant then Kulāchāra should be practised openly.

[6] Satya-dharma.

[7] Saphalang Karma.

than Truth,[1] there is no sin greater than falsehood; therefore should man seek protection under Truth with all his soul (75). Worship without Truth is useless, and so too without Truth is the Japa[2] of Mantras and the performance of Tapas.[3] It is in such cases just as if one sowed seed in salt earth (76).

Truth is the appearance of the Supreme Brahman; Truth is the most excellent of all Tapas[3]; every act is rooted in Truth. Than Truth there is nothing more excellent (77). Therefore has it been said by Me that when the sinful Kali Age is dominant, Kaula ways[4] should be practised truthfully and without concealment[5] (78). Truth is divorced from concealment. There is no concealment without untruth. Therefore is it that the Kaulika-sādhaka should perform his Kaulika-sādhana openly (79). What I have said in other Kaulika Tantras about the concealment[5] of Kaulika-dharma not being blameworthy is not applicable when the Kali Age becomes strong[6] (80).

In the (First or) Satya Age, O Devī! Virtue possessed the four quarters of its whole; in the Tretā Age it lost one-quarter of its Virtue; in the Dvāpara Age there was

---

[1] Na hi satyāt paro dharmaḥ.

[2] Recitation.

[3] Austerities (see Ch. LV, 21, and notes).

[4] Kulāchāra.

[5] *Vide ante*, note to verse 63, and Niruttara Tantra, chap. i, "Rātrau kula-kriyām kuryāt, divā kuryāt cha vaidikīm" (In the day do the Vaidika and in the night the Kaulika rites)—a rule of Vīrāchāra only, as Pashus are, however, prohibited from performing Sādhanā at night, as all such Sādhanā connotes Maithuna it has been said—Rātrau naiva yajed Devīng, sandhyāyāng vāparāhnake (Nityā Tantra). It is said "at night" not for concealment, but as denoting the particular form of worship then done. See Ch. X, verse 111. In this verse, Bhāratī says, a question is anticipated and answered.

[6] This is an ordinance abrogating during the period mentioned the law of secrecy, which had governed the Tāntrika Vīrāchāra ritual when the Vaidikāchāra prevailed.

of Virtue but two quarters, and in the Kali Age it has but one (81). In spite of that Truth will remain strong, though Tapas[1] and Charity become weakened. If the one quarter which is Truth goes Virtue goes also, therefore of all acts Truth should be the abiding support (82). O Sovereign Mistress of the Kaula-Dharma[2]! since men can in this Age have recourse to Kaulika Dharma only, if that doctrine be itself infected with untruth, how can there be Liberation? (83). With his soul purified in every way by Truth, man should, perform all acts enjoined by his caste and stage[3] of life, in the manner shown by Me (84). Initiation,[4] worship,[5] recitation of Mantras,[6] the offering of oblation to Fire with Ghee,[7] repetition of Mantras,[8] occasional devotions,[9] marriage,[10] the conception ceremony,[11] and that performed in the fourth, sixth, or eighth months of pregnancy,[12] the natal rite,[13] the naming[14] and tonsure[15] ceremonies, and obsequial rites upon cremation[16] and after death[17]—all such

---

[1] Austerity, etc.

[2] Kuleshvari.

[3] Āshrama.

[4] Dīksha.

[5] Pūjā.

[6] Japa.

[7] Homa.

[8] Purashcharana.

[9] Vrata.

[10] Udvāha. For this and the following, see Ch. IX, *post*.

[11] Pungsavana.

[12] Sīmantonnayana.

[13] Jāta-karma.

[14] Nāma-karana.

[15] Chūdā-karana. In all castes the Shikhā or tuft at the back of the head is kept. The Kshatriya preserves also the Kāka-paksha (the hair on the cheek).

[16] Mrita-kritya, or Mrita-kriyā.

[17] Shrāddha.

ceremonies should be performed in the manner approved by the Āgamas (85-86).

The ritual which I have ordained should be followed, too, as regards Shrāddha at holy places,[1] dedication of a bull,[2] the autumnal festival,[3] on setting out on a journey,[4] on the first entry into a house,[5] the wearing of new clothes or jewels, dedication of tanks, wells or lakes,[6] in the ceremonies performed at the phases of the Moon,[7] the building[8] and consecration of houses, the installation[9] of Devas, and in all observances to be performed during the day[10] or at night, or on special occasions[10] in each month, season, or year, and in observances both daily or occasional,[11] and also in deciding generally what ought and what ought not to be done, and in determining what ought to be rejected and what ought to be adopted (87-90).

Should one not follow the ritual ordained, whether from ignorance, wickedness, or lack of faith, then one is disqualified for all observances, and becomes a worm in dung (91).

---

[1] As at Gayā, Prayāga.

[2] *Vrish*otsarga Shrāddha of the second degree, the first being Dānasāgara (Ocean of gifts); the third is Chandana-dhenu (Sandalwood and Cows), which is performed only for women who leave surviving their husbands and sons; the fourth is Tila-kānchana (Til seed and Gold).

[3] Shāradotsava, *i.e.*, the Durgā Pūjā, in autumn (Sharat), the vernal (Vasanta) worship being called Vāsantī.

[4] Yātrā.

[5] *Gri*ha-pravesha—that is, entering into a house for the first time to live there.

[6] See chapter xiii, *post*, verse 166.

[7] Tithikarma.

[8] *Gri*hārambha = beginning to build a house, laying the foundation of a house.

[9] Prati*shth*ā.

[10] Divā*kri*tya, Nishi*kri*tya and Parva*kri*tya. The first is any rite required to be done in day time; the second what is enjoined to be done at night and the last as what is ordered to be done on special occasions (Parva) such as festival, day of eclipse and the like.

[11] Naimittika = That is rites necessary for the attainment of any special object.

O Maheshi[1]! if when the Kali Age has become very powerful any act be done in violation of My precepts, then that which happens is the very contrary of that which is desired (92). Initiation of which I have not approved destroys the life of the Sādhaka[2] and an act of worship not so approved is as fruitless as oblations poured on ashes,[3] and the Deva whom he worships becomes angry or hostile, and at every step he encounters danger (93). Ambikā[4]! he who during the dominance of the Kali Age, knowing My ordinances, yet performs his religious observances in other ways, is a great sinner (94). The man who performs any Vrata,[5] or marries according to other ways, will remain in a terrible Hell so long as the Sun and Moon endure (95). By his performance of Vrata he incurs the sin of killing a Brahma*n*a, and similarly a boy invested with the sacred thread becomes degraded.[6] He merely wears the thread, and is lower than a Cha*nd*āla[7] (96), and so too the woman who is married according to other ways than Mine is to be despised, and, O Sovereign Mistress of the Kaulas[8]! the man who so marries is her associate in wrong, and is day

---

[1] Feminine of Mahesha = Great Lord.

[2] Sādhakaprā*n*aghātinī; that is if the Sādhaka does Sādhana with a Mantra not communicated in manner approved by Mahādeva then it leads to his death.

[3] They should be poured on living Fire.

[4] A title of the Devī, meaning Mother of the Universe (see Lalitā-sahasra-nāma, verse 69). Devī is also called Holy Mother (Shrī-mātā). In a technical sense Ambikā is the name for the first movement of the Vimarsha Shakti.

[5] Occasional devotion.

[6] Vrātya = a degraded or disqualified Brāhma*n*a.

[7] See note under ch. iii, 84.

[8] Kula-nāyikā, used here in this sense (Mistress of the Tāntrikas), though also denoting the woman worshipped as Shakti in Latāsādhana by Vāmāchārīs.

after day guilty of the sin of going with a prostitute[1] (97). From him the Devatā will not accept food, water, and other offerings, nor will the Pitris[2] eat his offerings, considering them to be as it were mere dung and pus (98). Their children are bastards,[3] and disqualified for all religious, ancestral, and Kaulika[4] observances and rites (99) To an image dedicated by rites other than those prescribed by Shambhu[5] the Deva never comes. Benefit there is none either in this or the next world. There is but mere waste of labour and money (100).

A Shrāddha performed according to other rites than those prescribed by the Āgamas is fruitless, and he who performs it will go to Hell together with his Pitris[6] (101). The water offered by him is like blood, and the funeral cake[7] like dung. Let the mortal then follow with great care the precepts of Shangkara[8] (102). What is the need of saying more? Verily and verily I say to You, O Devī! that all that is done in disregard of the precepts of Shambhu[8] is fruitless (103). For him who follows not His precepts there is no future merit. That which has been already acquired is destroyed, and for him there is no escape from Hell (104). O Great Ruler[9]! the performance of daily and occasional duties in the manner spoken

---

[1] Maithuna purchased at a price (Kraya-krīta-maithuna) is greatly condemned.

[2] The departed Spirits of the Ancestors.

[3] Kānīna=son of an unmarried woman. Kānīnah kanyakā-Jāto mātāmaha-suto matah (Yājnavalkya).

[4] Observances of Kula worship.

[5] Shiva.

[6] The departed Spirits of the Ancestors (see note, ch. i, 20), for whose spiritual benefit Shrāddha is performed.

[7] Pinda.

[8] Title of Shiva (see note, ch. i, 5).

[9] Maheshāni, feminine of Maheshāna, title of Shiva.

of by Me is the same as worshipping Thee (105). Hear from Me O Devī! the particulars of the worship with its Mantras[1] and Yantras,[2] which is the medicine for the ills of the Kali Age (106).

End of the Fourth Chapter, entitled "Introduction of the Worship of the Supreme Prakriti".

---

[1] See Woodroffe's "Garland of Letters" and "Shakti and Shākta".

[2] Used in worship as Pratika or representative of the Devatā. Each Devatā has His or Her own Yantra. Yantra which literally means instrument is the instrument by which worship is done. Diagrams (see *Ibid.*).

CHAPTER V

MANTRAS AND PURIFICATION

SHRĪ SADĀSHIVA said:

Thou art the Ādyā Paramā Shakti,[1] Thou art all power.[2] It is by Thy power[3] that We (the Trinity) are powerful[4] in the acts of Creation, Preservation, and Dissolution. Endless and of varied colour and form are Thy appearances, and various are the strenuous efforts whereby (Thy Sādhakas) may realise them. Who can describe them? (1-2). In the Kula Tantras and Āgamas[5] I have, by the aid of but a small part of Thy mercy and with all My powers, described the Sādhana and Archana[6] of Thy appearances; yet nowhere else is this secret Sādhana revealed. It is by the grace of this (Sādhana), O Blessed One[7]! that Thy mercy in Me is so great (3-4). Questioned by Thee I am no longer able to conceal it. For Thy pleasure, O Beloved! I shall speak of that which is dearer to Me than even life itself (5). To all sufferings it brings relief.. It

[1] That is, Primordial Supreme Power. In this chapter Sadāshiva describes the particular worship (Vishesharādhana) of Devī in which Mantra and Yantra is used (Bhāratī).

[2] Sarva-shakti-svarūpinī. That is the Devī is the one Shakti which manifests itself in different forms.

[3] Tava shaktyā.

[4] Shaktāh.

[5] See "Principles of Tantra."

[6] As to the specific meaning of these terms, which, speaking generally, mean spiritual discipline and worship, see Woodroffe's "Shakti and Shākta".

[7] Kalyānī. This word has elsewhere been interpreted to mean "Giver of Liberation"— Mokshadāyinī.

wards off all dangers. It gives Thee pleasure, and is the way by which Thou art most easily obtained (6). For men rendered wretched by the taint of the Kali Age,[1] short-lived and unfit for strenuous effort, this is the greatest wealth (7). In this (Sādhana which will be described) there is no need for a multiplicity of Nyāsa,[2] for fasting or other practices of self-restraint.[3] It is simple and pleasurable, yet yields great fruit to the worshipper (8). Then first listen, O Devī! to the Mantroddhāra[4] of the Mantra, the mere hearing of which liberates man from future births while yet living[5] (9).

By placing "Prāṇesha" on "Taijasa," and adding to it "Bheruṇḍā" and the Bindu, the first Bīja[6] is formed.[7] After this, proceed to the second (10). By placing "Sandhyā" on "Rakta," and adding to it "Vāmanetra" and Bindu, the second Bīja is formed.[8] Now listen, O Blessed One! to the formation of the third Bīja.

---

[1] The last and worst age.

[2] See "Shakti and Shākta."

[3] Saṁyama.

[4] See note, ch. iii, 11, *ante*.

[5] Jīvanmukta.

[6] Or Mantra. As to the meaning of Bīja Mantra see Woodroffe's "Garland of Letters".

[7] For secrecy the letters are given different names which are only known to the learned. They may however also be got from the Bīja-koshas one of which is published as Tantrābhidhāna in vol. I of my series of "Tāntrik Texts". Prāṇesha means "the Lord of Life," and signifies the letter *Ha*. Ha-kāra may mean either Viṣhṇu or Shiva, or the latter alone, according to the Mantrābhidhāna. Ha-kāra is the Bīja of Ākāsha (Vyoma)—Shiva being Mahākāsha-rūpī: in the form of the Great Ether. Taijasa (Tejas) means Fire, and signifies the letter *Ra* (Rang being the Bīja of Fire). Bheruṇḍā, an attendant of Durgā, signifies the long vowel ī. Thus, Ha + Ra = Hra + ī = Hrī + the Bindu (point or sign Anusvāra) = Hrīng.

[8] Sandhyā = Sha, Rakta = Ra, Vāma-netra = the long vowel ī, and Bindu is the point Anusvāra. Thus, Sha + Ra = Shra + ī = Shrī + the Bindu = Shrīng. As to the significance of Bindu see "Garland of Letters".

"Prajāpati" is placed on "Dīpa," and to them is added "Govinda" and Bindu.[1] It yields happiness to the worshippers: After making these three Bījas add the word Parameshvarī[2] in the vocative, and then the word for Vahni-kāntā.[3] Thus, O Blessed One! is the Mantra of ten letters formed.[4] This Vidyā[5] is the Supreme Devī, is the substance which is all Mantras[6] (11-13).

The most excellent worshipper should for the attainment of wealth and all his desires make Japa of each or all of the first three Bījas[7] (14). By omitting the first three Bījas the Vidyā[8] of ten letters becomes one of seven.[9] By prefixing the Bīja of Kāma,[10] or the Vāgbhava,[11]

---

[1] Prajā-pati, or Brahmā, Lord of creation = Ka; Dīpa, or Fire (whose Bīja is Rang) = Ra; Govinda = long vowel ī; and Bindu is the sign Anusvāra which is Hasanta Makāra, *i.e.*, the letter M without the vowel. Thus, Ka + Ra = Kra + ī = Krī + Bindu = Krīng.

[2] Title of the great Devī, as the Supreme Lord.

[3] Consort of Vahni—Fire—that is, the Mantra "Svāhā," used in making oblation to Fire or at the conclusion of the feminine Mantras (see *post*).

[4] That is, Hrīng, Shrīng, Krīng Pa-ra-me-shva-ri Svā-hā. The vowels are the Shaktis of the consonants, which cannot be uttered without them. Therefore, consonant and vowel annexed are treated as one letter. See Ānanda-laharī, v. 1.

[5] Vidyā is the feminine Mantra, the sex of the Mantra changing with that of its presiding Devatā. The Shārada-tilāka says that if a Mantra is followed by Hung or Phat, it is a masculine Mantra (Purusha; Pung-Mantra). Those which end with Svāhā are feminine, and those ending with Namah are neuter.

[6] Sarva-vidyā-mayi is Sarvavidyāsvarūpā (Hari-harānanda Bhāratī). All the Vidyās are included in it (Tarkālangkāra). The Vidyā is identical with its Devatā; *Cf.* Devatā mantrarūpinī.

[7] Hrīng, Shrīng, Krīng. Bhāratī gives a variant—"for the attainment of piety (Dharma), desire (Kāma), wealth (Artha)".

[8] Feminine Mantra (*vide ante*).

[9] That is, omitting the first three letters, Hrīng, Shrīng and Krīng. The Mantra is then Pa-ra-me-shva-rī Svā-hā.

[10] The Bīja of Kāma—Deva of Desire—is Klīng.

[11] Vāgbhavā is Sarasvatī, Devī of Learning, Music, Speech, the Fine Arts, and so on. Her Bīja is Aing.

or the Tāra,[1] three Mantras of eight letters each or formed[2] (15).

At the end of the word[3] in the vocative in the Mantra of ten letters the word Kālike[4] should be uttered, and then the first three Bījas,[5] followed by the name of the Wife of Vahni[6] (16). This Vidyā[7] is called *Shod*ashī,[8] and is concealed in all the Tantras.[9] If it be prefixed by the Bīja of Badhū[10] or by the Pra*n*ava,[11] two Mantras of seventeen letters each are formed[12] (17).

O Beloved! there are tens of millions upon tens of millions,[13] nay an hundred millions,[14] nay countless Mantras that Thou hast. I have here but shortly stated twelve of them[15] (18). Whatever Mantras are set forth in the various Tantras, they are all Thine, since Thou art the

[1] That is, the Pra*n*ava=Oṁ.

[2] That is, to the Mantra of seven letters thus formed either of the following three Mantras are added—that is, Klīng, or Aing, or Oṁ—then separate Mantras of eight letters each are formed, which are Klīng Parameshvari Svāhā, Aing Parameshvari Svāhā, Oṁ Parameshvari Svāhā.

[3] *i.e.*, Parameshvari.

[4] Name of the Devī.

[5] That is, Hrīng, Shrīng, Krīng.

[6] That is, Svāhā.

[7] The Mantra thus formed is; Hrīng, Shrīng, Krīng, Parameshvari Kālike, Hrīng, Shrīng, Krīng Svāhā.

[8] Feminine of *Shod*asha, so called because composed of sixteen letters.

[9] But is disclosed by Sādashiva out of his affection for Pārvati (Bhāratī).

[10] That is, the Badhū (woman) Bīja—Strīng.

[11] Oṁ.

[12] That is, the Mantra in Note 5, *ante*, plus either "Strīng" or "Oṁ".

[13] Ko*t*i.

[14] Arvuda.

[15] Namely one of ten letters in v. 13, one of three letters and three of one letter in v. 14, one of seven letters and three of eight letters in v. 15 and in v. 16 two of seventeen letters each.

Ādyā Prakriti[1] (19). There is but one mode of Sādhana in the case of all these Mantras, and of that I shall speak for Thy pleasure and the benefit of humanity (20).

Without Kulāchāra,[2] O Devī! the Shakti-Mantra[3] is powerless to give success, and therefore the Sādhaka should practise Shakti Sādhanā with Kulāchāra rites (21). O Ādyā[4]! the five essential Elements in the worship of Shakti have been prescribed to be Wine,[5] Meat,[6] Fish,[7] parched Grain,[8] and the Union of man with woman[9] (22). The worship of Shakti without these five elements[10] is but the practice of evil magic.[11] That Siddhi which is the object of Sādhana is never attained thereby, and obstacles

---

[1] Tvam ādyā prakritir yatah. Primordial material cause as Māyā-Shaktī and efficient cause as Chit-Shakti. Here is established the connection between Prakriti and all Mantras (Tarkālangkāra). All Devas, Devīs, and Mantras have originated from the Parabrahma united with Prakriti either directly or mediately. They are not separate from Him. Therefore whatsoever Devas, Devīs or Mantras are worshipped it is the Ādyā Herself who is worshipped.

[2] Tāntrika doctrine in its Kaula form.

[3] The Mantra of the Devī—Shakti of Shiva.

[4] Ādyā, Who is from the beginning.

[5] Madya (or other fermented liquor).

[6] Māngsa.

[7] Matsya.

[8] Mudrā, a term here used in its technical Panchatattva sense, but which ordinarily means "ritual gestures with the fingers or postures of the body". See as to these last four Tattvas Woodroffe's "Shakti and Shākta".

[9] Maithuna.

[10] Ordinarily called the Pancha Makāra (Five M's), as to which see "Shakti and Shākta," *ante*. They are here called Pancha-tattva, and elsewhere Pancha-dravya.

[11] Abhichāra. Abhichāra is a ritual to injure or destroy, and is, according to Harīharānanda Bhāratī, the equivalent of Hingsākarma—an act injurious to others. Jaganmohana Tarkālangkāra says that if the special treatment prescribed by the Tantras is not followed then the sensual proclivities are not eradicated and the ritual is for the desired end of Tantra useless as magic which leads only to the injury of others. See also Woodroffe's "Shakti and Shākta".

are encountered at every step (23). As seed sown on barren rocks does not germinate, so worship[1] without these five elements is fruitless (24).[2]

---

[1] Pūjā.

[2] On this verse Tarkālangkāra says what Shiva says is plainly this: By the poison which kills all animals, by that same poison the physician destroys disease. The root of Homeopathy is to cure illness by that which causes illness. Amongst us also there is the tradition that poison is destroyed by poison. What then is that which makes man sin and die before his time the object of contempt of all: The first amongst these causes are wine and woman; meat, fish, Mudrā (fried rice, gram and other such things taken along with drinks) are accessories. These five Tattvas are the primary cause of the terrific incurable disease which is Sangsāra. Man under the influence of wine and the like becomes devoid of manliness and worthless. The stupefying power of wine and woman is so great as to attract even the pious and wise and hurl them into the abyss of darkness and ignorance. Here Shiva prescribes the poison which eradicates poison. We know as other Sādhakas do that this Homeopathic system of Shiva is infallible and yields speedy results. He who thirsts for wine or lusts after woman can be cured by this treatment within a very short time. But the physician, that is the Guru, must be experienced and skilful. A slight error in the administration of the poison may lead to fatal result. On this account Shiva has said that the path of Kulāchāra is more difficult than it is to walk on the edge of a sword or to embrace the neck of a tiger. Here we give a popular or exoteric explanation of the Tattvas. But if the esoteric meaning of them be also known then it will be seen that in the matter of Sādhanā they are absolutely necessary. No one who is not a Tattva-Jnānī can master their esoteric meaning. On this account Shiva has prohibited the disclosure of the Sādhanā to ordinary people. We have ourselves seen people who claim to be Kaulas but as a fact they are no better than drunkards and libertines. O Reader, blame not Kulāchāra on seeing these erring men. A libertine and drunkard can never be a Kaula. The Kaula method is unique. He cannot be a libertine and drunkard. On seeing a woman he sees his mother and I*sht*adevatā in her and in either mind or body makes obeisance to her. The saints Gaurāṁga, Nityānanda and Advaita are brilliant examples of the true Kaula. In the Mahābhārata and Vis*hn*upurā*n*a it has been said that desire cannot be quenched by the enjoyment of objects of that desire. On the contrary desire flames up like fire when Ghee is thrown upon it. This is very true. No one says that the drinking of poison will not kill. But the physician administers poison in such a wonderful way that it does not kill the patient but on the contrary the poison in the body is destroyed. The way in which the Guru administers the poison of wine and thus destroys the poison of Sangsāra cannot be disclosed before the unworthy (Anadhikārī) and so this is prohibited by Shiva.

Unless he has performed the morning rites [1] a man is not qualified to perform the others. And therefore, O Devī! I shall first speak of those which are to be performed in the morning (25). In the second half of the last quarter of the night [2] the Sādhaka should rise from sleep. Having shaken off drowsiness, he should seat himself in appropriate posture and meditate on the Guru as being in his head: [3]

Dhyāna

As two-eyed and two-armed, situate in the white lotus of the head [4] (26); clad in white raiment, engarlanded with white flowers, smeared with sandal paste. With one hand he makes the sign which dispels fear, and with the other that which bestows blessings. He is calm, and is the image of mercy. On his left his Shakti, holding in her hand a lotus, embraces him. He is smiling and gracious, the bestower of the fulfilment of the desires of the Sādhaka (27-28).

O Kuleshvari [5]! the Sādhaka should, after having thus meditated upon his Teacher and worshipped him with the articles of mental worship,[6] do Japa with the excellent Vāgbhava-Bīja [7] (29).

[1] Prātah-kritya, such as bathing, morning prayers, etc. (*vide post*).

[2] Arunodaya.

[3] For the purpose of meditation a definite picture is formed in the mind's eye, which is to be the subject of Dhyāna.

[4] One of the higher Chakras—the Lotus of twelve white petals under the Sahasrāra, resting on the Sushumnā Nādī.

[5] Feminine of Kuleshvara, a name of Shiva as Lord of Kala.

[6] Mānasa upachāra = articles of mental worship (see verses 142-157 of the Chapter).

[7] That is, "Aing," Vāgbhavā being Sarasvatī (*vide ante*). The mode of mental worship (Mānasapūjā) is Kanishthābhyāng Lang Prithivyātmakang gandhang samarpayāmi Namah Amgushthābhyāng Hang Ākāshātmakang pushpang samarpayāmi Namah and so on.

After doing Japa[1] of the Bīja as best lies in his power, the wise disciple should, after placing the Japa[2] in the right palm of his excellent Guru, bow to him, saying meanwhile the following (30):

MANTRA

I bow to thee, O Sad-guru,
Thou who destroyeth the bonds which hold us to this world,
Thou who bestoweth the vision of Wisdom,[3]
Together with worldly enjoyment and final Liberation,[4]
Dispeller of ignorance,
Revealer of the Kula-dharma,[5]
Image in human form of the Supreme Brahman[6]
Obeisance to the Shrī Guru (31-32).

The disciple, having thus made obeisance to his Guru, should then meditate upon his Is*h*t*a*-devatā,[7] and worship Her as aforesaid,[8] inwardly reciting the Mūla-mantra[9] meanwhile (33). Having done this to the best of his

[1] Recitation of the Mantra.

[2] That is, the merit of it.

[3] Jnāna-d*ri*s*h*t*i*.

[4] See Yoga-Vāshis*h*t*h*a, Nirvā*n*a-Prakara*n*a, III, chap. lxxxv.

[5] Tāntrika doctrine of the Kaulas.

[6] The Guru is not a mere man. It is not as such that obedience to Him is due. He is Shiva the Supreme Guru (Ādiguru) in human form.

[7] That is, the particular Devatā whom the particular disciple worships. "There" that is in the head (Bhāratī). Tarkālangkāra says this is unusual, for ordinarily Is*h*t*a*-devatā is worshipped in the heart. To Her also mental offerings should be made (*v. post*). They are not the same as those made to the Guru.

[8] That is, the way the Guru has been worshipped.

[9] That is, the root or primary Mantra—Hrīng, Shrīng, Krīng, Parameshvari Kālike, Hrīng, Shrīng, Krīng Svāhā. As regards mental

powers, he should place the Japa in the left palm of the Devī, and then make obeisance to his Ishta-devatā with the following (34):

MANTRA

To Thee I bow Who art one with, and the Supporter of, the Universe,
I bow to Thee again and yet again, the Ādyā Kālikā,[1] both Creatrix and Destructress[2] (35).

worship of the Ishta-devatā Tarkālangkāra says: Offer the lotus of the heart as seat (Āsana), the nectar from the Sahasrāra for Pādya (water for washing the feet) and the Mind for Arghya (offering to show honour) offer the same Nectar for Āchamanīya (water for rinsing the mouth) and Snānīya (bathing) give Ether (Ākāsha-tattva) for clothing and earth (Gandha-tattva) for perfume. The mind (Chitta) should be used in place of flowers and the vital forces (Prānas) for incense. For light give Tejas-tattva (Light) and for food the ocean of Nectar. In lieu of ringing the bell offer Anāhata-shabda (in the heart) and Vāyu-tattva (Air) for fanning. The Sahasrāra is the umbrella and Shabda-tattva singing. The functions and movements of the mind are dancing and the Sushumnā Nādī is a garland of lotuses (for in this are the Chakras or Padmas). She who is experienced through feeling (Bhāvagocharā) should be worshipped with the ten flowers of feeling (Bhāvapushpa). These are Amāya, Anahangkāra, Arāga, Amada, Amoha, Adambha, Advesha, Akshobha, Amātsarya, Alobha, Ahingsā or absence of deceit, egoism, attachment, pride, delusion, hypocrisy, hostility, agitation, envy, greed, respectively. Ahimsā (harmlessness), Indriya-nigraha (control of the senses), Dayā (mercy), Kshamā (forgiveness), Jnāna (spiritual knowledge), are five excellent flowers. Shivā (the beneficent one) should be worshipped with these fifteen flowers of feeling (Bhāva) and also with the ocean of Nectar, mountains of flesh and fish, piles of Mudrā well ground and fried in Ghee, Paramānna, Kula nectar, Kula flowers of five kinds and the washings of it. Worship should be done after lust and anger which are typified by the goat and buffalo are sacrificed. Whatsoever there be in heaven or earth, or the lower regions, in the firmament and in water, all that should be made an offering. Japa should be done in peace after making sacrifice to all beings who obstruct, be they in the lower regions, on earth or in the spaces above.

[1] *Vide* chap. iv, verse 81 *ante*.

[2] Kartrī and Hartrī. She both creates and withdraws creation into Herself.

Having thus made obeisance to the Devī, he should leave his house, placing his left foot first, and then make water, discharge his bowels, and cleanse his teeth (36). He then should go towards some tank or other large sheet of water, and make his ablutions in the manner prescribed. First of all let him rinse his mouth, and then enter the water (37), and stand therein up to his navel. He should then cleanse his body by a single immersal only, and then, standing up, rinse his mouth, saying the Mantra the while[1] (38). That best of worshippers, the Kula-Sâdhaka,[2] should then sip water[3] three times uttering:

THE MANTRAS

Ātma-tattvāya Svāhā.
Vidyā-tattvâya Svāha.
Shiva-tattvāya Svāhā,

after each sip.[4] Lastly, he should rinse the upper lip twice[5] (39).

Then, O Beloved! the wise disciple should draw on the water the Kula-yantra[6] with the Mantra[7] in its centre, and do Japa over it of the Mūla-mantra[8] twelve times (40).

[1] Māntram āchamanam, or rinsing the mouth and reciting the Tāntrika Mantras at the same time.

[2] Tântrika worshipper of the Kula Sampradaya.

[3] Āchamana.

[4] The worshipper here offers with the Mantra Svāhā oblation of water to the thirty six Shaiva-Shākta Tattvas or stages of involution into the supreme "I" (Pūrnāham) of duality, *viz.*, Ātma-tattva from Prithivī to Prakriti: Vidyā-tattva, *viz.*, Māyā Kanchukas, Sadvidyā and including Sadākhya Tattva: and Shiva Tattva including Shiva Tattva and Shakti Tattva. See Woodroffe's "Garland of Letters", p. 248.

[5] This is the method of rinsing one's mouth referred to in verse 88, and called Māntra manner of rinsing the mouth.

[6] Diagram.

[7] That is, the Bīja of the Devī.

[8] *Vide ante*, note under v. 88.

Then meditating on the Water[1] as the Image of Fire,[2] let him offer it thrice to the Sun in his joined palms. Sprinkling it thrice over his head, let him close the seven openings therein[3] (41). Then for the pleasure of the Devī he should immerse himself thrice, leave the water, dry his body, and put on two pieces of clean cloth[4] (42).

Tying up his hair whilst reciting the Gāyatrī,[5] he should mark on his forehead with pure earth or ashes the Tilaka[6] and Tri-pu*nd*ra,[7] with a Bindu[8] over it (43). The worshipper of the Mantra should then perform both the Vaidika and Tāntrika forms of Sandhyā[9] in their respective order. Listen while I now describe to you the Tāntrika Sandhyā (44).

After rinsing his mouth in the manner described, he should, O Blessed One! invoke into the water the Waters of the holy Rivers thus (45):

MANTRA

O Gaṁgā, Yamunā, Godāvarī, Sarasvatī, Narmadā, Sindhu, Kāverī, be in this water (40).[10]

[1] The water of the Kula-yantra—that is, the Yantra drawn as above.

[2] Tejorūpa. Tejas = Fire or radiance.

[3] That is, the two eyes, two ears, two nostrils, and mouth.

[4] Shuddha-vāsasī.

[5] Tāntrikī Gāyatrī Mantra is given later in this Chapter.

[6] The sectarian mark on the forehead or between the eyebrows.

[7] A mark consisting of three lines on the forehead, back, head, and shoulders, or three horizontal lines across the forehead, worn by Shaivas or Shāktas. The Prā*n*atosh*in*ī (2nd Ed., 198) gives a full account of these marks which are also dealt with in Kālāgnirudropanis*had*.

[8] Literally, drop, point; here, a mark like the point Anusvāra.

[9] The rite here described.

[10] The vocative forms in *e* and *i* are not given.

The intelligent worshipper having invoked the sacred Rivers with this Mantra, and made the Angkusha[1]-mudrā, should do Japa with the Mūla-mantra,[2] twelve times (47). Let him uttering the Mūla-mantra, and with the middle and third[3] fingers joined together throw drops of that water thrice upon the ground (48).

He should then sprinkle his head seven times with the water, and taking some in the palm of his left hand cover it up with his right (49). Then inwardly reciting the Bīja of Īshāna,[4] Vāyu,[5] Varuṇa,[6] Vahni,[7] and Indra,[8] four

[1] Angkusha is a hook used to drive an elephant. The first finger is bent at the second joint in the shape of a hook, the first being closed.

Cf. Jnānārṇava Tantra:

> Dakṣhamushṭing vidhāyātha tarjanyangkusha-rūpiṇī
> Angkushākhyā mahāmudrā trailokyākarṣhaṇakṣhamā.

[2] *Vide ante*, note under v. 33.

[3] The ring finger.

[4] Īshāna is the name of Shiva, and the presiding Deva of the Mantra Hang.

[5] Lord of the element of Air, and the presiding Deva of the Mantra Yang. "His noise comes rending and resounding, moving onward he makes all things ruddy. He comes propelling the dust of the earth. The gusts of air rush after him, and congregate upon him as women in an assembly. Hasting forward, he never reels. Friend of the waters first born, holy, in what place was he born! His sounds have been heard, but his form is not seen" (Hymn to Vāyu, Muir, O.S.T., verse 146).

[6] Varuṇa, originally Deva of the Heavens, and regarded later in the Purāṇas as Lord of the Waters (Jala-pati), whose Mantra is Vang (see as to Varuṇa, Muir, O.S.T., verses 58, 64, 78, 75, and Viṣhṇu Purāṇa).

[7] Agni, or Vahni (he who receives the Homa), is the presiding Deva of Fire, whose Mantra is Rang.

[8] Indra, Deva of the Firmament, King of Celestials, presiding over the Mantra Lang. He is Svarga-pati, Lord of Heaven (Svaḥ), whose home is on Mount Meru, in the City of gems and gold built by Vishvakarmā, amid shady gardens of fragrant flowers and luscious fruits, inhabited by beautiful Apsarās and resounding with song and music The five Bījas given are those of the Devatās of the five Chakras in the body from Vishuddha to Mūlādhāra.

times, the water should be transferred to the right palm[1] (50). Looking at the water in his hand and meditating upon the water as Fire,[2] the worshipper should draw it through the nose by *Idā*,[3] expel it through Pingalā[4] (into his palm), and so wash away all inward impurity (51).

The worshipper should then three times[5] dash the water (so expelled into his palm) against an (imaginary) adamant[6] at the same time uttering the Astra-Mantra,[7] and then let him wash his hands (52). Then rinsing his mouth, oblation of water should be offered to the Sun with the following (53).

MANTRA

Ong Hrīng Hangsa. To Thee, O Sun, full of heat, shining, effulgent, I offer this oblation. Svāhā[8] (54).

Then let him meditate upon the great Devī Gāyatrī,[9] the Supreme Devī, whose form changes in three ways in the morning, midday and evening according to the difference of the three Qualities[10] (55).

[1] The whole Mantra is then Hang, Yang, Vang, Rang, Lang.

[2] Tejomaya.

[3] That is, the left nostril.

[4] Or right nostril.

[5] In other Tantras, and as a matter of practice, it is only once.

[6] Vajra-Shilā. This process is known as "Agha-mar*shana*," or destruction of sin. Water is expelled with the sins through Pingalā, and then for the destruction of the latter dashed against an imagined adamant. In practice the water is dashed against the left palm, which the Sādhaka conceives to be of adamantine hardness. Tarkālangkāra inclines to the view that the Mantra Pha*t* should be thrice repeated and the water dashed once only.

[7] That is, the Weapon-Mantra, or "Pha*t*".

[8] Om Hrīng Hangsa, ghri*ni*sūrya idam arghyam tubhyam svāhā.

[9] The Devī of the Gāyatrī Mantra. In the Purā*n*as, Gāyatrī is represented as Consort of Brahmā. Gāyatrī is also Vāk, Mother of the Vedas. See Woodroffe's "Garland of Letters".

[10] Gu*n*a, or qualities—*viz.*, Sattva, Rajas, Tamas. In her Sāttvika form She is represented as Vai*shn*avī; in her Rājasika form as Brāhmī; and in her Tāmasika form as Shaivī.

DHYĀNA

In the morning meditate upon Her in Her Brāhmī form,[1] as a Maiden of ruddy hue, with a pure smile, with two hands holding a gourd[2] full of holy water in one hand and in the other a string of crystal beads, clad in the skin of a black antelope, seated on a Swan (56). At midday meditate upon Her in Her Vaishnavī form,[3] of a dark blue colour,[4] youthful, with full and rising breasts, situated in the Solar Disc, with four hands holding the conch-shell, discus, mace, and lotus, seated on Garuda, garlanded with flowers[5] to the knees (57-58). In the evening the Yati should meditate upon Her as of a white colour, clad in white raiment, old and long past her youth, with three eyes, beneficent, propitious, seated on a Bull, holding in Her lotus-like hands a noose, a trident, and a skull[6] (59-60), and making the gesture of granting boons.

[1] Rājasika as Brāhmī. The Shakti of Brahmā who is generally pictured as a red man with four hands, seated on a Hangsa, dressed in white.

[2] Kamandalu.

[3] Sāttvika as Vaishnavī. Vishnu is pictured as of a dark blue colour, four-armed, holding the articles mentioned, riding upon the bird Garuda, dressed in yellow robes. The Mahābhārata pictures Him as seated in Vaikuntha, the heaven of Vishnu, on a seat glorious as the midday sun, resting on white lotuses with his consort Lakshmī, who shines like a continued blaze of lightning, and from whose body the fragrance of the lotus extends 800 yojanas away.

[4] Shyāma-varnā. According to Commentator on *Shatchakranirūpana*, v. 21, it means of the colour of gold.

[5] Vanamālā which does not mean garland of forest or wild flowers but a garland of this particular size extending from neck to knee:

Ājānulambinī mālā sarvartukusumojjvalā
Madhye sthūlakadambādhyā vanamāleti kīrtitā.

[6] Tāmasika as Shaivī. Each Deva or Devī has His or Her Vāhana or vehicle. In this case the Bull Nandī. Shiva is always represented of a white colour, and is described in the Shiva-stotra as shining like a mountain of silver (Rajata-giri-nibha). Yati is the self-controlled worshipper.

Having thus meditated on the great Devī Gāyatrī, and offered water three times with the hollow of his joined hands, the worshipper should make Japa with the Gāyatrī mantra either ten or a hundred times (61). Listen now, O Queen of the Devas! while I out of my love for Thee recite the Gāyatrī (62).

After the word "Ādyāyai" say "Vidmahe," and then "Parameshvaryyai dhīmahi; tanna*h* Kālī prachodayāt"[1]. This is Thy Gāyatrī which destroys all great sins (63). The inward recitation of this Vidyā[2] thrice daily obtains the fruit of the performance of Sandhya. Water should then be offered to the Devas, *Rish*is,[3] and the Pit*r*is[4] (64). First say the Pra*n*ava,[5] and then the name of the Deva (the *Rishi* or the Pit*ri*) in the accusative case, and after that the words "Tarpayāmi nama*h*".[6] When however, oblation is offered

[1] "Let us think upon Ādyā; let us meditate on Parameshvarī (the Supreme Devī). May Kālī direct us (in the path of Dharma, Artha, Kāma, and Moksha)". Ādyā, Parameshvarī, and Kālī are one and the same. To the Shākta reciting this Gāyatrī the Ādyā is the only Divinity he thinks of, knows, and contemplates. To Her alone his whole soul is bent with a prayer for the attainment of the fourfold aim of sentient being. Bhāratī reads: "May Kālī Whom we seek to know and on Whom we meditate that we may attain the Ādyā Parameshvarī, may She Who is verily the Cause of this universe, direct us in the path of Dharma, Artha, Kāma and Moksha."

[2] Feminine Mantra.

[3] Seer.

[4] Forefathers.

[5] Oṁ.

[6] "Him I satisfy: Nama*h*." The Mantra for the offering is given in the verse which follows and runs: Oṁ Devān tarpayāmi Nama*h*, Oṁ *Rish*īn tarpayāmī Nama*h*, Oṁ Pit*r*īn tarpayāmi Nama*h*, Hrīṁ Ādyāng Kālīng tarpayāmi Svāhā, for Devas, *Rish*is, Pit*r*is and Ādyā Shakti respectively (Bhāratī). Tarkālankāra says the mode of Tarpa*n*a is not fully given, but following the authority of other Tantras it should be done with the Tattva Mudrā (formed by the union of the thumb and ring finger of the left hand). In doing Tarpa*n*a (as in Rahasya tarpa*n*a) to a male Devatā it should be done in the Sādhaka's

to Shakti, the Māyā Bīja[1] should be said in place of the Pranava, and in lieu of Namah the Mantra Svāhā[2] (65).

After reciting the Mūla-mantra,[3] say "Sarva-bhūta-nivāsinyai," and then "Sarva-svarūpā" and "Sāyudhā" in the dative singular, as also "Sāvaranā" and "Parātparā," and then "Ādyāyai, Kalikāyai, te, idam arghyam: Svāhā". (When the Mantra will be:)[4]

Mantra

Hrīng, Shrīng, Krīng, to Thee the Supreme Devī, Thou Who dwelleth in and art in the form of all things, Who art surrounded by Thy attendant Devatās, and Who bearest all Thy insignia, Who art above even the most high, to Thee, Who art the Ādyā Kālikā, I offer this oblation: Svāhā (66-67).

Having offered this Arghya to the Mahādevī the self-controlled Sādhaka should make Japa with the Mūla-mantra with all his powers, and then place the Japa in the left hand of the Devī[5] (68). Then let the Sādhaka bow to the Devī, take such water as is needed for the

---

own head within a triangle the apex of which is upwards and to a female Devatā in the heart the triangle having its apex downward. The triangle so placed is symbolic of the Yonī or Cause of all.

[1] That is, Hrīng or Hrim̐.

[2] That is, the Devas, Rishis and Pitris are worshipped with the Mantra prefixed by Om̐, and ending with Namah but a Devī with Hrīm̐, or whatever Her Bīja may be, concluding with Svāhā.

[3] The primary Mantra—that is, "Hrīng, Shrīng, Krīng, Parameshvarī Svāhā." Shiva proceeds to describe the formation of the Mantra for offering oblation.

[4] The Mantra is thus: "Hrīng, Shrīng, Klīng, Parameshvarī, Svāhā: Sarva-bhūta-nivāsinyai Sarva-svarūpāyai Sāyudhāyai Sāvaranāyai Parātparāyai Ādyāyai Kalikāyai te idam arghyam̐: Svāhā."

[5] That is, the merit of it is offered to Her.

worship, bowing to the water whence he has drawn it, and proceed to the place of worship,[1] earnestly meditating on and reciting hymns of praise to the Devī meanwhile. On his arrival there let him wash his hands and feet, and then make in front of the door the Sāmānyārghya[2] (69-70). The Sādhaka should draw a triangle, and outside it a circle, and outside the circle a square, and after worshipping the Ādhāra-shakti place the vessel on the figure[3] (71).

Let him wash the vessel with the Weapon-Mantra,[4] and while filling it with water let him say the Heart-Mantra.[5] Then, throwing flowers and perfume into the water, let him invoke the waters of the holy places into it (72). Worshipping Fire, Sun, and Moon in the water of the vessel, let him say[6] the Māyā Bīja[7] over it ten times (73). The Dhenu and Yoni Mudrās[8] should then be shown.[9]

---

[1] Yāga-maṇḍapa.

[2] Sāmānyārghya, the common or universal oblation—that is, the oblation which is to serve for the whole ritual worship which follows. The following verses to the seventy-fourth explain it.

[3] That is, the worship is to be of the Shakti which supports the vessel of oblation—Ādhāra-shakti. This worship is done with scents, flowers and the like and with the Mantra Oṁ. Ādhāra-shaktaye Namaḥ (Oṁ obeisance to the Shakti of support) for the universe is sustained in and by Her.

[4] That is the Astra-Mantra or Phaṭ.

[5] Hṛin-Mantra, or Namaḥ—said in the heart.

[6] Mantrayet, by which the power of the Mantra is discharged into it.

[7] That is, Hrīng.

[8] The Yoni Mudrā—symbolical of the sexual organ of woman—is used in the Durgā and Kālī Pūjā. The little finger is placed on little finger, the first finger on first finger, and the thumb on thumb. The knuckles of second and third fingers of each hand are bent, and rest on one another. A triangular Yantra is thus formed, of which the first fingers are the apex and the others the base. The Dhenu (Cow) Mudrā representing the udder of a cow is shown when offering food, water, etc., to the Devatā changing it to Amṛita. See, *post*, VI, verses 137-138.

[9] That is, over the vessel containing the Arghya.

This is known as Sāmānyārghya.[1] With the water and flowers of this oblation the Devatā of the entrance to the place of worship should be worshipped (74). They are Ga*n*esha, Ks*h*etrapāla,[2] Va*t*uka,[3] Yoginī,[4] Gaṁga, Yamunā, Laks*h*mī, and Vā*n*ī[5] (75). The Sādhaka, lightly touching that part of the door-frame which is on his left, should then enter the place of worship with his left foot forward, meditating the while on the lotus-feet of the Devī (76). Then, after worship of the presiding Devatā of the site, and of Brahmā in the south-west corner, the place of worship should be cleansed with water taken from the common offering[6] (77). Let the good Sādhaka then by steadily gazing[7] in front of him with winkless eyes remove all celestial obstacles,[8] and by the repetition of the Weapon-Mantra[9] and springling of water remove all obstacles in the Antarīks*h*a[10] (78).

Striking the ground three times with his heel, let him drive away all earthly obstacles, and then fill the place of

[1] *Vide* p. 101, note 2.

[2] The Deva protector of the ground. The Mantra for His worship is Ks*h*āng Ks*h*etra-pālāya Nama*h* and for Va*t*uka Vāng Va*t*ukāya Nama*h*.

[3] One of the manifestations of Bhairava.

[4] Yoginī is an influence or force recognised in Hindu Astrology which shifts from place to place in all the eight directions, like N., N.E., E., S.E., S., S.W., W., N.W.

[5] Laks*h*mī, of Shakti of Vis*h*nu, and Vā*n*ī or Sarasvatī, Shakti of Brahmā.

[6] Sāmānyārghya.

[7] Divya-d*r*is*h*ti—literally, "celestial gaze," which is achieved by practice of the process of Ha*th*a Yoga called Trā*t*aka. The Sādhaka without winking, gazes at some minute object until tears start from his eyes. Practice in Tra*t*aka secures Divya-d*r*is*h*ti (see the Second Upadesha of the Ghera*n*da Saṁhitā). A Deva's eyes do not wink. The gaze is steady. The Sādhaka's must be that.

[8] Divya-vighna—those obstructive beings which originate from Sva*h*.

[9] Astra-Mantra, or Pha*t*.

[10] The Plane Bhuva*h*, between earth and heaven (Sva*h*).

worship with the incense of burning sandal, fragrant Aguru,[1] saffron and camphor. He should then mark off a rectangular space as his seat, draw a triangle within it, and therein worship Kāma-rūpa with the

MANTRA

To Kāma-rūpa,[2] Namaḥ: (79-80).

Then for his seat spreading a mat[3] over it, let him worship the Ādhāra-Shakti[4] of the Mat with the

MANTRA

Klīng, Obeisance to the Ādhāra-Shakti of the lotus-seat[5] (81).

The Sādhaka well versed in Mantra should then seat himself according to the "Vīrāsana posture,"[6] with his face towards the East or the North, and should purify the Vijayā[7] (82) with the following

MANTRA

Ong, Hrīng, Ambrosia, that springeth from ambrosia, Thou that showerest ambrosia, draw ambrosia for me again

---

[1] Aguru a kind of aromatic wood obtainable in the Garo hills—much used in worship.

[2] Who is the Presiding Divinity or Adhishṭhātri Deva of the place.

[3] Āsana, generally a mat of Kusha grass.

[4] Shakti of the support.

[5] Klīng Adhāra-shakti-kamalāsanāya Namaḥ—that is, the power of support of the lotus-seat.

[6] Baddha-vīrāsana. *Cf.* Gheranḍa Samhitā:

> Ekapādam athaikasmin vinyased ūrusangsthitam
> Itarasming stathā pashchād vīrāsanam udāhṛitam.

[7] That is, the narcotic Bhāng (hemp) or siddhi, as it is called in Bengali, and which is used in all ceremonies.

and again. Bring Kālikā within my control. Give Success; Svāhā.[1]

This is the Mantra for the consecration of Vijayā (83-84). Then inwardly reciting the Mūla-mantra[2] seven times over the Vijayā, show the Dhenu,[3] the Yoni,[4] the Āvāhanī,[5] and other[6] Mudrās (85).

Then satisfy the Guru in the Lotus of a thousand petals[7] by thrice offering him the Vijayā with the Sangketa-Mudra, and the Devī in the heart by thrice offering the Vijayā with the same Mudrā, and reciting the Mūla-mantra[8] (86). Then offer oblations to the

---

[1] "Am*ri*te am*ri*todbhave am*ri*ta-vars*h*i*n*i am*ri*tam ākars*h*ayā-kars*h*aya: siddhim dehi: Kālikām me vasham ānaya svāhā".

[2] *Vide* p. 100, note 3.

[3] The Cow-Mudrā. The two little and ring fingers are joined, the latter crossing one another. The two middle cross one another, and join two index fingers. See note under v. 74.

[4] *Vide ante*, note 8 under v. 74.

[5] The two hands joined together, showing the palms with two thumbs turned in—the gesture with which honoured guests are received.

[6] The other Mudrās referred to, but not mentioned in the text, are—(1) Āvāhanī, (2) Sthāpanī, (3) Sannidhāpanī, (4) Sannirodhinī, and (5) Sammukhīkara*n*ī. These are meant by Āvāha*n*ī and others. *Cf.* Daks*h*i*n*amūrti Saṁhitā. These are gestures of—(1) invoking and welcoming, (2) placing, (3) fixing or placing on a seat, (4) restraining or detaining, and (5) confronting. All these gestures are made by the fingers and palms.

[7] That is, the Sahasrāra Lotus in the head. The Mantra when bowing to the Guru is Oṁ Shrīghrubhyo Nama*h*; to Ga*n*esha Oṁ Ga*n*eshāya Nama*h*; to Ādyā Kālikā Shakti Oṁ Sanātanyai Ādyāyai Kālyai Nama*h* (Bhāratī). Other lengthier Mantras are given by Tarkālangkāra.

[8] Bhāratī says: Reciting the Mantra, "Aing (*name of Guru*) Ānanda-nātha—Shrī-guru-Shrī-pādukāng tarpayāmi: Nama*h*," and with the peculiar gesture (Sangketa-Mudrā) taught by the Guru, the Guru should be satisfied three times by (offer of) Vijayā (Bhāng) and reciting the Mūla-mantra—*i.e.*, "Hrīng Ādyāng Kālīng tarpayāmi: Svāhā"—and with the Sangketa-Mudrā the Devī should be satisfied three times in the heart. The Sangketa Mudrā in the text is the Tattva-Mudrā taught by the Guru.

mouth of the Ku*nd*alī,[1] with the Vijayā reciting the following

MANTRA

Aing (O Devī Sarasvati), Thou Who controllest all life, do Thou inspire me, do Thou inspire me, and remain ever on the tip of my tongue. Svāhā[2] (87).

After drinking the Vijayā[3] he should bow to the Guru, placing his folded palms over the left ear, then to Ga*n*esha, placing his folded palms over his right ear, and lastly to the Eternal Ādyā Devī,[4] by placing his folded palms in the middle of his forehead, and should meditate meanwhile on the Devī (88).

The Sādhaka should place the articles necessary for worship[5] on his right, and scented water and other Kula articles[6] on his left (89). Saying the Mūla-mantra terminated by the Weapon-Mantra,[7] let him take water from the common offering and sprinkle the articles of worship with it, and then enclose himself and the articles in a circle of water.[8] After that, O Queen of Devas! let

---

[1] That is, the Shakti Ku*nd*alinī, as to whom see A. Avalon's "Serpent Power". Oblation is made to Ku*nd*alī by the Sādhaka, placing the Vijayā in his own mouth.

[2] "Aing vada vada Vāgvādini mama jivhāgre sthirībhava sarva-sattva-vashangkari: Svāhā."

[3] Bhāng.

[4] The primordial Devī.

[5] Pūjādravya, that is, flowers and the like.

[6] Kula-dravya—*i.e.*, wine, etc.

[7] Pha*t*.

[8] That is, water is taken in the hand, and a few drops allowed to drop at a time while the hand makes a circle. A streak of water is thus made to surround (according to the text) the articles of worship. According, however, to Tarkālangkāra's Bengali translation, the worshipper (Sādhaka) surrounds both himself and the articles with the water.

him by the Vahni Bija[1] surround them with a wall of Fire (90). Then for the purification of the palms of his hands he should take up a flower which has been dipped in sandal paste, rub it between the palms, reciting the while the Mantra Pha*t*, and then throw it away (to his left) (91).

Then in the following manner let him fence all the quarters so that no obstructions proceed from them.[2] Join the first and second fingers of the right hand, and tap the palm of the left hand three times, each time after the first with greater force, thus making a loud sound, and then snap the fingers while uttering the Weapon-Mantra[3] (92). He should then proceed to purify the elements of his body.[4] The good Sādhaka should place his hands in his lap with the palms upwards, and fix his mind on the Mūlādhāra Chakra[5] and rouse Ku*nd*alinī by uttering the Bīja "Hūng". Having so roused Her, he should lead Her with P*ri*thvī[6] by means of the Hangsa Mantra to the Svādhis*hth*āna Chakra,[7] and there unite[8] the Tattva (of P*ri*thivi or Earth and

---

[1] That is, Rang, the Bīja of Fire.

[2] This is the Dig-bandhana rite.

[3] Astra—that is, "Pha*t*".

[4] This is the Bhūta-shuddhi rite in which the component elements of the body are purified by an imagined process similar to the real Ku*nd*alinī Yoga. See A. Avalon's "Serpent Power" and "Shakti and Shākta".

[5] The lowest of the six Chakras in the human body (see "Serpent Power").

[6] Earth element. The P*ri*thivī Tattva together with whatever there is in the Mūlādhāra is brought up and dissolved in the Jala-tattva. The Tattva in each of the lower centres is first united with and then dissolved into that in a higher.

[7] The Chakra next above the Mūlādhāra at the sexual organs (see "Serpent Power"). In actual Yoga the vāyu is gently driven up the middle of the Sus*h*umnā Nādī, by the Hangsa Mantra and P*ri*thivī, which is in the Mūlādhāra, is absorbed in Ku*nd*alī.

[8] Niyojayet = Vilāpayet.

so forth) with the Tattva (of Jala or Water and the rest)[1] (93-94). Then let him dissolve Prithivī as also odour, and the organ of Smell into the Tattva of Water.[2] Dissolve Water and Taste, as also the sense of Taste itself,[3] into the Tattva of Fire (95). Dissolve Fire and Form, and the sense of Sight itself,[4] into Air.

Let Air and all connected therewith[5] and Touch, as also the sense of Touch itself be dissolved into Ether[6] (96). Dissolve Ether along with Sound into Ahangkāra[7] and the latter into Mahat,[8] Mahat itself into Prakriti, and Prakriti Herself into Brahman (97). Let the Sādhaka, having thus dissolved all the Tattvas,[9] then think of a black man in the left cavity of his abdomen the embodiment of all sin.[10] He is of the size of a thumb, with red beard and red eyes, holding a sword and shield, angry with his head ever held low (99).

---

[1] Here commences the description of the rite of Bhūta-shuddhi.

[2] The Guna of Prithivī is smell. This Guna and the sense of smell is dissolved in Water. Odour is the objective and the sense of Smell the subjective side of Prithivī. Both are dissolved in "Water" in the Svādhishthāna.

[3] The tongue. The objective physical quality of Water affects us as Taste. Subjectively the Tattva is the sense of Taste through the organ the tongue.

[4] The eyes. Both objective Fire and Form and subjective Vision are dissolved in Air.

[5] Everything that can be touched.

[6] Vyoma—that is, the void in which Ether is.

[7] The "I-making" faculty of Consciousness, from which the five subtle elements (already in the worship ideally dissolved) proceed.

[8] Mahat, or the Mahat-tattva, that is, Buddhi.

[9] There are altogether twenty-five Tattvas, categories, principles, or elements in the Sāmkhya Philosophy. The twenty-three emanations from Prakriti are dissolved into Her who is one with Brahman.

[10] Pāpātmakam deham=pāpam ātmani svasmin yasya evam bhūtam deham (Bhāratī)—the body wherein sin abides. This is the Pāpapurusha. See "Sinful body" next verse.

Then the foremost of Sādhaka should meditate on the smoky-coloured Vāyu Bīja[1] as in his left nostril, and as he inhales through that nostril mentally repeat it sixteen times, and thus dry the sinful body (100). Next, meditating on the red Bīja of Agni[2] which is in the navel, the (Sādhaka's) body with all its sinful inclinations should be burnt up by the fire born of the Bīja, assisted by sixty-four Kumbhakas[3] (101). Then, thinking of the white Varu*n*a Bīja[4] in his forehead, let him bathe (the body which has been so burnt) with the nectar-like water dropping from the Varu*n*a Bīja by thirty-two repetitions thereof whilst exhaling[5] (102).

Having thus bathed the whole body from feet to head, let him consider that a new born Deva body has come into being (103). Then, thinking of the yellow Bīja of the Earth[6] as situate in the Mūlādhāra circle,[7] let him strengthen his body by that Bīja and by a steadfast and winkless gaze[8] (104).

---

[1] That is, Yang. The colour Dhūmra is smoky grey—the reddish colour of fire seen through smoke. Vāyu is a friend of fire because it is necessary to and fans it.

[2] That is, Rang—Bīja of Fire.

[3] Kumbhaka. The technical name of inspiration is Pūraka: of expiration, Rechaka; and the restraining or holding of breath is known as Kumbhaka. Here, then, there are to be sixty-four Kumbhakas, at the same time sixty-four repetitions of the Agni Bīja, that is, the period is one requiring sixty-four repetitions of the Bīja.

[4] That is, Vang—Bīja of Water.

[5] Rechaka, which is also repetitions of Varu*n*a Bīja, is to be performed thirty-two times.

[6] P*ri*thivī Bīja—Lang.

[7] The Mūlādhāra Lotus, two digits below the sexual organ and two digits above the anus.

[8] Divya-d*ris*ti. Here ends the rite of Bhūta-shuddhi, and the Text proceeds to the rite known as Jīvanyāsa (see verses 106-108). Tarkālangkāra says that in this verse Jīvanyāsa is only given in brief. The full procedure is as follows. After Bhūta-shuddhi, the Sādhaka places his hand on his heart and says "He I am" (So'ham). The sense of the

Placing his hand on his heart and uttering the

MANTRA

Āng, Hrīng, Krong, Hangsa*h*, So'hang,[1]

let him infuse therewith, into his new body the life of the Devī (105).[2]

O Ambikā! having thus purified the elements[3] in his body the Sādhaka should realise that he is one with the

Mantra is "She I am". "I am the Ādyā Kālikā who is Brahman (Brahmamayī)." Thereafter he puts Kula Ku*nd*alinī and others in these places and with his hand on the heart recites the following Mantras—Ang, Hrīng, Krong, Yang, Rang, Lang, Vang, Shang, *Shang*, Sang, Haung Haung, Hangsa*h*, Shrīmadādya-Kālīkāyā*h* prā*n*ā iha prā*n*āh. (The Prā*n*as or vital airs of the glorious primordial Kālikā are the vital airs here). Then repeating the Bījās as above says Shrīmadādyā Kālikāyā jīva iha sthita*h*. (The Jīva or life of the glorious Ādyā Kālikā is here). Then same Bījās Shrīmadādyā-Kālikāyā*h* sarvendriyā*n*i ; same Bījas Shrīmadādyā Kālikāyā vāngmanashchaksh*uh* shrotra ghrā*n*a prā*n*āsh chāgatya sukhang chirang ti*shth*antu Svāhā (may all the senses of the glorious Ādyā Kālikā, may the speech, mind, vision, hearing, smell, life of the Ādyā Kālikā come here and abide in happiness always).

[1] That is, "He I am". Sa*h*=he, Aham=I. The two words, when combined, according to the rules of Sandhi, become So'ham, or the unity of the individual and Supreme Spirit.

[2] Literally, "Place the vital air of the Devī into his body." Taddehe Devyā*h* prā*n*ān nidhāpayet. The Sādhaka puts into the newly formed body of his the life of the Devī. He realises in his body the identity of himself with Her. This Shloka concludes Jīva-nyāsa, and then next proceeds to Mātrikā-nyāsa (see "Shakti and Shākta").

Cf.:

1. The Deva alone should worship Deva:
   A non-Deva (a-deva) should not worship Deva.
   —Gandharva Tantra.

2. An a-Vi*sh*nu (non-Vi*sh*nu), should he worship Vi*sh*nu, gains no merit thereby: Become Vi*sh*nu yourself before you worship Vi*sh*nu.—Yoga-vāshi*shth*a.

3. By worship of Rudra one becomes Rudra himself.
   By worship of Sūrya one becomes Sūrya himself.
   By worship of Vi*sh*nu one becomes Vi*sh*nu, and
   By worship of Shakti one becomes Shakti.
   —Agni Purāna.

[3] *i.e.*, performed Bhūta-shuddhi.

Devī,[1] and with mind intent do Māt*ri*kā-nyāsa.[2] The *Rishi*[3] of Māt*ri*kā[4] is Brahmā, and the verse is Gāyatrī,[5] and Māt*ri*kā[6] is the presiding Devī thereof; the consonants are the Seed,[7] and the vowels the Shaktis,[8] and Visarga[9] is the End. In Lipi-nyāsa,[10] O Mahādevī! it is necessary to state the object with which the rite is being performed. Having in this way performed *Rishi*-nyāsa, Kara-nyāsa and Aṅga-nyāsa should be performed (106-108).[11]

---

[1] Devībhāva-parāya*n*a.

[2] Disposition of the letters of the alphabet or body of the Devatā upon the body of the Sādhaka. The meaning of Māt*ri*kā-nyāsa is as follows: After the destruction of the body which is the product of Avidyā a Deva-body is created by Bhūta-shuddhi.

The identity of the individual and Brahman is realised. Then in the body of the Sādhaka which is a microcosm (Ks*h*udra-brahmā*nd*a) are produced the Devatās and the like of the six Chakras. Tarkālangkāra then quotes the following Texts: "From Shambhu who is the Bindu (Bindvātmā) the associate of Kāla (Kāla-bandhu) and Kalā (Kalātmā) originated Sadāshiva who is all pervading and witness of the world (Jagatsāks*h*ī). From Sadāshiva came Īsha, from Īsha, Rudra, from Rudra, Vis*hn*u and then Brahmā. Thus did they originate" (Shāradā-tilaka, I, vv. 15-16). After this by Jīva-nyāsa the Prā*n*a, Indriyas, and the like of the Brahmarūpā Devī are placed in the body of the Sādhaka. Thereafter he utters different letters which constitute the different parts of the body of the Devatā. They are placed in the corresponding parts of the Sādhaka's body. The body of the Devatā is composed of the letters of the Māt*ri*kā.

[3] Revealer; he who proclaimed the Mantra to the world.

[4] That is, the Māt*ri*kā-Mantra.

[5] A form of verse.

[6] That is, Sarasvatī, as the origin of the letters.

[7] Bīja.

[8] The vowels are the Shaktis, which enable the utterance of the consonants (the Bījas), which by themselves cannot be uttered. The latter merely interrupt the vowel sounds.

[9] Final hard-breathing *h*, which comes at the end of the letter, and is the end or Kīlaka. Kīlaka literally means a peg, a fence.

[10] Or Māt*ri*kā-nyāsa.

[11] In vv. 107 and 108 Sadāshiva wishing to show the mode of doing Māt*ri*kā-nyāsa speaks of *Rishi*-nyāsa and says that it is necessary to state the object (Viniyoga) of the rite. The preliminary Nyāsa called *Rishi*-nyāsa is done thus: Shirasi (on the head) Brahma*n*e Nama*h*

O Beauteous Face! the Mantras enjoined for *Shad*-aṁ-ga-nyāsa[1] are Ka-varga[2] between Ang and Āng,[3] Cha-varga[4] between Ing and Īng,[5] *Ta*-varga[6] between Ung and Ūng,[7] Ta-varga[8] between Eng and Aing,[9] and Pavarga[10] between Ong and Aung,[11] and the letters from Ya to K*sh*a[12] between Bindu[13] and Visarga[14] respectively (109-110).

(obeisance to Brahman). Mukhe (on the mouth) Gāyatryai chhandase Nama*h*. Hridaye (in the heart) Māt*r*ikāyai Sarasvatyai Devatāyai Nama*h* (to the Devatā Māt*r*ikā Sarasvatī). Guhye (in the anus which is in the region of the Mūlādhāra) Vyanjanebhyo Bījebhyo Nama*h* (obeisance to the Bījas the consonants). Pādayo*h* (on the two feet) Svarebhya*h* Shaktibhya*h* (the vowels which are the Shaktis) Nama*h*. Sarvāṁge*sh*u (on all the limbs) Visargāya Kīlakāya Nama*h* (to Visarga the Kīlaka). For the attainment of Dharma, Artha, Kāma and Mok*sh*a Lipi-nyāsa (=Māt*r*ikā-nyāsa) is employed (Viniyoga).

[1] *Shad*-aṁga-nyāsa is done by placing the hands on six different parts of the body, and Kara-nyāsa is done with the five fingers and palms of the hands only. The latter is also called Aṁgu*sh*th*ā*di-*shad*-aṁga-nyāsa. As to Kara-nyāsa *cf.* 1, 3, 25 Shatapatha Brāhma*n*a; and 3, 2, 1, 6, for Aṁga-nyāsa. For Dhyāna of letters, see Lā*tt*yāyana Shrauta Sūtras, 2, 9, 12, as to Nyāsa see Sh. Br., 7, 5, 2, 12. As to Mudrā *cf.* Kātyāyana Shrauta Sūtra, 16, 3, 4 also Sh. Br., 6, 8, 2, 6. This group is placed on the thumb in Kara-nyāsa and in the heart in Aṁga-nyāsa with nama*h*.

[2] That is, the five letters—Ka, Kha, Ga, Gha, and Nga.

[3] Short and long A of Sanskrit alphabet, with nasal Anusvāra superposed placed on the thumbs and the heart.

[4] That is, the letters Cha, Chha, Ja, Jha, and Nya on index fingers and head with Svāhā.

[5] Short and long I. On middle fingers and crown lock (Shikhā) with Va*sh*at.

[6] That is, hard *Ta*, *Tha*, *Da*, *Dha*, *N*a (Mūrdhanya).

[7] Short U and long Ū.

[8] That is, soft Ta, Tha, Da, Dha, Na (Dantya) on ring fingers and Kavacha with Hum.

[9] E and Ai of alphabet, with nasal Anusvāra.

[10] That is, letters Pa, Pha, Ba, Bha, and Ma on little fingers and three Eyes with Vau*sh*at.

[11] O and Au.

[12] That is, Ya, Ra, La, Va, Sha (Tālavya), *Sh*a (Mūrdhanya), Sa, (Dantya) Ha, *L*a (pronounced with a rolling sound), and K*sh*a placed on the palm and back of the hands

[13] The nasal sign.

[14] The hard-breathing *h*.

Having placed the letters according to the rules of Nyāsa, the Sādhaka should next meditate upon Sarasvati :

Dhyāna

I seek refuge[1] in the Devī of Speech, three-eyed encircled with a white halo, whose face, hands, feet, middle body, and breast are composed of the fifty letters of the alphabet, on whose radiant forehead is the crescent moon, whose breasts are high and rounded, and who with one of her lotus hands makes Jnāna-mudrā,[2] and with the other holds the rosary of Rudrāk*sh*a[3] beads, the jar of nectar, and learning[4] (112).

Having thus meditated upon the Devī Māt*r*ikā,[5] the Sādhaka places the letters in the six Chakras[6] as follows :

---

[1] Āshraye=Bhaje=I adore (Bhāratī).

[2] A gesture of the hands. The index finger is pointed upwards, and the fingers closed. She is represented with four arms. The text has Mudrā only which the Commentator says is Jnāna-mudrā.

[3] Rudrāk*sh*a is the stone of a fruit, which grows in Nepal, in use by Shaivas.

[4] Vidyā, learning, which consists of—(1) Ānvik*sh*ikī, Logic and Metaphysics; (2) Trayī, the three Vedas; (3) Vārtā, Practical Arts, such as Agriculture, Medicine, etc.; (4) Da*n*da-nīti, Science of Government. To these Manu adds (vii, 43) a fifth—Ātma-vidyā, Knowledge of the Spirit. Others divide Vidyā into fourteen sections: Four Vedas, Six Vedāṁgas, Purā*n*as, the Mīmāngsā, Nyāya, and Dharma-shāstra, or Law. Others, again, add the four Upa-vedas, making the division eighteen. The Vedāṁgas are Shik*sh*ā (Science of proper articulation), Kalpa (ceremonial), Vyākara*n*a (linguistic analysis, or Grammar), Nirukta (explanation of Vedic words), Jyoti*sh*a (Astronomy), and Chhandas (Metre). These are regarded as auxiliary to, and in this sense as part of, the Vedas. Some people interpret Vidyā to mean the Mudrā of that name.

[5] Sarasvatī.

[6] That is, the six Chakras or centres situate between the eyebrows (Ājnā), in the region of the throat (Vishuddha), heart (Anāhata), navel (Ma*n*ipūra), sexual organ (Svādhi*sh*t*h*āna), and in that portion of the perineum which lies two digits from that organ and the anus respectively (Mūlādhāra). The letters are said, and with suitable action placed in these six regions.

Ha and Ksha in the Ājnā[1] Lotus, the sixteen vowels in the Vishuddha[2] Lotus, the letters from Ka to *Tha* in the Anāhata[3] Lotus, the letters from Da to Pha in the Ma*ni*pūra[4] Lotus, the letters from Ba to La in the Svādhi*sh*-*th*āna[5] Lotus, and in the Mūlādhāra[6] Lotus the letters Va to Sa. And having thus in his mind placed these letters of the alphabet, let the Sādhaka place them outwardly (113-115).

Having placed them on the forehead, the face, eyes, ears, nose, cheeks, upper lip,[7] teeth, head, hollow of the mouth, back, the hump of the back,[8] navel, belly, heart, shoulders, (four) joints in the arms, ends of the arms,

---

[1] Ājnā Chakra, a Lotus of two petals, with the letters Ha and K*sh*a, whose presiding Shakti is Hākinī. Within the petal there is the eternal Seed, brilliant as the autumnal moon (Shiva Saṁhitā, chap. v, verses 96-119; and *Shat*chakra-nirūpa*n*a, A. Avalon's "Serpent Power").

[2] Vishuddha Chakra, the Lotus Circle of sixteen petals, with the sixteen vowels, whose presiding Shakti is Shākinī (see Shiva Saṁhitā, chap. v, verses 90-95).

[3] Anāhata Chakra, the Lotus Circle of twelve petals, with the letters Ka, Kha, Ga, Gha, Nga, Cha, Chha, Ja, Jha, Nya, *Ta*, *Tha*. (*Ibid.*, verses 83-89.)

[4] Ma*n*ipūra, a Lotus of ten petals, with the letters *Da*, *Dha*, *Na*, Ta, Tha, Da, Dha, Na, Pa, Pha. (*Ibid.*, verses 79-82.)

[5] Svādhi*shth*āna Chakra of six petals, situate at the root of the organ of generation. The six petals contain the letters Ba, Bha, Ma, Ya, Ra, La. Its Shakti is Rāki*n*ī.

[6] The Mūlādhāra, Root Lotus of four petals, with Va, Sha, *Sha*, Sa, two fingers above the anus and two below the genital organ, with its face towards the back. This space is called the root (mūla). In this Chakra dwells the Devī Ku*nd*alinī, embodied energy and like burning gold. There is the seed (Bīja) of Kāma (Kāma-Bija), beautiful as the Bandhūka flower, brilliant like burnished gold. Its Bīja is the great energy, subtle with a flame of fire. It encircles Svayambhu Liṁga (see "Serpent Power," by A. A.)

[7] See Woodroffe's "Shakti and Shākta". In the text only O*shth*a (upper lip) is mentioned, but the practice is as described in the work cited.

[8] Kakud. The hump of the bull is called Kakud. Here it means the portion of the back between the two shoulder-blades, where a hump, if it existed, would be,

heart, (four) joints of the legs, ends of legs, and on all parts from the heart to the two arms, from the heart to the two legs, from the heart to the mouth, and from the heart to the different parts as above indicated, Prāṇāyāma should be performed[1] (116-118). Draw in the air by the left nostril whilst inwardly uttering the Māyā Bīja[2] sixteen times, then fill up the body by Kumbhaka by stopping the

---

[1] See "Serpent Power" and Woodroffe's "Shakti and Shākta". Mode of doing Mātrikā nyāsa is as follows. With middle and third finger place letter A on forehead and say Ang Namah. With first, middle and third fingers put round the mouth and say Āng Namah. With thumb and third place I on right eye and say Ing Namah. Same fingers on left eye Īng Namah. Back of thumb on right ear Ung Namah and left ear Ūng Namah. Little finger and thumb on right nostrils *Ring* Namah: on left nostrils *Rring* Namah. First, second, third on right cheek *Lling* Namah: on left *Ling* Namah. Middle finger upper lip Eng Namah. On lower lip Aing Namah. Third fingers upper teeth Ong Namah. Lower teeth Aung Namah. Middle finger head Āng Namah. Third finger on opened mouth Ah Namah.

Then passing to the consonants, with middle, third and little fingers joined together place on right shoulder Kang, on elbow Khang, on wrist Gang. With same fingers place on lower forms of fingers of right hand Ghang and on tips of fingers Ngang in the same way on left arm place Chang, Chhang, Jang, Jhang and Nyang. Then on right leg on hip-joint knee ankle, lower joints and tips of toes place *Tang, Thang, Dang, Dhang, Nang* and on the left place Tang, Thang, Dang, Dhang and Nang. With same fingers on right side place Pang on left Phang, on back Bang, With thumb middle third and little fingers place Bhang on navel. On belly place Mang with all the fingers. On the heart put Yang saying Tvagātmane Namah with the palm of the hand. On the right shoulder with palm put Rang saying Asrigātmane Namah. With palm place Lang on the hump saying Māngsātmane Namah. On left shoulder place Vang with palm saying Meda ātmane Namah. From the heart to the right shoulder place Shang saying Asthyātmane Namah. From the heart to the left shoulder *Shang* saying Majjātmane Namah. From heart to right leg place Sang saying Shukrātmane Namah. From heart to left leg place Hang and say Prāṇātmane Namah. From heart to belly place Llang and say Jīvātmane Namah. From heart to mouth place *Kshang* and say Paramātmane Namah. This is the Vahiruyāsa of Mātrikā (Tarkālangkāra). For those who cannot do the prescribed Mudrās a flower may be used. (*Cf.* Ullāsa, iii, 44 *et seq.*)

[2] That is Hrīng. See as to this and other Bījas as Saguṇa Shakti Woodroffe's "Garland of Letters".

passage of both the nostrils with the little, third finger, and thumb whilst making Japa of the Bīja sixty-four times, and, lastly, exhale the air through the right nostril whilst making Japa of the Bīja thirty-two times[1] (119-120). The doing of this thrice through the right and left nostrils alternately is Prā*n*āyāma.

After this has been done, *Rish*i-nyāsa[2] should be performed (121). The *Rish*is[3] of the Mantra are Brahmā and the Brahmar*sh*is,[4] the metre is of the Gāyatrī and other[5] forms, and its presiding Devatā is the Ādyā Kālī (122).[6] The Bīja is the Bīja of the Ādyā,[7] its Shakti is the Māyā Bīja,[8] and that which comes at the end[9] is the Kamalā Bīja[10]. Then the Mantra should be assigned[11] to the head, mouth, heart, anus, the two feet, and all the parts

---

[1] This is Pūraka, Kumbhaka, Rechaka. The air inhaled by Pūraka increases in volume by the heat of the body five times during Kumbhaka, and, when exhaled, two-fifths only passes out, and the remaining three-fifths is retained, the object of Prā*n*āyāma being the increase of the vital forces and the lightness of the body. The more the air (vital breath) is kept in, the lighter becomes the body and the stronger the vitality.

[2] As to the meaning of Nyāsa see "Shakti and Shākta".

[3] *Rishi*, the inspired Teacher by whom it has been originally *seen*—that is, to whom it has been revealed.

[4] Mind-born sons of Brahmā.

[5] U*sh*n*ik, Anu*sh*t*up, *Bri*hatī, Pangkti, Tri*sh*t*up, and Jagatī, are with Gāyatrī, the seven metres.

[6] VV. 122, 123 give the *Rish*yādi-Nyāsa of the Mantra that is the *Rish*i-Nyāsa and other kinds of Nyāsa which are required to be done.

[7] *I.e.*, Krīng.

[8] *I.e.*, Hrīng.

[9] *I.e.*, the Kīlaka.

[10] *I.e.*, Shrīng.

[11] Nyāsa. To these different parts these Bījas should be assigned—that is, when the Mantra is said, it is thought of as being located in the head, mouth, etc., the hands touching the part in question. Vinyaset = Nyāsa should be done = should be placed.

of the body (123).[1] The passing of the two hands three or seven times over the whole body from the feet to the head, and from the head to the feet, making Japa meanwhile of the Mūla-mantra,[2] is called Vyāpaka-nyāsa,[3] which yields the declared result (124).

O Beloved! by adding in succession the six long vowels to the first Bīja[4] of the Mūla-mantra, six Vidyās[5] are formed. The wise worshipper should in Aṁga-kalpanā[6] utter in succession these or the Mūla-mantra[7] alone (125), and then say "to the two thumbs," "to the two index fingers," "to the two middle fingers," "to the two ring fingers," "to the two little fingers," "to the front and back of the two palms," concluding with Nama*h*, Svāhā, Va*sh*a*t*, Hūng, Vau*sh*a*t*, and Pha*t* in their order respectively[8] (126).

---

[1] The mode of doing *Rish*yādi Nyāsa of the Mantra Hrīng, Shrīng, Krīng, Parameshvari Svāhā is as follows: On the head place the hand saying salutation to Brahmā, the Brahmar*sh*is and other *Rish*is. On the Mouth salutation to the metres Gāyatri and others. On the heart salutation to the Shrīmad Ādyā Kālikā the Devatā. In the Mūlādhāra salutation to the Bīja Krīng. On the two feet salutation to the Shaktī Hrīng and on every part of the body salutation to the Kīlaka Shrīng. The *Rish*is of this Mantra are Brahmā and the Brahmar*sh*is. The metres are Gāyatrī and others. Shrīmad Ādyā Kālikā is the Devatā. Krīng is Bīja (of Kālī), Hrīng is Shakti and Shrīng is Kīlaka. The object of using this Mantra is attainment of the four Puru*sh*ārthas by *Rish*yādi-Nyāsa.

[2] The chief Mantra of the Rite.

[3] From Vyāpaka, meaning diffusive, comprehensive, spreading all over, which is Yathokta-phala-siddhi-da. Here follows Kara-nyāsa which is done with the fingers.

[4] Hrīng.

[5] That is, Hrāng is assigned to the thumb, Hrīng to the first finger, Hrūng to the middle finger, Hraing to the fourth finger, Hraung to the little finger, Hra*h* to the palm and back of each hand.

[6] That is, Aṁgu*shth*ādi-h*ri*dayādi-*sh*a*d*aṁga-nyāsa. The Nyāsa of the whole body, as distinguished from that of the fingers, is called H*rid*ayādi-*sh*a*d*aṁga-nyāsa.

[7] Hrīng Shrīng Krīng Parameshvari Svāhā.

[8] These verses speak of Aṁgu*shth*ādi-*sh*a*d*aṁga-nyāsa, beginning with thumb as Kara-nyāsa. The Mantras are Hrāng Aṁgu*shth*ābhyāng

When touching the heart[1] say "Namah," when touching the head, "Svāhā," and when touching the crown lock say "Vashat". Similarly when touching the two upper portions of the arms, the three eyes[2] and the two palms, utter the Mantras Hūng and Vaushat and Phat respectively. In this manner Nyāsa of the six parts of the body should be practised, and then the Vīra should proceed to Pīthanyāsa[3] (127-128). Then let the Vīra[4] place in the Lotus of the Heart,[5] the Ādhāra-shakti,[6] the Tortoise,[7]

Namah, Hrīng Tarjanībhyāng Svāhā, Hrūng Madhyamābhyāng Vashat, Hraing Anāmikābhyāng Hūng, Hraung Kanishthābhyāng Vaushat, Hrah Karatala-prishthābhyāng Phat.

Kara Nyāsa is done as follows: Hrāng Namah to the two thumbs, Hrīng Svāhā to the two first fingers, Hrūng Vashat to the two middle fingers, Hraing Hūng to the two third fingers, Hraung Vaushat to the two little fingers Hrah Phat to the palm and back of the hand. In ordinary Kara Nyāsa the thumbs and fingers abovementioned are used. But the method is different in different Sampradāyas.

In vv. 125, 126 direction is given as regards Karanyāsa and Amganyāsa.

[1] The ceremony which now follows is called Hridayādi-shadamga-nyāsa—that is, Nyāsa done with the six parts of the body, beginning with the heart—*viz.*, heart, head, the crown lock, Kavacha (literally, armour, the covered hands touch arms above the elbow), the three eyes (see next note), and two palms. The Mantra is Hrāng Hridayāya Namah, Hrīng Shirase Svāhā, etc.

[2] The central eye, situated in the forehead between the other two. The eye of Wisdom (Jnāna-chakshu).

[3] Here the Pīthas take the place of the Mātrikā. These Pīthas are the ten from Ādhāra Shakti to Padmāsana.

[4] From here to verse 135 Pītha-nyāsa is dealt with.

[5] Hridayāmbuje. The Lotus, with all it contains, is called Ānanda Kanda (*vide post*). This is the Sthūla aspect for worship of that which exists in the twelve-petalled lotus.

[6] Ādhāra-shakti, Shakti of support. Everything in the universe has a support, or energy by which it is upheld.

[7] Kūrma on which the worlds are said to rest. The Kūrma is the emblem of patient endurance. *Cf.* Sh. Br., vii, 5, 1.

Shesha (the serpent),[1] Prithivī,[2] the Ocean of Ambrosia,[3] the Gem Island,[4] the Pārijāta tree,[5] the Chamber of Gems which fulfil all desires,[6] the Jewelled Altar,[7] and the Lotus Seat (129-130). Then he should place on the right shoulder, the left shoulder, the right hip, the left hip, respectively

---

[1] Which is on the Tortoise. The Deva, King of Serpents, with a thousand hoods, crown on its head, red like the leaf of a mango-tree, brown-bearded, brown-eyed, wearing yellow silk cloth, holding lotus, mace, conch, and discus, adorned with ornaments lying in the ocean of milk (Bhavishya Purāna). He supports the worlds (Kūrma Purāna, verse 48, where the Dhyāna is given).

[2] Prithvī, or Prithivī, Devī Earth. Supported by Shesha. In the body it is in Mūlādhāra below which in the lower limbs are the previous supporting Shaktis.

[3] Sudhāmbudhi.

[4] Isle of Gems (Mani-dvīpa) in the Ocean of Ambrosia. There are seven oceans, of milk and other substances. The Rudra-yāmala says: "Outside and beyond the countless myriads of gross world-systems, in the centre of the Ocean of Nectar, more than 1,000 crores of Yojanas in extent, is the Gem Island, 100 crores of Yojanas in area, the lamp of the world. There is the supreme city of Shrī-vidyā, three lakhs of Yojanas in height, adorned with twenty-five halls, representing the twenty-five Tattvas."

[5] A Tree with scented flower in the Heaven of Indra. One of the five celestial Trees in the garden of Indra—*viz.*, Mandāra, Pārijāta, Santāna, Kalpa-vriksha, Hari-chandana. Here a tree in the Isle of Gems.

[6] Chintāmani-griha. Chintāmani is that gem which yields all objects desired. Of that the chamber or house is built in the Isle of Gems. In the house of Chintāmani, which is on the northern side of Shringāra-vana, all is Chintāmani. In the commentary on the Gaudapāda Sūtra (No. 7) the Chintāmani house is said to be the place of origin of all those Mantras which bestow all desired objects (Chintita). The Lalitāsahasra-nāma speaks of the Devī as residing there (Chintāmani-grihantahsthā).

[7] The jewelled altar is in the Chintāmani Griha and on the altar is the Lotus-seat on which is Devī with whom the Jīvātmā is one. She is Svasamvit-tripurā Devī (see Yoginīhridaya Tantra). The Mantra for placing them in the heart lotus is: Hridayāmbuje (in the heart lotus (Adhāra-shaktaye Namah, Kūrmāya Namah, Sheshāya Namah, Prithivyai Namah, Sudhāmbudhaye Namah, Mani-dvīpāya Namah, Pārijāta-tarave Namah, Chintāmani grihāya Namah, Manimānikya-vedikāyai Namah, Padmāsanāya Namah.

and in their order, Dharma,[1] Jnāna,[2] Aishvarya,[3] and Vairāgya[4] (131), and the excellent worshipper should place the negatives of these qualities on the mouth, the left side, the navel, and the right side respectively[5] (132). Next let him place in the heart, Ānanda Kanda,[6] Sun, Moon, Fire,[7] the Three Gu*n*as[8] preceded by the first of their letters with the Bindu added thereto[9], the filaments and pericarp of the Lotus, and the eight Nāyikās[10] of the Pī*th*as on the petals. The eight Nāyikās are Maṁgalā, Vijayā, Bhadrā,

---

[1] The universal and special Law.

[2] Knowledge.

[3] Dominion and Power.

[4] Dispassion, the state of freedom from all desires.

[5] The Mantra is: Dak*sh*a-skandhe Dharmāya Nama*h*, Vāma-skandhe Jnānāya Nama*h*, Vāma-ka*t*au Aishvaryāya Nama*h*, Daksha-ka*t*au Vairāgyāya Nama*h*, Mukhe Adharmāya Nama*h*, Vāma-pārshve Ajnānāya Nama*h*, Nābhau Anaishvaryāya Nama*h*, Dak*sh*a-pārshve Avairāgyāya Nama*h*.

[6] Literally "Root of Bliss" which gives the name to an eight-petalled lotus in the heart (which, however, is not one of the six Chakras), where the I*sh*ta Devatā is thought of. It is immediately beneath the Anāhata Chakra, facing upwards to the Anāhata Chakra, which faces downwards. The eight petals of this lotus are the eight Siddhis. The eight Nāyikās whose names are given in the Text are the eight Shaktis, and the eight Bhairavas their consorts are emanations of Shiva.

By Sūrya, Soma, and Hutāshana (Eater of Oblations) are meant the Sthūla aspect of "Sun," "Moon" and "Fire" in the head: as to which see Chapter so-named in Woodroffe's "Garland of Letters" and "Serpent Power". In the early stage of Sādhana the Devatā is here invoked. On attainment of Yoga-siddhi the lotus is merged in the Sahasrāra.

[7] Standing for I*d*ā, Piṁgalā, and Su*sh*umnā.

[8] That is, Sattva, Rajas, Tamas.

[9] That is, the Sādhaka says: Sang Sattvāya Nama*h*, Rang Rajase Nama*h*, and Tang Tamase Nama*h*.

[10] The Nāyikas like all other subordinate Shaktis represent different aspects and portions (Angsha) of the general Power in beneficence, supremacy, happiness, continuance in victory, invincibility, pleasing (Nandinī=daughter so called because pleasing to parents), majesty and might (Nārasiṁhī); Shakti of Kārtikeya (Kaumārī) or of Vi*sh*nu (Vai*sh*navi) which last name is given ch. vi, vv. 99, 100 *post*.

Jayantī, Aparājitā, Nandinī, Nārasiṁhī, Vaishnavī.[1] The eight Bhairavas[2] are Asitāṁga, Chanda, Kapālī, Krodha, Bhīshana, Unmatta, Ruru, Saṁhārī. These should be placed on the tips of the petals of the lotus and then after Pīthanyāsa is done in this way Prānāyāma should be done (133-135).

Then the Sādhaka should, after forming his hands into the Kachchhapa Mudrā,[3] take perfume and flower, and, placing his hands held in the same Mudrā on his heart, meditate upon the eternal Devī (136). The nature of meditation upon Thee, O Devī! is of two kinds, according as Thou art thought of as formless or with a form.[4] As formless Thou art ineffable and incomprehensible, unmanifest, all-pervading. Of Thee it cannot be said that Thou art either this or like this. Thou art omnipresent, transcendent, attainable only by Yogīs through austerities such as the many acts of self-restraint and the like (137-138).[5] I will next speak of meditation upon Thee in

---

[1] The ceremony is accompanied by the following Mantra: Hridaye Ānanda-kandāya Namah, Sūryāya Namah, Somāya Namah, Agnaye Namah, Sang Sattvāya Namah, Rang Rajase Namah, Tang Tamase Namah, Kesarebhyo Namah, Karnikāyai Namah, Hritpadma-patrebhyo (to the petals of the heart lotus) Namah, Maṁgalāyai Namah, Vijayāyai Namah, etc. Hritpadma-patrāgrebhyo (to the tips of the petals of the heart lotus) Namah, Asitāṁgāya Namah, etc.

[2] He of the black body, the Fierce One, the Wearer of skulls, the Angry One, the Terrific One, the Mad One, Ruru, and the Destroyer. These Bhairavas are aspects or emanations of the God Shiva (see notes under ch. II. v. 23 and ch. VI. v. 2). Some texts read Bhayaṁkara for Unmatta.

[3] The Sādhaka first makes with his hands the Kachchhapa or Kūrma (Tortoise) Mudrā (as to which, see Tantrasāra, p. 689), and, keeping his hands in this position, picks up the flower.

[4] Dhyāna is Sa-rūpa or A-rūpa.

[5] Shama=control of the inclinations (Antahkarana). Dhyāna is of two kinds, namely, Sthūla gross or with form and Sūkshma or subtle. If the Brahman is thought of with form and attributes then it is Sthūla Dhyāna. Dhyāna of the formless (Nirākāra) and attributeless (Nirguna) is Sūkshma Dhyāna. The latter again is of two kinds: (a) Bindudhyāna, (b) Shūnyadhyāna. The Bindu or Point has neither length nor height nor depth nor breadth. It is however united with Māyā (Māyāyukta).

corporeal form in order that the mind may learn concentration, that the desired end be speedily achieved, and that the power to meditate according to the subtle form may be aroused [1] (139).

The form of the greatly lustrous Kālikā, Mother of Kāla,[2] Who is without form, is imagined according to Her qualities [3] and actions [4] (140).

DHYĀNA

I adore the Ādyā Kālikā Whose body is of the hue of the (dark) rain-cloud, upon Whose forehead the Moon gleams, the three-eyed One [5] clad in crimson raiment,[6] Whose two hands are raised—the one to dispel fear, and

---

It is from this Bindu that Brahmā, Vishnu and Maheshvara and others originated. Meditation on that which is undifferentiated (Aparichchhinna), attributeless, formless, changeless, incomprehensible Sat Chit Ānanda is Shūnyadhyāna. This is beyond the scope of mind and speech. When by Yoga practice another "sense" is awakened then Yogīs by Yoga-power experience the Bindu or Shunya. This is called Brahma-sākshātkāra (Tarkālangkāra).

[1] That is, the meditation of the Devī as the Formless One. Dhyāna is of two kinds. Some speak of three kinds of Dhyāna; Sthūla, Sūkshma and Para. The Gheranda Sanghitā speaks of *three* forms of Dhyāna—Sthūla, Jyotih, and Sūkshma.

[2] Kālamātā which may mean as in Text or she who "measures," that is, creates time (Kāla).

[3] Sattva, Rajas and Tamas.

[4] Creation, Preservation, and Destruction, Anugraha and Nigraha or Nirodha. In this verse is given the answer to the anticipated question. "One may meditate on form in Sthūla Dhyāna but how can there be Sthūla Dhyāna of Her who is formless without beginning or end?"

[5] Symbolising the Past, Present and Future of Time, of whom she is the Mother.

[6] The Āsana of the Devī is also red, which is the Rājasika colour. Red is an active (Rājasika) colour. The flower of these Tāntrikas is the red Jabā-pushpa (hibiscus), and in the ritual of Latāsādhana the Madanāgāra is sprinkled with red sandal. Red indicates Will and Desire (Ichchhā) and Vimarshha Shakti and so it is said Sarvasya etasya lauhityam Vimarshah. See Introduction to Tantrarāja, Vol. VIII Tantrik Texts, Ed. A. Avalon.

the other to bestow blessing[1]—Who is seated on a red lotus in full bloom, Her beautiful face radiant, watching Mahā-Kāla,[2] Who, elated with the delicious wine of the Madhūka flower,[3] is dancing before Her (141).

After having meditated upon the Devī in this manner and placed a flower on his head, the Sādhaka should with all devotion worship Her with the articles of mental worship (142). Let him offer the Lotus of the heart[4] for Her seat, the Ambrosia trickling from the Lotus of a thousand petals[5] for the washing of Her feet, and his mind as offering[6] (143). Then let him offer the same ambrosia as water for rinsing of Her mouth and bathing of Her body, and the essence of the Ether as raiment of the Devī, the essence of smell for the perfumes, his own heart[7] and vital airs,[8] fire,[9] and the Ocean of nectar respectively as the flowers, incense, light and food offerings (of worship). (144-145.)

---

[1] That is, She makes the Abhaya-mudrā and Vara-mudrā.

[2] Shiva as the destroyer or as the embodiment of Time. In Tantrarāja (ch. 86, v. 40) Shiva says "whatever the letters in the word Kāla signify that is my body."

[3] The Madhūka flower, of which an intoxicating liquor is made. The Kaulikāchāra-bheda Tantra, which speaks of the different wines which should be drunk on different occasions, says: "On a joyful occasion should Mādhvika be drunk." Mahā-kāla is dancing because of the benignant state of the Ādyā. Here the worship is mental (Mānasa) not exterior (Bāhya).

[4] The eight-petalled lotus—Ānanda-kanda (see verse 133, *ante*).

[5] The Lotus which is situated in the Brahma-randhra (Cavity of Brahma) is called Sahasrāra (the thousand-petalled).

[6] Arghya = offering of worship.

[7] Chitta—the heart considered as the seat of intellect as modified by the sentiments. Ākāshatattva (Ether) or space itself is offered as raiment because the Devī being all-pervading, it is limitless space alone which can be imagined as Her garment. Outer space is the objectification of the infinite extensity of the supreme experience.

[8] Prā*n*āh.

[9] Tejastattva in Manipura. The ocean which follows (Sudhāmbudhi) is one of the seven oceans by which the universe is surrounded.

Let him offer the Sound in the Anâhata Chakra[1] for the ringing of the bell, the essence of the Air for the fan and fly-whisk,[2] and the functions of the Senses and the restlessness of the mind for the dance before the Devī[3] (146). Let various kinds of flowers (of mind) be offered for the attainment of purity of mind[4]: Amāya,[5] Anahangkāra,[6] Arāga,[7] Amada,[8] Amoha,[9] Adambha,[10] Advesha,[11] Akshobha,[12] Amātsarya,[13] Alobha,[14] and thereafter the five flowers—namely, the most excellent flowers, Ahiṁsā,[15]

---

[1] The Yogīs hear the sound as of a bell in this Chakra (See Mānasollāsa, verse 39 and ninth Shloka of the Dakshina-mūrti Stotra). The Chakra is so called because there without a sound-producing cause—*e.g.*, a stroke—sounds are heard, emanating from the Shabda Brahma. This is the Pulse of the Universal Life.

[2] Chāmara, which is used in the worship of the image.

[3] In full worship there is always dancing and singing before the Devatā for its entertainment. This is Rajasika-pūjā. The Pūjā of the text is Sāttvika, the dance being the ideal one of the mind and senses. All things offered are in the human body, which is called the Kshudra Brahmāṇda, or small egg or spheroid, of Brahmā.

[4] Bhāva-siddhi. That is leading to Shuddha-bodha or Brahmajnāna. Svābhipreta-padartha-nishpatti (Bhāratī).

[5] Guilelessness.

[6] Absence of egotism. Ahangkāra=Ātmani atipriyatvābhimānaḥ.

[7] Detachment. According to Bhāratī=absence of anger.

[8] Absence of pride=Dhanavidyādi-nimittakan chittasyag utsukatvam (Bhāratī).

[9] Freedom from delusion. Viveka—Power to discriminate the real and unreal, coupled with dispassion.

[10] Absence of duplicity: straightforwardness or absence of hypocrisy (Dambha=Kapaṭata).

[11] Want of all enmity.

[12] Freedom from mental disturbance or repentance.

[13] Absence of envy.

[14] Absence of greed. Desire for more even when possessed of what is necessary.

[15] Harmlessness. No oppression of others.

Indriya-nigraha,[1] Dayā,[2] K*sh*ama,[3] and Jnāna.[4] With these fifteen flowers, which are fifteen qualities of disposition,[5] he should worship the Devī (147-149).

Then let him offer (to the Devī) the Ocean of Ambrosia,[6] a mountain of meat and fried fish, a heap of parched food,[7] grain cooked in milk with sugar and ghee, the Kula nectar,[8] the Kula flower,[9] and the water which has been used for the washing of the Shakti.[10] Then, having sacrificed all lust and anger, the cause of all impediments, let him do Japa (150-151).

The Mālā (rosary) prescribed consists of the letters of the alphabet, strung on Ku*nd*alinī[11] as the thread (152). After reciting each of the letters of the alphabet from A[12]

---

[1] Control of the senses such as of the eyes over their objects.

[2] Mercy, pity, kindness. The desire to remove the pain and suffering of others without hope of reward.

[3] Forgiveness.

[4] Spriritual knowledge. Knowledge of what is essential and non-essential (Sārāsāravivekanaipu*n*yam).

[5] Bhāvarūpa: Bhāratī says Bhāvyante, chintyante iti bhāvā*h* tadrūpai*h* bhāvyamānair ity arthah. Bhāvarūpa is the mental attitude and content of the Sādhaka.

[6] Wine.

[7] Mudrā.

[8] Kulām*ri*ta nectar produced by means of Shakti. It is defined by Hariharānanda as Shakti-gha*t*itam am*ri*tavishe*sh*am.

[9] Tatpu*sh*pa that is, Strī-pu*sh*pa or Kulapu*sh*pa. When a girl attains puberty and its symptoms, she is said to have "borne the flower". A ceremony is celebrated in the inner apartments on this occasion, which is called Pu*sh*potsava.

[10] Pī*th*a-k*sh*ālana-vāri, or water which has been used in washing the Pī*th*a of the Kula-nāyikā, of which it is said that he who offers an Arghya of the same becomes a great Yogī (see Tantrasāra, 698 *et seq.*). Hariharānanda says Stryamga-vishe*sh*adhāvanāmbha*h*.

[11] The Devī awakened in the Mūlādhāra. Usually a rosary is used for Japa. Here the beads are the letters of the Alphabet, and the string is Ku*nd*alinī herself.

[12] Which is called Shrī-ka*nth*a. The letter A is so called because it is an enquivalent of Vi*sh*nu, and Shrī-ka*nth*a is one of His names.

to *La*, with the Bindu[1] superposed upon each, the Mūla-mantra[2] should be recited. This is known as Anuloma.[3] Again, beginning with *La* and ending with A, let the Sādhaka make Japa of the Mantra. This is known as Viloma.[3] Ksha-kāra[4] is called the Meru[5] (153-154).

Japa should be done of the Mūla-mantra[6] eight times adding it to each of the last letters of the eight group of letters[7] and having thus done one hundred and eight Japas the same should be offered (to the Devī[8]) with the following (155)

MANTRA

O Ādyā Kālī! Who abidest as the Spirit in all,[9] Who art the innermost Light,[10] O Mother! accept this inner Japa of my heart.[11] I bow to Thee (156).

Having offered the Japa, with the foregoing Mantra, he should mentally prostrate himself, touching in his mind the ground with the eight parts[12] of his body. Having

---

[1] The nasal sound. The verse answers the question as to the kind of rosary to be used in this internal Japa by saying that it is to be the letters of the alphabet strung on Kundalī.

[2] Hrīng, Shrīng, Krīng, Parameshvari Svāhā.

[3] That is, the ordinary order, as Viloma is the reversed order.

[4] The letter Ksha.

[5] The central and most prominent bead in the rosary (Mālā, or Japa-mālā).

[6] *Vide* above, note 2.

[7] Varga. The eight Vargas are A, Ka, Cha, *Ta*, Ta, Pa, Ya, Sha, which are the first letters of each group; the last letters are A*h*, Nga, Nya, *Na*, Na, Ma, Va, *La*.

[8] It is offered to the left hand.

[9] Antarātmā.

[10] Antar-jyoti*h*—that is, the divine Light seen by the inward or central eye of the Siddha when the others are closed.

[11] Antar-japa, that is said within.

[12] Feet, hands, knees, breast, head, eyes, mind (Manas), and word (Vāch).

concluded the mental worship, let him commence the outer worship (157).

I am now speaking of the consecration of the Vishesh-ārghya,[1] by the mere placing whereof the Devatā is exceedingly pleased. Do Thou listen (158). At the mere sight of the cup of this offering the Yoginīs,[2]

[1] The Visheshārghya is the special offering, as contrasted with the Sāmānyārghya, placed in front of the room where worship is being performed.

[2] Attendants of numerous kinds of the Devī, who is Herself called Yoginī. Generally however the Yoginīs are the Āvarana Devatās of various classes. The Yoginīs (see Jnānārnava Tantra, Ch. XVI, 140 *et seq.*, also Tantrarāja, Tāntrik Texts, Vol. VIII) are of nine classes as appearing in the nine Chakras of the great Shrīyantra, *viz.* (proceeding from the outermost Chakra, inwards) Prakatā, Guptā, Guptatarā, Atiguptatāra, Kula-kaulā, Nigarbhā, Rahasyā, Parārahasyā, Parāpara-rahasyā. The first is in the outermost Chakra called Trailokya-mohana and the last in the innermost, called Sarvānandamaya. In the same order the names of the Devatā worshipped are Tripurā, Tripureshī, Trīpurasundarī, Tripuravāsinī, Tripurāshrī, Tripuramālinī, Tripura-siddhā, Tripurāmbā, Mahātripurasundarī. The names of the Chakra in the same order are: (1) Trailokya-mohana; (2) Sarvāshāpūraka; (3) Sarvasangkshobhana, (4) Sarva-saubhāgyaprada; (5) Sarvārtha-sādhaka; (6) Sarvarakshākara; (7) Sarvaroghara; (8) Sarva-siddhiproda; (9) Sarvānandamaya.

In (1) are eight Yoginīs, *viz.*, Brāhmī, Māheshvarī, Aindrī, Kaumārī, Vaishnavī, Vārāhī, Chāmunda, Mahālakshmī, eight Mātrikā Yoginīs and eight Siddhis. Worship is of these as it is of the others in their respective Chakras.

In (2) there are sixteen, *viz.*, Kāmākarshinī, Buddhvākarshinī, Ahmgkārākarshinī, Shabdākarshinī. Sparshākarshinī Rūpākarshinī, Rasākarshinī, Gandhākarshinī, Chittākarshinī, Dhairyākarshinī, Smrityākarshinī, Nāmākarshinī, Bījākarshinī, Ātmākarshinī, Amritākarshinī, Sharīrākarshinī.

In (3) there are eight, *viz.*, Anamgakusumā, Anamgamekhalā, Anamgamadanā, Anamgamadanāturā, Anamgarekhā, Anamgaveginī, Anamgāngkushā, Anamgamālinī.

In (4) there are fourteen, Sarvasangkshobhinī, Sarvavidrāvinī, Sarvākarshinī, Sarvāhlādinī, Sarvasammohinī, Sarvastambhinī, Sarvajambhinī, Sarvavashangkarī, Sarvaranjinī, Sarvonmādinī, Sarvārthasādhanī, Sarvasampattipūrinī, Sarvamantramayī, Sarvadvandvakshayangkarī.

In (5) there are ten, *viz.*, Sarvasiddhipradā, Sarvasampatpradā, Sarvapriyangkarī, Sarvamamgalakārinī, Sarvakāmapradā, Sarvasaubhāgyadāyinī, Sarvamrityuprashamanī, Sarvavighnanivārinī, Sarvāmgasundarī, Sarvaduhkhavimochanī.

Bhairavas,[1] Brahmā and other Devatās dance for joy and grant Siddhi[2] (159). The disciple should on the ground in front of him and on his left draw with water taken from the Sāmānyārghya[3] a triangle, with the Māyā Bīja[4] in its centre, outside the triangle a circle, and outside the circle a square, and let him there worship the Shakti[5] of the Ādhāra[6] with the

MANTRA

Hrīng Obeisance to the Shakti of the support[7] (160-161).

He should then wash the support, and place it on the Ma*nd*ala,[8] and worship the region of Fire with the

In (6) there are ten, *viz.*, Sarvajnā, Sarvashaktipradā, Sarvaishvaryapradā, Sarajnānamayī, Sarvavyādhivināshinī, Sarvādhārā, Sarvapāapaharā, Sarvānandamayī, Sarvaraksh*h*ā, Sarvepsitaphalapradā.

In (7) there are eight, *viz*, Vashinī, Kāmeshvarī, Modinī, Vimalā, Aru*n*ā, Jayinī, Sarveshvarī, Kaulinī.

In (8) there are three, *viz.*, Kāmeshvarī (Rudrā*n*ī Shakti) Vajreshvarī (Vais*h*navī-shakti) Bhagamālinī (Brāhmī Shakti).

In the (9) there is only one that is the supreme Yoginī who is Mahātripurasundarī. This Chakra is Brahmabindu, Chitsvarūpa, Samvid-vedya. The above total 78.

[1] See note under ch. I, 28.

[2] Success. Accomplishment of one's aim. The next verse proceeds to consecration of Vishes*h*ārghya.

[3] The Vishes*h*ārghya is the special offering, as contrasted with the Sāmānyārghya, placed in front of the room where worship is being performed. In Kālīkula there is no Vishes*h*ārghya but in Shrīkula there is. Ādyākālī belongs to the latter.

[4] That is, Hrīng.

[5] Devī of the Ādhāra.

[6] A tripod.

[7] Hrīng Ādhāra-shaktaye Nama*h* (see note 6, p. 117). Here the tripod is the support.

[8] The diagram drawn as above.

MANTRA

Mang! Obeisance to the Mandala of Fire with its ten Kalās.[1]

And having washed the Arghya vessel with the Mantra Phat, the worshipper should place it on the Ādhāra[2] with the Mantra Namah (162-163).

He should then worship the cup with the

MANTRA

Ang! Obeisance to the Mandala of Sun with its twelve Kalās.[3]

And fill the vessel (in which the offering is made) whilst repeating the Mūla-mantra,[4] three parts with wine and one part with water, and having placed scent and flower in it, he should there worship, O Mother![5] with the (164-165)

MANTRA

Ūng Obeisance to the Mandala of the Moon with its sixteen Kalās[6] (166).

[1] Mang Vahni-mandalāya dasha-kalātmane Namah. Ten aspects or digits of manifestation are mentioned in Chapter V, verse 25. As to Kalā see Woodroffe's "Garland of Letters".

[2] The tripod or other support on which the Kalasha is placed.

[3] Ang Arka-mandalāya dvādasha-kalātmane Namah. The Kalās are referred to in Chapter VI, verses 32, 33.

[4] That is, the chief Mantra of the particular Devī worshipped, e.g., here it is Hrīng, Shrīng, Krīng, Parameshvarī Svāhā.

[5] Ambikā, a title of the Devī.

[6] Ūng Soma-mandalāya shodasha-kalātmane Namah. The sixteen digits or Kalās are given in Chapter VI, verse 32, 33.

He should then place in front of the special offering, on bael leaves[1] Dūrvā grass,[2] flowers, and sun-dried rice[3] dipped in red sandal paste (167).

Having invoked the holy waters (of the sacred Rivers into the Arghya) by the Mūla-mantra and Angkusha-mudrā, the Sādhaka should meditate upon the Devī as in it and worship Her with incense and flowers, and make Japa of the Mūla-mantra twelve times (168). After this let him display over the Arghya[4] the Dhenu Mudrā,[5] and the Yoni Mudrā,[6] incense sticks and light. The worshipper should then pour a little water from the Arghya into the vessel[7] kept for that purpose, and sprinkle himself and the offering therewith. The vessel containing the offering[8] must not, however, be moved[9] until the worship is concluded (169-170). O Thou of pure Smiles! I have now spoken of the consecration of the special offering.[10]

I will now pass to the Yantra-rāja[11] which grants the aims of all human existence[12] (171).

---

[1] The bael leaf (Bilva-patra) is sacred to Shiva.

[2] The bael leaves, grass, and flowers are placed at the end of, and projecting from, the vessel, their stems being in the wine and water. Dūrvā is *Panicum dactylon*.

[3] Akshata. This is commonly called Ātapa rice.

[4] Arghya, consisting of Jabā flower (hibiscus or Rosa Sinensis), bael leaf, grass, rice, and red sandal, with wine and water.

[5] *Vide* p. 104, note 8.

[6] *Vide* p. 101, note 8.

[7] Prokshanī-pātra = a vessel for holding water to sprinkle.

[8] Arghya.

[9] Lest by so doing the Devatā be disturbed.

[10] Visheshārghya.

[11] Yantra-rāja, the King of all Yantras. This Yantra or Diagram of worship is similar in form to that figured at p. 782 of the Tantrasāra as the Rudra-Bhairavī Yantra. Yantra-rāja = King of all Yantras so called in order to emphasise its importance in this particular form of Sādhana.

[12] Samasta-purushārtha—*i.e.*, the fourfold aim of existence—Dharma, Artha, Kāma, Moksha.

Draw a triangle with the Māyā Bīja[1] within it, and around it two concentric circles (the one outside the other). In the space between the two circumferences of the circles draw in pairs the sixteen filaments, and outside these the eight petals of the lotus, and outside them the Bhū-pura,[2] which should be made of straight lines with four entrances, and be of pleasing appearance (172-173). In order to cause pleasure to the Devatā[3] the disciple should (reciting the Mūla-mantra[4] the meanwhile) draw the Yantra either with a gold needle, or with the thorn of a bael tree on a piece of gold, silver, or copper, which has been smeared with either the Svayambhu, Ku*nd*a, or Gola flowers,[5] or with sandal, fragrant aloe,[6] Kungkuma,[7] or with red sandal paste. It may also be made by a clever carver on crystal, coral, or lapis lazuli (174-176).

After it has been consecrated by auspicious rites, it should be kept inside the house; and on this being done all wicked spirits, all fear from (adverse) planets, and diseases are destroyed; and by the beneficent influence of

---

[1] That is, Hrīng. The triangle is equilateral with apex downward.

[2] That is, the base upon which the Yantra is drawn.

[3] Devatā-bhāva-siddhaye, which may also mean "for the attainment of a celestial disposition"; but the interpretation adopted in the text is that of Bhāratī.

[4] *Vide ante*, note under v. 16.

[5] These are three kinds of the Kula-pus*h*pa, the Tāntrika significance of which is given in note under ch. iv, v. 66. Svayambhu is the Kula-pus*h*pa of any woman; Ku*nd*a, that of a girl born of a married woman by any other than her husband: and Gola, that of the daughter of a widow. In conformity with its general character, this Tantra (Chapter VI, verse 15) substitutes for the Kula-pus*h*pa (of whatever kind) red sandal paste.

[6] Aguru.

[7] The red powder made from a fruit, which is thrown in the Holi (Dola-yātrā) Festival; also saffron.

this Yantra the worshipper's house becomes the source of happiness. With his children and grandchildren, and with happiness and dominion,[1] he becomes a bestower of gifts and charities, a protector of his dependants, and his fame goes abroad (177-178). After having drawn the Yantra and placed it on a jewelled altar[2] in front of the worshipper, and having worshipped the Devatās of the Pī*th*a[3] according to the rules of Pī*th*a-nyāsa, the principal Devī[4] should be adored in the pericarp of the Lotus[5] (179).

I will now speak of the placing of the jar[6] and the formation of the circle of worship[7] by the mere institution of which the Devatā[8] is well pleased, the Mantra[9] becomes fruitful, and the wishes[9] of the worshipper are accomplished (180). The jar is called Kalasha, because

---

[1] Aishvarya (see p. 119, note 3).

[2] Ratna-siṁhāsanā, *lit.* jewelled lion-seat or throne.

[3] That is, the supporting Devatā of the Yantra. As to Pī*th*anyāsa, *vide ante.*

[4] Mūla-Devatā : here Ādyā Shakti or Kālī.

[5] *i.e.*, the lotus in the Yantra.

[6] Kalasha, a jar made of mud or metal, used for the drawing of water from the river, etc., and in worship, and in which—according to Kaulika ritual—the Tattva of wine is kept in the Chakra. He now begins to speak of the rules of worship of the Mahādevī with the Panchatattva.

[7] Chakra. The text here refers to the celebrated circles of Tāntrika worship. The chief Sādhaka and his Shakti—who may be, but not necessarily are, the host and hostess (G*r*ihi*n*ī) in whose house the circle takes place—sit in the centre, the Shakti on the Sādhaka's left. Between and in front of them are the articles of worship referred to in the text, and the large jar (Kalasha) of wine, which is called by the Tāntrikas Kāra*n*a-vāri and Tīrtha-vāri. In the Jnānār*n*ava Tantra it is said that the Kula articles of worship should—when purified—be considered as the image of Brahman and the I*sh*t*a*-devatā worshipped. The other worshippers sit round in a circle, men and women alternating, the latter on the left of the former.

[8] *i.e.*, I*sh*t*a*-devatā.

[9] Mantra-siddhi and Ichchhā-siddhi.

Vishvakarmā[1] made it from the different parts[2] of each of the Devatās (181).

It should be thirty-six fingers breadth (in circumference) in its widest part, and sixteen in height. The neck should be four fingers breadth, the mouth six fingers, and the bottom five fingers breadth. This is the rule for the design of the Kalasha (182). It should be made either of gold, silver, copper, bell-metal, mud, stone, or glass, and without patch or blemish. In its making all miserliness[3] should be avoided, since it is fashioned for the pleasure of the Devas (183). A Kalasha made of gold, one of silver, one of copper, and one of bell-metal give prosperity, emancipation, contentment, and nourishment respectively to the worshipper. One of crystal is good to produce Vashīkara*n*a,[4] and one of stone to produce Stambhana.[5] A Kalasha made of mud is good for all purposes. Whatever it is made of it should be clean and of pleasing design (184, 185).

On his left side the worshipper should draw a hexagon with a Shūnya[6] in its centre, around it a circle, and outside

---

[1] The Celestial Architect.

[2] Kalā. The meaning is that the Kalasha contains the properties of the different Devatās.

[3] Vitta-shā*th*ya=parsimony, that is, one who is able to afford a costly metal should not make it of a cheap material.

[4] Vashīkara*n*a is one of the six *shat*karma or magical powers (siddhis), the bringing of a thing or person under control—*e.g.*, causing a woman to love a man.

[5] Stambhana is another of such powers, such as stopping forces of nature, making a person speechless, etc. The other powers are Māra*n*a, Uchchā*t*ana, Vidve*sh*a*n*a, Svastyayana (Shāntikriyā). Tarkālangkāra says that the defect of a stone jar is that wine kept therein in a short time loses its elating qualities in a considerable measure. Hence in some Tantras it is prohibited. Possibly the stone here spoken of is a variety free from this defect.

[6] Brahma-randhra, *i.e.*, a small circle like °. The Hexagon is a figure made of two equilateral triangles one with the apex upwards and the other downwards. Some Tantras speak of a triangle within the hexagon.

the circle a square (186). These figures should be drawn either with vermilion or Kula flower[1] or red sandal paste; the Devatā of the support should then be worshipped thereon by the (187)

MANTRA

Hrīng, salutation to the Shakti of the Support[2] (188). The support[3] for the jar should be washed with the Mantra Nama*h*, and placed on the Ma*nd*ala, and the jar[4] itself with the Mantra Pha*t*, and then placed on the support (189).

Let the Sādhaka then fill the Kalasha with wine, uttering meanwhile the Mūla-mantra preceded by the letters of the alphabet—commencing with the letter Ks*h*a and ending with A with the Bindu superimposed[5] (190). The wise one realising in himself the presence of the Devī[6] should worship the Ma*nd*alas of Fire, Sun, and Moon in the support, in the jar and in the wine[7] in the manner already described (191). After decorating the jar with vermilion, red sandal paste, and a garland of crimson flowers,[8] the worshipper should perform Panchīkara*n*a[9] (192).

---

[1] Rajas or Kula-pus*h*pa, see p. 130, note 5.

[2] Hrīng Ādhāra-shaktaye Nama*h*.

[3] The tripod (see *ante*).

[4] Kalasha. This term, as well as Gha*t*a, are used in the text for the Kalasha, which in the translation is employed throughout.

[5] The Viloma Māt*r*ikā followed by the Mūla-mantra Hrīng Shrīng Krīng Parameshvari Svāhā. Viloma Māt*r*ikā is the Māt*r*ikā (letters) uttered in a reversed order, beginning with Ks*h*ang and ending with Ang. Japa should be done of this when filling the jar with wine.

[6] Devī-bhāva-parāya*n*a—that is, the mind and body are full of the presence of the Devī.

[7] Tīrtha, a ritualistic term for Madya. There are other names such as Kāra*n*avāri, Sudhā, etc.

[8] Such as the Jabā Pus*h*pa, the Tāntrika Shākta flower of the Devī.

[9] Literally, mixing of five things, or the doing of five ceremonies. The ceremony is described in the next verse.

Strike the wine-jar with a wisp of Kusha grass, saying Phat; then, whilst uttering the Bīja Hung, veil it by the Avagunthana Mudrā[1]; next utter the Bīja Hrīng, and look with unwinking eye upon the jar, then sprinkle the jar with the Mantra "Namah". Lastly, whilst reciting the Mūla-mantra, smell the jar three times:[2] this is the Panchīkarana ceremony[3] (193).

Making obeisance to the jar, purify the wine[4] therein by throwing red flowers into it, and say the following (194)

MANTRA

Oṁ, O Devī Sudhā! The Supreme Brahman, One without a second[5] is verily both gross[6] and subtle.[7] By That I destroy Thy sin of slaying a Brāhmana which attached to

---

[1] Or Gesture of the Veil.

[2] Gandham trirdadyāt, which literally means offer scent three times. The translation given in the text is that of Tarkālangkāra, who supports it by the observation that the practice amongst all the different communities (Sampradāya) of Tāntrika Sādhakas is to close the right nostril and to inhale the scent from the Kalasha three times by Īdā, and then to exhale it by Piṁgalā to a place away from the jar.

[3] Tarkālangkāra says that whatever is done in Pūjā has a meaning. The ritual significance of Panchīkarana is to make the wine in the jar the celestial nectar (Divyasudhā) which manifests Brahman-bliss. This Kārana (wine or cause) is the Ajnāna which is the cause of the material world produced of the collectivity of the five subtle Bhūtas. The Sādhaka in doing Panchīkarana (making fivefold) of the five unmixed (Apanchīkrita) Bhūtas first of all realises sound the property of Ākāsha by striking the jar. Then he limits or condenses Ākāsha by the veiling gesture (Avagunthana Mudrā) and mentally realise the sense of touch. Then by looking with winkless eyes he unites Tejas with the last and sees form. Thereafter by dropping a little water he realises taste. Lastly thinking of the earth-element he becomes aware of smell which is the property of Prithivī. By smelling this celestial nectar the Nādīs of the Sādhaka are purified and then impurities are thrown out through Piṁgalā to a distance.

[4] Surā: the first of the five Tattvas of the Tāntrika ritual.

[5] Oṁ ekam eva parang Brahma. The Brahman is verily one that is without a second: Ekameva=Advaitam eva.

[6] Sthūla.

[7] Sūkshma.

Thee (the wine) by reason of the death of Kacha[1] (195). O Devī (Sudhā) Who hast Thy abode in the region of the Sun,[2] and Thy origin in the dwelling-place of the Lord of Ocean,[3] Thou who art one with the Amā[4] Bīja, mayest Thou be freed from the curse of Shukra (196). O Devī! as the Pranava which is the seed of the Vedas is one with the Bliss of Brahman,[5] may by that truth be destroyed Thy sin of slaying a Bráhmana (197)

MANTRA[6]

Hrīṁ:[7] The Hangsa[8] dwells in the pure sky.[9]

[1] Son of Brihaspati and disciple of Shukra, Priest of the Demons. Kacha was burnt by the Asuras, and his ashes mixed with the wine that Shukra drank. The latter, when he discovered what he had done cursed wine. *Krishna* also cursed wine because the Yādavas took to drinking and began quarrelling and killing one another so much so that the Dynasty became extinct.

[2] The allusion is to the concealment of Amrita by the Devas in the Sūrya-mandala (Mahābhārata, Ādi Parva).

[3] Varuna. As to the Churning of the Ocean, from which Amrita was produced, see Mahābhārata, Ādi Parva, chap. xviii. The place of Varuna is the ocean.

[4] Amā is the sixteenth digit (Kalā) of the Moon.

[5] Brahmānandamaya.

[6] This is the celebrated Hangsavatī *Rik* of the *Rigveda*.

Hrīṁ Hangsah Shuchisad Vasur Antarīkshasat
Hotā Vedisad Atithir Duronosat
Nrisad Varasad *Ritasad* Vyomasad Abjā
Gojā *Ritajā* Adrijā *Ritam* Brihat.

Rigveda Saṁhitā Mandala 4, Adhyāya 4, Sūkta 40, *Rik* 5, Max Muller, 1st Ed., Vol. III, p. 195; and Yajurveda X, 24 and XII, 24. See also Kathopanishad, II. 2. As to the Mantra *cf.* Ait. Br., 420; Sh. Br., 5. 4-3, 22, 6, 7, 3, 11.

[7] This is the Māyā Bīja which Tantra prefixes to the Vedic Mantra. See Woodroffe's "Garland of Letters".

[8] Shangkara (Commentary on Kathopanishad) says that Hangsa is either Sūrya the solar deity or Paramātmā (of whom it is a form). Sūrya is Āditya so called, according to Sāyana, from Hanti (=Gachchhati) because he is in perpetual motion and also because he destroys Ahambhāva. Hangsa is the Ajapā Mantra said in breathing. By the Sun all life is maintained. Hangsah is So'ham reversed.

[9] Shuchisat or dweller (as the Sun) in the sky (Shangkara). By this its position in Svah is shown (Sāyana). Or is in the sun in the sky (Tarkālangkāra).

It is in the air and in the middle region.[1]

It[2] is in the sacrificial[3] and Gārhapatya[4] and household[5] fires.

It is honoured in the guest.[6]

It is in man,[7] in the great and worshipful ones.[8] It is in *Rita*,[9] in the ether,[10] in the waterborn,[11] in the earthborn.[12]

[1] Vasur Antarīksh*h*asat. Its light pervades the airs. Sāyana says it is Vasu because it dwells (Vas) everywhere as does the all-pervading air (Vāyu) in the middle region, the Bhuv*a**h* or Antarī*sh*a. Shangkara says Vasu is He who maintains the beings of the world and Antarīks*h*asat—who (in the form of Vāyu, (air) dwells in the space mid Heaven (Sv*a**h*) and Earth (Bhū).

[2] Hotā Vedisad Atithir Duro*n*asat. The Mantra now goes on to show that the Supreme is not only in Heaven (Sv*a**h*) and the mid-region between Heaven and Earth (Antarīks*h*a) but also on Earth (Bhū).

[3] Hotā is as Shangkara says fire or who dwells in the senses and experiences sounds and so forth.

[4] The Gārhapatyāgni is kept constantly burning by a class of Brāhma*n*as. According to Shangkara, Vedisat=who is on the altar which is the P*ri*thivī.

[5] Duro*n*āsat (Sāyana). According to Shangkara it means that "That which is in the jar of Somarasa or who is in Houses."

[6] Atithir is a guest so called because he does not stay longer than one Tithi that is fifteenth part of the lunar half month. Shangkara says it means here Somarasa.

[7] N*ri*sat. It is the Consciousness (Chaitanya) of man (Shangkara). By this, says Sāyana, the Paramātmā is indicated for man's Consciousness is the highest manifestation of the Supreme Consciousness or Chit.

[8] Varasat. Shangkara says the reference is here made to Brahmā and other Devas. Tarkālangkāra interprets Varasat as the Sūrya Ma*n**d*ala or solar circle.

[9] *Ri*tasat. The term *Ri*ta means the Brahman, Truth (Satya) or Yajna (Sacrifice). That which is there is *Ri*tasat (Sāyana). Shangkara says *Ri*tasat=He who is in Yajna or in Veda which is Satyasvarūpa.

[10] Vyomasat (Shangkara).

[11] Abjā. Shangkara says that this means who is in waterborn things such as shellfish and other aquatic animals. Tarkālangkāra says that the reference is made to the submarine fire Va*d*avāgni or to the Vidyudagni in water.

[12] Gojā such as (Shangkara says) rice and other things grown on earth. Tarkālangkāra says the fire which is in the stones and the like.

It is seen in *Rita*[1] who rises from the eastern mountain[2] who is *Rita*.[3]

The great[4] all-pervading Cause of all.

Exchange the vowel of the Varu*n*a Bīja[5] for each of the long vowels,[6] then say "Salutation to the Devī Ambrosia, who is freed from the curse of Brahmā."[7] By the repetition of the entire Mantra seven times, the curse of Brahmā is removed (198-199). Substituting in their order

[1] *Ritajā* (see as to *Rita* note, ante) because as Shangkara says it manifests in the parts (Aṁga) of the Yajna, or because as Sāyana says, it is visible to all and does not (like Indra and others) come and go.

[2] Adrijā: That is Udayāchala from behind which the sun is said to rise. It sets behind Astāchala. He as Āditya arises therefrom and goes thereto (Tarkālangkāra). According to Shangkara this means "Who is the rivers which have their source in the mountains."

[3] *Ri*tam = Satyam or that which the Vedas prove (Shangkara). It is said by Sāyana to be the Brahmatattva or great consciousness (Mahānubhava). Tarkalangkāra says it is known as the Truth Reality which is everywhere and which can neither be hidden nor limited. It is the all-pervading Brahmatattva whose Sattā or Being is everywhere seen (Upalabdha).

[4] B*ri*hat as He is the Cause of all (Sarva-kārana) according to Shangkara. B*ri*hat comes from the root B*ri*h or B*ri*nh which is the root of the word Brahman. The object of the Mantra is to establish the unity of the Paramātmā without attributes, the Sagu*n*a Īsvara and of all things which have proceeded from Him. As used here it indicates the unity of the Devī Sudhā (wine) with all the Devatās mentioned in the Ma*nd*ala. Wine is Tārā Devī in liquid form (Dravamayī). The Devī who thus manifests is displayed in all things in Īshwarī the sovereign Lady the Cause and Ruler of all and in her *Svarūpa* as Chinmayī one with the Supreme Shiva or Paramātmā.

[5] That is, Vang Bīja of the Lord of Waters.

[6] That is, Vāng, Vīng, Vūng, Vaing, Vaung, Va*h*.

[7] Brahma-shāpa-vimochitāyai Sudhā-devyai Nama*h*. Brahmā, under the influence of liquor, lusted after his own daughter, and therefore cursed it, saying that he that should drink it was as guilty as one who killed a Brāhma*n*a, and would go to hell. "Non-Tāntrikas say that, even when the curses are removed, wine should not be drunk, to which the Tāntrikas reply that Pashus are ignorant (Ajnānī), and that if their views were correct then no one should make Japa of the Gāyatrī, which also is afflicted with three curses. Yet, after the curses are removed, worshippers make Japa of the Gāyatrī" ("Pancha-tattva-Vichāra," by Nīlama*n*i Mukhyopādhyāya, Calcutta, p. 19).

the six long vowels in place of the letter o in Angkusha,[1] and adding thereto the Shrī and Māyā Bījas,[2] say the following

MANTRA

"Remove the curse of *Krishna*[3] in the wind: pour nectar[4] again and again: Svāhā"[5] (200).

Having thus removed the curse of Shukra, of Brahmā, and of *Krishna*, the Sādhaka should with mind controlled worship the Deva Ānanda-Bhairava and Ānanda-Bhairavī[6] (201). The Mantra of the former is:

[1] That is, the Bīja Krong.

[2] That is, the Bījas Shrīṁ and Hrīṁ. Shrī is a name of Lak*sh*mī.

[3] *Krishna*'s family, the Yadu-kula, was destroyed through drink, which he therefore cursed.

[4] Am*ri*ta, the ambrosia of immortality.

[5] The Mantra is thus: Krāng, Krīng, Krūng, Kraing, Kraung, Kra*h* Sudhā-*Krishna*-shāpang mochayām*ri*tam srāvaya srāvaya: Svāhā.

[6] Shiva and His Shakti are so called when the worshippers are in a joyful mood. The Tantrāntara gives the following meditations on Ānanda Bhairava and Ānanda Bhairavī. The former is lustrous like ten million suns and cool like ten million moons. The Deva has five faces with three eyes in each and eighteen arms. He is on a Brahmapadma in the middle of the ocean of nectar. His throat is blue. He is decked with ornaments and seated on a bull. He holds a skull and Kha*t*vāṁga (The club surmounted by the skull; a piece of wood half burnt from a funeral pyre is also so called) and makes a music with bell and drum (*D*amaru). He holds the noose (Pāsha), goad (Angkusha), mace (Gadā), spear (Mushala), sword (Kha*d*ga), shield (Khe*t*aka), axe (Pa*tt*isha), hammer (Mudgara), trident (Shūla) and staff (Da*nd*a). He holds a Vajra (Thunderbolt) and a severed head and makes the Mudrā (gesture) of granting boons and dispelling fear.

Ānandabhairavī, the Devī Sudhā, should be meditated upon as lustrous as a hundred thousand million moons white as snow and the Kunda flower. She has five faces with three eyes in each and eighteen arms. She is eager to give joy to all, She is large-eyed smiling and seated in front of the Devadevesha. The rest is as above.

MANTRA

"Ha - Sa - Ksha - Ma - La - Va - Ra- Yūng: To Ānanda-Bhairava:[1] Vashat" (202).

In the worship of the Ānanda-Bhairavī the Mantra is the same, except that its face is reversed, and in place of the Ear the left Eye should be placed, and then should be said

MANTRA

"Sa - Ha - Ksha - Ma - La - Va - Ra- Yīng: To the Sudhā Devī: Vaushat"[2] (203).

Then, meditating upon the union of the Deva and Devī[3] in the wine, and thinking that the same is filled with the ambrosia of such union, Japa should be made over it of the Mūla-mantra twelve times (204). Then, considering the wine to be the Devatā,[4] handfuls of flowers should be offered with Japa of the Mūla-Mantra. Lights and incense-sticks should be waved before it to the accompaniment of the ringing of a bell[5] (205). Wine should be always thus purified in all ceremonies, whether Pūjā[6] of the Devatā, Vrata,[7] Homa,[8] marriage, or other festivals (206).

---

[1] That is, the seven Sanskrit letters, followed by Yūng Ānanda-Bhiravāya Vashat.

[2] That is, the same seven letters (the first two letters being reversed)—Sa-Ha-Ksha-Ma-La-Va-Ra- Yīng (instead of Yūng)—followed by Sudhādevyai vaushat. The "ear" and "eye" mean Ū-kāra and Ī-kāra, which they resemble.

[3] Sāmarasya of Ānanda-Bhairva and Ānanda-Bhairavī.

[4] Devatābuddhyā. For wine is the saviour (Tārā) in liquid form. The Buddhi or higher mind of the worshipper should be such that he believes the wine to be Devatā.

[5] This is called Ārati. In the right hand is held the light or burning incense-stick, and as these are being waved round and round the bell is rung with the left hand.

[6] See "Shakti and Shākta," by Woodroffe.

[7] See *Ibid.*

[8] See *Ibid.*

The disciple, after placing the meat [1] on the triangular Ma*nd*ala in front of him, should sprinkle it with the Mantra Pha*t*, and then charge it thrice with the Bījas of Air [2] and Fire [3] (207). Let him then cover it up with the Gesture of the Veil,[4] uttering the Kavacha-Mantra,[5] and protect it with the Weapon-Mantra Pha*t*. Then, uttering the Bīja of Varu*n*a,[6] and displaying the Dhenu-Mudrā,[7] make the Meat like unto nectar [8] with the following (208)

MANTRA [9]

May that Devī whose abode is in the breast of Vis*hn*u and in the breast of Shankara [10] purify this my meat, and give me a resting-place in the Supreme abode of Vis*hn*u [11] (209).

In a similar manner, placing the fish [12] and sanctifying it with the Mantras already prescribed, let the wise one say over it the following [13] (210)

[1] Then follows the purification (shuddhi) of meat, the second Tattva of the five.

[2] The Vāyu-Bīja "Yang".

[3] The Vahni-Bīja "Rang".

[4] The Avagu*nth*ana Mudrā.

[5] Or Armour Mantra "Hung".

[6] *i.e.*, "Vang".

[7] Or Cow gesture (*vide* p. 104, note 8).

[8] Literally, "having made into nectar"—Am*r*itīk*r*itya.

[9] Vis*hn*or vaks*h*asi yā devī yā devī Shangkarasya cha
Māṁsaṃ me pavitrīkuru kuru tad Vis*hnoh* paramampadam

[10] Shiva.

[11] Or perhaps "make it sacred like that which is in the abode of Vis*hn*u".

[12] The following is the ritual for the purification of the third Tattva —Fish (Matsya).

[13] This is a *Rik* from *Rig*-Veda, Seventh Ma*nd*ala, fourth chapter, forty-ninth Sūkta, twelfth Mantra. The translation and interpretation given is that of the Bengali translation by Tarkālangkāra. It occurs also in Ullāsa viii, verse 244, *post*.

Mantra [1]

We worship Tryambaka [2] sweet-scented increaser of nourishment.[3] May He free us from the bond of death just as the Urvāruka [4] is detached from its stock. May He not cast us away from [5] immortal Life [6] (211). Then O Beloved, the disciple should take and purify the parched grain [7] with the following

Mantras [8]

Oṁ: As is seen (the sun) the round [9] eye of heaven spreading its rays on all sides, so worshippers [10] ever see the

[1] Oṁ Tryambakang yajāmahe sugandhing pu*sh*ṭibardhanam
Urvārukam iva bandhanān m*r*ityor muk*sh*īya māmṛitāt.

[2] A name of the three-eyed Shiva esoterically the mother of the "Three" that is Brahmā, Vi*shn*u and Rudra.

[3] That is who is as the seed of the world nourishing the body and increasing the wealth of the worshipper and whose beneficent deeds are manifested everywhere,

[4] Bandhana: that is the bond of death. Urvāruka is a kind of melon which when ripe detaches itself from the stalk. The fruit though detached from the stalk is not dead. Cf. Sanatsujātīyam *Pari passu.*

[5] Literally "May he not free us".

[6] That is, Sāyujyamukti (see Chap. VIII *post*). This Mantra is called M*r*ityunjaya (Death-conquering).

[7] Mudrā—the fourth Tattva.

[8] Oṁ Tad Vi*shn*o*h* paramam padang sadā pahyanti sūraya*h*.
Divīve chak*sh*urātatam.
Oṁ Tadviprāso vipa*n*yavo jāg*r*ivāngsa*h* samindhate.
Vi*shn*or yat paramam padam.

These two *Riks* are from the *Rig*-veda, Ma*nd*ala, IV, Chap. V, Sūkta 22, *Rik*, 20, 21. They occur in N*r*isiṁha Pūrva Up., V, 13 and in other places also.

[9] Ātataṁ—Circular, spreading, revealing (Vartulam, Prakāshātmakang, Sarva-prakāshābhibhavakāra*n*am).

[10] Sūraya*h*—Upāsakā*h* anu*shth*ātāro japtāro'dhyetāro vā.

abode [1] of Vis*h*nu. Brâhma*n*as with firmly centered mind ever [3] glorify [4] the supreme abode of Vis*h*nu [5] (212, 213).

Or all the Tattvas [6] may be consecrated by the Mûla-Mantra itself. To him who has belief in the root, [7] of what use are the branches and leaves? [8] (214).

I say that anything which is sanctified by the Mûla-Mantra alone is acceptable for the pleasure of the Devatâ (215). If the time be short, or if the disciple be pressed for time, everything should be sanctified with the Mûla-Mantra, and offered to the Devî (216). Truly, truly, and again truly, the ordinance of Shangkara [9] is that if the Tattvas be so offered, there is no sin or shortcoming [10] (217).

End of Fifth Chapter, entitled "The Formation of Mantras, Placing of the Jar, and Purification of the Elements of Worship".

[1] Yat paramam padam—The place which is the Ocean of Milk. Ks*h*îrodâr*n*avasthânam.

[2] Vipa*n*yava*h*—such as have Dhâra*n*â-shakti in Samâdhi (Medhâvina*h* samâdhau dhâra*n*âshaktiyuktâ*h*).

[3] Jâg*ri*vângsa*h*—diligent.

[4] Samindhate—Sam*ri*ddhing kurvanti.

[5] These *Riks* are for the Nis*h*kâma Sâdhaka. The Parampada is the ocean of milk, the hub (Nâbhi) of the wheel of the universe. He who has reached there attains Sâyûjya-phala, union with the Supreme. By the expression "Supreme abode of Vis*h*nu" (Vis*h*noh paramam padam) is to be understood the Supreme abode which is Vis*h*nu (Shangkarâchârya).

[6] *i.e.*, the five Tattvas.

[7] Mûla.

[8] Mûle tu shrad-dadhâno ya*h*, kiṁ tasya dala-shâkhayâ?

[9] Shiva.

[10] Literally, wanting of parts—Aṁga.

CHAPTER VI

MANTRAS AND RITES

SHRI DEVĪ said:

As Thou hast kindness for Me, pray tell Me, O Lord! more particularly about the Pancha-tattva[1] and the other observances of which Thou hast spoken (1).

Shrī Sadāshiva said:

There are three kinds of wine which are excellent—namely, that which is made from molasses,[2] rice,[3] or the Madhūka flower.[4] There are also various other kinds

[1] The Pancha-tattva (the five elements of worship)—wine, meat, fish, parched food, and woman, which in the Shyāmā rahasya are said to destroy great sins (Mahā-pātaka-nāshana).

For the preparation of surā (wine) see Kātyāyana, XIX, 1, 20, 21. As to Ānanda, *vide* Sh. Br., XII, 7, 8, 11, 12: not propitious but made so by Mantra: Sh. Br., XII, 8, 1, 5; XII. 8, 1, 16; XII, 8, 1, 4. See also *Rig*-Veda, VIII, 2, 12; X, 107, 9; IX, 1, 1. Ait. Br., VIII, 37, 4; VIII, 39, 6. As to Pātra Sthāpana, *cf.* Ait. Br., III, 1, 5; Sh. Br., V, 5, 4, 23. Paddhati in Sautrāma*n*i Yāga, Sh. Br., XII, 7, 3, 14. As to the eating of flesh and animal sacrifice see Sh., Br., XI, 7, 1. Food is of three kinds: Sh. Br., VIII, 5, 3, 3; VIII, 6, 2, 2; XII, 7, 3, 20. As to sexual intercourse: Agnihotra āhuti Sh. Br., XI, 6, 2, 10. See also V, 2, 1, 10; III, 2, 1, 10, 11.

[2] Gau*d*ī (Gu*d*a = Molasses).

[3] Pai*sht*ī.

[4] Mādhvī. Wine made from grapes is also called Mādhvī. Tarkālangkāra says that wine made from molasses is Gau*d*ī. What is made from half cooked rice, paddy and the like is called Pai*sht*ī. This is made in French Chandernagore. Wine made from grapes, raisins, honey, different kinds of flower particularly the Madhūka flower is called Mādhvī. Wine can also be made from Tulasī and Bael leaves, the bark of the Bael tree, betel nuts, coriander seed, nutmeg, myrabolam, Bhāng, ginger, bamboo, bananas, bark of the ber fruit tree and acacia tree and other substances. The Bhutias make an excellent wine from some kind of leaf. In fact in everything there is Sat, Chit, Ānanda of the Sachchidānanda Brahma. If the part which is the basis of Ānanda in Molasses and the like be separated then it becomes known as wine.

made from the juice of the palmyra and date tree, and known by various names according to their substance and place of production. They are all equally appropriate in the worship of the Devatā (2, 3).

Howsoever it may have been produced, and by whomsoever it is brought, the wine, when purified, gives to the worshipper all Siddhi. There are no distinctions of caste in the taking of wine so sanctified[1] (4). Meat, again, is of three kinds, that of animals of the waters, of the earth, and of the sky. From wheresoever it may be brought and by whomsoever it may have beeen killed, it gives without doubt, pleasure to the Devatās (5). The wish of the Sādhaka determines what should be offered to the Devatās.[2] Whatsoever he himself likes, the offering of that conduces to his well-being (6). Only male animals should be killed in sacrifice.[3] It is the command of

It is on this account that it is helpful in Sādhanā of the Brahman who is Sachchidānanda and it is on this account that the knower of Brahman looks upon it as sacred and worships it.

[1] On this verse Tarkālangkāra says that in one of the Tantras it has been said that shortly after the churning of the ocean the inexhaustible jār of Amrita or nectar was placed in the hands of Ganesha. Whenever any of the Devatās wanted to drink the nectar, Ganesha would pour it out for him. In this way he got no leisure. On one occasion Ganesha became very tired and some impurity (Mala) came out of his trunk, out of that a man came. Because he came out of the trunk (Shunda) he was called a Shaundika or brewer. Ganesha placed the jar of nectar in the hands of this man and granted him the following boon, *viz.*, that as the Devatās churned the ocean after throwing into it drugs and other substances and thus produced nectar so the brewer and his descendants would put into water different things and churning it would produce nectar which they were to give to other people but never drink it themselves. In the drinking of this no one should make any distinction of caste. If the brewer of the present day make wine from the prescribed articles according to the method laid down in the Tantras then man becomes long lived and free of ailments. Old men by the use of wine become young again.

[2] Sādhakechchhā valavatī deye vastuni daivate.
i.e., The wish of the Sādhaka is the main factor in determining what should be offered to the Devatā.

[3] Vali-dāna. As to male animals, see Sh. Br., XI, 7, 1, 3.

Shambhu that female animals should not be slain (7). There are three superior kinds of Fish—namely, Shāla, Pāthīna,[1] and Rohita.[2] Those which are without bones are of middle quality, whilst those which are full of bones are of inferior quality. The latter may, however, if well fried, be offered to the Devī (7-8).

There are also three kinds of parched food, superior, middle, and inferior. The excellent and pleasing kind is that made from Shāli rice,[3] white as a moonbeam, or from barley or wheat, and which has been fried in clarified butter.[4] The middling variety is made of fried paddy and the like. Other kinds of fried grain are inferior (9-10). Meat, fish, and parched food, fruits and roots, or anything else offered to the Devatā along with wine, are called Shuddhi[5] (11). O Devī! the offering of wine without Shuddhi, as also Pūja and Tarpana (without Shuddhi), become fruitless, and the Devatā is not propitiated (12). The drinking of wine without Shuddhi is like the swallowing of poison. The disciple is ever ailing, and lives for a short time and dies[6] (13). O Great Devī! when the weakness of the Kali Age becomes great, one's own Shakti or wife should alone be known as the fifth Tattva, This is devoid of all defect[7] (14). O Beloved of My Life! in

---

[1] & [2] The two latter are commonly called Boāl and Ruhi respectively in the vernacular.

[3] A variety of rice of very small grain and very white.

[4] Ghee.

[5] The meat, fish, grain, etc., are called Shuddhi. Shuddhi is also commonly used for anything which is eaten to take away the taste after drinking wine, such as salt or pān-leaf. Milk and water cannot be used as Shuddhi. As to the effect of drinking without Shuddhi, see verse 13.

[6] Another check upon indiscriminate wine-drinking, for it cannot be indulged in until Shuddhi is obtained, prepared, and eaten with the necessary rites.

[7] Shesha-tattvang Maheshāni! nirvīrye prabale Kalau.
Svakīyā kevalā jneyā sarva-dosha-vivarjitā.

The allusion here is to the three classes of women who might be Shaktis: Svīyā (one's own wife), Parakiyā (the wife of another), and

my injunctions relating to this (the last Tattva) I have spoken of Svayambhu and other kinds of flower.[1] As substitutes for them, however, I enjoin red sandal paste (15). Neither the Tattvas nor flowers, leaves, and fruits should be offered to the Mahādevī unless purified. The man who offers them without purification goes to hell (16).

The Shrī-pātra[2] should be placed in the company of one's own virtuous Shakti;[3] she should be sprinkled with the purified wine[4] or water from the common offering[5] (17). (For the sprinkling of the Shakti use the)—

MANTRA

Aing, Klīng, Sauḥ. Salutation to Tripurā; purify this Shakti, make her my Shakti;[6] Svāhā (18-19).

If she who is to be Shakti is not already initiated, then the Māyā Bīja[7] should be whispered into her ear, and

---

the Sādhāranī (one who is common). This Tantra (according to the present text) discountenances Shaktis of the second and third kind, and ordains that the Shakti should be the wife of the Sādhaka (worshipper). With her the fifth Tattva or coition (maithuna) should be done.

[1] See verse 174 of Chapter V—that is, Svayambhu, Gola, and Kunda. Kathitam tatpratinidhau kushīdam parikīrtitam. A form of ritual which will disgust all but those who practise it whose principle however it is to free themselves of all *Ghrinā* and other Pāshas.

[2] See note under ch. X, v. 148. If the Bhogyā Shakti be absent, the Shrīpātra may be placed for worship with the aid of the Pūjyā Shakti after the Pūjyā Shakti has been worshipped and her leave obtained.

[3] The wife is Saha-dharminī (co-worshipper with the husband), and shares the merit acquired by the husband.

[4] Kārana.

[5] Sāmānyārghya. The Shakti should be sprinkled if she is not already an initiate.

[6] Aing Klīng Sauh Tripurāyai Namah: imāng shakting pavitrīkuru mama shakting kuru: Svāhā.

[7] Hrīng. "Initiated" in this verse is used as equivalent for Dīkshitā.

other Shaktis who are present should be worshipped and not enjoyed[1] (20).

The worshipper should then, in the space between himself and the Yantra, draw a triangle with the Māyā Bīja[2] in its centre, and outside the triangle and in the order here stated, a circle, a hexagon, and a square (21). The excellent disciple should then worship in the four corners of the square the Pīṭhas, Kāma-rūpa,[3] Pūrṇa-shaila Jālandhara, Uḍḍīyāna, with the Mantras formed of their respective names, preceded by Bījas formed by the first letter of their respective names, and followed by Namaḥ[4] (22).

---

[1] Nārhāstāḍana-karmaṇi. The reference is to sexual intercourse. Shaktis are of two kinds: Bhogyā, to be enjoyed; and Pūjyā, to be worshipped. The first sit on the left, and the second on the right. If the worshipper yields to desire for the latter, he commits the sin of incest with his own mother and becomes fallen (see Bhakta, 214). By "other Shaktis" is meant Parakīyā, as opposed to Svīyā (one's own).

[2] *i.e.*, Hrīng.

[3] These Pīṭhas are the correspondences in the outer world (Bāhyataḥ) of the four Shāktik manifestations of the general Vimarsha Shakti called Ambikā, Vāmā, Jyeshṭhā, Raudrī. The first denotes the "seeing" of the Divine Mother of Her own forthcoming (Sphuraṇa) when She is Parā Vāk. Vāmā is the state when she is outward turned (Unmukhī) Shakti being then in its seed or Bīja state. She is then Ichchhā Shakti and pashyantī in which she is in the form of a goad (Angkusha). Jyeshṭhā is Jnāna Shakti, Madhyamā Vāk, in the form of a straight line (Ṛijurekhā). Raudrī is Kriyā Shakti and Vaikharī Vāk in the form of Shṛiṁgāṭa (Pyramidal and triangular) and as Saṁhāra Shakti is in the form of Bindu in the return movement (Pralaya). These Pīṭhas are the Kanda, Pada, Rūpa and Rūpātīta respectively. The first is the root of the Sushumnā Nāḍī or Mūlādhāra. Pada is Hangsa in Anāhata chakra the seat of Jīva. Rūpa is Bindu in Ājnā Chakra, Rūpātīta is Nishkala in the Brahmrandhra. The outer subtle manifestations are here the inner Chakras of the body. The gross Chakras are the holy places, named in the Text, great seats of Shākta worship.

See Nityāshoḍhashikārṇava, vi—36 to 42 verses and Commentary of Bhāskararāya. This part of the Nityā is also known as Yoginīhṛidaya. (Ānandāshrama Series of Sanskrit Texts, vol. 56, pp. 209-212.)

[4] Thus, Pūng Pūrṇa-shailāya Pīṭhāya Namaḥ, Ung Uḍḍīyānāya Pīṭhāya Namaḥ, Jāng Jālandharāya Pīṭhāya Namaḥ, Kāng Kāma-rūpāya Pīṭhāya Namaḥ. These Pīṭhas are in the Sādhaka's own body and are Shaktis and forms of Shakti. See Nityāshoḍashikārṇava, Ch. VI, vv. 37-42.

Then the six parts of the body should be worshipped in the six corners of the hexagon.[1] Then worship the triangle,[2] with the Mūla-Mantra, and then the Shakti of the Support with the Māyā Bīja and Nama*h*[3] (23). Wash the receptacle with the Mantra Nama*h*, and then place it (as in the case of the jar) on the Ma*nd*ala, and worship in it the ten Kalās of Vahni with the first letters of their respective names as Bījas (24). These Kalās,[4] which are ten in number—*viz.*, Dhūmrā, Archi*h*, Jvalinī, Sūks*h*mā, Jvālinī, Vis*h*phuliṅginī, Sushrī, Surūpā, Kapilā, Havya-kavya-vahā[5]—should be uttered in the Dative singular, and followed by the Mantra Nama*h* (25-26).

Then worship the region[6] of Vahni[7] (in the Ādhārā or receptacle) with the following

MANTRA

Mang: Salutation to the Ma*nd*ala of Vahni with His ten Kalās[8] (27).

[1] The Mantra which is used is as follows: Hrāng H*ri*dayāya (to the heart) Nama*h*, Hrīng Shirase (to the head) Svāhā, Hrūng Shikhāyai (to the crown lock on the head) Va*shat*, Hraing Kavachāya (to the upper body) Hung, Hraung Netra-trayāya (to the three eyes) Vau*shat*, Hra*h* Kara-tala-p*rishth*ābhyāng (to the back and palm of the hands) Pha*t*. Kavacha means literally armour, but the action of the worshipper is to cover the arms over the chest, touching the shoulders with the hands. It is thus translated "upper body".

[2] *i.e.*, the Presiding Devatā thereof.

[3] Hrīng Ādhāra-Shaktaye Nama*h*—Salutation to the Shakti of the support.

[4] For Kalā see Woodroffe's "Garland of Letters".

[5] These ten Kalās respectively mean—(1) Smoky Red; (2) Flame; (3) Shining; (4) Subtle; (5) Burning; (6) Shining with sparks; (7) Beautiful; (8) Well-formed; (9) Tawny; (10) That which is the carrier of oblations to Devas and Pit*ri*s.

[6] Ma*nd*ala.

[7] Lord of Fire.

[8] Mang Vahni-ma*nd*alāya dasha-kalātmane Nama*h*. The Kalās are the ten in v. 26. They are particular Shaktis of Fire.

Then, taking the vessel[1] of offering and purifying it with the Mantra Pha*t*, place it on the tripod, and, having so placed it, worship therein the twelve Kalās of the Sun with the Bījas, commencing with Ka-Bha[2] to Tha-Da (28). These twelve Kalās are—Tapinī, Tāpinī, Dhūmrā, Marīchi, Jvālinī, Ruchi, Sudhūmrā, Bhoga-dā, Vishvā, Bodhinī, Dhāri*n*ī, Ks*h*amā[3] (29). After this, worship the region[4] of Sun in the vessel[5] of offering with the following

MANTRA

Ang: Salutation to the Ma*nd*ala of the Sun with His twelve Kalās (30).

Then the Sādhaka should fill the cup of offering as was done with the jar three-quarters full with wine taken from the jar, uttering the Māt*ri*kā Bījas in the reverse[6] order (31). Filling the rest of the cup with water taken from the special offering, he should worship with a well-controlled mind the sixteen digits[7] of the Moon, saying as Bījas each of the sixteen vowels before each of the sixteen digits spoken in the dative singular, followed by the Mantra Nama*h* (32).

[1] Arghya-pātra.

[2] The Mantras are thus: Kang Bhang Tapinyai Nama*h*, Khang Bang Tāpinyai Nama*h*, Gang Phang, etc., Ghang Pang, Ngang Nang, Chang Dhang, Chhang Dang, Jang Thang, Jhang Tang, *Ny*ang *N*ang, *T*ang *Dh*ang, *Th*ang *D*ang.

[3] The Kalās of Sun respectively literally mean "Containing heat," "Emanating heat," "Smoky," "Ray-producing," "Burning," "Lustrous," "Smoky red," (as of fire seen through smoke) "Granting enjoyment," "Universal," "Which makes known," "Illuminating". Dhāri*n*ī and Ks*h*amā denote the qualities in virtue of which the Sun draws water from the Earth to himself, and showers it again on the Earth as rain.

[4] The Mantra is Ang Sūryama*nd*alāya dvādashakalātmane Nama*h*.

[5] Arghyā-pātra.

[6] *i.e.*, from Ks*h*a to Ā.

[7] Kalā—*e.g.*, Ang Am*ri*tāyai Nama*h*, Āng Prā*n*adāyai Nama*h*, etc.

The sixteen desire-granting Kalās of Moon are—Amritā, Prānadā, Pūshā, Tushti, Pushti, Rati, Dhriti, Shashinī, Chandrikā, Kānti, Jyotsnā, Shrī, Prīti, Aṁgadā, Pūrnā and Pūrnāmritā[1] which grant fulfilment of desires (33). As in the manner afore-mentioned,[2] the disciple should then worship the region of the Moon with the following

MANTRA

Ūng: Salutation to the Mandala[3] of Moon wherein are His sixteen digits[4] (34).

Dūrvā grass, sun-dried rice, red flowers, Varvarā leaf,[5] and the Aparājitā[6] flower should be thrown into the vessel with the Mantra Hrīng, and the sacred waters should be invoked into it (35). Then, covering the wine and the vessel of offering with the Avagunthana Mudrā,[7] and uttering the Armour Bīja,[8] protect it with the

[1] The literal meaning of the sixteen Kalās of Moon (Soma) are—(1) Amritā = Ambrosial; (2) Prānadā = life-giving; (3) Pūshā = nourishing growth, Pūshas is a Vedic Deity associated with Soma; (4) Tushti = Contentment; (5) Pushti = Nourishment; (6) Rati = Attachment; (7) Dhriti = Constancy; (8) Shashinī = Containing the hare ("Man in the Moon"); (9) Chandrikā = beam spreading; (10) Kānti = effulgence, beauty; (11) Jyotsnā = Moonlight; (12) Shrī = Prosperity; (13) Prīti = delight; (14) Aṁgadā = Body or limb developing; (15) Pūrnā = Full, Complete; (16) Pūrnāmritā = Full of Nectar. Bhārati reads Mānadā for Prānadā.

[2] That is the moon circle is to be worshipped in the wine in the cup as was done in the case of the wine in the jar.

[3] Mandala.

[4] Ūng Soma-mandalāya shodasha-kalātmane Namah.

[5] A kind of basil.

[6] Aparājitā, the flower Clitoria, which is shaped like the female organ, is used in the worship of Durgā and other Devīs. By putting Karavī (Karavīra) flower (representative of the Liṁga) dipped in red sandal paste into Aparājitā flower, the Maithuna-tattva is performed. The two are offered as Arghya.

[7] Gesture of the veil.

[8] The Kavacha Bīja or Hung.

Weapon-Bīja,[1] and converting it into ambrosia with the Dhenu-Mudrā,[2] cover it with the Matsya-Mudrā[3] (36). Making Japa of the Mūla-Mantra ten times, the *Ishta*-devata[4] should be invoked and worshipped with flowers offered in the joined palms.

Then charge[5] the wine with the following five Mantras, beginning with Akha*nd*a:[6] (37).

MANTRAS

O Kula-rūpi*n*ī![7] infuse its natural joy[8] into this excellent wine which is the source of uniform and unbroken bliss joy.[9]

Thou who art Pure Jnāna art also the nectar which is in Anaṁga,[10] place into this liquid substance ambrosia[11] which is Brahma bliss (39).

[1] This is done by uttering the Mantra Pha*t*, tapping three times with the fore and middle fingers of the right hand on the palm of the left hand above, on a level with, and under the Pātra.

[2] Gesture of the Cow. Dhenu-Mudrā is described in note under ch. v. 85.

[3] Or Fish Mudrā. The right hand is placed flat on the back of the left hand, and the thumbs are outstretched like fins.

[4] The particular Devatā of the worshipper: here Kālī.

[5] Abhimantrayet.

[6] The first word of the next verse.

[7] Image of Kula: Brahma-rūpi*n*ī (*cf.* Kula = Sanātana Brahman).

[8] Svachchhanda-Sphura*n*ām—The words are difficult to translate but the sense seems as stated. Svachchhanda = of one's own will independently, spontaneous, natural; Sphura*n*a = bursting forth and joy. That is the joy or thrill which is a form of Brahman bliss.

[9] Akha*nd*aikarasānandākare parasudhātmani.
Svachchhandasphura*n*ām atra nidhehi kularūpi*n*i.

[10] A name of Kāma = God of Love. That is the Svarūpa of the nectar which is in Kāma. Kāma is here the cosmic Kāma the Will or Desire which produced the universe with all its desires. It is nectar for Nectar is the source of life and joy accompanies it. This cosmic Will is in the individual sexual desire from which proceeds individual life. The interpretation adopted is that of Hariharānanda Bhāratī. Tarkālangkāra's runs as follows: Although this liquid substance is for those who have desire do Thou yet place in it the nectar which is Brahman Bliss.

[11] Am*r*ita = here Brahmānanda (Bhāratī).
Anaṁgasthām*r*itākāre shuddhajnānakalevare
Am*r*itatvaṁ nidhehyasmin vastuni klinnarūpi*n*i.

O Thou, who art That![1] do Thou make[2] this Arghya one in substance with That, and having become the Kulamrita,[3] manifest in me[4] (40).

Bring into this great cup, which is full of wine, the essence of ambrosia produced from the essence of all that is in this world with all its differing kinds of taste[5] (41).

I offer as oblation into the Fire of the Supreme Self (Parāhantāmaye) the excellent nectar of Thisness (Idantā)[6]

[1] Tatsvarūpinī = Tattatsvarūpashālinī (Bhāratī).

[2] Tadrūpena eka-rasyang kritvā arghyāng = Having unified this Arghya with That. Eka-rasyang = State of being in the same Rasa (emotion, sentiment). Tadrūpena = Pradhānamādhurya-rūpena (Bhāratī) that is, with supreme Bliss. Ekarasyam = Pradhāna mādhurya-vishishtam, *i.e.*, endowed with supreme Bliss. Arghyam = the consecrated wine. The Sādhaka here invokes Brahman bliss into the wine he is about to use for the purpose of his Sādhanā. Tat = Brahman = Supreme Bliss. The Sādhaka prays that through that wine he may be united with that Bliss.

[3] Consecrated wine.

[4] *i.e.*, Bring me joy.

Tadrūpenaikarasyancha kritvrāghyam tatsvarūpini
Bhūtvā kulāmritākāram mayi vishphuranam kuru.

[5] Brahmāndarasa-sambhūtam asheshha-rasa-sambhavam
Āpūritam mahāpātram pīyūsha-rasam āvaha.

[6] Ahantāpātra-bharitam idantāparamāmritam :
Parāhantāmaye vahnau homa-svīkāra-lakshanam.

Aham = I. Ahantā = "I-ness" (Ahangkāra). Idam = this. Idantā = Thisness. These two as duality are offered to the one supreme Self beyond "I" and "This". See as to Idantā, Taitt.-Up. *Cf.* Jnānārnava Tantra, XXI, v. 25.

A is the first and Ha the last letter of the alphabet, Ma (M) being the usual terminal; Aham then represents all the letters of the alphabet which is the manifested Shabda Brahman. Aham = Jivātmā; Parāham = Brahman, So it is said Tato'hamnāma abhavat. (Br.-Up., 1, 4, 1, 55, 4). When a man is asked "who are you?" (Kastvam) he replies "it is I" (Aham) and then gives his name. When he says Aham or I he affirms that he is Brahman. He refers to his individual self when he gives his name. "This" arises when the Ātmā as "I" posits itself over against it. Idantā = universe which is in the Aham and yet appears separate from it. Parāhantā = the Supreme "I-ness" as Paramātmā. By this Mantra the Sādhaka endeavours to realise the oneness of the individual self (Ahantā) with the Supreme Self (Parāhantā). The joy (Ānanda) which is in the wine is a form of the supreme Bliss (Paramānanda) of which it is a manifestation.

with which the cup of I-ness is filled. (Ahantāpātra-bharitam).

Having thus consecrated the wine with the Mantra, think of the union [1] in it of Shiva and Shivā [2] and worship it by waving lights and burning incense-sticks before it [3] (43).

This is the consecration of the Shrī-pātra [4] in Kaulika worship. Without such purification the disciple is guilty of sin, and the worship is fruitless [5] (44). The wise one should then, according to the rules prescribed for the placing of the common offering,[6] place between the jar and the Shrī-pātra, the Guru-pātra, the Bhoga-pātra, the Shakti-pātra, the Yoginī-pātra, the Vīra-pātra, the Vali-pātra, the Pādya-pātra and the Āchmanīya-pātra [7] making nine cups in all (45-46).

Then, filling the cups three-quarters full of wine from the jar, a morsel of Shuddhi [8] of the size of a pea should be placed in each of them (47). Then, holding the cup between the thumb and the fourth finger of the left hand, taking [9] the morsel of Shuddhi [8] in the right hand, and making the Tattva-mudrā, Tarpaṇa should be done. This is the practice which has been enjoined (48). Taking an excellent

[1] Sāmarasya = Eka-rasya (*vide* 152, note 2).

[2] Shiva and His Shakti.

[3] Ārati.

[4] See p. 111, note 2.

[5] See, as to Pancha-tattva, Woodroffe's "Shakti and Shākta".

[6] Sāmānyārghya.

[7] The Bhoga-pātra, Shakti-pātra, Yoginī-pātra, Vīra-pātra, Vali-pātra, Pādya-pātra, and Āchamanīya-pātra (see Ullāsa, x, 148) are cups used for different purposes in the Chakra ritual. The use to which they are put are set out in the Text.

[8] See p. 145, note 5.

[9] Bhāratī adds: "With the wine from the cup"—Pātra-sthitāmṛitam. In the Tattva-mudrā the thumb and fourth finger are joined Jnānārṇava Tantra, XVI, 185.

drop of wine from the Shrīpātra[1] and a piece[1] of Shuddhi,[2] Tarpa*n*a[3] should be made to the Deva Ānanda-Bhairava and the Devī Ānanda-Bhairavī[4] (49).

Then, with the wine in the Guru-pātra, should be offered oblations to the line of Gurus:[5] in the first place to the Sādhaka's own Guru seated together with his wife on the lotus of a thousand petals, and then in the same way to the other three Gurus who are the Parama Guru, the Parāpara Guru, the Parame*sh*thi Guru successively.[6] In offering oblations to the four Gurus, the Vāgbhava Bīja[7] should first be pronounced, followed in each case by the name of each of the four Gurus[8] (50). Then, with wine from the Bhoga-pātra, the worshipper should, in the lotus of his heart, offer oblations to the Ādyā-Kālī. In this oblation Her own

[1] The practice is to take it between the thumb and third finger of the right hand.

[2] See p. 145, note 5.

[3] Oblation. Made for the satisfaction of the Devatās or Pit*ri*s, the word being derived from *Trip* = to please or gratify.

[4] The Mantra for this Tarpa*n*a is as given under ch. v, verses 201 and 202 with the words Anandabhairavam tarpayāmī Nama*h* in the case of Ānandabhairava and Ānandabhairavīm tarpayāmi Nama*h* in the case of the Devī.

[5] Guru-santati. The Parama Guru is the Guru's own Guru; Parāpara Guru is the Guru of the latter; Parame*sh*thī Guru is the Guru of the last.

[6] See last note. The Guru is seated in the twelve-petalled lotus in the region of the Sahasrāra.

[7] *i.e.*, Aing.

[8] It is customary also to add the Guru's wife's name, the wife being the Shakti. The Mantra thus runs Aing Sashaktika Guru Shrī (name) + ānandanatha + name of Guru's wife + devyambā shrī pādukāng tarpayāmī Nama*h* and so with Parama guru and the rest. In doing Tarpa*n*a to a Devatā the nectar should be held in the left hand, the fingers of which are formed into the Tattva-mudrā. The Shuddhi is in the right hand the fingers being in Tattva-mudrā. The two hands are then brought together and carried to the Brahmarandhra and offering made thereon. On the Brahmarandhra previously draw a reversed triangle if the Devatā is female and upturned if male.

Bīja [1] should precede, and Svāhā should follow Her name.[2] This should be done thrice (51).

Next, with wine taken from the Shakti-pātra, oblation should be similarly offered to the Aṁga Devatās and the Āvaraṇa Devatās [3] of the Devī (52). Then, with the wine in the Yoginī-pātra, oblation should be offered to the Ādyā-Kālikā carrying all her weapons and with all Her followers.

Then should follow the sacrifice to the Vaṭukas [4] (53). The wise Sādhaka should draw on his left an ordinary rectangular figure, and after worshipping it, place therein food with wine, meat, and other things (54). With the Bījas of Vāk, Māyā, Kamalā,[5] prefixed to the Mantra:

"Vang,[6] Salutation to Vaṭuka," [7]

[1] *i.e.*, Krīng.

[2] Krīng Ādyāng Kālīng tarpayāmi Svāhā. Bhāratī says that the Mantra for the Tarpaṇa of the Devī is—Hrīng, Shrīng, Krīng, Parameshvari Svāhā Ādyāng Kālīng tarpayāmi Svāhā.

[3] The word is Aṁgāvaraṇa = Aṁga + Āvaraṇa—that is, the Devatā of both classes (Bhakta, 226). By Aṁga is here meant the six limbs (*Shaḍanga*), of the Mūla devatā considered as Devatās, *e.g.*, Angīnityā and Aṁganityā and by Āvaraṇa-Devatās, the attendant Devatās (see verse 96, *post*).

[4] Between the Tarpaṇa to the Devī, as in verse 58, and before the sacrifice to Vaṭuka, the practice is to perform—(1) Tattva-shuddhi, which is done by seven Mantras, in each of which the following pentads: Prāṇa, Apāna, Vyāna, Udāna, Samāna-Pṛithivī, Ap, Tejas, Vāyu, Ākāsha—Prakṛiti, Ahangkāra, Buddhi, Manas, Shrotra—Tvak, Chakshu, Jihvā, Ghrāṇa, Vachas—Pāṇi, Pāda, Pāyu, Upastha, Shabda-Sparsha, Rasa, Rūpa, Gandha, Ākāsha—Vāyu, Tejas, Salila, Bhūmi, Ātmā are mentioned by name, with the prayer that the same may be purified, and a declaration by the worshipper that he is the Jyotiḥ (Light) and free from sin ; (Jyotiḥ aham virajā vipāpmā) and (2) Tattva-svīkāra ; and (3) Bindu-Svīkāra. See Bhakta's edition, at p. 226. These rites are described at p. 227. Verse 54 describes the mode of sacrifice.

[5] *i.e.*, Aing, Hrīng, Shrīng.

[6] *i.e.*, Bīja of Vaṭuka.

[7] Aing, Hrīng, Shrīng, Vang, Vaṭukāya Namaḥ.

Summarising Tarkālangkāra's Commentary; in Tattva-Svīkāra a triangle is drawn on the palm of the right hand. A piece of Shuddhi of the size of a pea is a placed upon it. This is taken up with thumb and

Vaṭuka should be worshipped in the East of the rectangle, and then offering should be made to him (55).

Then, with the

MANTRA

"Yāng to the Yoginīs Svāhā,"

offering should be made to the Yoginīs,[1] on the South (56), and then to Kshetra-pāla[2] on the West of the rectangle, with the

MANTRA

"To Kshetra-pāla Namah,"

preceded by the letter Ksha, to which in succession the six

middle finger of left hand. Uttering the Mūla-mantra together with the words Shiva, Shakti, Sadāshiva, Īshvara, Vidyā, Kalā, the Sādhaka says "I purify the gross body with Ātmā-Tattva" (that is, the Tattvas of the 36 Tattvas from Prakriti to Prithivī). Then he consumes the Shuddhi. He next takes up another piece of Shuddhi and uttering the Mūla-mantra together with the words Māyā, Niyati, Shuddha-vidyā, Rāga, Purusha says "I purify the subtle body of Vidyā-Tattva" (that is, the Tattvas from Māyā to Purusha of the 36 Tattvas). He consumes the Shuddhi. Then he takes a third piece of Shuddhi and saying the Mantra as before with the words commencing with Prakriti and ending with Bhūmi says "With the Shiva Tattva (*i.e.*, the Tattvas of the 36 commencing with Shiva Tattva and ending with Sadvidyā Tattva) I purify my paradeha" (that is, causal body). Then saying the Mūla-mantra and all the 36 Tattvas the vowels and consonants says "I purify the Jīva the Āshraya of which (in which) are the Tattvas with all the Tattvas."

In Bindu Svīkāra, the Sādhaka realises that Kundalinī extends from the Mūlādhāra to the tip of the tongue and so meditating on Her becomes filled with Her presence (Tanmayo bhavet: that is, becomes Her). Then taking the Bindu from the Bhogapātra uttering meanwhile the appropriate Mantra he should say "The liquid burns (Jvalati) I am the Light (Jyotih). The Light is flaming (Jyotih jvalati). Brahma am I (Brahmāhamasmi) He I am (So'ham) I am I (Aham eva aham). I make offering (Juhomi) Svāhā. Then taking the Bindu he says "I will speak of the Pratyaksha Brahma, of Ritam Satyam. May He protect me. May he protect the speaker. May he protect me, May he protect the speaker. Svāhā." Then having taken Bindu as before he says: Oṁ Chhandasām rishayo yachchhando hyamritā bhūvasā mandro medhayā sprinotu bhuvi sruvam menopāyatu Svāhā.

[1] See note 11 under ch. v. 159.

[2] Protecting Devatā of the ground.

long vowels are added with the Bindu[1] (57). Following this, offering should be made to Gaṇa-pati on the North, with the Mantra formed by adding to the letter Ga the six long vowels in succession with the Vindu thereon, followed by the name of Gaṇesha in the dative singular, and ending with Svāhā.[2] Lastly, offering should be made inside the rectangle to all Bhūtas,[3] according to proper form (58-59).

Uttering "Hrīng, Shrīng, Sarva-vighna-kṛidbhyaḥ," add "Sarva-bhūtebhyaḥ," and then "Hūng Phaṭ Svāhā"; this is how the Mantra is formed[4] (60). Then an offering to Shivā[5] should be made in manner ordained with the following

MANTRA

Oṁ, O Devī! O Shivā, O Exalted One, Thou art in the form of the final Conflagration[6] at the Dissolution of things, deign to accept this sacrifice, and to reveal clearly to me the good and evil which I am to receive. Hrīng,

[1] The Mantra is—Kshāng, Kshīng, Kshūng, Kshaing, Kshaung, Kshah Kshetra-pālāya Namaḥ. The offering to Vaṭuka consists of food with wine.

[2] *i.e.*, Gāng, Gīng, Gūng, Gaing, Gaung, Gaḥ Gaṇa-pataye Svāhā.

[3] Sarva-bhūta (explained in the Mantra in next note). The manner of offering Sarva-bhūta-vali is described in following Shloka. The offering is the same as to Vaṭuka.

[4] *i.e.*, Hrīng, Shrīng, sarva-vighna-kṛibdhyaḥ sarva-bhūtebhyaḥ Hūng Phaṭ Svāhā, or Hrīng, Shrīng, Salutation to all Beings which cause obstruction, Hūng Phaṭ Svāhā—that is, cause obstruction to the worship. The ritual will be found described in detail in Bhakta's Edition, at p. 280.

[5] This is Shivāvali or offering to the jackal. The word means a jackal, and in the commentary of Bhāratī the word is said here to be the equivalent of Phet-kārikā (=Howling), which means a jackal. There is a well-known Tantra of this name. The jackal accompanies the Devī, and feasts on the leavings. It is a Tāntrika usage to feed female jackals at and after midnight. The jackal feeds on carcases and frequents cremation grounds and hence is emblematic of final dissolution.

[6] Kālāgni-rūpiṇī.

Shrīng, Krīng, Parameshvari, Svāhā. This offering is for Thee: Obeisance to Shivā.

O Holy One! I have now described to Thee the mode of formation of the circle of worship [1] (and the placing of the cups [2] and other rites) (61-62). Then, making with the two hands the Kachchhapa-Mudrā,[3] let the Sādhaka take up with his hands a beautiful flower scented with sandal, fragrant aloes, and saffron and holding it against his heart, let him meditate upon the most supreme Ādyā [4] in the lotus of his heart (63-64).

The Sādhaka should next lead the Ādyā Kālī (in the heart) along the path [5] which leads to Brahman and which is within the Sushumnā Nādī [6] to the great lotus of a thousand petals [7] and there make Her joyful [8] (by Her union with Her Lord). Then bringing Her forth through his nostrils (as if another Ādyā Kālī [9] emanates from Her) as light from light let the Sādhaka place Her on the flower [10]

[1] Chakrānushthāna. The Mantra of offering to Shivā consists of the two lines beginning with *Grihna* and ending valing tava following Hrīng, Shrīng, Krīng, Parameshvari Svāhā *Esha* Bali*h* Shivāyai*h* Nama*h*.

[2] The Shrī-pātra and other Pātras.

[3] Tortoise Gesture. The right thumb is left free, the first finger of right hand is placed on the first finger of left, the second and third fingers of the right are placed between the thumb and first finger of left, the little finger of right hand is placed on first finger of left, and the remaining three fingers of left are placed on the back of the right hand, which is slightly curved.

[4] Parātparām Ādyām = The Supreme Ādyā or Kālī.

[5] The central "nerve" in the Merudanda or spine. See A. A. "Serpent Power".

[6] Brahma-vartman: just as Rāja-vartman means the King's highway.

[7] See "Serpent Power" as to this Sahasrāra Padma.

[8] For Her Lord and Husband is there, with whom She is there united. See "Serpent Power", v. 52, and notes under it.

[9] Aparāng Ādyāng Kālīng (Bhāratī).

[10] Referred to in verses 63, 64.

(which is in his hand). The Sādhaka versed in the Mantra with firm faith should then place the flower [1] on the Yantra, [2] and with folded hands pray with all devotion to his *Ishta*-devatā [3] thus (65-66)

MANTRA

O Queen of the Devas! Thou who art easily attained by devotion.[4] Remain here, I pray Thee, with all Thy following, the while I worship Thee (67).

Kring, O Ādyā Devī Kālikā! come here [5] with all Thy following, come here, stay here, stay here (68); place Thyself here, and be Thou detained here. Accept my worship (69).

Having thus invoked (the Devī) into the Yantra,[6] the Life [7] of the Devī should be infused therein by the following Pratis*hth*ā Mantra (70)

MANTRA

Āng, Hrīng, Krong, Shrīng, Svāhā: May the Life [8] of this Devatā [9] be here: Āng, Hrīng, Krong, Shrīng, Svāhā:

---

[1] To which the presence of the Devī has been communicated.

[2] Diagram of worship. See " Shakti and Shākta ".

[3] The particular Devatā of the Sādhaka.

[4] Bhakti—*i.e.*, by Bhakti-mārga.

[5] As the Worshipper says the Mantra he makes the gestures (Mudrā)—(1) Avāhanī, (2) Sthāpanī, (3) Sannidhāpanī, (4) Sammukhī-kara*n*ī, and (5) Sannirodhinī.

[6] Diagram (*vide ante*).

[7] This is the Prā*n*a-prati*shth*ā ceremony. According to the general belief of all Hindu worshippers of images, the latter are not made the object of worship until this ceremony is performed, whereby the life or presence of the Deva or Devī is invoked into it. That is, in the consciousness of the worshipper the presence of the Devatā in the image is recognised. The Prā*n*a-prati*shth*ā Mantra follows in next verse. The five Mudrās should also be shown.

[8] Prā*n*a*h*-Life. Life presupposes the presence in the body of the five vital airs, namely, Prā*n*a, Apāna, Samāna, Udāna, and Vyāna.

[9] *i.e.*, Ādyā Kālī.

May Her Jīva[1] be here: Āng, Hrīng, Krong, Shrīng, Svāhā: May all Her senses be here: Āng, Hrīng, Krong, Shrīng, Svāhā: The Speech, Mind, Sight, Smell, Hearing, Touch, and the Vital Airs[2] of the Ādyā-Kālī Devatā,[3] may they come here and stay happily here for ever: Svāhā (72-74).

Having recited the above three times, and having in due form placed the Life[4] (of the Devī) in the Yantra[5] with the Lelihāna[6] Mudrā, with folded palms, he (the worshipper) should say (75)

MANTRA

O Ādyā Kālī! hast Thou had a good journey? Is this coming pleasing to Thee? O Parameshvari! mayest Thou be seated on this seat[7] (76)?

Then, for purification of the Devatā whilst repeating the Mūla-Mantra, the Sadhaka should sprinkle thrice the water of the special oblation[8] over the Devī, and next make

---

[1] Life individualised.

[2] Prā*n*āh (see note 7, p. 159).

[3] The Ever-glorious Primordial Devī Kālī—*i.e.*, Ādyā Kālī Devatā.

[4] Prā*n*a-pratis*hth*ā.

[5] Diagram.

[6] Literally, showing the Lelihāna-Mudra. Lelihāna is derived from the root Liha=to lap, to lick. It is also a name of Shivā. Lelihāna-Mudrā is of two kinds. In the Daks*hin*ā-mūrti-Samhitā it is described to be as follows: Hold the index, middle, and ring finger straight downward; hold the little finger out straight. The thumb should touch the root of the ring finger. Bhāratī refers to the Daks*hin*ā-mūrti-Samhitā. The other kind is as follows: The two closed fists are placed near the two ears, the mouth is opened wide, and the tongue protruded and moved about. In the notes in the Edition of Bhakta it is said by Tarkālangkāra that it is the practice among worshippers to show Lelihāna-Mudrā, Kha*d*ga (sword) Mudrā, Mu*n*da (head) Mudrā, Vara-Mudrā, and Abhaya-Mudrā after Prā*n*a-pratis*hth*ā.

[7] A usual form of welcome.

[8] Vishes*h*ārghya.

Nyāsa[1] with the six limbs of the Devī. This ceremony is called Sakalīkriti. Then Devī should be worshipped with all the sixteen offerings (77). These are: water for washing the feet, water for the offering, water for rinsing the mouth and for Her bath, garments, jewels, perfume, flowers, incense-sticks, lights, food, water for washing the mouth,[2] nectar,[3] *pān*,[4] water of oblation,[5] and obeisance. In worship these sixteen offerings are needed (78-79).[6]

Uttering the Ādyā Bīja,[7] and then saying "This water is for washing the feet of the Ādyā: To the Devatā Nama*h*," offer the water at the feet of the Devī. In making the offering of Arghya the same should be placed at the head of the Devī and the Mantra should end with Svāhā (80). Then the Sādhaka versed in Mantra should offer the water for rinsing the mouth[8] to the mouth of the Devī and the Mantra should end with the word Svadhā and then the worshipper should offer to the lotus-mouth of the Devī, Madhu-parka[9] with the Mantra ending with the word Svadhā. He should then offer water to rinse the mouth a second time with the Mantra ending with "Vang

---

[1] See "Shakti and Shākta". This is the Shakalīk*r*iti or Sakalīkara*n*a rite: "Devatāmge *shada*mgānāng nyāsa*h* syāt sakalīk*r*iti*h*."

[2] There are two offerings of this water Āchamanīya, as water is used for rinsing the mouth both before and after the repast of the guest, to whom also water is offered for washing the feet.

[3] Wine.

[4] Tāmbūla—*i.e.*, Areca nut, lime, catechu, cardamum, cinnamon etc., wrapped up in betel-leaf and fastened with a clove.

[5] Tarpa*n*a—literally, satisfaction, or satisfying act.

[6] If the rite is performed in the day time Madhuparka is substituted for wine. For as the Tantrāntara says the night rites should be done according to Kulāchāra and during the day according to Vedāchāra: Rātrau kulakriyāng kuryāt divā kuryāchcha vaidikīm.

[7] *i.e.*, Hrīng Shrīng Krīng Parameshvari Svāhā.

[8] Āchamanīya.

[9] A mixture of curd, ghee, and honey.

Svadhā" (81). Then the Sādhaka should offer water for bathing, apparel and jewels, saying the

MANTRA

Hrīng Shrīng Krīng Parameshvari Svāhā: I offer this water for bathing, this apparel, these jewels, to all parts of the body of the Primordial Kālīkā, Svāhā (82).

Then the worshipper should, with the same Mantra, but ending with Namah, offer scent with his middle and third finger to the heart-lotus (of the Devī), and with the same Mantra, but ending with Vaushat, he should similarly offer to Her flowers[1] (83). Having placed the burning incense and lighted lamp in front of Devī, and sprinkling them with water, they should be given away to Her with the

MANTRA

Hrīng Shrīng Krīng Parameshvari Svāhā: This incense-stick and this light I humbly offer to Ādyā Kālikā.

MANTRA

After worship of the Bell with scent and flower and with the

MANTRA

The scent and flower are offered to the Mantra which is sound and rings the triumph of the Mother, Svāhā.

he should ring the bell with his left hand, and, whilst so ringing it, he should take up the incense-stick with his right hand, and wave it up to the nostrils of the Devī.[2]

---

[1] Bael-leaves are also offered.

[2] Ārati is done by waving the light and incense-stick in an elliptical circle in front of the image, the top of the circle being under the nostrils or the eyes (see next verse).

Then, placing the incense-stick on Her left, he should raise and wave the light ten times before the Devī[1] from Her feet up to Her eyes (84-86). Then, taking the Cup and the Shuddhi[2] in his two hands, the Sādhaka should, whilst uttering the Mūla-Mantra, offer them to the centre[3] of the Yantra (87).

MANTRA

O Thou who hast brought to an end a crore[4] of Kalpas![5] take this excellent wine,[6] as also the Shuddhi, and grant to me endless Liberation (88).

Then, drawing a figure (in front of the Yantra), according to the rules of ordinary worship, place the plate with food thereon (89). Sprinkle the food (with the Mantra

---

[1] And then, according to the ritual, he should place it on the right. Tarkālangkāra says: After recitation of the Bīja say: This Pādya (water for the feet) to the Ādyā Kālīka Devatā Namaḥ. Then place it at Her feet. The Bīja should be repeated at every offering. Thus "This Arghya to—Namaḥ and then the Arghya should be offered to Her head: Then Āchamanīya should be offered to Her mouth with the Mantra This Āchamanīya to—Svāhā. Then offer Madhuparka to the mouth to—Svadhā. Similarly with the second Āchamanīya. In offering bathing water sprinkle it all over Her. In offering wearing apparel (Vasana) cover Her therewith. Dedicate ornaments to Her and place them on different parts of the body. Then offer scent, flower and sandal paste. Bael leaves should be offered and then incense and light.

[2] *Vide* p. 104, note 5.

[3] *i.e.*, to the Devī in the Yantra (diagram).

[4] Ten millions.

[5] Duration of the life of Brahmā, or 4,320,000 human years at the end of which the universe comes to an end. By Koṭikalpāntakāriṇi is meant that the Devī is the cause of endless creations, maintenance and withdrawal thereof.

[6] Vāruṇī-kalpa is "like Vāruṇī". It is excellent because it is like Vāruṇī. Vāruṇī is like the Shakti of Varuṇa, Deva of Ocean by the churning of which nectar was produced. Vāruṇi=Varuṇastrī (Vāchaspatya) Vāruṇīpriya and Vāruṇīkānta are names of Vishṇu. Vāruṇī= Lakshmī who also came out of the water at the churning of the ocean. Vāruṇī is liquor made from rice.

Pha*t*) and veil it with the Avagu*nth*ana-Mudrā[1] (and the Mantra Hūng[2]), and then again protect it (by the Mantra Pha*t*[2]). (Saying Vang[2] and exhibiting the Dhenu-Mudrā[3] over it), it should be made into nectar of immortality.[4] Then, after recitation of the Mūla-Mantra seven times, it should be offered to the Devī with the water taken from the vessel of offering[5] (90).

The worshipper, after reciting the Mūla-Mantra,[6] should say: "This cooked food, with all other necessaries, I offer to the Ādyā-Kālī, my I*sh*ta-devī." He should then say: "O Shivā! partake of this offering" (91). Then he should make the Devī eat the offering by means of the five Mudrās called Prā*n*a, Apāna, Samāna, Vyāna, and Udāna[7] (92).

Next, form with the left hand the Naivedya[8]-Mudrā, which is like a full-blown lotus. Then, whilst reciting the Mūla-Mantra, the jar filled with wine should be offered to the Devī for Her to drink. After that again offer of water for rinsing the mouth, and following that a threefold oblation should be made to the Devī with wine from the

---

[1] Gesture of veiling.

[2] The Mantras are not in the text, but are in fact those used with sprinkling, veiling, and protecting.

[3] See notes under vv. 74 and 85, ch. v.

[4] Am*r*ita.

[5] Arghya. That is Arghya water.

[6] See p. 161, note 7.

[7] It is said that there are five different kinds of Vāyus, working various functions in the human body—manifestations of Prā*n*a in its generic sense, constituting a part of the life sac or Prā*n*amaya-kosha. In the Prā*n*a Mudrā the tip of thumb, middle, and third finger are joined together; in Apāna Mudrā the thumb, index, and middle finger are similarly joined; in Samāna Mudrā the little finger, third, and thumb are so joined; in the Udāna Mudrā the thumb, index, middle, and third; and in the Vyāna Mudrā all the fingers are so joined. After the Mudrās is said Apānāya, etc., Svāhā.

[8] With left hand the palm is shown, and all fingers kept straight.

cup of the Shrī-pātra[1] (93-94). Then, reciting the Mūla-Mantra, let the Sādhaka offer five handfuls of flowers to the head, heart, Mūlādhāra Lotus,[2] the feet, and all parts of the body of the Devī (95), and thereafter with folded palms he should pray to his I*sht*a-devatā thus:

MANTRA

O I*sht*a-devatā! I am now worshipping the Devatās who surround Thee,[3] Nama*h* (96).

The six parts of the body[4] of the Devī should then be worshipped at the four corners of the Yantra,[5] and in front and behind it in their order; and then the lines of Gurus should be worshipped[6] (97). Then, with scent and flowers,

---

[1] See p. 110, note 10.

[2] See p. 80, note 6.

[3] Āvara*n*a-devatā—*i.e.*, the minor Devatās accompanying the Devī. The worshipper asks the leave of the Devī to worship them.

[4] The six Aṁgas are the heart, head, tuft (Shikhā)—when Hindu women worship they gather together a lock of their hair, and knot it as their Shikhā—Kavacha (see note under III, 57), three eyes (see note under ch. v, 125), and two sides of the hand (palm and back). The Mantras for the worship of the six limbs of the Devī are: (1) Hrāng H*ri*dayāya Nama*h*, (2) Hrīng Shirase Svāhā, (3) Hrūng Shikhāyai Va*sh*a*t*, (4) Hraing Kavachāya Hūng, (5) Hraung Netratrayāya Vau*sh*a*t*, (6) Hrna*h* Karatala-p*ri*sh*th*ā bhyām Pha*t*.

[5] Diagram—*i.e.*, at Agni, S.E.; Nair*ri*ta, S.W.; Vāyu, N.W.; and Ishāna, N.E. Agni is Fire, Nair*ri*ta is a name of Yama, Vāyu is Wind, and Īshāna, Shiva as Ruler.

[6] There are three lines of Guru—Divyaugha (Heavenly line). Siddhaugha (Siddha line), Mānavaugha (Human line or type). The Gurus of the first class are four—Mahādevānanda-nātha, Mahākālānanda-nātha, Bhairavānanda-nātha, Vighneshvarānanda-nātha. There are five of the second, class, and ten of the third class. Of the second class are —Brahmānanda-nātha, Pūr*n*adevānanda-nātha, Chalachchittānanda-nātha, Chalāchalānandā-nātha, Kumārānanda-nātha. Of the third class are—Vimalānanda-nātha, Bhīmasenānanda-nātha, Sudhākarānanda-nātha, Nīlānanda-nātha, Gorak*sh*ānanda-nātha, Bhoja-devānanda-nātha, Vighneshvarānanda-nātha, Hutāshanānanda-nātha, Samayānanda-nātha, and Nakulānanda-nātha. See also Tantrarāja, Ch. II, Introduction, Vol. 8, A. Avalon's Tantrik Texts. Jnānār*n*ava Tr., XVI,

worship the four Kula-gurus—namely, Guru, Parama-guru, Parāpara-guru, Parameshthi-guru[1] (98).

Then, with the wine in the Gurupātra make three Tarpanas[2] to each, and on the lotus of eight petals worship the eight Mothers, who are the eight Nāyikās—namely, Maṁgalā, Vijayā, Bhadrā, Jayantī, Aparājita, Nandinī, Nārasiṁhī, and Kaumārī[3] (99-100), and on the tips of the petals worship the eight Bhairavas—Asitāṁga, Ruru, Chanda, Krodhonmatta, Bhayaṁkara, Kapālī, Bhīshana, and Saṁhāra[4] (101-102). Indra and the other Dik-pālas[5] should be worshipped in the Bhū-pura,[6] and their

---

50, *et seq.*, gives both additions and variations of these. These are the names of the three classes of Gurus for Sādhakas of Ādyākālī. For Sādhakas of other Devatās the name differs. See Tantrarāja, Ch. I, where names of the Gurus of the Sādhakas of Tripurā are given. These three lines are Āvarana of the Ishtadevatā. When a Sādhaka does Sannyāsa then the Guru selects for him out of the names of his Ishtadevatā group (the Kaulāvadhūta need not do Sannyāsa) such name as he is qualified to receive. Some Gurus select a name from the eight Bhairavas and add ānandanātha to it.

[1] *Vide* p. 154, note 5.

[2] Oblation.

[3] *Cf.* Chapter v, verse 184.

Tarkālangkāra gives the Mantras for the Tarpana of the four Kulagurus. He says that in almost all Tantras the rule is to worship and do Tarpana of the fifteen Yoginīs and eight Shaktis. The former are Kālī, Kapālinī, Kullā, Kurukullā, Virodhinī, Viprachittā, Ugrā, Ugraprabhā, Dīptā, Nīlā Ghanā, Valākā, Mātrā, Mudrā, Mitā. The latter are Brāhmī, Nārayanī, Māheshvarī, Chāmundā, Kaumārī, Aparājitā, Vārāhī and Nārasiṁhī. The Mantra for worship is Ong Kālīdevyambā Shrīpādukāng pujayāmi Namah Svāhā and so with the rest, when saying the Mantra wine is taken from the Yoginīpātra and cup is held in the left hand with Tattva Mudrā. The Shuddhi is similarly held in the right hand. The two hands are united and Tarpana is done on an inverted triangle drawn on the Sādhaka's heart. The Tarpana of the other Yoginīs is done in the same way.

[4] *Cf.* Chapter v, verse 185.

[5] Protectors of the ten sides—that is, North, East, South, West, Above and Below, South-East, South-West, North-East and North-West. The Dikpālas are Indra, Agni, Yama Yaksha, Varuna, Vāyu, Kuvera, Īshāna, Brahmā, Ananta.

[6] See Introduction to Prapanchasāra (vol. III, Tantrik Texts).

weapons[1] outside the Bhū-pura, and then Tarpa*n*a should be made to them (103).

After worshipping the Devī with all the offerings,[2] the Sādhaka should make sacrifice of an animal to Her (104). The ten approved beasts which may be sacrificed are—deer, goat, sheep, buffalo, hog, porcupine, hare, iguana,[3] tortoise and rhinoceros (105); but other beasts may also be sacrificed if the worshipper so desires (106). The Sādhaka versed in the rules of sacrifice should select a beast free from disease and defect, and, placing it before the Devī, should sprinkle it with the water from the Vishes*h*ārghya,[4] and by the Dhenu-Mudrā[5] should make it into nectar.[6]

Let him then worship the goat (sheep, or whatever other animal is being sacrificed) with (the Mantra) "Nama*h*[7] to the goat, which is a beast," and with perfumes, flowers, vermillion, food, and water. Then he should whisper into the right ear of the beast the Gāyatrī Mantra, which severs the bond of its life as a beast ((107-108). The Pashu-Gāyatrī, which liberates a beast from its life of a beast,[8]

---

[1] The weapons are, Vajra of Indra, Shakti of Vahni, Da*n*da of Yama, Kha*d*ga of Yaks*h*a, Pāsha of Varu*n*a, Angkusha of Vāyu, Gadā of Kuvera, Shūla of Īshāna, Padma of Brahmā, Chakra of Ananta.

[2] Upachāra, that is offerings beginning with Pādya.

[3] Godhā (in Bengali, Go-sarpa). Sometimes cocks and pigeons are sacrificed. According to the Nīla Tantra and Annadā-kalpa, a triangular Yantra representing the Yoni of the Devī is drawn on a mud platter, and the head of the bird is held in such a way that when severed the blood falls on the Yantra, and is then offered to Va*t*uka, the Yoginīs, etc.

[4] *i.e.*, Special offering, at the same time saying the Mantra "Pha*t*".

[5] Cow Mudrā (see p. 104, note 3).

[6] Am*ri*ta—*i.e.*, food fit for the Immortals (Immortalising Food).

[7] Nama*h* Chhāgāya pashave.

[8] The sacrifice is as much for the benefit of the beast sacrificed as for the benefit of the sacrificer, since the beast, though sacrificed,

is as follows: After the word "Pashupāshāya" say "Vidmahe," then, after the word "Vishvakarma*ne*," say "Dhīmahi," and then "Tanno jīva*h* prachodayāt".[1]

MANTRA

Let us bring to mind the bonds of the life of a beast. Let us meditate upon the Creator of the Universe. May He liberate thee from out of this life (of a beast) (109-110).

Then, taking the sacrificial knife,[2] the excellent Sādhaka should worship it with the Bīja "Hūng," and worship Vāgīshvarī and Brahmā at its end, Laks*h*mī and Nārāya*n*a[3] at its middle, and Umā and Maheshvara[4] at the handle (111-112). Then the sacrificial knife should be worshipped with the

MANTRA

Nama*h*: To the sacrificial knife infused with the presence of Brahmā, Vis*h*n*u, Shiva, and their Shaktis (113).

---

attains after death a higher state of existence. The sacrificer says to the beast the Gāyatrī of release.

[1] Translation follows.

[2] Khad*g*a: A heavy knife with a straight blade and a curved end like a crescent. The cutting is done with the straight blade.

[3] Vis*h*n*u—a compound word made of Nāra (water) and Ayana (abode)—"He Whose abode was in water in the beginning of the creation." The Supreme Lord first created water, on which He reposed Himself. It is said also that the Lord descended on earth as the Sages Nara and Nāraya*n*a, sons of Mūrti—daughter of Daks*h*a and Dharmma (Shrīmad-bhāgavata, ii, 77). According to the Kālikā Purā*n*a, Nārāya*n*a is the Siṁha portion of the Nara-siṁha Avatāra. Vāgīshvarī is a name of Sarasvatī.

[4] Shiva—"the Great Lord."

Then, dedicating it with the Mahāvākya[1] he should with folded hands, say: "May this dedication to Thee be according to the ordained rites" (114).

Having thus offered the beast to the Devī, it should be placed on the ground[2] (115). The worshipper then, with devotion to the Devī, should sever the head of the beast with one sharp stroke. This may be done either by the worshipper himself or by his brother, brother's son, a friend,[3] or a kinsman,[4] but never by one who is inimical (116). The blood, when yet warm, should be offered to the Va*t*ukas.[5] Then[6] the head with a light on it[7] should be offered to the Devī with the following:

MANTRA

"Krīng: This head with the light upon it I offer to the Devī: Nama*h*"[8] (117).

---

[1] Mahā-vākya—ordinarily means a great Vedic saying pre-eminently "Tat tvam asi"; but here Vākya=Saṁkalpa, declaration, expression of purpose of rite, *i.e.*, the following Mantra: Vi*sh*n*u*rong tatsat adya (to-day; here the worshipper inserts the date, month, Paksha, or half of the lunar month, and the position of the Sun in the Zodiac) samastābhīpsita-padārtha-siddhi-kāma*h* (desirous of obtaining success and the object of all desires; here is given the name and Gotra of the performer of the sacrifice) aham I*sh*t*a*-devatāyai pashum imam sampradade (I give away to the Ishta devatā this beast). Hariharānanda Bhāratī.

[2] Hitherto the animal has been standing, but before sacrifice it is raised and held before the Devī, and then placed on the ground.

[3] Su-h*r*id—a well disposed person.

[4] Sapi*nd*a—an agnate.

[5] See p. 28, note 1. The Mantra for offering to the Va*t*ukas is: Ong *esha*h kavo*sh*n*a*-rudhira-vali*h* Va*t*ukādibhyo Nama*h*.

[6] Krīng.

[7] After the head is severed, a light is placed on it between the horns.

[8] Krīng E*sha*h sa-pradipa-shīr*sh*a-vali*h*: Shrīmadādyā-Kālikāyai Devyai Nama*h*.

This is the sacrificial rite of the Kaulikas[1] in Kaula worship. If it be not observed, the Devatā is never pleased (118). After this, Homa[2] should be performed. Listen, O Beloved One! to the rules which relate to it (119). The worshipper should, with sand, make on his right a square, each side of which is one cubit. Let him, then, while reciting the Mūla-Mantra,[3] gaze at it, stroke it with a wisp of Kusha grass, uttering the Weapon-Bīja,[4] and then sprinkle it with water to the accompaniment of the same Bīja (120).

Then, veiling it with the Kūrchcha[5] Bīja, he should say: "Obeisance to the Stha*nd*ila of the Devī," and with this Mantra worship the square[6] (121). Then, inside the square three lines should be drawn from East to West, and three lines from South to North, of the length of a Prādesha.[7] When this has been done, the following Devatās, (whose names are hereinafter given) should be worshipped over these lines (122). Over the lines from West to East worship Mukunda,[8] Īsha,[9] and Purandara:[10] over the lines from South to North, Brahmā, Vaivasvata,[11] and Indu[12] (123).

---

[1] Tāntrikas of that Āchāra.

[2] Sacrifice in fire.

[3] See ante, ch. v, 66, and note.

[4] Pha*t*.

[5] Hūng. It is to be veiled by the veil (Avagu*nth*ana) Mudrā.

[6] Stha*nd*ila—*i.e.*, the square piece of raised ground marked off as above. The Mantra here for worshipping it is: Shrimadādya-Kālikā-devatā-stha*nd*ilāya Nama*h*. The worship is with scent and flower.

[7] *i.e.*, the length between the tip of the thumb and that of the first finger when fully stretched out.

[8] Vi*sh*n*u—"Giver of liberation."

[9] Shiva—Īsha is God, the Ruler.

[10] Indra, so called as destroying the Asura Tripura.

[11] Yama—Son of the Sun.

[12] Chandra—the Moon, the pleasing one.

Then a triangle should be drawn within the square, and within the triangle the Bīja Hsau*h* [1] should be written. Outside the triangle draw a hexagon, outside this a circle, and outside the circle a lotus with eight petals, and outside this a (square) Bhū-pura,[2] with four entrances; so should the wise one draw the excellent Yantra [3] (124). Having worshipped, with the Mūla-Mantra [4] and with offerings of handfuls of flowers, the space thus marked off [5], and washed the articles [6] for the Homa sacrifice with the Pra*n*ava,[7] the intelligent one, should, after first uttering the Māyā Bīja,[8] worship in the pericarp of the lotus the Ādhāra-shakti [9] and others,[10] either individually

---

[1] This is the Mahā-preta Bīja, the formation of which is shown in the eighth verse of the Ānanda-laharī of Shangkarāchārya and in the 2nd Ch. of Jnānār*n*ava Tantra. The Mahā-Pretas are the five Shivas—Brahmā, Vis*h*n*u, Rudra, Īshāna and Sadāshiva (Rudra-yāmala Tantra). Ha-kāra=Shiva, and Sa-kāra=Shakti, Au-kāra=Sudhāsindhu. (Ocean of Nectar).

[2] Bhū (Earth), Pura (town, city, etc.). This is the part of the diagram outside the drawing, the marked-off space within which the special diagram is drawn (see Introduction).

[3] Diagram.

[4] See note under ch. v, 66, 67.

[5] Ma*n*d*ala, or Yantra.

[6] *i.e.*, Ghee, plantain, rice, fried paddy (Bengali khai, or Lāja in Sanskrit), bael-leaf, flowers, curd, and charu (rice boiled with milk), stick of Palāsha-tree, and leaves of Shamī (a thorn).

[7] Oṃ.

[8] Hrīng.

[9] Shakti of the Support.

[10] *i.e.*, Prak*r*iti, Kūrma (tortoise), Ananta (Serpent), P*r*ithivī (Earth), Sudhāmbudhi (Ocean of Nectar), Ma*n*i-dvīpa (Island of Gems), Chintāma*n*i-g*r*iha (Room of Chintāma*n*i stones, which grant all desires), Pārijāta (Tree so called), Kalpa-v*r*iks*h*a (The tree which grants all desires), Ratnā-vedikā (Jewelled altar), Ratna-siṁhāsana (Lion seat of gems), Ma*n*i-pīt*h*a (Gem-set seat)—all to be worshipped in the pericarp (see *ante*, p. 118). To which Tarkālangkāra adds Muni, Deva Vahumāṁsāsthimodamānashivā (she-jackals), Shavamu*n*d*a (Head of a corpse), Chitāngkārāsthi (fuel and bones from the funeral pyre), Dharma, Jnāna, Vairagya, Aishvarya, Adharma, Ajnāna, Avairāgya,

or collectively (125). Piety, Knowledge, Dispassion, and Dominion[1] should be worshipped in the Agni, Īshāna, Vāyu, and Nairrita corners of the Yantra respectively,[2] and the negation of the qualities in the East, North, West, and South respectively, and in the centre Ananta and Padma[3] (126-127). Then let him worship Sun with his twelve digits, and Moon with her sixteen digits,[4] and, on the filament commencing from the East,[5] worship Pītā, and then Shvetā, Arunā, Krishnā, Dhūmrā, Tibrā, Sphulimginī, Ruchirā, in their order, and in the centre Jvalinī[6] (128-129). In the worship of these Pranava[7] should

---

Anaishvarya, Samvinnāla (the stalk which is Samvid), Prakriti-mayapatra (the leaves which are Prakriti), Vikāra-maya-keshara (the filaments which are Vikāra), Tattva-mayakarnikā (the Tattva which is the pericarp) Arkamandala (the solar circle with 12 Kalās), Somamandala (Lunar circle with 16 Kalās), Vahni-mandala (the fire circle with 10 Kalās), Sattva, Rajas, Tamas, Ātmā, Antarātmā, Paramātmā, Jnānātmā (see "Shakti and Shākta," Ch. 1), Ichchhā, Jnāna, Kriyā, Kāminī, Kāmadāyinī, Rati, Ratipriyā, Ānandā, Manonmanī, Parā, Parāparā, Sadashiva-mahāpretapadmāsana.

These are given from the Shyāmārahasya, Shyāmapradīpa and other Tāntrik works.

[1] *i.e.*, Dharma, Jnāna, Vairāgya, Aishvaryya. The latter term, which comes from Īshvara (Lord, God), a divine attribute of Īshvara, of which there are eight (see p. 5, note 5). It means also the prosperity, power, might.

[2] *i.e.*, the South-East, North-East, North-West, South-West, of which the Devas named are regents.

[3] Ananta, the endless one—Vishnu. Padma, the lotus from navel of Vishnu.

[4] Kalās. See for the Kalās of Sun and Moon, pp. 107, 108.

[5] Prāgādi-keshara. The others are Īshāna (Shiva), North-East, Uttara (North), Vāyu (Wind), (North-West), Pashchima (West), Nairrita (South-West, whose regent is Yama), Dakshina (South), Agni (Fire), or South-East.

[6] *i.e.*, Yellow, White, Tawny-red, Black, Smoky (Red seen through smoke), Fierceness, Having Sparks of Fire, Brilliant, Flaming, the names or Fire. Shvetā is worshipped in N.E., Arunā in N., Krishnā in N.W., Dhūmrā in W., Tīvrā in S.W., Sphulimginī in S., and Ruchirā in S.E.

[7] Ong.

commence the Mantra, and Nama*h* should end it. The seat of Fire[1] should be worshipped with the

MANTRA

Rang: Salutation to the seat of Fire.[2]

Then the Mantrin[3] should meditate upon the Devī Vāgīshvarī as after She has bathed,[4] with eyes like the blue lotus, on the seat of Fire in the embrace of Vāgīshvara;[5] and worship them in the seat of Fire with the Māyā-Bīja[6] (130, 131).

After worshipping Vāgīshvarī and Vāgīshvara on the seat of fire with the Māyā Bīja the Sādhaka should bring Fire in the manner prescribed,[7] and gaze intently on it, and, whilst repeating the Mūla-Mantra, invoke Vahni into it with the Mantra Pha*t*[8] (132). Then the seat of Fire should be worshipped in the Yantra with the

MANTRA

Ong: Salutation to the Yoga-pī*th*a of Fire,[9]

---

[1] Vahni.

[2] Rang Vahner āsanāya Nama*h*.

[3] One versed in the Mantras—the worshipper, sacrificer.

[4] *R*itu-snātā Vāgīshvarī. This refers to the first bath after the monthly period, during which no bath of immersion is taken, such as bathing in the river, tank, etc. Vāgīshvarī or Sarasvati—Devī of Speech, Learning, Fine Arts, etc.

[5] *i.e.*, Brahmā.

[6] Hrīng.

[7] *i.e.*, either on a mud or bell-metal platter.

[8] Tarkālangkāra says that "Pha*t*" is here incongruous in that it is the Astra or Weapon Mantra used to avert danger, and there can be no invocation by Pha*t*. He would therefore read "pha*t*ā tā*d*anam," or "pha*t*ā raksha*n*am," in lieu of "pha*t*āvāhanam". It would then mean driving out or protecting by Pha*t*.

[9] Ong Vahner Yoga-pī*th*āya Nama*h*. Yoga-pī*th*a is Yoga Seat.

and on the four sides, beginning on the East and ending on the South, Vāmā,[1] Jyeshthā,[2] Raudrī,[3] Ambikā,[4] should be worshipped in the order given (133).

Then the marked-off space[5] should be worshipped with the

MANTRA

Salutation: To the Sthaṇḍila of the revered Devatā, the Primeval Kālikā[6]

and then within this place the worshipper should meditate upon the Devī Vāgīshvarī[7] under the form of the Mūla-Devatā.[8] After lighting the Fire with the Bīja Rang, and reciting the Mūla-Mantra, and then the

MANTRA

Hūng Phaṭ: To the eaters of raw flesh[9], Svāhā,

---

[1] and [2] See next note. Vāmā is Ichchhā, Jyeshthā Jnāna, and Raudrī is Kriyā Shakti.

See Ch. I. Yoginīhṛidaya Tantra, vv. 36-42.

[3] *Cf.* Bhūta-shuddhi Tantra, chap. iv: "O Maheshāni! Vāmā is Brahmā and Jyesththā is called Vishnu, and by Raudrī is to be understood Rudra. Vāmā dwells in the navel, Jyeshthā in the heart, and Raudrī always in the head. These are the Bindus from which everything has originated. Brahmā, Vishnu, and Rudra are Prakṛiti Herself. And O Parameshāni! it is the Bindu which prompts them to action. It is by Bindu that everything is created, protected, and absorbed (Sṛishti, Sthiti, Laya). The Bindu is the Bīja (Cause) of Brahmā, Vishnu, and Mahesha.") Possibly "navel" may indicate the whole region from Mūlādhāra to the heart.

[4] Mother. Here the state when the creative Shakti first saw Her own Sphurana.

[5] Sthaṇḍila.

[6] Shrīmad-Adyā-Kālikāyāḥ Devatāyāḥ Sthaṇḍilāya Namaḥ.

[7] Devī of Speech—Sarasvatī.

[8] *i.e.*, Kālī.

[9] Kravyādebhyaḥ—that is, to the Demonic, Rākshasas. Hūng is Kūrchha Bīja.

the share of the raw meat eaters (Rākshasas) should be put aside. Gaze at the Fire, saying the Weapon-Mantra,[1] and surround it with the Veil Mudrā,[2] uttering the Bīja Hūng (134-136). Make the Fire into nectar with the Dhenu-Mudrā.[3] Take some Fire in both palms, and wave it thrice in a circle over the Sthandila from right to left. Then with both knees on the ground, and meditating on Fire as the male seed of Shiva, the worshipper should place it into that portion of the Yoni Yantra[4] which is nearest him (137-138). Then, the Sādhaka should first worship the Image of Fire with the

MANTRA

Hrīng: Salutation to the Image of Fire,[5] Namah

and after that the Spirit[6] of Fire with the

MANTRA

Rang: to the Spirit of Fire, Namah[7] (139).

The Mantrin[8] will then think in his mind of the awakened form of Vahni,[9] and kindle Fire with the following (140)

---

[1] *i.e.*, Phat.

[2] Avaganthana-Mudrā (see note under ch. v, 192).

[3] Cow Mudrā (see p. 104, note 8).

[4] Female organ diagram—*i.e.*, the triangle, which is symbolical of the Yoni.

[5] Hrīng Vahni-mūrtaye Namah.

[6] Chaitanya derived from chit=to awaken, to be conscious.

[7] Rang Vahni-chaitanyāya Namah.

[8] See p. 173, note 2.

[9] Fire.

MANTRA

Ong: Ruddy Spirit of Fire, which knows all, destroy, destroy, burn, burn, ripen, ripen,[1] command: Svāhā.

This is the Mantra for kindling Fire. After this, with folded hands, Fire should again be adored (141-142).

MANTRA

I adore the lighted and kindled Fire of the colour of gold, free from impurity, burning, Jāta-veda,[2] the devourer of oblations,[3] which faces every quarter[4] (143).

After adoration of Fire in this manner, cover the marked-off space[5] with Kusha grass, and then the worshipper, giving Fire the name of his own, I*sh*t*a*-devatā,[6] should worship[7] him with the (144).

---

[1] Ong chit-pingala, hana hana, daha daha, pacha pacha, sarvajnājnāpaya: Svāhā. "Ripen," either in the sense that Fire should assimilate the oblation, or convey them matured to the other Devas.

[2] See p. 177, n. 1, and *Rig*-veda (x, 79, 80).

[3] Hūtāshana is a name of sacrificial Fire.

[4] Agning prajvalitang vande Jāta-vedang Hutāshanang:
Suvar*n*a-var*n*am amalang samiddhang sarvatomukham.

[5] Stha*nd*ila.

[6] See note under ch. v, 33. This is done thus: "Agne! tvam Ādyā-Kālikā-nāmāsi"=Agni, Thy name is Adyā Kālikā.

[7] Archchanā: in external Archchanā scent and flower are offered. The Mantra is: "Ete gandha-pus*h*pe Ādyā-Kālikā-nāmāgnaye Nama*h*" (These the flower and scent are to Āgni, whose name is Ādyā Kālikā); and before Archchanā the Deva must be invoked with the Āvāhana Mantra, which is as follows: "Ādyā-kālikā-nāmāgne! ihāgachchha ihāgachchha; iha tis*h*t*h*a iha tis*h*t*h*a, iha sannidhehi, iha sannidhehi; iha sammukhībhava, iha sammukhībhava; iha sanniruddho bhava, iha sanniruddho bhava; mama pujāng g*r*ihā*n*a" (O Agni! whose name is Adyā-Kālikā, come here, come here, stay here, stay here, fix thyself here, fix thyself here, be here and face towards me, be here and face towards me, be here detained, be here detained. Accept my worship.)

MANTRA

Ong, Vaishvānara, Jāta-veda, come here, come here, O Red-eyed One, accomplish all works: Svāhā.[1]

In this way the seven Tongues[2] of Fire, Hiranya and others, should be worshipped (145-146). The worshipper should next adore the six Limbs of Vahni,[3] uttering the word "of a thousand rays" in the dative singular, and also "obeisance to the heart".[4]

Then the wise one should worship the forms of Vahni (147). The eight[5] forms are Jāta-veda and others (148). Then the eight Shaktis—namely, Brāhmī[6] and others,

---

[1] Ong Vaishvānara Jātaveda ihāvaha ihāvaha; lohitāksha, sarvakarmāni sādhaya: Svāhā. Vishvānara = "Ruling or benefiting all men," is a name of Savitri. Vaishvānara = Son of Vishvānara, an epithet of Agni. As to Jātaveda, see below, note 5.

[2] *i.e.*, Kālī, Karālī, Mano-javā, Su-lohitā, Sudhūmra-varnā, Ugrā or Sphulimginī, Pradīptā. The Mantra is Ong Vahner Hiranyādi-saptajihvābhyo Namah.

[3] Fire. The worshipper should do Hridayādi-shadamga-nyasa of Fire. The first Mantra applicable to the heart is given. The rest is understood (see next note).

[4] The full Mantra runs thus: Oṁ Sahasrārchishe Hridāyāya Namah (Oṁ salutation to the heart of a thousand rays), Oṁ Svasti-pūrnāya Shirase Svāhā (salutation to the head full of prosperity), Oṁ Uttishthapurushāya Shikhāyai Vashat (salutation to the crown lock where abides the Supreme Purusha or Being), Oṁ Dhūma-vyāpine Kavachāya Hūng (to the smoke-spreading body), Oṁ Sapta-jihvāya Netra-trayāya Vaushat (to the seven-tongued and three-eyed), Oṁ Dhanurdharāya Astrāya Phat (carrying the bow and his weapon).

[5] The eight forms of Vahni (Fire) are—(1) Jāta-veda (which, according to the Nirukta=all knowing (Sarvajna); (2) Saptajihva (Seven-tongued); (3) Vaishvānara (from Vishvānara, see note 1, above); (4) Havya-vāhana (Carrier of oblations); (5) Ashvodara-ja (Bādavānala, or Bādavāgni—literally, Mare's fire=Submarine fire said to come from a cavity called the mare's mouth); (6) Kaumāra-tejah (The Fire or Seed from which Kumāra or Kārttikeya was born, see note to Shlokas 14-16, Chapter I, *ante*); (7) Vishvamukha (since it can devour the universe); (8) Deva-mukha (because as all oblations are offered to him he is the mouth of the Devas).

[6] *i.e.*, Brāhmī, Nārāyanī, Māheshvarī, Chāmundā, Kaumārī, Aparājitā, Vārāhī, Narasiṁhī (*cf.* Ashta-nāyikās, Ch. v, 184 and Ch. vi, 100). The Ashta-nāyikās are also Ashta-mātris, or eight Mothers.

the eight Nidhis[1]—namely, Padma and others, and the ten Dik-pālas[2]—namely, Indra and others should be worshipped (149).

After worshipping the Thunderbolt and other weapons,[3] the sacrificer should take two blades of Kusha grass of the length of the space between his stretched-out thumb and forefinger,[4] and place them lengthwise in the Ghee[5] (150). He should meditate on the Nādī Iḍā[6] in the left part of the Ghee, and on the Nādī Piṁgalā[7] in the right portion, and on the Nāḍī Sushumnā[8] in the centre, and with a well-controlled mind take Ghee from the right side, and offer it to the right eye of Fire[9] with the following

---

[1] Treasures of Kuvera (Deva of Wealth), of which mention is made of eight—Padma, Mahā-padma, Shaṁkha, Makara, Kachchhapa, Mukunda, Nanda, and Nīla. Tarkālangkāra quoting Mārkaṇḍeya Purāṇa says these are the Ādhāra of Lakshmī.

[2] Regents of the Quarters—Indra, Agni, Yama, Nairṛita, Varuṇa, Vāyu, Kuvera, Īshāna, Brahmā, and Vishṇu (Ananta).

[3] Of the guardians or regents (Dik-pālas) of the quarters—*viz.*, Indra's Vajra (thunderbolt), Agni's Shakti (spear, dart), Yama's Daṇḍa (staff or stick), Nairṛita's Khaḍga (sword), Varuṇa's Pāsha (fetter), Vāyu's Angkusha (hook), Kuvera's Gadā (mace), Īshāna's Trishūla (trident), Brahmā's Padma (lotus), Vishṇu's Chakra (discus).

[4] Prādesha.

[5] Clarified butter used for oblation in the Homa sacrifice. The two blades of grass should be placed in such a way as to divide the ghee into three equal parts.

[6] Iḍā and Piṁgalā are the two Yoga-"nerves" (Nāḍī) on each side of the central Sushumnā Nāḍī. See "Serpent Power" by A. Avalon.

[7] See last note.

[8] See *ibid.*

[9] Hutāshitā=Easter of oblations. Fuel is the ear of fire, the smoky part is the nose; where the flame is dim that is the eye. The head is the glowing coal and the light flame is the tongue of Fire. If Homa be done without knowing this and the order in which the offering is to be made then harm results; see Tantrasāra.

MANTRA

Oṁ: to Agni Svâhâ.[1]

Then, taking Ghee from the left side, offer it to the left eye of Vahni with the

MANTRA

Oṁ: to Soma Svāhā[2] (151-153).

Then, taking Ghee from the middle portion, offer it to the forehead of Vahni with the

MANTRA

Oṁ: to Agni and his flame Svāhā[3] (154).

Then, saying Nama*h*, take the Ghee again from the right side, say first the Pra*n*ava,[4] and then the

MANTRA

To Agni the Svi*sht*i-k*ri*t[5] Svāhā.

With this Mantra he should offer oblation to the mouth of Vahni.[6] Then, uttering the Vyāh*ri*tis[7] with the Pra*n*ava at the commencement, and Svāhā at the end, the

---

[1] Oṁ Agnaye Svāhā.

[2] Oṁ Somāya Svāhā.

[3] Oṁ Agni-*sh*omābhyām Svāhā.

[4] Oṁ.

[5] Oṁ Agnaye svi*sht*i-k*ri*te Svāhā. Svi*sht*i-k*ri*t=one who causes good sacrifice; a form of Fire.

[6] Fire.

[7] The names of the three worlds,—Bhū*h* (Earth), Bhuva*h* (Space between Earth and Heaven), and Sva*h* (Heaven). These, with Oṁ and the Gāyatrī, are according to Manu, the principal part of the Vedas. By these, says Yājnavalkya, the Most High, the Source of all, should be worshipped. To remove doubt whether or not that cause,

Homa sacrifice should be performed (155-156). Then he should offer oblations thrice with the

MANTRA

Oṁ, O Vaishvānara, Jātaveda, come hither, come hither, O Red-eyed One! fulfil all my works Svāhā[1] (157).

Then, invoking the *Ishta*-Devatā with the proper Mantra into the Fire, let him worship Her and the Pī*tha*-Devatā.[2] Twenty-five oblations should then be offered uttering the Mūla-Mantra with Svāhā at the end, and, contemplating on the union (or identity) of his own Self with Vahni and the Devī, eleven more oblations should be offered with the Mūla-Mantra. Oblations should next be made to the Aṁga-Devatās (158-159).

Then, with a mixture of Ghee, Tila-seed, honey, or with flowers and bael-leaves, or with (other prescribed) articles, oblation[3] should be made for the attainment of one's desire. This oblation should be made according to one's ability not less than eight times, and with every attention and care (160-161). Then, reciting the Mūla-Mantra ending with Svāhā, complete oblation should be made (with a full ladle[4]) with fruits and leaves.[5] Then the worshipper, with the

---

signified by Oṁ, exists separately from the effects, the text of the Vyāh*r*iti is next read explaining that God, the sole Cause, eternally exists pervading the Universe (Rām Mohan Rāy, "Prescript for Worship by Means of the Gāyatrī," 1827).

[1] Oṁ Vaishvānara! Jātaveda! ihāvaha ihāvaha: Lohitāk*sh*a sarva-karmā*n*i sādhaya: Svāhā. See p. 177, notes 1 and 5.

[2] The I*sh*ta-devatā is here the Primordial Kālī. The Mantra is given by Tarkālangkāra. As to Pī*th*a Devatā, see p. 147, note 3. But here Ādhārashakti, Shes*h*a and the rest are meant.

[3] This should also be with the Mūla-Mantra ending with Svāhā.

[4] Literally, Pūr*n*āhuti should be offered—*i.e.*, complete oblation made with a full ladle, in testimony of the completion of the rite.

[5] Leaf: Tāmbula or Pān-leaf (Bhāratī).

Saṁhāra-Mūdrā,[1] transferring the Devī from the Fire to the lotus of his heart (162), should say "Pardon me," and dismiss[2] Him who feeds on oblations.[3] Then, distributing presents,[4] the Mantrin should consider that the Homa has been duly performed (163). Then the excellent worshipper should place between the eyebrows what is left over of the oblations[5] (164). This is the ordinance relating to Homa in all forms of Āgama[6] worship.

After performance of Homa the worshipper should proceed to do Japa[7] (165). Now, listen, O Queen of the Devas! to the mode of doing Japa by which the Vidyā[8] is pleased. During Japa, the Devatā, the Guru, and the Mantra should be fully realised as one (166). The letters of the Mantra are the Devatā, and the Devatā is in the form of the Guru. He who worships them as one and the same, his is the highest success[9] (167).

---

[1] Saṁhāra-Mūdrā. Left hand placed with palm downward, the right hand is placed on it, the back of the right hand touching the back of the left. The fingers of one hand are placed between the fingers of another; then the hands are given a turn, and the two index fingers are joined. In bringing the Devī to the heart a flower from those offered should be taken up with the tips of the index fingers, and brought near the nose, and, when smelling it, the worshipper should think that he has brought Her to the heart.

[2] Visarjana.

[3] Hutāshana—*i.e.*, Vahni, Fire.

[4] Dakshinā. At the conclusion of Homa the officiating priest tells the assembled people to consider that everything has been faultlessly done. This is Achchhidrāvadhāra*n*a ("K*r*itam idam homakarmāchchhidram astu").

[5] *i.e.*, he should mark his forehead with the mixture of ashes and Ghee left. This is called Tilaka.

[6] Tāntrika.

[7] Part of Mantra-sādhanā.

[8] *i.e.*, the Devi Ādyā Shakti.

[9] Siddhi. As the Mantra is made of letters, the Devatā has a celestial and the Guru a human body it may be asked, says Tarkālangkāra, where is their identity. He answers. Suppose in three houses three images of Jagaddhātrī are worshipped. If I bow to the materials

The worshipper should then meditate upon his Guru as being in his head, the Devī in his heart, the Mūla-Mantra in the form of Tejas[1] on his tongue, and himself as identified[2] with the glory of all three (168). Japa should then be done of the Mūla-Mantra seven times adding to the beginning and at the end of it the Tāra.[3] Having done this, Japa should be done of it with the Mātrikā letters placed before and after it[4] (169). The wise worshipper should make Japa of the Māyā-Bīja[5] over his head ten times, and of the Pranava ten times over his mouth, and of the Māyā-Bīja again seven times in the lotus ofhis heart, and then perform Prānāyāma[6] (170).

---

of these images then obeisance to them is obeisance to three separate things. But I did not bow to the materials. I do not bow before life is placed in the image (Jīvanyāsa). I bow to the one Jagaddhātrī who is invoked into all the three images. The Guru again is not merely a human being. As the material of the image is the place of the Devatā so is the human form of the Guru. The Mantra is the body of the Devatā and is therefore the place (Adhishthāna) of the Devatā. Now eliminate the material of the image, the human form, and the letter form or Shabdabrahman of the Mantra and look for the object of worship. That is the one Brahman in the form of all three. The Guru, Devatā, and Mantra are one and the same Brahman.

[1] Light, and energy. The Mantra is thought of at the root of the tongue.

[2] Mantra and Devatā are one: Mantrārnā Devatā proktā, Devatā Gururūpinī. See Woodroffe's "Garland of Letters".

[3] *i.e.*, the Pranava—Oṁ.

[4] A to Ksha, the Anuloma and Ksha to A, the Viloma Mātrikā.

[5] *i.e.*, Hrīng.

[6] Breath control (See "Serpent Power"). Making Japa (as in verse 169) of the Mūla-Mantra, preceded and followed by the Pranava, is called Ashaucha-bhaṁga (=breaking or removing uncleanliness), and making Japa as above with the Mātrikā Bīja in the Mani-pūra is called Nirvāna. Making Japa over the head is Kullukā (see Chapter iii, 119); making Japa of the Pranava is Mukhashodhana (purification of the mouth); making Japa of Māyā-Bīja in the heart is Setu (bridge). Meditating on the Mūlamantra with the Bīja Hūṁ before and after it, in the Sahasrāra, in the Heart, in the Mūlādhāra and then again in the Sahasrāra is called Mantrachaitanya. To do Japa seven times of the Mūlamantra preceded and followed of the Bīja Īng is Nidrābhaṁga.

Then, taking a rosary of coral, or other substance, let him worship it thus:

MANTRA

O Rosary,[1] O Rosary, O great Rosary, thou art the form of all Shaktis.[2] Thou art the repository of the fourfold blessings.[3] Do thou therefore be the giver to me of all success.[4]

Having thus worshipped the rosary, and also made oblation[5] to it thrice with wine taken from the Shrī-pātra,[6] accompanied by recitation of the Mūla-Mantra, the worshipper should, with well-controlled mind, make Japa one thousand and eight, or at least one hundred and eight times (171-173). Then, doing Prā*n*āyāma, he should offer into the left lotus-hand of the Devī the fruit of his Japa,

---

To meditate on the Ish*t*adevatā from feet to head as composed of the letters of the Mantra is called Mantrārtha-bhāvanā.

To do Japa of the Bīja Krīng or Ong Krīng in the heart or throat seven times is called Mahāsetu. To meditate on the Guru in the head and on the Ish*t*adevatā in the heart and to think of the Yonirūpā Bhagavatī as pervading one from the head to the Mūlādhāra and the reverse and then doing Japa of the Bīja Eng ten times is Yonimudrā. Doing Japa of the Mantra seven times formed by three repetitions of the Bīja, three of the Pra*n*ava and three of the Bīja again is Jihvā-shodhana. Prā*n*ayoga is done by Japa seven times of the Bīja preceded and followed each time by Hrīng. Dīpanī is Japa of the Bīja seven times preceded and followed in each case by the Pra*n*ava. Doing this seven times is Ashaucha-bhaṁga. There are other terms such as Mantra-shikhā which relate to Japa-rahasya.

[1] Mālā.

[2] Sarvashakti svarūpi*n*i, that is, all the Shaktis are in Thee.

[3] *i.e.*, Dharma, Artha, Kāma, Mok*sh*a.

[4] Siddhi.

[5] Tarpa*n*a.

[6] See p. 146, note 2.

which is Tejas[1] together with water[2] and flowers from the Shrī-pātra,[3] and, bowing down his head to the ground, say the following :

MANTRA

O Great Queen![4] Thou Who protectest that which is most secret, deign to accept this my Japa. May by Thy grace, success attend my effort.

After this, let him with folded hands recite the Hymn[5] and the Protective Mantra[6] (174-176). Then the Sādhaka with the special oblation[7] in his hand should go round the Devī, keeping Her to his right, say the following, and dedicate his Self[8] to Her by offering Vilomārghya[9] (177).

MANTRA

Oṁ: Whatsoever ere this I have done through the vital airs, mind or body, whether when awake, in dream or dreamless sleep, whether by mind, word or deed, whether by my hands, feet, belly, or organ of generation, whatsoever I have thought or said—may all that be an offering

---

[1] The fruit of the Japa, is like Tejas itself.

[2] *i.e.*, Jala, here Wine and water mixed.

[3] See p. 146, note 2.

[4] Maheshvarī.

[5] Stotra.

[6] Kavacha. The text of this and the hymn are given in the next Chapter.

[7] Vishe*sh*ārghya.

[8] Ātma-samarpa*n*a. This should be done by reciting the Mantra in Verses 178-181.

[9] Vilomārghya is offering of Arghya at the feet of the Devī. Arghya is generally offered at the head, but the worshipper, in offering his own self as Arghya, offers same at the feet. Vilomārghya = reversed Arghya.

to Brahman. Me and all that is mine I lay at the lotus-feet of the Ādyā Kālī. Ong Tat Sat[1]. After saying this dedication should be made of the Self.[2] (178-181).

Then, with folded hands, let him supplicate his I*sh*ta-devatā[3] and reciting the Māyā-Mantra,[4] say:

MANTRA

"O Primordial Kālikā! I have worshipped Thee with all my powers and devotion," and then saying, "Forgive me," let him bid the Devī go.[5] Let him then with his hands formed into Saṁhāra-Mudrā[6] take up a flower, smell it, and place it on his heart (182-183). A triangular figure well and clearly made should next be drawn in the North-East corner, and there he should worship the Devī Nirmālya-vāsinī[7] with the

MANTRA

Hrīng To the Devī Nirmālya-vāsinī[8] Nama*h* (184).

---

[1] Ita*h* pūrvam pra*n*a-buddhi-deha-dharmādhikārato jagratsvapna-susha*h*uptyavasthāsu manasā vāchā karma*n*ā hastābhyām padbhyām, udare*n*a shishnayā yat k*r*itam yat sm*r*itam yaduktam tat sarvam brahmārpa*n*am bhavatu mām madīyam sakalam Ādyā Kālīpadāmbhoje arpayāmi. Oṁ Tat Sat. See p. 21, note 2, as to the concluding words.

[2] Ātma-samarpa*n*am.

[3] The particular Deity of the worshipper; here Kālī.

[4] Hrīng.

[5] Visarjana. This is the dismissal of the Devī to Her seat in the eight-petalled Lotus in the heart of the worshipper. He asks to be forgiven both because of the trouble he has given Her as also for his shortcomings in worship. At this time the jar is slightly tilted by the Sādhaka.

[6] The Mudrā of Dissolution (see p. 181, note 1).

[7] Nirmālya is the remains of the offerings made to a Devatā. The flowers, etc., used in the ceremony. These, too, are sacred, and of them Nirmālya-vāsinī is the Devī.

[8] Hrīng Nirmālya-vāsinyai Nama*h*.

Then, distributing Naivedya[1] to Brahmā, Vishnu, and Shiva, and all the other Devas, the Sādhaka and his Shakti should partake of it (185). Then, placing his Shakti[2] to his left, on a separate seat or on the same seat with himself, he should take a pleasing cup (186). The cup should be so formed as to hold not more than five and not less than three Tolās (about two ounces) of wine, and may be of either gold or silver (187), or crystal, or made of the shell of a cocoa-nut. It should be kept on a support[3] on the right side of the plate containing the Shuddhi[4] (188).

Then either the gentle Sādhaka himself or his brother's sons should serve the sacred food[5] and wine among the worshippers according to the order of their seniority[6] (189). The purified wine should be served in the drinking-cups, and the purified food in plates kept for that purpose,

---

[1] Anything offered to the deity, usually cooked or uncooked food.

[2] The wife or other woman with whom the worship is done.

[3] *i.e.*, a tripod.

[4] *i.e.*, the Shuddhi-pātra, or dish containing the prepared meat, fish, etc., the cup being called Pāna-pātra.

[5] Mahā-prasāda.

[6] Here, seniority=priority in initiation and not in years. The practice is, as given in the Kaulikārchanadīpikā, as follows: The worshipper first serves his own Guru, then the Shakti of the Guru, then his own Shakti, then the elders on the right and the juniors on his left, and then he helps himself. In Kālīkula, the Shaktī of the Guru is served before the Guru. If in a Chakra a Sādhaka has a Mahāpātra (cup made of human skull) the wine should be put into that first.

Manu says that a man is not old because his hairs are grey. The Devas call him old who though young in years is possessed of wisdom (Jnāna). In ascertaining seniority the Pūrnābhishikta is senior to the Shāktābhishikta. The Kramadīkshita is senior to the Pūrna-bhishikta. The Sāmrājyābhishikta is senior to the Kramadīkshita. Mahāsāmrājya is superior to Sāmrājya, Sāmrājyātīta is superior to Mahāsāmrājya. The Pūrnadīkshita is superior to the former. Of the Pūrnadīkshita, he who is a Pūrnayogī, who is fully adept in Mantra and Yoga is above all. The Guru of the particular Chakra is above the Pūrnayogī. He is above all as representing the Ādiguru.

and then food and drink should be taken with such as are present at the time (190). First of all, some Shuddhi should be eaten to make a foundation[1] (for the wine which is to be drunk). Let the assembled worshippers then joyously take up each his own cup filled with excellent nectar.

Then let them take up each his own cup and meditate upon the Kula-Ku*nd*alinī,[2] who is the Chit,[3] and who is spread from the Mūlādhāra[4] lotus to the tip of the tongue, and, uttering the Mūla-Mantra,[5] let each, after taking the others' permission, offer it as oblation to the mouth of the Ku*nd*alī[6] (191-193). When the Shakti is of the household,[7] the smelling of the wine is the equivalent of drinking it. Worshippers who are householders may drink five cups only (194).[8] Excessive drinking prevents the attainment of success by Kula worshippers[9] (195).

---

[1] For drinking on an empty stomach would more strongly effect the worshipper and maybe render him unfit for worship. This practice is not (I am told) followed, at any rate at present, by the Vi*sh*nukrāntā worshippers. They hold the cup of wine in the left, and the Shuddhi in the right, and as they drink they take the Shuddhi. With the first cup they take meat, with the second fish, with the third Mudrā, and with the fourth all these, and with the fifth cup anything they may desire.

[2] The Shabda-Brahman in bodies.

[3] Divine Consciousness as to which term, see "Shakti and Shākta".

[4] The abode of Ku*nd*alinī in the Pi*nd*a or body.

[5] See note under ch. v, 66.

[6] The offering to the mouth of the Ku*nd*alī is done by pouring the wine down the throat of the worshipper in whom the Ku*nd*alī resides.

[7] Kula-strī—*i.e.*, where the wife of the worshipper is his Shakti, as opposed to cases where the Shakti is Parakīyā or Sādhāra*n*ī, a practice discountenanced by this Tantra.

[8] Sādhakānāṁ *gri*hasthānām pancha-pātram prakīrtitam.

[9] Ati-pānāt kulīnānāng siddhi-hāni*h* prajāyate.

They may drink until the sight or the mind is not affected.[1] To drink beyond that is bestial[2] (196). How is it possible for a sinner who becomes a fool through drink and who maligns the Sādhaka of Shakti to say "I worship the Ādyā Kālikā"[3]? (197). As touch[4] cannot affect food and the like offered to Brahman, so there is no distinction of caste in food[5] offered to Thee (198).

As I have directed, so should eating and drinking be done. After partaking of food offered[6] to Thee, the hands should not be washed,[7] but with a piece of cloth or a little water remove that which has adhered to the hands (199). Lastly, after placing a flower from the Nirmālya[8] on his head, and wearing a Tilaka mark[9] made from the remnants of the oblation on the Yantra between his eyebrows, the intelligent worshipper may roam the earth like a Deva (200).

End of the Sixth Chapter, entitled "Placing of the Shrī-pātra, Homa, Formation of the Chakra, and other Rites."

---

[1] Literally, "does not go round".

[2] Yāvan na chālayed dṛshṭing, yāvan na chālayen manaḥ,
Tāvat pānang prakurvīta, pashu-pānamataḥ param.

[3] Pāne bhrāntir bhaved yasya ghṛinī cha shakti-sādhake.
Sa pāpishṭhaḥ kathang bruyāt ādyāng Kālīng bhajāmyaham.

[4] Of a person of an inferior caste.

[5] Prasāda.

[6] Naivedya.

[7] The hands are always washed after meals. It is customary to use water to wash and clear the throat and mouth after meals.

[8] Remnants of offerings (*vide* p. 185, note 7). By Nirmālya is usually meant flowers, but in some temples (as in Purī) food offerings are so called. The word is from Nir-mala=stainless or dirtless. Things offered to the Devatā become stainless.

[9] The sectarian mark.

CHAPTER VII

HYMN AND AMULET

PĀRVATĪ was pleased at hearing the revelation of the auspicious Mantra of the Ādyā Kālikā, which yields abundant blessings, is the only means of attaining to a knowledge of the Brahman and leads to prosperity and Liberation[1]; as also at hearing of the morning rites, the rules relating to bathing, Sandhyā, the purification of Saṁvid, the methods of external and internal Nyāsa[2] and worship, the sacrifice of animals,[3] Homa, the formation of the circle of worship,[4] and the partaking of the holy food.[5] Bowing low with modesty, the Devī questioned Shaṁkara (1-3).

Shrī Devī said:

O Sadāshiva![6] Lord[7] and Benefactor of the Universe! Thou hast in Thy mercy spoken of the mode of worship of the Supreme Prakṛiti[8] (4), which benefits all being, is

---

[1] Saubhāgya, Moksha.

[2] See "Shakti and Shākta".

[3] Vali.

[4] Chakra (see *ibid.*).

[5] Mahā-prasāda. Any offering of food made to a Deva is called Prasāda which literally means graciousness or kindness: for the food on being offered to the Deva is infused with His grace. In Chakra worship the offering has the same sanctity.

[6] See p. 5, note 6.

[7] Jagannātha, Jagatāṁ hitakāraka.

[8] Parā-prakṛiti-sādhanā. Prakṛiti (Pra=before, kriti=creation). That which precedes creation. The Devī is so called. From Her, in association with Purusha, the creation (*Srshti*) has come. The process by which She is realised is Sādhanā.

the sole path both for enjoyment and final Liberation, and which gives, in this Age,[1] in particular, immediate success (5). My mind, immersed in the ocean of the nectar of Thy word, has no desire to rise thereform, but craves for more and more (6). O Deva, in the directions Thou hast given relating to the worship of the great Devī, Thou hast but hinted at[2] the hymn of praise and of the protective Mantra.[3] Do Thou reveal them now (7).

Shrī Sadāshiva said:

Listen, then, O Devī, Who art the adored of the worlds, to this unsurpassed hymn, by the reciting of or listening to which one becomes the Lord of all the Siddhis[4] (8) (a hymn) which allays evil fortune, increases happiness and prosperity, destroys untimely death, and removes all calamities (9), and is the cause of the happy approach to the gracious Ādyā Kālikā. It is by the grace of this hymn, O Shivā, that I am Tripurāri[5] (10).

O Devī! the *Rishi*[6] of this hymn is Sadāshiva,[7] its metre is Anu*sht*up,[8] its Devatā is the Ādyā Kālikā, and the object of its use is the attainment of Dharma, Artha, Kāma and Mok*sh*a[9] (11).

---

[1] Kali Yuga.

[2] See ch. vi, 176.

[3] Kavacha (see note under ch. iii, 57 and ch. vi, 176).

[4] "Powers" such as the eight—A*n*imā and the rest.

[5] Tri-pura+ari (enemy). A title of Shiva as the destroyer of the Tri-pura, the Asura. It was by the Devī's grace that He became the Destroyer of the Tri-pura. Tripura was so called because he conquered the heaven, earth and nether world and held them as his three cities.

[6] Or Revealer. He sees and reveals to others.

[7] Shiva. See p. 5, note 6.

[8] *Vide*, p. 115, note 5.

[9] Morality and Piety, Wealth, Fulfilment of Desire, Liberation.

Hymn Entitled Ādyā-Kālī-svarūpa[1]

Hrīng,[2] O Destroyer of Time,[3]
Shrīng,[4] O Terrific One,[5]
Krīng,[6] Thou Who art beneficent,[7]
Possessor of all the Kalās,[8]
Thou art Kamalā,[9]

---

[1] See v. 51 *post*. It will be observed that all the names of the Devī here commence with K. Hence it is called Kādistotra. Kādi is that which has Kā in the beginning. In the Tantrarāja Shiva says to Devī: "The syllable Kādi is in Thy form, and that Shakti confers all Siddhis" (see Lalitā-sahasra-nāma, verse 18, where a number of the following names appear). See as to the letter Ka and Kādimata, A. Avalon's Introduction to Tantrarāja, Vol. 8, Tāntrik Texts.

[2] Māyā-Bīja (see Chapter v, verse 10). H. (=Shiva) and R. (=Fire) and Ī (Mahāmāyā) and Ng (=Nāda visvamātā and Bindu Du*h*khahara).

[3] Kālī (see Chapter IV, verse 30 *et seq.*) She is thus also called Kāla-kar*sh*i*n*ī. Lak*sh*mīdhara in his commentary to Saundarya-laharī, says that Kālī is Saṁhara*n*a Shakti.

[4] Bīja of Lak*sh*mī, Goddess of Prosperity.

[5] Karālī.

[6] Ka=Kālī, Ra=Brahmā, I=Mahāmāyā (She Who conquers Māyā). The half-circle of Chandra Bindu (ँ) is the Universal Mother and the point is the Destroyer of misery (Bījābhidhāna).

[7] Kalyā*n*ī—*i.e.*, She Who utters words of kindness and bestows peace, happiness and Liberation. According to the Padma Purā*n*a, Devī is worshipped as Kalyā*n*ī in the Malaya Mountain (see also Lalitā-sahasra-nāma, verse 78).

[8] Kalā-vatī (see *ibid.*, verse 74). As to Kalās in the Mantra Shāstra sense, see "Garland of Letters," by Woodroffe. Kalā also means the Arts which are sixty-four in number. The Shakti should always be Kalā-vatī. Devī is also called Kalā-mālā, or Garland of the Kalās (Lalitā-sahasra-nāma, verse 151). Kalā-vati may also mean "possessed of all Kalās. complete, perfect." For She as Brahman is Pūr*n*ā, the whole.

[9] Kamalā is a name of Lak*sh*mī, (see Lalitā-sahasrā-nāma, verse 73, where the Devī is called Kāma-kalā-rūpā). On this Bhāskararāya says that there are three Bindus and the Hārdhakalā. The first Bindu is Kāma, and the last Kalā; according to the rules of Pratyāhāra, Kamalā includes all four who are seated on a Lotus (Kamala). The Kālikā purā*n*a says Devī alone is indicated by Kāma. Devī is Kamalā, as She is all Shaktis.

Destroyer of the pride of the Kali Age,[1]
Who art kind to Him of the matted hair,[2] (12)
Devourer of Him Who devours,[3]
Mother of Time,[4]
Thou Who art brilliant as the Fires of the final Dissolution,[5]
Consort of Him of the matted hair,[6]
O Thou of formidable countenance,[7]
Ocean of the nectar of compassion,[8] (13)
Merciful,[9]
Vessel of Mercy,[10]
Whose Mercy is without limit,[11]
Who art attainable alone by Thy mercy,[12]
Who art Fire,[13]
Tawny,[14]
Black of hue,[15]

---

[1] Kali-darpa-ghnī.

[2] Kapardīsha-*kri*pānvitā. Kapardīsha is a title of Shiva, derived from His matted hair.

[3] Kālikā, because She devours Shiva as Mahā-kāla (see Chapter IV, verse 31).

[4] Kāla-mātā. Time devours all things. She devours Time which again issues from Her.

[5] Kālānala-sama-dyuti.

[6] Kapardinī, wife of Shiva, so called Kapardī from His matted hair (see Lalitā-sahasra-nāma, verse 151). The Vishva says that Kaparda means the matted hair of Shiva.

[7] Karālāsyā. Literally with protruding teeth.

[8] Karu*n*ām*ri*ta-sāgarā (see Lalitā-sahasra-nāma, verse 78).

[9] K*ri*pā-mayī.

[10] K*ri*pādhārā.

[11] K*ri*pāpārā.

[12] K*ri*pāgamā, that is through Shakti-pāta or descent of grace.

[13] K*ri*shānu. K*ri*shānu-retas is an epithet of Shiva whose male seed is fire. See notes under I, 14.

[14] Kapilā. Kapilā is also Queen of the Eastern and Southern corners.

[15] K*ri*sh*n*ā.

Thou Who increasest the joy of the Lord of Creation,[1] (14)
Night of Dissolution,[2]
In the form of (creative) Desire,[3]
Yet Liberator from the bonds of (earthly) desire,[4]
Thou Who art (dark) as a bank of Clouds,[5]
And are sustainer of all Kalās,[6]
Destructress of sin in the Kali Age,[7] (15)
Thou Who art pleased by the worship of virgins,[8]

---

[1] K*ri*sh*n*ānanda-vivardhinī. K*ri*sh*n*a here is apparently the Supreme Lord.

[2] Kāla-rātri. Lalitā-sahasra-nāma, verse 101, speaks of the Devī as attended by hosts of Shaktis, Kāla-rātrīs, etc.—that is, the twelve Shaktis from Kāla-rātrī to *Ta*ṁkārī, one in each petal of Anāhata Padma. The Varāha Purā*n*a says that Raudrī (the Shakti causing dissolution), who was born from darkness and went to the Blue Mountains to perform penance, is called Kāla-rātri. She absorbs all things.

[3] Kāma-rūpā (see Lalitā-sahasra-nāma, verse 78). The Kālikā Purā*n*a says that Devī is called Kāmā because she came to the secret place in the Blue peak of the Great Mountain (Kailāsa) along with Shiva for the sake of desire, and because She fulfils desires and destroys and restores the body of Kāma. As to Kāma-rūpa see p. 147, n. 4. Kāma also=Ichchhā or Creative Will. Devī first manifests as Kāmeshvarī in the Shrīchakra. See Introduction, Tantrarāja, Vol. 8, Tantrik Texts, ed. A. Avalon and Kāmakalāvilāsa, vol. 10 in same series.

[4] Kāma-pāsha-vimochinī.

[5] Kādambinī. In the heat of India the rain-cloud is welcomed.

[6] Kalādhārā. As to Kalā see Avalon's "Garland of Letters," Kalā is a fraction of the total Shakti, a division or aspect of the temporal process in its cause and the 64 Arts. In the Lalitā (v. 210) Devī is called Kalāmitrā where Kalā is defined as the Kalās Niv*ri*tti, Pratish*th*ā, etc., also Kalānidhi where Kalā is said to refer to "Sun," "Moon" and "Fire".

[7] Kali-kalma*sh*a-nāshinī (see Lalitā-sahasra-nāma, verse 118). The Kūrma Purā*n*a says that the repetition of the names of Devī destroys the multitude of sins in the Kali Age.

[8] Kumārī-pūjana-prītā. The Kumārī Pūjā, or worship of virgins, is a Pūjā common among Shāktas. The worship is by men, whereas the Sadhavā-pūjā, or worship of married women, is done by women. A girl in her eighth year is called Gaurī. The Devī as Pārvatī was married to Shiva in her eighth year. Girls of eight are considered Gaurīs and forms of the Devī. Or Kumārī may refer directly to the

Thou Who art the Refuge of the worshippers of virgins,[1]
Who art pleased by the feasting of the virgins,[2]
Who art in the form of the virgin,[3] (16)
Thou Who wanderest in the Kadamba forest,[4]
Who art pleased with the flowers of the Kadamba forest,[5]
Who hast Thy abode in the Kadamba forest,[6]
Who wearest a garland of Kadamba flowers,[7] (17)
Thou Who art youthful,[8]

Devī Herself. She is known as the "Virgin" (Kumārī). One of the Shiva Sūtras runs: "Ichchhā-shakti*h* Umā Kumārī" (the power of Will is Umā, the Virgin). Bhāskara-rāya, in his Commentary, in the Lalitā-sahasra-nāma, pp. 54, 76, gives the following explanations: As play She creates the Universe, Kumāra=to sport, hence She is Kumārī, or She destroys (Mārayati) the ground (Ku) of the Great illusion, hence She is Ku-mārī. Kumārī is the Enjoyer, and not to be enjoyed, as She is One with the Yogī, Who is the Enjoyer. These interpretations are taken by him from the Shiva-sūtrā vimarshinī (under Sūtra 13).

[1] Kumārī-pūjakālayā.

[2] Kumārī-bhojanānanda. At the Kumari-pūjā sweets, a basket made of shells, and a new Sari are given to the little girls, the soles of whose feet are then painted with Alakta (lac-dye).

[3] Kumārī-rūpa-dhāri*n*ī.

[4] Kadamba-vana-sanchārā. It was under and on the Kadamba-trees, with their beautiful yellow blossom, that K*ris*h*n*a played with the Gopinīs. Tantrarāja, ch. xxxiv, 84, speaks of Devī Tripurā becoming K*ris*h*n*a.

[5] Kadamba-push*h*pa-santosh*h*ā (see Lalitā-sahasra-nāma, verse 23).

[6] Kadamba-vana-vāsinī (see Lalitā-sahasra-nāma, verse 23). The palace of Chintāma*n*i is surrounded by a wall of gems (Ma*n*i-ma*n*tapa). Around this is the grove of Kadamba-trees, which in the Purā*n*as are said to be seven Yojanas in height in the space between the walls of gold and silver. The Bhairava-yāmala says: "The abode of Bindu is the ocean of nectar. The five Yonis—that is, five Shakti angles in the Shrī-chakra—are the divine trees. There is the grove of Nīpa-trees. Within that is the wall of gems. Within that is the palace of Chintāma*n*i."

[7] Kadamba-push*h*pa-mālinī. The Lalitā-sahasra-nāma, verse 8, speaks of Devī as decked above her ears with clusters of Kadamba flowers.

[8] Kishorī.

Deep throated,[1]
Whose voice is resounding,[2]
Who drinkest[3] and art pleased with the Kādambarī
wine,[4] (18)
Whose favoured cup is a skull,[5]
Who wearest a garland of bones,[6]
Who art pleased with,[7]
And Who art seated on the Lotus,[8] (19)
Who abidest in the midst of the Lotus,[9]
Whom the fragrance of the Lotus pleases,[10]
Who movest with the swaying gait of a Hangsa,[11]
Destroyer of fear,[12]

---

[1] Kāla-ka*nth*ā. Bhāratī gives the meaning as Kala=Gambhīra-shabda-yukta. She is also Kāla-ka*nth*ī (Lalitā-sahasra-nāma, verse 96), or wife of Kāla-ka*nth*a, a name of Shiva, whose throat was coloured by poison. According to the Devī Purā*n*a, Kāla-ka*nth*a was worshipped at Kālanjara.

[2] Kala-nāda-ninādinī: as in fighting uttering Hūng see p. 198, n. 6.

[3] Kādambarī-pāna-ratā.

[4] Kādambarī-priyā (see Lalitā-sahasra-nāma, verse 74). Kādambarī is a kind of wine distilled from the Kadamba flower, it is Uttamā madirā. The Tripurā Upani*sh*ad refers to wine, fish, flesh, cooked cereals being offered in the Yantra to the Great Devī. Bhāskara-rāya's Commentary on this Upani*sh*ad says that it enjoins those who are allowed to take wine, flesh, etc., that they should do so first after dedicating them to the Devī, and minimize the habit by gradation. The same idea is expressed in Manu Sm*ri*ti, verse 56; Bhāgavata Purā*n*a, xi, 5-11.

[5] Kapāla-pātra-niratā.

[6] Kaṁkāla-mālya-dhāri*n*ī.

[7] Kamalāsana-santu*sh*tā.

[8] Kamalāsana-vāsinī. Kamalāsana is a name of Brahmā whose Shakti as Brāhmī She is.

[9] Kamalālaya-madhya-sthā. Kamalālaya may mean Vi*sh*nu out of whose navel the Lotus came or the ocean in which He lay in either of which cases Vai*sh*navī Shakti is referred to.

[10] Kamalāmoda-modinī.

[11] Kala-hangsa-gati. Hangsa is variously translated goose, swan, etc. A swaying waddle like that of a duck is admired,

[12] Klaibya-nāshinī.

Who assumest all forms at will,[1]
Whose abode is at Kāma-rūpa,[2] (20)
Who ever plays at the Kāma-pī*th*a,[3]
O beautiful One,[4]
O Creeper Which givest every desire,[5]
Who art decked with beautiful ornaments,[6] (21)
Adorable as the Image of all tenderness,[7]
Thou with a tender body,[8]
And Who art slender of waist,[9]
Who art pleased with the nectar of purified wine,[10]
Giver of success to them whom purified wine rejoices,[11] (22)

---

[1] Kāma-rūpi*n*ī. See Lalita, 146.

[2] Kāmarūpa-k*ri*tāvāsā. Kāma-rūpa, the great Shākta centre in Assam, one of the Mahā-pī*th*as, where the genital organ of the Devī fell on the severance of Her body by Vis*h*nu. Kāma-rūpa is also one of the Ādi-pī*th*as, which are in the Mūlādhāra and other power centres (see Lalitā-sahasra-nāma, p. 159). In external creation (Bāhyas*rishti*) it is the first, esoterically it is in the Mūlādhāra. See p. 147, note 8, as to Kāma-rūpa being representative of Ambikā, an aspect of Vimarsha Shakti.

[3] Kāma-pī*th*a-vilāsinī—that is, the Yoni-pī*th*a at Kāma-rūpa in Assam and also Mūlādhāra where She is as Ku*nd*alinī, or the Kāmakalā may be meant.

[4] Kamanīyā.

[5] Kalpa-latā. The Kalpa-tree is a tree in the heaven of Indra, which yields whatever one desires. Woman is likened to a creeper (see note under i, 53). See also Lalitā-sahasra-nāma, where the Devī is called Bhakti-mat-kalpa-latikā=the Kalpa creeper of the devotee. Latā is by some defined as Is*ht*adevatā.

[6] Kamanīya-vibhūs*ha*nā.

[7] Kamanīya-gu*n*ārādhyā; or it may mean that the Devī is to be worshipped by the worshipper with all best and tender feeling.

[8] Komalāṅgī.

[9] K*ri*shodarī, literally, small of belly. *Cf.* Ā-pīvara-stana-ta*t*īṁ tanuv*ri*tta-madhyām (Bhuvaneshvarī Stotra): Tanu-madhyā (Lalitā-sahasra-nāma, verse 79).

[10] Kāra*n*ām*ri*ta-santos*h*ā. Kāra*n*a is the name given to the purified wine used in the Tāntrika ritual. Kāra*n*a=Cause. Wine is the cause of material bliss. When the Sādhaka drinks he thinks of the Cause of all causes or Brahman as Kāra*n*a.

[11] Kāra*n*ānanda-siddhi-dā.

The own Deity of those who do Japa of Thee when joyed with wine,[1]
Who art gladdened by the worship of Thyself with purified wine,[2]
Who art immersed in the Ocean of Kāraṇa,[3]
Who art the Protectress of those who accomplish Vrata with wine,[4] (23)
Whom the fragrance of musk gladdens,[5]
And Who art bright with a tilaka-mark of musk,[6]
Who likest worship with musk,[7]
Who lovest those who worship Thee with musk,[8] (24)
Who art a Mother to those who burn musk as incense,[9]
Who art fond of the musk-deer[10] and art pleased to eat its musk,[11]
Whom the scent of camphor gladdens,[12]
Who art adorned with garlands of camphor,[13]

---

[1] Kāraṇānanda-jāpeshṭā.

[2] Kāraṇārchchana-harshitā.

[3] Kāraṇārṇava-sangmagnā. Throughout there is a play on the word Kāraṇa as Brahman and as wine.

[4] Kāraṇa-vrata-pālinī.

[5] Kastūrī-saurabhāmodā. Musk is used in worship to scent Chandana, etc. See Lalitā, 5. Some say Kastūrī = Saffron.

[6] Kastūrī-tilakojjvalā. The Tilaka is the mark worn by sectarian Hindus on the forehead. Men of different sampradāyas wear different marks and use different materials.

[7] Kastūrī-pūjana-ratā.

[8] Kastūrī-pūjaka-priyā.

[9] Kastūrī-dāha-jananī.

[10] Kastūrī-mṛiga-toshiṇī.

[11] Kastūrī-bhojana-prītā. Musk is powdered and put into wine. It is a stimulant.

[12] Karpūrāmoda-moditā. (Camphor is burnt in worship during Ārati, and is used to scent the Pādya, betel leaf, etc., offered to the Devī.) Medicinally in small quantities it is a stimulant but in excess produces impotence.

[13] Karpūra-mālābharaṇā.

And Whose body is smeared with camphor and sandal paste,[1] (25)
Who art pleased with purified wine flavoured with camphor,[2]
Who drinkest purified wine flavoured with camphor,[3]
Who art bathed in the ocean of camphor,[4]
Whose abode is in the ocean of camphor,[5] (26)
Who art pleased when Japa is done with the Bīja Hūng,[6]
Thou Who threatenest with the Bīja Hūng,[7]
Kulīnā,[8]
Adored by Kāulikas,[9]
Benefactress of the Kaulikas,[10] (27)
Observant of Kulāchāra,[11]
Joyous One,[12] Revealer of the path of the Kaulikas,[13]
Queen of Kāshī,[14]

---

[1] Karpūra-chandanoksh*it*ā or sprinkled with powdered camphor and sandal.

[2] Karpūra-kāra*n*āhlādā.

[3] Karpūrām*ri*ta-pāyinī.

[4] Karpūra-sāgara-snātā.

[5] Karpūra-sāgarālayā.

[6] Kūrchcha-bīja-japa-prītā. "Hūng" is the Kūrchcha Bīja.

[7] Kūrchcha-japa-parāya*n*ā—that is, She Who mutters Hūng. When conquering the demons, the Goddess constantly made the Hūng-kāra, the threatening roaring sound.

[8] Kulīnā (see Lalitā-sahasra-nāma, p. 71). Kula, according to the Tantra, means Shakti, Akula = Shiva, and the union of Kula with Akula is called Kaula. Hence Devī is called Kaulinī or Kulīnā. Commonly Kulīnā means 'one of noble family'. As to the use of Kula see Lalitā, verses 87, 88, 190, 217. Kula also = Sajatīya-samūha, consisting in the equality of Jnātā, Jnāna and Jneya.

[9] Kaulikārādhyā; and so also in the Lalitā-sahasra-nāma, verse 71, the Devī is addressed as Dak*shin*ādak*shin*ārādhyā.

[10] Kaulika-priya-kāri*n*ī.

[11] Kulāchārā.

[12] Kautukinī.

[13] Kula-mārga-pradarshinī.

[14] Kāshīshvarī. Kāshī is Benares, the sacred city of Shiva.

Allayer of sufferings,[1]
Giver of blessings to the Lord of Kāshī,[2] (28)
Giver of pleasure to the Lord of Kāshī,[3]
Beloved of the Lord of Kāshi,[4] (29)
Thou Whose toe-ring bells resound as Thou movest,[5]
Who art adorned with a girdle of tinkling bells,[6]
Who abidest in the mountain of gold,[7]
Who art the moon-beam on the mountain of gold,[8] (30)
Who art gladdened by the recitation of the Mantra Klīng,[9]
Who art the Kāma Bīja,[10]
Destructress of all evil inclinations,[11]
And of the afflictions of the Kaulikas,[12]
Lady of the Kaulas,[13] (31)
Who by the three Bījas, Krīng, Hrīng, Shrīng, art the Destructress of the fear of Death.[14] (To Thee I make obeisance.)

---

[1] Kash*t*a-hartrī—and thus the Lalitā, verse 79, speaks of the Devī as "the moonlight which soothes those burned by the triple fire of misery".

[2] Kāshīsha-vara-dāyinī. Lord of Kāshī=Shiva.

[3] Kāshīshvara-k*r*itāmodā.

[4] Kāshīshvara-manoramā.

[5] Kala-manjīra-chara*n*ā.

[6] Kva*n*at-kānchī-vibhū*sh*a*n*ā

[7] Kānchanādrī-k*r*itāgārā, the mountain Kānchana—*i.e.*, Sumeru.

[8] Kānchanāchala-kaumudī.

[9] Kāma-bīja-japānandā. Klīng is the Kāma Bīja. When Ka and La are eliminated, the remaining Īng is called Kāma-kalā, which is in the Turīya state. In the Lalitā-sahasra-nāma, verse 125, Devī is called "The form of the Mantra Klīng" (Klīng-kārī). Klīng-kāra is Shiva-Kāma, and She is his Spouse.

[10] Kāma-bīja-svarūpi*n*ī—that is, She is Klīng itself.

[11] Kumati-ghnī. Devī is also (Lalitā, verse 78) Sadāchāra-pravartakā, because She incites to right action.

[12] Kulīnārtī-nāshinī.

[13] Kula-kāminī.

[14] Krīng, Hrīng, Shrīng, mantra-var*n*ena kāla-ka*n*t*a*ka-ghātinī—literally, "Thorn of Death".

These are proclaimed as the Hundred Names of Kālikā (32). They begin with the letter Ka and hymn the nature of Kālī [1] (33). He who in worship recites these names with his mind fixed on Kālikā, for him Mantrasiddhi [2] is quickly obtained, and with him Kālī is pleased (34). By the mere bidding of his Guru he acquires intelligence, knowledge, and becomes wealthy, famous, munificent, and compassionate (35). Such an one enjoys life happily in this world with his children and grandchildren with wealth and dominion (36). He who, on a new moon night,[3] when it falls on a Tuesday, worships the great Ādyā Kālī, Mistress of the three worlds, with the five Ma-kāras,[4] and repeats Her hundred names, becomes suffused with the presence of the Devī,[5] and for him there remains nothing in the three worlds which is beyond his powers [6] (37-38).

He becomes in learning like Bṛihaspati [7] himself, in wealth like Kuvera.[8] His profundity is that of the ocean, and his strength that of the wind (39). He shines with the blinding brilliance of the Sun, yet pleases with the soft glamour of the Moon. In beauty he becomes like the Deva of Love,[9] and reaches the hearts of women (40). He comes forth as conqueror everywhere by the grace [10] of this

---

[1] Kālīrūpasvarūpakam.

[2] Mantra-success, proficiency in Mantra.

[3] Nishā—that is, Mahā-nishā=Midnight.

[4] The five M's (Pancha-ma-kāra) of worship—Wine, Meat, Fish, Parched Food, and Woman, or Pancha-tattva.

[5] Sākshāt Kālīmayo bhavet. Literally he is directly Kālī himself.

[6] Asādhya=Impracticable, Inaccessible.

[7] The Guru of the Celestials.

[8] Deva of Wealth.

[9] Kāma.

[10] Stava.

hymn of praise.[1] Singing this hymn, he attains all his desires (41). All these desires he shall attain by the grace of the gracious Ādyā, whether in battle, in seeking the favour of Kings, in wagers, or in disputes, and when his life be in danger (42) at the hands of robbers, amidst burning villages, lions, or tigers (43), in forests and lonely deserts, when imprisoned, threatened by Kings or by adverse planets, in burning fever, in long sickness, when attacked by fearful disease (44), in the sickness of children caused by the influence of adverse planets,[2] or when tormented by evil dreams, when fallen in boundless waters, and when he be in some storm-tossed ship (45). O Devī! he who with firm devotion meditates upon the Paramā Māyā[3] who is the Supreme Ādyā Kālī—is without a doubt relieved of all dangers. For him there is never any fear, whether arising from sin[4] or disease (46-47). For him there is ever victory, and defeat never. At the mere sight of him all dangers flee (48). He expounds all Scriptures, enjoys all good fortune, and becomes the leader in all matters of caste and duty, and the lord among his kinsmen (49). In his mouth Vānī[5] ever abides, and in his home Kamalā.[6] Men bow with respect at the mere mention of his name (50). The eight Siddhis,[7] such as Animā and others, he looks upon as but mere bits of grass.[8]

---

[1] See verses 2 and 22 of the Karpūrādi-stotra.

[2] Bāla-graha, or Planets malignant to children.

[3] The Devī as one with the Supreme Brahman.

[4] Pāpa.

[5] Vānī, or Saraswatī, is the Devī of Speech. It is commonly said that learning and wealth do not go together. Here they do.

[6] Kamalā, or Lakshmī, is the Devī of Prosperity. *Cf.* Karpūrādi Stotra, verse 6—"In their moonlike face the Devī of Speech ever wanders, and in their lotus-like eyes Kamalā ever plays."

[7] *i.e.*, the eight Powers—Animā, Mahimā, Laghimā, Garimā, Prāpti, Prākāmya, Ishitva, Vashitva.

[8] *i.e.*, as mere trifles, they being to him so easy of accomplishment.

This hymn of a hundred names, is called "Ādyā-Kālī-svarūpa"[1] (51).

Purashcharana[2] of this hymn, which is its repetition one hundred and eight times, yields all desired fruit (52). This hymn of praise of a hundred names, which is the Primeval Kālī Herself, if read, or caused to be read, if heard, or caused to be heard, frees from all sins and leads to union with Brahman (53-54).

Shrī Sadāshiva said:[3]

I have spoken of the great hymn of the Prakriti[4] of the Supreme Brahman,[5] hear now the Protective Mantra[6] of the sacred Ādyā Kālikā (55). The name of the Mantra is "Conqueror of the three Worlds,"[7] its *Rishi*[8] is Shiva, the verse is Anushtup,[9] and its Devatā is Ādyā Kālī (56).

Its Bīja[10] is the Māyā Bīja,[11] its Shakti[12] is Ramā Bīja,[13] and its Kīlaka[14] is Krīng. It should be used for the attainment of all desired objects[15] (57).

---

[1] Ādyā-Kālī-svarūpa—name of the Hymn. It is to be observed that the letter Ka which begins each name has in Bengali a triangle (ক). This triangle=Yoni=Shakti. The three sides are Brahmā, Vishnu, Rudra.

[2] This is a ritualistic method in Mantra Sādhanā. See *ante*, ch. III, vv. 114 *et seq.*, also *post*, v. 75.

[3] He is now about to speak of the Kavacha Mantra.

[4] Shakti as material cause of the World.

[5] Or Prakriti, who is the Shakti aspect of Brahman.

[6] Kavacha (see p. 46, note 4).

[7] Trailokya-vijaya.

[8] Revealer.

[9] See p. 41, note 1.

[10] Seed Mantra.

[11] Hrīng.

[12] That is, greatness (Prâbhâva).

[13] Shrīng.

[14] Literally, the bolt--that is, that which shuts out, closes, and finishes the Mantra.

[15] Kāmya-siddhi.

THE PROTECTIVE MANTRA (KNOWN AS TRAILOKYA-VIJAYA)

Hrīng,[1] may the Ādyā protect my head;
Shrīng,[2] may Kālī protect my face;
Krīng,[3] may the Supreme Shakti protect my heart;
May She Who is the Supreme of the Supreme[4] protect my throat (58);
May Jagaddhātrī[5] protect my two eyes;
May Shaṁkarī[6] protect my two ears;
May Mahāmāyā[7] protect my power of smell;
May Sarva-maṁgalā[8] protect my taste (59);
May Kaumārī[9] protect my teeth;
May Kamalālayā[10] protect my cheeks;
May Kshamā[11] protect my upper and lower lips;
May Chāru-hāsinī[12] protect my chin (60);
May Kuleshānī[13] protect my throat;
May Kripā-mayī[14] protect the nape of my neck;
May Bāhu-dā[15] protect my two arms;

---

[1] The Māyā Bīja.

[2] Bīja of Lakshmī.

[3] The Supreme Shakti is the Ādyā Kālī. Krīng is the Kālī Bīja.

[4] Parātparā. She as one with Para Brahman.

[5] The Devī, as Producing Mother and Supporter of the Universe.

[6] Consort of Shaṁkara—epithet of Shiva—He Who confers prosperity or who does good.

[7] The Devī as Māyā is one with and veils the greatness of the Brahman.

[8] Epithet of Devī as "The All-auspicious".

[9] Devī as Shakti of Kumāra, or Kārtikeya, Deva of War, Son of Shiva.

[10] Devī in the form of Lakshmī, "Whose abode is the lotus."

[11] Benevolence, or Forgiveness—a title of Devī.

[12] Devī, "Sweetly smiling."

[13] The Sovereign Mistress of the Kaulas.

[14] The Merciful One.

[15] Bāhu-dā="Arm-Giver:" Who gives strength to the arms.

May Kaivalya-dāyinī [1] protect my two hands; (61)
May Kapardinī [2] protect my shoulders;
May Trailokya-tāri*n*ī [3] protect my back;
May Apar*n*ā [4] protect my two sides;
May Kama*th*āsanā [5] protect my hips (62);
May Vishālāk*sh*ī [6] protect my navel;
May Prabhā-vatī [7] protect my organ of generation;
May Kalyānī [8] protect my thighs;
May Pārvatī [9] protect my feet;
May Jaya-durgā [10] protect my vital breaths;
And Sarva-siddhi-dā [11] protect all parts of my body (63).

As to those parts as have not been mentioned in the Kavacha, and are unprotected, may the Eternal Primeval Kālī protect all such (64).

I have now spoken to Thee of the wonderful heavenly Protective Mantra of the Ādyā Devī Kālikā, which is known as the "Conqueror of the three Worlds" (65). He who repeats it at his devotions with his mind fixed upon the

---

[1] Giver of Emancipation. Kaivalya is the fifth state. Bhoja-rāja, Commentator on the Yoga Sūtra, chap. iv, sūtra, 33, explains Kaivalya to be that state in which mental modification (V*ri*tti) is extinct, and when the Self remains alone with its own nature.

[2] Feminine of Kapardin, an epithet of Shiva, "The wearer of knotted or braided hair" (Ja*t*ā). *Vide ante*, p. 192, note 6.

[3] Saviour of the three Worlds.

[4] She Who had not even leaves for food during the performance of her austerities prior to the birth of Kārtikeya.

[5] She who is in Kama*th*a, the Tortoise on which the world rests is emblem of patience. She is sustainer of the universe.

[6] Large-eyed, Beautiful-eyed—an epithet of Pārvatī.

[7] The Radiant One.

[8] The Propitious One, Giver of Liberation or who is Liberation itself.

[9] Daughter of Himālaya (*vide* p. 2, note 9).

[10] The Conquering Durgā.

[11] The Giver of all kinds of Siddhi.

Ādyā[1] obtains all his desires, and She becomes propitious unto him (66). He quickly attains Mantra-siddhi.[2] The lesser Siddhis[3] become, as it were, his slaves (67). He who is childless gets a son, he who desires wealth gains riches. The seeker of learning attains it, and whatsoever a man desires he attains the same[4] (68).

The Purashcharana[5] of this Protective Mantra[6] is its repetition a thousand times, and this gives the desired fruit (69). If it be written on birch-bark,[7] with the paste of sandal, fragrant aloe, musk, saffron, or red sandal, and encased in a golden ball, worn either on the right arm, round the neck, in the crown lock,[8] or round the waist, then the Ādyā Kālī becomes devoted to its wearer, and grants him whatsoever he may desire (70-71). Nowhere has he fear. In all places he is a conqueror. He becomes ready of speech,[9] free from ailments, long-lived and strong, endowed with all power of endurance[10] (72), and an adept in all learning. He knows the meaning of all Scriptures,[11] has kings under his control, and holds both Enjoyment and Liberation in the hollow of his hand (73).

[1] Ādyādhikrita-mānasa=(His) mind occupied by the Ādyā.

[2] Mantra-success, Control over the Mantra (see p. 200, n. 2).

[3] Kshudra-siddhī=*i.e.*, the eight siddhis—Animā, Laghimā, etc. They are lesser as compared with the Great Siddhi—Liberation.

[4] Kāmī kāmān avāpnuyāt.

[5] See 'Shaktī and Shākta,' Tarkālamkāra says 1,008 times.

[6] Varman=Armour, or Kavacha (see p. 46, note 4).

[7] Birch-bark—Bhūrjja—is brought from the Himālaya, and is used for the writing of Mantras instead of paper, etc., on account of its sanctity.

[8] Shikhā, the long tuft of hair which is left uncut at the tonsure ceremony, and which is retained by the orthodox through life. Like a flag-staff it indicates the presence of the Brahman in the Brahmarandhra.

[9] Kavi, which also means Poet, wise. *Cf.* Karpūrādi-Stotra, verse 1.

[10] Dhārana-kshama, which however, Tarkālamkāra interprets to mean "Master of various Shāstras".

[11] Sarva-shāstrārtha-tattva-vid=One who knows the meaning (Artha) and essence (Tattva=true significance) of all the Shāstras.

For men affected with the taint of the Kali Age it is a most excellent Mantra for the attainment of final Liberation[1] (74).

Shrī Devī said:

Thou hast, O Lord! in Thy kindness told me of the Hymn and Protective Mantra; I now desire to hear of the rules relating to Purashoharaṇa[2] (75).

Shrī Sadāsiva said:

The rules relating to Purashcharaṇa in the worship of the Ādyā Kālikā are the same as those relating to the Purashcharaṇa in the worship with the Brahma-Mantra[3] (76). For Sādhakas who are unable to do them completely, both Japa, Pūjā and Homa, and Purashcharaṇa[4] may be curtailed (77), since it is better to observe these rites on a small scale than not to observe them at all.

Now listen, O Gentle One! the while I describe to Thee the shortened form of worship (78). Let the wise one rinse his mouth with the Mūla-Mantra, and then perform *Rishi*-nyāsa.[5] Let him purify the palms of the hands, and proceed to Kara-nyāsa[6] and Aṁga-nyāsa[7] (79). Passing the hands all over the body,[8] let him practise

---

[1] Niḥshreyasakara.

[2] Purashcharaṇa, or Puraḥkaraṇa, means literally "the act of placing in front". By repetition of the name or Mantra of the Deity, His or Her presence is invoked before the worshipper. See as to the rite the "Purashcharyārṇava" of the King of Nepal. As a term of social usage, Purashkāra means the singling out of a person from a number, and placing him in a position of honour. The word in the text is Purascharyā-vidhi = Method of Purashcharyā (= Purashcharaṇa). Tarkālaṁkāra says that in wearing or reciting Kavacha, Purashcharaṇa must be done without which no fruit is attained.

[3] See Chapter III, verse 114, *ante*.

[4] For the meaning of these terms, see "Shakti and Shākta".

[5] See *ibid.*

[6] *Ibid.*

[7] *Ibid.*

[8] This is called Vyāpaka-nyāsa. After this Prāṇāyāma is to be done.

Prā*n*āyāma,[1] and then meditate,[2] worship,[3] and inwardly repeat the Mantra.[4] This is the ceremonial for the shortened form of worship (80).

In this form of Purashcharana, in lieu of Homa[5] and other rites, the Mantras should be recited four times the number prescribed for the particular rite itself (81). There is also another mode of doing Purashchara*n*a. A Sādhaka who, when the fourteenth day of the dark half of the lunar month[6] falls on a Tuesday or Saturday, worships Jaganmayī[7] on any such day with the five elements of worship,[8] and recites with fully attentive mind the Mantra ten thousand times at midnight and feasts believers in the Brahman has performed Purashchara*n*a (82-83). By doing Japa of the Mantra from one Tuesday to another Tuesday daily a thousand times, the Mantra having thus been recited eight thousand times is (also) the performance of Purashchara*n*a (84-85).

In all Ages, O Devī! but particularly in the Kali Age, the Mantras of the Sacred Ādyā Kālikā are of great efficacy, and yield complete success (85-86). O Pārvatī! in the Kali Age, Kālī in her various forms is ever watchful,[9] but when the Kali Age is in full sway, then the form of Kālī Herself is for the benefit of the world (87). In initiation

---

[1] See "Serpent Power".

[2] Dhyāna.

[3] Pūjā.

[4] Japa. These terms are explained in "Shakti and Shākta".

[5] Homa is necessary and the alternative of additional Japa is for one who cannot for some reason do it.

[6] *Krishnā* chaturdashī, the fortnight in which the Moon wanes.

[7] A name of Devī as pervading the Universe, which is Her form.

[8] Pancha-tattva—*i.e.*, wine, meat, fish, parched grain, and Shakti.

[9] In this Kali Age (says Shiva-chandra Bha*tt*āchārya Vidyār*n*ava) only Kālī, *Krishna*, Gopāla, and Kālikā are Jāgrata (awakened, watchful, efficacious) Devatās (Principles of Tantra).

into this Kālikā Mantra there is no necessity to determine whether it be Siddha or Su-siddha, or the like, or favourable or inimical.[1] If Japa is made of it, whether according to Niyama[2] or not[3] the Ādyā Devī is pleased (88). The mortal, by the grace of the glorious Ādyā, attains Brahman Knowledge[4] and, possessed of such knowledge, is, without a doubt, liberated even while living[5] (89). Beloved, there is no need here for much exertion or endurance or penances. The

---

[1] See p. 35, note 4. *Cf.* Chapter III, verse 15. The manner in which the successful, friendly, or inimical character of the Mantra is determined is described in the Tantra-sāra in dealing with the A-ka-tha-ha, A-ka-*d*a-ma and Siddhāsiddha Chakras at p. 34. Calculations are made with reference to the "house" of the Chakra within which the first letter of the worshipper's name and the first letter of the Mantra respectively fall. The Mantra which falls within a certain "house" is called Siddha, that on the next house Sādhya, that in the next Susādhya, and that in the fourth Ari. Siddha and Susādhya Mantras are favourable, and of easy accomplishment. Sādhya is difficult of accomplishment. Ari is inimical, and leads to disaster. These and the like calculations are not necessary either in the Brahman (Chapter III) or the Ādyā Mantras of the present chapter. These Mantras are always favourable.

[2] Niyama=Prescribed rules—that is, Japa should first be done according to the Pashu method (Pashvāchāra) by living on Havi*sh*yānna (a pure form of food), continence, restraint of the senses, and so forth.

[3] Aniyamena=Literally not according to the prescribed form. It may mean that in this Sādhanā strict observance of rules is not necessary. Tarkālamkāra reads "Niyama" and Aniyama" in which case the dual form should be used. According to him Aniyama means, not according to the ordinary prescribed rules, but according to Vīrāchāra, by drinking wine, eating meat and fish, and union with Shakti. The Karpūrādi-Stotra says: "O Mother! he who during the day remains self-controlled, lives on Havi*sh*yānna, and, meditating on Thy two feet, does Japa of Thy Mantra one lakh times, and thereafter (abandoning his Pashu-bhāva) at night unclothes, and whilst with Shakti does Japa another lakh times, shall become on earth like the Destroyer of Smara (Kāma)—*i.e.*, Shiva, who destroyed Kāmā, Deva of Desire)." It is elsewhere said: "In the daytime remaing chaste, Japa should be done one lakh of times, and at night in bed, with mouth full of *pān*, another lakh of Japas should be done" (See *ante*, Chapter III, verse 14, also Purashchara*n*a-rasollāsa, Durgārchana-mukūra, Āgama-tattva-vilāsa, Kālikārchana-dīpikā). By "mouth full of pān" is implied that Japa is done after a meal, and whilst enjoying oneself in a restful position.

[4] Brahma-jnāna.

[5] Jīvan-mukta.

religious exercises of the worshippers of the Ādyā Kālī are pleasant to accomplish (90). By the mere purification of the heart and mind[1] the worshipper attains all that he desires (91). So long, however, as the impurity of the heart is not removed, so long must the worshipper practise the rites with devotion to Kula.[2] (92).

The carrying out of the practices ordained, verily produces purification of the heart. The Mantra should, however, first be received from the mouth of the Guru as in the case of the Brahma-Mantra (93). O Great Queen! Purash*h*kriyā[3] should be done after the performance of the necessary worship and of other prescribed rites.[4] In the purified heart knowledge of Brahman grows.[5] And when Knowledge of Brahman is attained, there is neither that which should, nor that which should not, be done[6] (94).

Shrī Pārvatī said:

O Great Deva! what is Kula, and what is Kulāchāra? O Great Lord! what is the sign[7] of each of the five elements of worship?[8] I desire to hear the truth relating to these (95).

Shrī Sadāshiva said:

Thou hast asked well, O Sovereign Lady of Kula.[9] Thou art indeed the Benefactress of the Sādhakas. Listen!

---

[1] Chitta. By Chitta-shuddhi is here meant the removal from the mind and heart of all that is impure and likely to interfere with devotion.

[2] *i.e.*, Brahma sanātanam, also see *post*, vv. 96, 97.

[3] *i.e.*, Purashcharan*a*.

[4] Prāta*h*-k*r*ityādi-niyamā*n*=rules relating to morning and other daily rites.

[5] Chitte shuddhe Maheshāni! Brahma-jnānang prajāyate.

[6] Brahma-jnāne samutpanne *k*r*ityāk*r*ityang* na vidyate: All ritual rules are then surpassed.

[7] Laks*hana*.

[8] Pancha-tattva (Wine, Meat, Fish, Parched Food, and Woman).

[9] Kuleshāni = Directrix of Kulāchāra,

For Thy pleasure I shall accurately describe to Thee these things (96). Kula is Prakriti, Jīva, Space, Time, Ether, Earth, Water, Fire, and Air[1] (97). O Primeval One! the looking upon all these as Brahman is Kulāchāra, and produces Dharma, Artha, Kāma, and Moksha[2] (98). Those whose sins are washed away by merits acquired in various previous births by penances, alms, and faithful observance of worship, it is they whose minds are inclined to the Kaula way[3] (99). When the mind[4] realizes the essence of Kula Āchāra, it becomes at once purified, and inclines to the lotus-feet of the Primeval Kālī (100). The excellent Sādhaka versed in Kaula doctrine, who has received this most excellent Vidyā[5] by the service of a good spiritual teacher,[6] if he remains firmly attached to the Kaula path[7] and to the worship, with the five elements[8], of the Primeval

[1] *i.e.*, Jīva, Prakriti-tattva, Dik (literally, points of the compass), Kāla, Ākāsha, Kshiti, Ap, Tejah, and Vāyu. Jīva is the embodied spirit. As to Prakriti, see "Shakti and Shākta". The produced principles are, as the Vāmakeshvara Tantra says, the displayed form of the Avyakta Prakriti. Kula is Brahman (see Ed. Bhakta, p. 299). Kula is Kundalinī Shakti, Shiva is Akula (*ibid.*, p. 102).

[2] Piety, Wealth, Fulfilment of desire, and Emancipation (see Introduction).

> Brahma-buddhyā nirvikalpam eteshvācharanam cha yat,
> Kulācharah sa ev' Ādye dharma-kāmārtha-moksha-dah.
> "The conduct of the Sādhaka based on the certainty of his belief in the oneness of all these with the Brahman gains for him Dharma, etc."

[3] Appertaining to the Kaulas: Tāntrika worshippers according to Kulāchāra (Āchāra). According to Kulāchāra all men and things are manifestations of Brahman and must be so treated.

[4] Buddhi.

[5] Bhārati says Vidyā here=Mantra. Vidyā is technically Mantra of a Devī.

[6] Guru-sevā. It was by service that disciples in olden time secured the favour of their Guru. And even now, when the Guru visits and stays with the disciple, all that is done for the Guru is considered to be the service (Sevā) of Brahman, and daily practices are in consequence dispensed with during the time the Guru is with his disciple.

[7] See note 3, above.

[8] Pancha-tattva: Wine, Meat, Fish, Parched Food, and Woman.

Kālikā, the Queen of Kula, will enjoy all blessings in this life, and attain final Liberation at its close[1] (101-102).

The characteristic of the first element[2] is that it is the great medicine for humanity, helping it to forget deep sorrows, and is the cause of joy (103). But, O Dearest One! the element which is not purified stupefies and bewilders, breeds disputes and diseases, and should always be rejected by the Kaulas (104). Beasts bred in villages,[3] in the air[4] or forest,[5] which are nourishing, and increase intelligence, energy, and strength. are the second element[6], (105). O Beautiful One! of the animals bred in water, that which is pleasing and of good taste, and increases the generative power of man, is the third element[7] (106). The characteristics of the fourth element[8] are that it is easily obtainable, grown in the earth, and is the root of the life of the three worlds (107). And, O Devī, the signs of the fifth element[9] are that it is the cause of intense pleasure, is the origin of all breathing creatures and the root of the world which is without either beginning or end[10] (108).

---

[1] Brajantyante nirāmayam : *lit.* goes to where there is no ailment and pain.

[2] Wine.

[3] Such as Goat and Sheep.

[4] Birds.

[5] Deer and the like.

[6] Meat,

[7] Fish.

[8] Mudrā—Parched Food.

[9] Sexual intercourse called as part of worship (Latā-Sādhana).

[10] Mahānanda-karang Devi! Prā*n*inā*n*g s*r*ish*t*i-kāra*n*am,
Anādyanta-jaganmūlang shes*h*a-tattvasya laks*h*a*n*am.

Sexual union is the root of all which breathes. As the Universe is without beginning or end, so is this energy, which is the root of it. It is in the microcosm (Ks*h*udrabrahmā*n*d*a*) a particle of the supreme creative energy. Seed (Retas) is a material precipitate of the Will to Life.

Know, Dearest One! that the first element is fire, the second is air, the third is water, the fourth is the earth (109), and, O Beauteous Face! as to the fifth element, know it to be ether, the support of the Universe (110). O Sovereign Mistress of Kula, he who knows Kula,[1] the five Kula-tattvas,[2] and Kula worship, is liberated whilst yet living[3] (111).

End of the Seventh chapter entitled "Hymn of Praise (Stotra), Amulet (Kavacha), and the description of the Kula-tattva."

[1] *i.e.*, the matters mentioned in verse 97.

[2] Wine, Meat, Fish, Parched Food and Woman.

[3] Jīvan-mukta. He is then possessed of Supreme or Tāttvika knowledge, and freed from the necessity of all rites.

CHAPTER VIII

CASTES AND ASHRAMAS

AFTER hearing of the various forms of Dharma, Bhavānī,[1] Mother of the worlds, Destructress of all worldly bonds, spoke again to Shaṁkara (1).

Shrī Devī said:

I have heard of the different Dharmas which bring happiness in this world and the next, and bestow piety,[2] wealth, fulfilment of desire, ward off danger, and are the cause of the realisation of oneness with the Supreme[3] (2). I wish now to hear of the castes[4] and of the stages of life.[5] Speak in Thy kindness, O Omnipresent One! of these, and of the mode of life which should be observed therein (3).

Shrī Sadāshiva said:

O Thou of auspicious Vows! in the Satya and other Ages there were four castes; in each of these were four stages of life; and the rules of conduct varied according to the caste and stages of life.[6] In the Kali Age, however, there are five castes—namely, Brāhmaṇa, Kshatriya, Vaishya, Shūdra, Sāmānya.[7] Each of these five castes,

---

[1] Feminine of Bhava—a title of Shiva.

[2] Dharma. [3] Nirvāṇa-kāraṇam. [4] Varṇa.

[5] Āshrama, that is of Student (Brahmacharya), Householder (Gṛihastha), Forest, dweller (Vānaprastha), and Mendicant (Bhikshu, Avadhūta, Sannyāsī). [6] *Ibid.*

[7] The ordinary division is into the first four castes. The Tantra adds a fifth—Sāmānya—which means common, or low-born. The new caste is not based on any essential difference, but is a hybrid from the others. *Vide post*, v. 118.

O Great Queen![1] have two stages of life.[2] Listen then, O Ādyā! whilst I narrate to Thee their mode of life, rites, and duties[3] (4-6). I have already spoken to Thee of the ways of men born in the Kali Age. Unused as they are to penance,[4] and devoid of learning in the Vedas, incapable of doing the rites, short-lived, and incapable of strenuous effort,[5] how can they endure bodily labour? (7)

O Beloved! there is in the Kali Age no Brahmachārya[6] nor Vānaprastha.[6] There are two stages only, those of Gṛihastha and Bhikshuka[7] (8). O Auspicious One! in the Kali Age the householder[8] should in all his acts be guided by the rules of the Āgamas.[9] He will never attain success[10] by other ways[11] (9). And, O Devī! at the stage of the mendicant[12] there is no carrying of the staff as enjoined in the Veda, since, O Thou Who knowest the Truth![13] that is a practice which is Vedic[14] (10). O Gentle One! the adoption

[1] Maheshvarī.

[2] *i.e.*, Gārhasthya and Sannyāsa. The first Brahmachārya and the third Vānaprastha are abrogated, owing to the strictness of their rules and the conditions they involve. The latter does not exist, and the morally and physically weak and fallen beings of the Kali Age are incapable of observing the former as was done in better ages.

[3] Dharma.

[4] Tapas.

[5] *i.e.*, such performances as involve great physical labour beyond the capacity of the weaklings of the Kali Age.

[6] See p. 213, n. 5.

[7] Householder and mendicant.

[8] Gṛiha-stha.

[9] *i.e.*, the Tantras to use in a generic sense a more commonly known term.

[10] Siddhi.

[11] *i.e.*, by following Vedic or Smārta rites.

[12] Bhikshuka.

[13] Tattva-jne.

[14] Shrauta-saṁskṛiti. Shrauta is the adjective derived from Shruti (the Vedas), and Saṁskṛiti, or Saṁskāra, are the purificatory ceremonies of the twice-born castes. The Tantra thus further emphasizes

of the life of an Avadhūta,[1] according to the Shaiva rites,[2] is in the Kali Age equivalent to the entry into the life of a Sannyāsin[3] (11). When the Kali Age is in full sway, the Vipras[4] and the other castes have equal right to enter into both these stages of life (12). The purificatory rites of all are to be according to the rules ordained by Shiva, though the particular practices of the Vipras and other castes vary (13).

A man becomes a householder the moment he is born. It is by Saṁskāra,[5] that he enters upon the other stage of life.[6] For this reason, O Great Queen![7] one should first be a householder, following the rules of that mode of life (14). When, however, the Brahman is known and one is

the degeneracy of the Kali Age, since even in those two stages (Āshrama) which are prescribed during its continuance, there is a dispensation from rites which the men of that Age are incapable of observing. The Āshrama is in vogue in the Kali Age but the carrying of the staff (Da*n*da dhāra*n*a) is not permitted, as the rites attending investiture with the Da*n*da are Vedic. Some however do carry the Da*n*da.

[1] Literally, shaken off, cast aside, washed off, one who has separated from the world. An Avadhūta has been thus defined:

Yo vilanghyāshramān var*n*ān ātmanyeva sthita*h* pumān,
Ati-var*n*āshramī yogī avadhūta*h* sa uchyate.

"A man who is above both caste and stage of life (āshrama), and ever contemplating the Supreme Soul only, he is called Avadhūta". The Brāhma*n*a must study, teach, give and take alms, worship and perform worship for others. The Avadhūta, if a Brāhma*n*a, however, does not follow these injunctions, or, if he is a Ks*h*atriya or Vaishya, the duties laid down for these castes (see "Shakti and Shākta").

[2] Shaiva-Saṁskāra—*i.e.*, purificatory ceremonies according to the Shaiva rites *I.e.*, in the Kali Age the broad principles are to be found in the Shaiva rules, though there must be differences of ritual in the different sects.

[3] One who adopts Sannyāsa—renunciation; an ascetic.

[4] Brāhma*n*as.

[5] A Consecratory rite.

[6] *i.e.*, marrying and living the ordinary life of society is the usual destiny of man. It is his exertions and merit which determine the possibility of his entrance into the other Āshrama.

[7] Maheshvarī.

freed of worldly desires,[1] it is then that one should abandon all and seek refuge in the life of an ascetic[2] (15). In childhood one should acquire knowledge; in youth, wealth and wife. The wise man in middle age will devote himself to acts of charity and piety, and in his old age he should retire from the world (16).

No one should retire from the world who has an old father or mother, a devoted and chaste wife, or young and helpless children[3] (17). He who becomes an ascetic[4] leaving mothers,[5] fathers,[6] infant children, wives, agnates and cognates,[7] is guilty of a great sin (18). He who becomes a mendicant without first satisfying the need of his own parents and relatives is guilty of the sins of killing his father and mother, a woman, and a Brāhma*n*a[8] (19). The Brāhma*n*as and men of other castes should perform their respective purificatory rites according to the ordinances laid down by Shiva. This is the rule[9] in the Kali Age (20).

Shrī Devī said:

O Omnipresent One! tell Me what is the rule of life[10] for the householder and mendicant, and what are the purificatory rites[11] for the Vipras[12] and other castes (21).

---

[1] Tattva-jnāne Samutpanne vairāgyam jāyate Yadā.

[2] Sannyāsin.

[3] Before renouncing the world the Avadhūta must take care to see that no one suffers by such renunciation.

[4] Ya*h* prabrajati, who goes forth, that is, out of the world.

[5] *i.e.*, the Mother and all who occupy the same place as the Mother —*e.g.*, Aunt.

[6] See last note—*e.g.*, Uncle.

[7] *i.e.*, the helpless and dependent on him.

[8] These are called Mahā-pātakas, "great sins".

[9] Dharma.

[10] *Ibid.*

[11] Saṁskāra.

[12] Brāhma*n*as.

Shrī Sadāshiva said:

The state of an householder is for all the descendants of Manu [1] the first duty. I shall, therefore, first speak of it, and do Thou listen to Me, O Lady of the Kaulas [2] (22). A householder should be devoted to the Brahman and have his mind turned towards the knowledge of Brahman, and should dedicate whatever he does to Brahman (23). He should not tell an untruth, or practise deceit, and should ever be engaged in the worship of the Devatās and guests [3] (24). Regarding his father and mother as to visible incarnate deities, he should ever and by every means in his power serve them [4] (25). O Shivā! O Pārvatī! if the mother and father are pleased, Thou too art pleased, and the Supreme Being [5] is propitious to him (26). O Primeal One! Thou art the Mother of the Worlds, and the supreme Brahman is the Father; what better religious act [6] can there be than that which pleases You both? (27). One should offer, as desired, seats, beds, clothes, drink, and food

[1] The representative man and father of the human race. There are fourteen mentioned in the Manu Smṛiti.

[2] Kaulinī. This word is defined by Bhāskararāya under verse 88 of Lalitā as follows:

Kula = Shakti, Akula = Shiva. The relation between these two is Kaula, Kaula = Shiva-Shakti-Sāmarasya. She who is possessed of this is Kaulinī.

[3] Atithi. Tithi is a lunar day, and the A-tithi is the stranger guest seeking shelter and a meal, who stays not longer than one Tithi.

[4] It is said:

Pitā svarga*h* pitā dharma*h*, pitā hi paramaṁ tapa*h*.
Pitari prītim āpanne prīyante sarva-devatā*h*.

i.e., Father is heaven, father is Dharma, father is the highest Tapas or object of devotion. When father is pleased, all Devas are pleased. But the mother is even more honoured. Garbha-dhāra*n*a-posh*ā*bhyām pitur mātā garīyasī—*i.e.*, Mother is superior to father on account of her bearing and also nourishing the child. Also Jananī janma-bhūmish cha svargād api garīyasī: Mother and the land of one's birth are superior to heaven itself.

[5] Para-brahman.

[6] Tapas: penance.

to mother and father. They should always be spoken to in a gentle voice, and their children's demeanour should ever be agreeable to them. The good son who ever obeys the behests of his mother and father hallows the family (28-29). If one desires one's own welfare, all arrogance, mockery, threats and angry words should be avoided in the parents' presence (30). The son should remain obedient to his parents and should, on seeing them bow to them and out of reverence to them, stand up in their presence, and should not take his seat without their permission (31). He who, intoxicated with the pride of learning or wealth, slights his parents, is beyond the pale of all Dharma, and goes to a terrible Hell (32). Even if the vital breath were to reach his throat,[1] the householder should not eat without first feeding his mother, father, son, wife, guest, and brother[2] (33). The man who, to the deprivation of his elders and equals, fills his own belly is despised in this world, and goes to Hell in the next (34). The householder should cherish his wife, educate his children, and support his kinsmen and friends. This is the eternal duty[3] (35). The body is nourished by the mother. It originates from the father. The kinsmen, out of love, teach. The man, therefore, who forsakes them is indeed vile (36). For their sake should an hundred pains be undergone. With all one's ability they should be pleased. This is the eternal duty[3] (37). That man who in this world turns his mind to Brahman and adheres faithfully to the Truth in his conduct is above all a man of good deeds, and knows the Supreme, and is blest in all the worlds (38). The householder should never punish his wife, but should cherish her

[1] Prāṇaiḥ kaṇṭhagatairapi = Even if the vital airs stick inside the throat and cannot be drawn into the lungs. This is called Kaṇṭhashvāsa, the stage before death.

[2] Uterine—Sodara: "Born from the same womb."

[3] Sanātana Dharma.

like a mother. If she is virtuous and devoted to her husband, he should never forsake her even in times of greatest misfortune (39). The wise man, whilst his own wife is living, should never with wicked intent touch another woman, otherwise he will go to hell (40). The wise man should not, when in a private place, live and sleep or lie down close to another man's wife. He should avoid all improper speech and braggart boldness in her presence (41). By riches, clothes, love, respect and pleasing words should one's wife be pleased. The husband should never do anything displeasing to her (42). The wise man should not send his wife to any festival, concourse of people, pilgrimage or to another's house, except she be attended by his son or an inmate of his own house [1] (43).

O Maheshvarī! that man whose wife is both faithful and happy is surely looked upon as if he had performed all Dharma, and is truly Thy favourite also (44). A father should fondle and nurture his sons until their fourth year, and then until their sixteenth they should be taught learning and their duties [2] (45). Up to their twentieth year they should be kept engaged in household duties, and thenceforward, considering them as equals, he should ever show affection towards them (46). In the same manner a daughter should be cherished and taught with great care, and then given away with money and jewels to a good husband [3] (47).

The householder should in the same way also cherish and protect his brothers and sisters and their children, his

---

[1] Amātya—Friend, or counsellor.

[2] Charity, self-abnegation, self-control, truthfulness, beneficence, etc.

[3] Vara (Bridegroom), from "Vri"="to adore," because the bride's father pays homage to him. Vara also means the "Chosen One". The girl should be married before puberty but the Shāstras say that the girl should be kept unmarried unless a qualified husband be secured. (Tarkālaṁkāra).

kinsmen, friends, and servants (48). He should also maintain his fellow-worshippers,[1] fellow-villagers, guests and unexpected strangers[2] (49). If the wealthy householder does not so act, then let him be known as a beast, a sinner, and one despised in the worlds (50). The householder should not be inordinately addicted to sleep, idling, care for the body, dressing his hair, eating or drinking, or attention to his clothes (51). He should be moderate as to food, sleep, speech, and sexual intercourse, and be sincere, humble, pure,[3] free from sloth,[4] and perserving[5] (52). Chivalrous to his foes, modest before his friends, relatives, and elders, he should neither respect those who deserve censure nor slight those who are worthy of respect (53). Men should only be admitted to his trust and confidence after association with them and observation of their nature, inclination, conduct, and friendly character (54). Even an insignificant enemy should be feared, and one's own power[6] should be disclosed only at the proper time. But on no account should one deviate from the path of duty[7] (55). He who knows Dharma[8] should not speak of his own fame and prowess, of what has been told him in secret, nor of the good that he has done for others (56). A man of good name should not engage in any quarrel with an unworthy

---

[1] Sva-dharma-nirata, which, however, may also mean "faithful to one's own religious observances and duties".

[2] Udāsīna—one who is neither a friend nor an enemy (Bhāratī).

[3] Shuchi = Vāhyābhyantara-shaucha-sampanna(Bhāratī)—*i.e.*, should be outwardly and inwardly clean.

[4] Daksha = Nirālasya (Bhāratī).

[5] Yukta = Udyogavān (Bhāratī)

[6] Ātma-bhāva—*i.e.*, one's own intentions, power, resources, etc. Bhāratī says that the term equals Sva-prabhāva. According to the Amara-kosha, Pra-bhāva is the power arising from wealth or ability to inflict punishment.

[7] Dharma.

[8] Dharma-jna.

motive,[1] nor when defeat is certain, nor with one who is either superior or inferior to himself (57). He should diligently earn knowledge, wealth, fame, and religious merit,[2] and avoid all vicious habits,[3] the company of the wicked, falsehood, and treachery[4] (58). Ventures should be undertaken according to the circumstances and one's condition in life, and actions should be done according to their season. Therefore, in everything that a man does he should first consider whether the circumstances and time are suitable[5] (59). The householder should employ himself in the acquisition of what is necessary and in the protection of the same. He should be judicious, pious, good to his friends. He should be moderate in speech and laughter, in particular in the presence of those entitled to his reverence[6] (60). He should hold his senses under control, be of cheerful disposition, think

[1] In Bhakta's edition it is said: "An unworthy quarrel should be avoided, even if victory is certain." There is, however, an "And" (Cha). Tarkālangkāra renders the verse thus: "The man possessed of a good name should not, even when victory is certain, engage in a dispute with his superior or inferior with an unworthy motive."

[2] Dharma.

[3] Vyasana. Defined in the Amara-kosha: Vyasanaṁ vipadi bhrangshe doshe kāmaja-kopaje—*i.e.*, calamity or disaster, fall or defeat, and vicious habits engendered by lust or anger, of which there are ten and eight kinds respectively. The last-mentioned meaning is applicable here. There are various kinds, such as excessive addiction to women, intoxicating drinks, gambling, hunting, etc. (see Kāmandakīya-Nītisāra, Chapter XI, verse 12). The term is a comprehensive one, and is sometimes used generally for all defects—sleeping in the day, over-addiction to dancing and singing, etc.

[4] Or unjust persecution of others.

[5] It is a common saying that an action should only be undertaken after considering Desha (place), Kāla (season), and Pātra (the party concerned in it).

[6] The rules of etiquette amongst the ancient Hindus were rigorous, as amongst other races during the past age of manners. Yawning, loose speech, or postures were forbidden.

of what is good,[1] be of firm resolve, attentive, far-sighted, and discriminating in the use of his senses[2] (61).

The wise householder's speech should be truthful, mild, agreeable, and salutary, yet pleasing, avoiding both self-praise and the disparagement of others[3] (62). The man who has dedicated tanks, planted trees, built rest-houses on the roadside, or bridges, has conquered the three worlds[4] (63). That man who is the happiness of his mother and father, to whom his friends are devoted, and whose fame is sung by men, he is the conqueror of the three worlds (64). He who has taken the vow of truth, whose charity is ever for the poor, who has mastered lust and anger,[5] by him are the three worlds conquered (65). He who covets not others' wives or goods, who is free of deceit and envy, by him the three worlds are conquered (66). He who is not afraid in battle nor to go to war when there is need, and who dies in battle undertaken for a sacred cause, by him the three worlds are conquered (67). He whose soul is free from doubts, who is devoted to and

---

[1] Which Bhāratī explains as meaning "keep his thoughts fixed on the Shāstras," etc.

[2] The senses are the doors through which the mind perceives the outer world. It should be cautious as to the objects with which it brings itself in contact, and not expose itself to temptation. Bhāratī says, Mātrā=Indriyav*r*itti and Sparsha is the relationship of the senses to external objects.

[3] So it is said: Satyam bruyāt priyam bruyāt na bruyāt satyam apriyam (Say what is true and pleasant, but not what is unpleasant even if true); also, Hitam manohāri cha durlabham vacha*h* (Kirātārjunīya of Bhāravī)—*i.e.*, Rare is the word both salutary and pleasing.

[4] By pleasing others the Paramātmā, who is in all, is pleased. When any of these acts is done, it is accompanied by the Prati*shth*ā ceremony. The tree, pond, etc., are dedicated to the Deity, and the consecrated object becomes public property. Public utility is served and religious merit is acquired by the dedication. Would that such acts were done in our day!

[5] The first two of the six sins—Kāma, Krodha, Lobha, Moha, Mada, Mātsarya.

a faithful follower of the ordinances of Shiva, and remains under My control, by him the three worlds are conquered (68). The Knower[1] who looks upon all alike and acts merely for the guidance of his fellowmen, has conquered the three worlds (69).

O Devī! purity is of two kinds, external and internal. The dedication of oneself to Brahman is known as internal purity (70) and the cleansing of the impurities of the body by water or ashes, or any other matter which cleanses the body, is called external purity (71). O Dearest One! the waters of Gaṁgā, or of any other river, lake, tank, pond, well, or pool, or of the celestial River, are equally purifying[2] (72). O Thou of auspicious Vows! the ashes from a place of sacrifice and cleansed earth or excellent, and the skin of an antelope, a clean cloth and grass are as purifying as earth (73). O Auspicious One![3] what need is there to say more about the rules of purity and impurity? Whatever[4] purifies the mind that the householder should do (74). Let there be external purification upon awakening from sleep, after sexual intercourse, making water, voiding the bowels, and at the close of a meal, and whenever dirt of any kind has been touched (75).

Sandhyā, both Vaidika and Tāntrika,[5] should be performed thrice daily, and according as the worship[6] changes

---

[1] Jnānī=he who has Brahman Knowledge or Tattvajnāna.

[2] *i.e.*, Water everywhere is as purifying as that of the sacred Ganges, which cleanses one of sin. The celestial Ganges is Mandākinī, or the Milky Way. The translation follows Tarkālaṁkāra's interpretation.

[3] Shivā.

[4] Whatever purifies the mind—Mana*h*-pūtaṁ bhaved yena. This is a common expression used to signify anything which brings a feeling of satisfaction to the mind, a feeling that the thing is rightly done.

[5] Sandhyā, the three daily (at Prāta*h*, Madhyāhna, Sāyam) and obligatory ceremonies (see "Shakti and Shākta") which are either Vaidika (which again varies according to the Veda followed) and according to the Tāntrika ritual.

[6] Upāsanā.

so does the ritual[1] (76). The Sādhakas of the Brahma Mantra have performed their Sandhya when they have made Japa of the Gāyatrī realizing within themselves the identity of the Gāyatrī and Brahman (77).[2] In the case of those who are not Brahma-worshippers, Vaidika Sandhya consists of the recitation of the Gāyatrī after offering of oblations to the Sun[3] (78).

O Gentle One! in all daily prayers[4] Japa should be done one thousand and eight, or a hundred and eight, or ten times (79). O Devi! the Shūdras and Sāmānyas[5] may observe any of the rites proclaimed by the Āgamas, and by these they attain that which they desire (80). The three times (of performance of Sandhyā) are at sunrise, at noon, and at sunset (81).

Shrī Devī said:

Thou hast Thyself said, O Lord! that when the Kali Age is in full sway then for all castes, commencing with the Vipras, Tāntrika rites are alone appropriate. Why, then, dost Thou enjoin on the Vipras[6] the Vedic rites? It behoveth Thee to explain this fully to Me (82-83).

Shrī Sadāshiva said:

O Thou Who knowest the essence of all things! truly hast Thou said that Tantrik rites produce enjoyment and Liberation for all men in all observances (84). The

---

[1] Pūjā. Both terms refer to worship, but here the former term has reference to the Deva adored, and the latter to the mode or material of the Upāsanā. So the worship of Shiva is Shiva-upāsanā, and his pūjā consists of special Mantras and special offerings, such as the leaf of the bael-tree, etc.

[2] By the knowledge that the Gāyatrī proves the Brahman (Bhāratī)

[3] Sūrya.

[4] Ahnika-karma.

[5] See p. 218, note 7.

[6] Brāhmaṇas.

Brahma-Sāvitrī,[1] is as much Vaidika, as Tāntrika, and is appropriate in both Vaidika and Tāntrika rites (85). It is, therefore, O Devī! that I have said that when the Kali Age is in full sway, the twice-born shall alone be entitled to the Gāyatrī, but not the other Mantras[2] (86). In the Kali Age the Sāvitrī[3] should be said by the Brāhmaṇas, preceded by the Tāra,[4] and by the Kshatriyas and Vaishyas, preceded by the Kamalā[5] and Vāgbhava[6] Bījas respectively (87). In order, O Supreme Devī! that a distinction may be drawn between the twice-born and the Shūdras, the daily duties[7] are directed to be preceded by Vaidika Sandhyā[8] (88). Success, however, may also be attained by the mere following of the ordinances of Shambhu.[9] This is verily true, and I repeat it is true and very true, and there is no doubt about it (89). O Adored of the Devas! even if the stated time for the doing of the daily Sandhyā is past, all, who desire Emancipation but are otherwise prevented, should do it by saying, "Oṁ That Ever-lasting Brahman"[10] (90). The seat, clothes, vessels, bed, carriages, residence, and

---

[1] *i.e.*, The great Vaidika Gāyatrī:

Oṁ bhūr bhuvaḥ svaḥ:
Tat savitur vareṇyam bhargo devasya dhīmahi:
Dhiyo yo naḥ prachodayāt.

(See "Garland of Letters".)

[2] That is, to the Gāyatrī preceded by Oṁ. The Hangsa-vatī and other Vaidik Mantras have been included in the Tantras, but the privilege of the twice-born to the Gāyatrī is retained.

[3] *i.e.*, Brahma-Gāyatrī.

[4] Oṁ.

[5] *i.e.*, Shrīng.

[6] *i.e.*, Aing.

[7] Āhnika-karma. When one says of another that he is at his "Āhnika," it is understood that the latter is saying his prayers or doing his Pūjā.

[8] *i.e.*, only the first three castes are entitled to the Vaidika Sandhyā.

[9] *i.e.*, the Tāntrika ritual ordained by Shiva.

[10] Oṁ Tat Sat Brahma = That, the Being, the Brahman.

household furniture of the worshipper should be as clean as possible (91). At the close of the daily prayers the householder should keep himself occupied with household duties or the study of the Vedas; he should never remain idle (92). In holy places, on holy days, or when the Sun or Moon is in eclipse,[1] he should do inward recitation,[2] and give alms, and thus become the abode of all that is good (93).

In the Kali Age, life is dependent on the food that is eaten[3] fasting is therefore not recommended;[4] in lieu of it, the giving of alms is ordained (94). O Great Queen![5] in the Kali Age, alms are efficacious in the accomplishment of all things. The proper objects of such alms are the poor devoted to meritorious acts (95). O Mother![6] the first days of the month, of the year, of the lunar half-months,[7] the fourteenth day of the lunar half-month,[8] the eighth day of the light half of the lunar month,[9] the eleventh day[10] of the lunar half-month, the new moon,[11] one's birthday, the anniversary of one's father's

[1] When the Moon or Sun are devoured by Rāhu. One of the names of the latter is Bhū-chhāya (Earth-Shadow), which shows that the ancients were not so foolish in this respect as some suppose them to have been.

[2] Japa.

[3] The reference here is to the belief that in the Satya Yuga the vital functions were dependent on the brain, in the Tretā Age on the bones, in the Dvāpara on the blood, and in the Kali Age on food.

[4] Fasting is not prohibited, and those may do so who can. For those who cannot, acts of charity are substituted.

[5] Maheshvarī.

[6] Ambikā.

[7] Paksha.

[8] Chaturdashī.

[9] Shuklāshtamī.

[10] Ekādashī.

[11] Amāvasyā. The day on which the Sun and Moon dwell together or are in the same line.

death, and days fixed as those of festivals, are holy days (96-97).

The River Gaṅgā and all the great Rivers, the house of the religious Teacher, and the places of the Devas [1] are holy places. But for those who, neglecting the study of the Vedas, the service of mother and father, and the protection of their wife, go to places of pilgrimage, such holy places are changed to Hell (98-99). For women there is no necessity to go on pilgrimage, to fast, or to do other like acts, nor is there any need to perform any devotion except that which consists in the service of their husband (100). For a woman her husband is the place of pilgrimage, the performance of penance, the giving of alms, the carrying out of vows, and her spiritual teacher. Therefore should a woman devote herself to the service of her husband with her whole Self (101). She should ever by words and deeds of devotion act for the pleasure of her husband, and, remaining faithful to his behests, should please his kinsmen and relations (102).

A woman whose husband is her vow [2], should not look at him with hard eyes, or utter harsh words before him. Not even in her thought should she do anything which is displeasing to her husband (103). She who by body, mind, and word, and by pleasant acts, ever pleases her husband, attains to the abode of Brahman [3] (104). Remaining ever faithful to the wishes of her husband, she should not look upon the face of other men, or have converse with them, or uncover her body before them (105). In childhood she should remain under the control of her parents, in her

---

[1] Devatā-kshetra. When they are worshipped such as Shrīkshetra (Puri) the land of Vishnu; Arkakshetra (Konarak) the land of the Sun God.

[2] Pati-vratā—*i.e.*, a chaste and dutiful wife.

[3] Brahmapada = Brahmatva.

youth of her husband, and in her old age of the relatives of her husband. She should never be independent[1] (106).

A father should not marry his daughter if she does not know her duty to a husband and how to serve him, as also the other rules[2] of woman's conduct (107).

Neither the flesh of human beings, nor of the animals resembling them,[3] nor the flesh of the cow, which is serviceable in various ways, nor the flesh of carnivorous animals, nor such meat as is tasteless, should be eaten (108). O Auspicious One![4] fruits and roots of various kinds, whether grown in villages or jungles, and all that is grown in the ground, may be eaten at pleasure (109).

Teaching and the performance of sacrifices are the proper duties of a Brāhma*n*a. But if he be incapable of these, he may earn his livelihood by following the profession of a Ks*h*atriya or Vaishya (110). The proper occupation of a Rājanya[5] is that of fighting and ruling. But if he be incapable of these, he may earn his livelihood by following the profession of a Vaishya or Shūdra (111). If a Vaishya cannot trade, then for him the following of the profession of a Shūdra involves no blame. For a Shūdra, O Sovereign Queen![6] service is the prescribed means of livelihood (112). O Devī! members of the Sāmānya[7] class may for their maintenance follow all occupations except such as are specially reserved for the Brāhma*n*a (113). The latter, void of hate and

---

[1] *i.e.*, her own mistress, with none to guide and protect her. This is the text of Manu.

[2] Dharma.

[3] *i.e.*, apes, monkeys, etc.

[4] Shivā.

[5] Ks*h*atriya.

[6] Parameshāni.

[7] *Vide* p. 218, note 7.

attachment,[1] self-controlled, truthful, the conqueror of his senses, free of envy and all guile, should pursue his own avocations (114). He should ever be the same to, and the well-wisher of, all men, and teach his well-behaved pupils as if they were his own sons (115). He should ever avoid falsehood, detraction, and vicious habits,[2] arrogance, friendship for low persons, the pursuit of low objects, and the use of language which gives offence (116). Where peace is possible, avoid war.[3] Peace with honour is excellent. O Beauteous One![4] for the Rājanya it should be either death or victory in battle[5] (117). A man of the kingly caste should not covet the wealth of his subjects, or levy excessive taxes, but, being faithful to his promises, he should ever in the observance of his duty[6] protect his subjects as though they were his own children (118). In administration, war, treaties, and other affairs of State the King should take the advice of his Ministers (119). War should be carried on in accordance with Dharma.[7] Rewards and punishments should be awarded justly and in accordance with the Shāstras. The best treaty should be

[1] Nirmama. Mama, or Mama-tā, is a sense of "Mineness," attachment to self, to one's property, etc.

[2] Vyasana (see p. 221, note 3). Manu enumerates ten evil habits as arising from pleasure, and eight from anger. Under the first head are: hunting, gambling, sleeping in the daytime, gossip, women, intoxicants, dancing, singing, instrumental music, and idle roaming; and under the second: slander, violence, insidious injury, envy, detraction, unjust seizure of property, violent language and assault. The word translated as "falsehood" (Mithyālāpa) in the text may also mean "frivolous conversation."

[3] The Sanskrit may also mean, "Desire for war when there is peace is blameworthy".

[4] Varānanā.

[5] A K*sh*atriya should not flee from the field of battle.

[6] Aṁgīk*r*itaṁ dharman *i.e.*, duty undertaken or promise made.

[7] Because men have to fight, they should not do so like beasts.

concluded which his power allows (120). By stratagem[1] should the end desired be attained. By the same means should wars be conducted and treaties concluded. Victory, peace, and prosperity follow stratagem (121). He should ever avoid the company of the low, and be good to the learned. He should be of a calm disposition, judicious of action in time of trouble, of good conduct, and reasonable in his expenditure (122).

He should be an expert in the maintenance of his forts, well trained in the use of arms. He should ever ascertain the disposition of his army, and teach his soldiers military tactics (123). O Devī! he should not in battle kill one who is stunned, who has surrendered his arms, or is a fugitive, nor those of his enemies whom he has captured, nor their wives or children (124). Whatever is acquired either by victory or treaty should be distributed amongst the soldiers in shares according to merit (125).

The King should make known to himself the character and courage of each of his warriors, and if he would care for his interests he should not place a large army under the command of a single officer (126). He should not put his trust in any single person, nor place one man in charge of the administration, nor treat his inferiors as equals, nor be familiar with them[2] (127). He should be very learned, yet not garrulous; full of knowledge, yet anxious to learn; full of honours, yet without arrogance. In awarding both reward and punishment he should be calm and discriminating (128). The King ahould either himself or through his spies watch his subjects, kinsmen, and servants (129). A wise master should not either reward or punish anyone in a fit of passion or arrogance

[1] Upāya.

[2] Nīchaiḥ krīḍopahāsaṁ vivarjayet = eschew playing and joking with the low.

and without due cause (130). Soldiers, commanders, ministers, wife, children and servitors he should protect. If guilty, they should be punished according to their deserts (131). The King should protect, like a father, the insane, the helpless, children and orphans,[1] and those who are old and infirm[2] (132).

Know that agriculture and trade are the appropriate callings of the Vaishya. It is by agriculture and trade that man's body is maintained (133). Therefore, O Devī! in agriculture and trade all negligence, vicious habits,[3] laziness, untruth, and deceit should be avoided in every way (134).

Shivā! when both buyer and seller are agreed as to the object of sale and the price thereof, and mutual promises have been made, then the purchase becomes complete (135). O Dearest One! the sale or gift of property by one who is a lunatic, out of his senses,[4] under age, a captive, or enfeebled by disease, is invalid (136). The purchase of things not seen is concluded by hearing the description thereof. If the article be found to differ from its description, then the purchase is of no effect (137). The sale of an elephant, a camel, and a horse is effected by the description of the animal. The sale is, however, set aside if the animal does not answer its description (138). If in the purchase of elephants, camels, and horses a latent vice becomes patent within the course of a year from the date of sale, then the purchase is set aside, but not after the lapse of one

[1] M*ri*ta-bāndhava, those whose protectors are dead.

[2] The text is Jvarābhibhūta, but probably should be read (and is so translated) as Jarābhibhūta, the latter being the adjective of V*ri*ddha. But, read as in the original, the meaning would be "stricken by disease".

[3] Vyasana (see p. 229, note 2).

[4] *e.g.*, by drink.

year (139). O Devī of Kula! the human body is the receptacle of piety, wealth, desires, and final Liberation. It should therefore never be the subject of purchase; and such a purchase is by reason of My commands invalid (140).

O Dear One! in the borrowing of barley, wheat, or paddy, the profit of the lender at the end of the year is laid down to be a fourth of the quantity lent, and in the case of the loan of metals one-eighth (141). In monetary transactions, agriculture, trade, and in all other transactions, men should ever carry out their undertakings. This is approved by the laws[1] (142).

A servant should be skilful, clean, truthful, wakeful, careful and alert, and possess his senses under control (143). He should, as he desires happiness in this and the next world, regard his master as if he were Vis*hn*u Himself, his master's wife as his own mother, and respect his master's kinsmen and friends (144). He should know his master's friends to be his friends, and his master's enemies to be his enemies, and should ever remain in respectful attendance upon his master, awaiting his orders (145). He should carefully conceal his master's dishonour, the family dissensions, anything said in private or which would hurt the mind of his master (146). He should not covet the wealth of his master, but remain ever devoted to his good. He should not make use of bad words or laugh or play in his master's presence (147). He should not, with lustful mind, even look at the maidservants in his master's house, or lie down with them, or play with them in secret (148). He should not use his master's bed, seat, carriages, clothes, vessels, shoes, jewels, or weapons (149). If guilty, he should beg the forgiveness of his master. He should not be forward, impertinent, or attempt to place himself on an equal footing with his master (150).

[1] Shāstras.

Except when in the Bhairavī-chakra[1] or Tattva-chakra,[1] persons of all castes should marry in their caste according to the Brāhma form,[2] and should eat with their own caste people (151). O Great Queen! in these two circles,[3] however, marriage in the Shaiva form is ordained,[4] and as regards eating and drinking, no caste distinctions exist (152).

Shrī Devī said:

What is the Bhairavī-chakra, and what is the Tattva-chakra? I desire to hear about them, and it behoves Thee kindly to speak of them (153).

Shrī Sadāshiva said:

O Devī! in the ordinances relating to Kula worship I have spoken of the formation of Circles.[5] That should be done by the excellent worshippers at times of special worship (154). O Dear One! there is no strict rule relating to the Bhairavī-chakra. This auspicious Circle may at any convenient time be formed (155). I will now speak of the rites relating to this Circle, which benefits the worshippers, and in which, if the Devī be worshipped, She speedily grants the prayers of Her votaries (156).

The Kulāchārya[6] should spread an excellent mat in a beautiful place, and, after purifying it with the Kāma[7]

---

[1] See below.

[2] There are eight forms of marriage, of which the Brāhmodvāha is that most generally adopted.

[3] *i.e.*, the Bhairavī-Chakra and Tattva-Chakra.

[4] Shaivodvāha*h* prakīrtita*h*. In the Tantrāntara it is said that in Shaiva marriage a Brāhma*n*a can marry a woman of all the classes, a Ks*h*atriya can marry all classes except a Brāhma*n*a, a Vaishya all classes except Brāhma*n*a and Ks*h*atriya. A Shūdra may marry a Shūdra or Sāmānya, a Sāmānya may marry a Sāmānya alone (ed. Bhakta, p. 338).

[5] Chakra.

[6] The instructor in Kula worship versed in the Tantras and Mantras and in the knowledge of the Brahman.

[7] *i.e.*, "Klīng."

and Astra[1] Bījas, should seat himself upon it (157). Then the wise one should draw a square with a triangle in it with either vermilion or red sandal-wood paste, or simply water (158). Then, taking a painted jar, and smearing it with curd and sun-dried rice, and placing a vermilion mark on it, let him put a bunch of leaves and fruit upon it[2] (159). Filling it with perfumed water whilst uttering the Pra*n*ava,[3] the worshipper should place it on the Ma*nd*ala,[4] and exhibit before it lights and incense-sticks (160). The jar should then be worshipped with scent and flowers. The I*sht*a-devatā[5] should be meditated upon as being in the jar. The ritual according to the shortened form should then be done (of the I*sht*a-devatā) (161). Listen, O Adored of the Immortals! whilst I speak to Thee of the peculiar features of this worship. There is no necessity of placing the nine cups for the Guru and others (162). The Sādhaka should then take such of the elements of worship as he wishes,[6] and place them in front of himself. Then, purifying them with the Weapon Mantra,[7] let him gaze upon them with steadfast eyes[8] (163).

Then, placing scent and flowers in the wine-jar, let him meditate upon the Ānanda-Bhairavī[9] and Ānanda-Bhairava in it (164).

---

[1] *i.e.*, "Pha*t*."

[2] Usually a mango twig with leaves and a cocoa-nut is placed on the mouth of the jar. The water is perfumed with camphor and the like.

[3] Om. The first word: from Pra=before, Nu=to speak.

[4] *i.e.*, the square and triangle referred to in verse 158, which is ordinarily perfumed with camphor.

[5] The special form of Deity of the worshipper.

[6] *i.e.*, such Tattvas as one prefers if all cannot be had, but there should be the first (Wine) and one of the Shuddhis.

[7] "Pha*t*."

[8] Divya-d*rishti*.

[9] *Vide* p. 188, note 8.

DHYĀNA

He should meditate upon the Ānanda-Bhairavī as in the full bloom of youth, with a body rosy as the first gleam of the rising Sun. The light of nectarlike sweetness of Her charming smile illumines Her face as beautiful as a full-blown lotus.[1] Decked with jewels, clad in beauteous coloured raiment, delighting in dance and song,[2] She with the lotus of Her hands makes the signs which confer blessings and dispel fears (165-166).

After thus meditating on the Blissful Devī[3] let the worshipper thus meditate upon the Ānanda Bhairava (167).

DHYĀNA

I meditate upon the Deva Who is white as a Stream of camphor, Whose eyes are large and beautiful like lotuses, the lustre of Whose body is adorned with celestial raiments and jewels, Who holds in His left lotus-like hand the cup full of nectar, and in the right a ball of Shuddhi[4] (168).

Having thus meditated upon Them both, and thinking of Them in a state of union[5] in the wine-jar, the worshipper should then worship Them therein, with Mantra, beginning with the Pranava and ending with Namah, the names of the Devatās being placed between,[6] and with perfume and flower. Let him then sanctify the wine (169).

---

[1] Bhāratī reads it to mean, 'Her charming smile and the sweetness of her words illumine Her face'.

[2] The Shakti should be versed in the Arts (Kalā). There are sixty-four of these—learning, singing, dancing, playing, painting, kissing, embracing, collecting flowers, etc. (see Raghu-vangsha, Canto 8, verse 67).

[3] Ananda-mayi.

[4] Shuddhi-gutikā—that is, a ball of purified Shuddhi or Tattva which is eaten.

[5] Sāmarasya, which means identity, or in the ordinary material sense sexual union.

[6] The Mantra would thus be Ete gandha-pushpe: Ong Ānanda-Bhairavāya Namah and Ete gandha-pushpe Ong Ānande-Bhairavyai Namah.

The Kula worshipper should sanctify the wine by repeating over it the Pāshādi-trika Bīja and Svāhā[1] a hundred and eight times (170). When the Kali Age is in full sway, in the case of the householder whose mind is entirely engrossed with domestic desires, the three sweets should be substituted in the place of the first element of worship (wine) (171). Milk, sugar, and honey are the three sweets.[2] They should be deemed to be the image of wine, and as such offered to the Deity (172). Those born in the Kali Age are by their nature weak in intellect, and their minds are distracted by lust. By reason of this, they do not recognize the Shakti to be the image of the Deity[3] (173). Therefore, O Pārvatī! for such as these let there be, in place of the last element of worship (sexual union), meditation upon the Lotus-feet of the Devī and the inward recitation of their[4] Ish*t*a-mantra[5] (174).

Therefore such of the elements of worship as have been obtained should be consecrated by the recitation, over each of them, of the same Mantra one hundred times (175). Let the worshipper, with closed eyes, meditate upon them

---

[1] *i.e.*, the Mantra, consisting of three Bījas, beginning with Pāsha, or Āng—" Āng Hrīng Krong : Svāhā."

[2] Madhura-traya. Some say ghee, honey, sugar. It has been previously said that the Sādhaka householder may drink up to five cups. Here it is said that a householder is not to drink at all. The apparent contradiction is resolved by Tarkālamkāra, who says that a householder whose mind is engrossed in his Sādhanā may drink five cups but he whose mind is occupied with worldly matters and rites for the attainment of worldly advantages should not drink.

[3] Sva-bhāvāt kali-janmāna*h* kāma-vibhrānta-chetasa*h*.
Tadrūpe*n*a na jānanti Shakting sāmānya-buddaya*h*.

[4] Atasteshāng pratinidhau shesh*ā*-tattvasya Pārvati !
Dhyānang Devyā*h* padāmbhoje svesh*t*a-mantra-japas tathā.

[5] *i.e.*, the Mantra given at initiation. Here it is the Kālikā Mantra Hrīng, Shrīng, Kring, Ādyākālikāyai Nama*h*.

as suffused by Brahman,[1] then offer them as before to Kālī, and, lastly, eat and drink the consecrated elements (176). O Gentle One![2] this is the Bhairavī-chakra, which is not revealed in the other Tantras. I have, however, spoken before Thee of it. It is the essence of essences, and more excellent than the best (177).

Pārvatī! in Bhairavī-chakra and Tattva-chakra the excellent worshipper should be wedded to his Shakti, according to the laws prescribed by Shiva[3] (178). The

---

[1] Brahma-maya.

[2] Bhadre.

[3] Vivāho bhairavī-chakre tattva-chakre'pi Pārvati
Sarvathā sādhakendrena kartavyah Shaiva-vartmanā.

Two forms of marriage are, Brāhma (the usual kind) and Shaiva. There is in the last no restriction as regards age or caste. A widow can also so marry. The only restriction is that the woman has not already a husband (ix, 279). The latter marriage is of two kinds, one terminated by the Chakra and the other lifelong (ix, 269 and in verse 280). The persons so married are Shaktis. A Shakti again may be Pūjyā or Bhogyā. The latter may be enjoyed and not the former who merely acts as Uttara-sādhikā, that is, assists in the ritual the man whose Shakti she is. A Pūjyā Shakti is never for life. The Bhogyā Shakti may be for life or for the Chakra only. In all cases some form of marriage precedes intercourse where it takes place. On verse 174 Tarkālamkāra says that the Brāhma wife is called Svashakti or Aparashakti (that is not Parashakt). The Shaiva wife is called Parashakti. The Brāhma wife, if purified by Shaiva marriage ritual or taken as a Shakti in the Bhairavī-chakra, becomes a Parashakti. Parashakti should (he says) be treated as the Sādhaka's mother and as Divinity (Ishta-devatā). If the thought of wife relationship (Bhāryābhāva) arise in the mind there is a fall. Here (he says) Shiva has prohibited the last Tattva ere long for men of ordinary intelligence and weak control over their desire (Kāma). Such are not competent to take a Shakti. (This is not clear. But presumably what is meant is that they are not in a position to do Sādhanā with a Shakti. For such a man the presence of a woman is rather an obstacle—Vighna—than a help). Those, however, who by Sādhanā have conquered lust, may do Sādhanā with Shakti. The Uttara and other Tantras say that after doing Sādhanā with Svashakti and obtaining success (Siddhi) then when the mind is free of temptation, Sādhanā may be done with Parashakti. Guptasādhanā Tantra says that "in Kulāchāra the Siddhamantrin should worship (Prapūjayet) the Kula women."

I may add that the various grades of competency and Chakra must be considered. There are men who do Sādhanā with a woman

Vīra[1] who without marriage worships by enjoyment of Shakti[2] is, without doubt, guilty of the sin of going with another man's wife[3] (179). When seated in the Bhairavī-chakra men of all castes composing it are like the best of the twice-born; but when the circle is broken, they revert again to their own respective castes (180). In this Circle there is no distinction of caste nor impurity of food.[4] The Vīra worshippers in the Circle are My image; there is no doubt of that (181). In the formation of this Circle there is no rule as to time or place or question as to fitness.[5] The necessary articles may be used by whomsoever they may have been brought (182). Food brought from a long distance, whether it be cooked or uncooked,[6] whether brought by a Vīra[7] or a Pashu,[8] becomes pure, immediately it is brought within the Chakra (183).

While the Chakra is being formed, all dangers flee in confusion, awed by the Brāhma*n*ik[9] lustre of its Vīras (184).

---

who never have sexual intercourse with her nor thought of it. The Parashakti in human form is identified not the Parashakti in Supreme Power.

For status of Shaiva wife and her children, see Chapter IX, verse 267, *et seq.*

[1] See "Shakti and Shākta". The worshipper in whom the Rajogu*n*a predominates, and for whom worship must be in the Vīrāchāra form.

[2] Shakti-sevā.

[3] Vinā Pari*n*ayang vīra*h* shakti-sevāng samācharan
Para-strī-gāminām̐ pāpam̐ prāpnuyān nātra sam̐shaya*h*.

[4] Literally, there is nothing to be considered Uchchhi*sh*ta. This term means food left on the plate of a person after he has finished eating. These leavings are considered impure.

[5] Pātra-vichāra*n*a.

[6] Pakka, a-pakka, which also means ripe or unripe, here means cooked or uncooked. Cooked food should not be taken from the place where it has been cooked; if so, it becomes impure.

[7] See "Shakti and Shākta".

[8] See *Ibid.* Cooked food should not be touched by a lower caste; if so, it becomes impure. But the rule does not apply to uncooked food.

[9] Brahma-tejas. The word Brāhma*n*ik is here to be understood in its primary meaning, "Brahma jānāti sa Brāhma*n*a*h*"—*i.e.*, he who knows the Brahman is a Brāhma*n*a, and not as signifying the Brāhma*n*a caste,

Upon the mere hearing that a Bhairavī circle has been formed at any place, fierce Pishāchas, Guhyakas, Yak*sh*as, and Vetālas[1] depart afar off in fear (185). Into the circle come all the holy places,[2] the great and holy places,[3] and with reverence Indra[4] and all the immortals (186). Shivā! the place where a circle is formed is a great and holy place, more sacred than each and all the other holy places. Even the Thirty-three[5] desire the excellent offerings[6] made to Thee in this circle (187). Whatever the food be, whether cooked or uncooked, and whether brought by a Mlechchha,[7] Cha*nd*āla,[8] Kirāta,[9] or Hūna,[10] it becomes pure as soon as it is placed in the hand of a Vīra[11] (188). By the seeing of the circle and of the worshippers therein, who are but images of Myself, men infected with the taint of the Kali Age are liberated from the bonds of the life of a Pashu[12] (189). When, however, the Kali Age is in full sway, the circle should not be concealed. The Vīra should at all places and at all times practise Kula[13] rites and make Kula worship (190).

---

[1] See note under Ch. III, v. 25.

[2] Tīrtha—Shrines, places of pilgrimage.

[3] Mahā-tīrtha.

[4] King of the Celestials.

[5] Tri-dasha—*i.e.*, the thrity-three Devas—*viz.*, twelve Ādityas, eight Vasus, eleven Rudras, and two Ashvins. The word also means "Devas," as they do not go through the three (Tri) stages (Dashās): growth, maturity, decay.

[6] Naivedya.

[7] Non-aryan.

[8] See p. 52, note 1.

[9] Untouchables, living by hunting.

[10] Hun.

[11] See "Shakti and Shākta".

[12] See "Shakti and Shākta". Man is liberated from the bonds which bind his humanity to the animal element in him. A Pashu is one in whom the Tamogu*n*a is dominant. He is not fit for Vīra Sādhanā.

[13] Tāntrika rites of the Kaula form.

In the Circle all distinction of caste, frivolous talk, levity, garrulity, spitting, and breaking wind should be avoided (191). Such as are cruel, mischievous, Pashu,[1] sinful, atheists, blasphemers of Kula doctrine, and calumniators of the Kula[2] Scriptures, should be kept far away from the Circle (192). Even the Vīra[3] who, induced by affection, fear, or attachment, admits a Pashu[4] into the circle falls from his Kula duty,[5] and goes to hell (193). All who have sought refuge in the Kula Dharma, whether Brāhma*n*as, Ks*h*atriyas, Vaishyas, Shūdras, or Sāmānyas, should ever be worshipped like Devas (194). He who, whilst in the Circle, makes, from pride in supremacy of his caste, distinctions of caste, descends to a terrible hell even though he should have gone to the very end of the Vedānta[6] (195). How within the Circle can there be any fear of sin for Kaulas,[5] who are good and pure of heart, and who are manifestly the very image of Shiva? (196). Vipras[7] and others who are followers of Shiva[8] should, so long as they are within the circle, follow the ordinance of Shiva[9] and the observances prescribed by Him[10] (197).

---

[1] See "Shakti and Shākta" also see p. 239, note 12.

[2] See p. 289, note 13, *ante*.

[3] Tāntrika of the Vīra class. The Vīra is a man of strong impulses and passions. In him the Rajoguṇa is dominant. Tāntrik Sādhanā is mainly aimed at using these impulses and passions in such a way that they help the man in the upward path.

[4] See "Shakti and Shākta".

[5] That is, his duty as a kulasādhaka.

[6] *i.e.*, even though he be a master of Vedāntic doctrine.

[7] 'Here the word is used as the equivalent of the Brāhmanik caste.

[8] Shaiva-mārgin, he who follows the mode of life and worship ordained by Shiva.

[9] Shiva-shāsana.

[10] Shāmbhavāchāra. Emanating from Sambhu (Shiva) both words = beneficent.

Without the Circle each should follow his own calling according to his caste and stage of life,[1] and should discharge his respective duty for the ordered continuance of the world (198). One Japa[2] made by a devout[3] man, when seated within the circle, bears the fruit attainable by the performance of a hundred Purashcharana[4] and by Shavāsana Mundāsana, and Chitāsana[5] (199). Who can describe the glory of the Bhairavī-chakra? Its formation, though but once only frees of all sins (200). The man who for six months worships in such a circle will become a King, he who so worships for a year becomes the Conqueror of Death,[6] and by the daily performance of such worship he attains to Nirvāna (201).

What is the need, O Kālikā! of saying more? Know this for certain, that for the attainment of happiness in this or the next world there is only the Kula-dharma, and no other (202). When the Kali Age is dominant and men are devoid of all Dharma, even a Kaula merits hell by concealment of the Kula-dharma[7] (203).

I have spoken of the Bhairavī-chakra, which is the sole means of attaining enjoyment and final Liberation. I will now speak to Thee, O Queen of the Kaulas! of the Tattva circle. Do Thou listen (204).

The Tattva-chakra is the king of all Chakra. It is also called the Divine Circle.[8] Sādhakas who have not attained

[1] Āshrama.

[2] Repetition of Mantra.

[3] Sudhī (Su=good; dhi=intellect), or Wise.

[4] A Mantra rite. See *ante*, p. 56, n. 8.

[5] These are particular postures—on a corpse, on skulls, and funeral pyre respectively. In the case of Japa done on these the Mantra if of one letter should be said 10,008, if of two letters 8,008, if of three letters 5,008, and of more letters 1,008 times.

[6] M*ri*tyunjaya, a title of Shiva, means "Conqueror of Death".

[7] Gopanāt kuladharmasya kaulo'pi nārakī bhavet.

[8] Divya-chakra: possibly so called because those who join it are of the Divyabhāva.

to a Knowledge of Brahman[1] may not take part in it (205). Only those worshippers of the Supreme Brahman[2] are competent to take part in this circle who have attained to Knowledge of Brahman, who are devoted to Brahman,[3] pure of heart, tranquil,[4] devoted to the good of all beings, who are unaffected by the external world,[5] who see no differences, but to whom all things are the same,[6] who are merciful, faithful to their vows,[7] and who have realized the Brahman[8] (206-207).

O Knower of That![9] only those who, possessing the Knowledge of the Real,[10] look upon this moving and motionless Existence as one with Brahman, such men are competent to take part in this Circle (208). They who regard everything in the Tattva Circle as Brahman,[11] they alone, O Devī, are qualified[12] to take part therein (209). In the formation of this Circle there is no necessity for placing the wine-jar, no lengthy ritual. It can be formed everywhere in a spirit of devotion to Brahman (210). O Dearest One! the worshipper of the Brahma-Mantra[13] and a devout believer in Brahman should be the Lord[14] of the Circle,

[1] Brahma-jna.

[2] Parabrahmopasaka.

[3] Brahma-tatpara—He to whom the Brahman is his highest Aim.

[4] Thānta=Free from attachment and envy (Bhāratī).

[5] Nir-vikāra—Changeless.

[6] Nirvikalpa--no distinction, to whom there is no longer "I" and "Thou," "I" and "This," but to whom all things are the Brahman.

[7] Satya-saṁkalpaka.

[8] Brāhma.

[9] Tattva-jna. Tat=That=Brahman. Tattva=Brahman state or Thatness. Tattva is the real. Tattvajna=the knower of That.

[10] Tattva-vid=Tattva-jna, or Brahma-jna: Knower of the Brahman.

[11] Brahma-maya.

[12] Tattva-chakri*nah*.

[13] Brahma-Mantra—Ong Sachchidekang Brahma.

[14] That is, Chakreshvara.

which he should form of other worshippers who know the Brahman[1] (211). In a beautiful and clean place, pleasant to the worshippers, should be spread beautiful carpets for seats[2] (212). There, O Shivā! the Lord of the Circle should seat himself with the worshippers of Brahman, and have the elements of worship brought and placed in front of him (213). The Lord of the Circle should inwardly recite the Mantra, beginning with the Tāra[3] and ending with the Prā*n*a-bīja,[4] a hundred times, and then pronounce the following Mantra over the elements (214):

MANTRA

The act of offering is Brahman. The offering itself is Brahman. Into the Fire which is Brahman offering is made by him who is Brahman. By him alone, who is absorbed in the offering to Brahman, is unity with Brahman attained[5] (215).

All the elements should be purified by the inward recitation of this Mantra seven or three times (216). Then, with the Brahma-Mantra,[6] making an offering of the food and drink to the Supreme Spirit, he should partake thereof with the other Sādhakas, Knowers of the Brahman (217).

---

[1] That is, who have realized the identity of all things with Brahman.

[2] Vichitra=Beautifully made or coloured-Āsana=mats, carpets.

[3] Oṁ.

[4] That is, Hangsa*h*—the Mantra, "Ong Hangsa*h*." The Hangsa Mantra is called Ajapā. Hangsa is Prā*n*abīja (Life mantra). *Ha* is outgoing breath and Sa=Indrawn breath. Breathing is the Mantra which is constantly said of itself: Hangkāre*n*a Vahir yāti sa*h*-kāre*n*a vishet puna*h*. According to some Sa*h* is the outgoing and Hang the indrawn breath.

[5] Brahmārpa*n*aṁ Brahma-havir Brahmāgnau Brahma*n*ā hutam,
Brahmaiva tena gantavyaṁ Brahma-karma-samādhinā.
vide ante, p. 45.

[6] That is, Oṁ sachchidekang Brahma. The words "Brahma*n*i arpa*n*am astu" are also added.

O Great Queen![1] there is no distinction of caste in the Brahma Circle,[2] nor rule as to place or time or cup.[3] The foolish men who in their ignorance, make distinctions of birth[4] or caste[5] when seated in the Divyachakra go upon the downward path[6] (218-219). And therefore should those excellent worshippers, possessed of the Knowledge that the Supreme Brahman pervades all things, perform the rites of the Tattva Circle with every care for the attainment of religious merit, fulfilment of desire, wealth, and Liberation[7] (220).

Shrī Devī said:

Lord! Thou hast spoken in full of the duties of the householder; it now behoves Thee kindly to speak of the duties appropriate to the ascetic life[8] (221).

Shrī Sadāshiva said:

Devī! the stage of life of an Avadhūta[9] is in the Kali Age called Sannyāsa. Now listen while I tell Thee what should be done (222).

When a man who is versed in Spiritual Wisdom[10] acquires Brahman knowledge, and distaste for all Karma he should seek refuge in the life of an ascetic (223). If,

[1] Maheshāni.

[2] That is, Tattva-chakra.

[3] Pātra (Tarkālamkāra). It may also mean worthiness—that is, there is to be no distinction as to persons deserving, or undeserving, to take part in the Chakra. The expression Desha-kāla-pātra is very often used, and there it means the worth of the person one deals with.

[4] Kula—family, or rank.

[5] Varna.

[6] Adhamā gati.

[7] Dharma, Artha, Kāma, Moksha.

[8] Sannyāsa.

[9] Avadhūtāshrama (Avadhūta + Āshrama). Avadhūta = Ava + dhū + kta = Shaken off, rejected; hence, one who has separated himself from the world (see p. 215, note 1, and "Shakti and Shākta.") Āshrama = hermitage, place of rest or refuge, also stage of life.

[10] Adhyātma-vidyā-nipuna = Ātmavidyābhijna.

however, one abandons an old mother or father, infant children and a devoted wife, or helpless dependents, and adopts the life of a wandering mendicant, one goes to Hell[1] (224). All, whether Brāhma*n*a, Ks*h*atriya, Vaishya, Shūdra, or Sāmānya, are equally entitled to take part in the purificatory ceremony of the Kula ascetic[2] (225).

After the performance of all the duties of a householder, and after satisfying all dependents and others,[3] one should go forth from his house, indifferent, free from desires, with all his senses conquered (226). He who wishes thus to leave his house should call together his kinsmen and friends, his neighbours and men of his village, and lovingly ask of them their permission (227). Having obtained it, and made obeisance to his Is*ht*a-devatā,[4] he should go round his village, and then without attachment, set forth from his house (228). Liberated from the bonds of household life, and immersed in exceeding joy,[5] he should approach a Kula ascetic of divine knowledge, and pray to him as follows: (229)

O Supreme Brahman! all this life of mine has been spent in the discharge of household duties. Do Thou, O Lord! be gracious to me in this my adoption of the life of an ascetic (230).

---

[1] See Bhakta, p. 857. Tarkâlaṁkāra says that Veda teaches that when there arises the sense of detachment in a man he should take the ascetic path (Sannyāsa). The verse may seem to conflict with this. But the answer is that the prohibition there does not apply where there is intense dispassion (Vairāgya such as that of Shuka-deva, Buddha-deva, Chaitanya, Shaṁkarāchārya and other great men like them.

[2] Kulāvadhūta-sangskāra, or purificatory rites upon entrance into life of an Avadhūta.

[3] Literally, persons outside the domestic circle.

[4] The text has Para-devatā, which literally means the Supreme Deva (Brahman), but which is translated by Tarkālangkāra as Abhī*sht*a-devata (or Is*ht*a-devatā), such Devatā being to each worshipper his Supreme Devatā. So far as the Tantra is concerned the Is*ht*adevatā is either the Brahman or Supreme Devī Kālikā.

[5] Paramānanda, or in the Brahman who is Supreme Bliss.

The religious Preceptor[1] should thereupon satisfy himself that the disciple's duties as a householder have all been accomplished, and, on finding him to be of calm mind and full of discernment, initiate him into the second stage (231). The disciple should then, with a well-controlled mind, make his ablutions and say his daily prayer, and then, with the object of being absolved from the threefold debt[2] due to them, worship the Devas, the *Rishis*,[3] and the Pitris (232).

By the Devas are meant Brahmā, Vishnu, and Rudra, with their followers[4]; by the *Rishis*[3] are meant Sanaka and others, as also the Devarshis[3] and the Brahmarshis[3] (233). Listen, whilst I now enumerate the Ancestors[5] who should be worshipped (234). The father, paternal grandfather, paternal great-grandfather, mother, the maternal grandfather, and others in the ascending line, and the maternal grandmother and others in the ascending line (235). At the time of adoption of the life of an ascetic,[6] the Devas and *Rishis* should be worshipped in the East, the paternal ancestors in the South, the maternal ancestors in the West

---

[1] Guru.

[2] The threefold debt is that due to the Devas, *Rishis*, and Pitris for protection, teaching, parentage; the fourth debt (Mānava) is that to men for their help. The first is discharged by Yajna, the second by Brahmacharya, the third by giving birth to children, and the fourth by the performance of the duties of the Āshrama.

[3] *Rishi* according to some comes from that root Drish = to see for they are seers. Vāchaspatya derives it from root Rish = to go, that is, one who has gone to the end of Sangsāra by Jnāna is a *Rishi*. Bhārati classifies them as follows: the highest are the Mānasa-putras of Brahmā who are Sanaka, Sanandana, Sanātana and others. The second class are the Devarshis—Nārada and others. The third class are the Brahmarshis Bhrigu and others. Others give a different classification, Bhrigu is there a Mānasaputra which is then the same as Brahmarshi. Another class of *Rishis* is the Kings who are *Rishis* (Rājarshi).

[4] Bhāratī says that "their followers" should be "his", that is, Rudras followers.

[5] Pitris.

[6] Nyāsakarma=Sannyāsakarma.

(236). Spreading two seats on each of these sides, beginning from the East, and invoking the Devas and others thereto, they should therebe worshipped[1] (237). Having worshipped them in proper form, Pi*nd*as[2] should be offered to each of them separately according to the rules relating thereto. And then, with folded palms, let the disciple thus supplicate the Devas and Ancestors (238):

MANTRA

O Fathers! O Devas! O *Rish*is! O Mothers! be you satisfied. Do you absolve me, about to enter upon the path of Renunciation[3] from all debts[4] (239).

Having thus prayed to be free from all debts, bowing again and again, and being thus freed of all debts, he should perform his own funeral rites[5] (240). The father and paternal grandfather and great-grandfather are one's Self. In offering, therefore, the individual Self to the Supreme Spirit, he who is wise should perform his own funeral rites (241). O Devī! sitting with his face to the North, and invoking the spirits of his ancestors[6] upon the seats which he has prepared for them, he should, after doing them homage, offer the funeral cakes[7] (242). In so offering he should spread Kusha grass with the ends towards the East,[8]

---

[1] That is, the Devas and *Rish*is in the East, the paternal Ancestors in the South, and the maternal Ancestors in the West. And each should be worshipped there separately.

[2] Funeral cakes.

[3] Gu*n*ātīta-pada—literally, beyond the life of attributes.

[4] *Vide* verse 232, *ante*.

[5] Shrāddha in order to realise his severance from the world and to consign the individual Self (Ātmā) into the Supreme Self (Paramātmā).

[6] Who are his Sva-rūpa (Bhāratī).

[7] Pi*nd*a.

[8] For the Devas and *Rish*is. The Pi*nd*as are placed on the Kusha grass.

South,[1] West,[2] and towards the North for himself[3] (243). After completion, according to the directions of the Guru, of the funeral rites, the seeker after Liberation should, in order to purify his heart inwardly, recite the following Mantra a hundred times (244):

MANTRA

Hrīṁ, Let us worship Tryaṁbaka[4] sweet-scented increaser of nourishment. May He free us from the bond of death just as the Urvāruka[5] is freed of its stalk. May He not cast us away from immortality (245).

Then the religious Preceptor[6] should draw a Ma*nd*ala[7] on the altar of a shape in accordance with the form of worship of the I*sh*t*a*-devatā of the Sādhaka,[8] and then place the jar on the altar and commence worship (246). Then the Guru, possessed of Brahma knowledge, should meditate upon and worship the Supreme Spirit in the manner prescribed by Shambhu, and place fire on the altar (247). The Guru should then offer unto the fire so sanctified the oblation according to his own Kalpa,[9] and then make his disciple perform the complete Homa[10] (248). He

---

[1] For the paternal Ancestors.

[2] For the maternal Ancestors.

[3] For his own Shrāddha, offering Pi*nd*a to himself as dead.

[4] Tryambaka, which, according to Tarkālangkāra, means the Father of the three Devas—Brahmā, Vi*sh*n*u, and Rudra—though the *Rig*-vidhāna uses it as an equivalent of Mahādeva (see Chapter v, 210).

[5] A kind of melon (see as to Mantra, *Rig* Veda, vii, 59, 12). See *ante* p. 141.

[6] Guru.

[7] Ma*nd*ala, or diagram which should be that of the I*sh*t*a*-devatā of the disciple.

[8] That is, the shape of the figure will vary with the Devatā worshipped. The Vedī or altar should be made according to the form of worship.

[9] See *post*, under ch. x, v. 139.

[10] Sākalya Homa—the universal oblation or sacrifice to Fire.

should first offer oblation with the Vyāhritis, and then with the vital airs, Prāna, Apāna, Samāna, Udāna, Vyāna [1] (249).

For the destruction of the false belief that the body, whether gross or subtle, is the Ātmā, the Tattva-Homa [2] should be performed, uttering the following words:

MANTRA

"Earth, Water, Fire, Air, Ether; (then) Smell, Taste, Vision, Touch, Hearing; (then) Mouth, Hands, Feet, Anus, and Organ of generation; (then) Ears, Skin, Eyes, Tongue, and Smell; (then) Manas, Buddhi, Ahamkāra, and Chitta; [3] (and lastly) all involuntary acts the functions of the senses and of life, [4]"

He should then say (after each group):

"May all these of mine be purified;" (adding)

"Hrīṁ: [5] I am the Light, may I be free from Desire [6] and from the Sin of Ignorance: Svāhā" [7] (250-254).

Having consigned as oblations into the fire the twenty-four Tattvas and the functions of the body, he who is now actionless should consider his body as dead (255).

---

[1] The Vyāhriti are Bhūh, Bhuvah, Svah. See p. 250, note 1.

[2] *Cf.* Tattva-Shuddhi, Chapter VI, verse 53.

[3] Constituting the mental Self, or Antahkarana.

[4] The twenty-four Tattvas have been grouped under their different heads—(five) Prithivī, Salila, Vahni, Vāyu, Ākāsha; (five) Gandha, Rasa, Rūpa, Sparsha, Shabda; (five) Vāk, Pāni, Pāda, Pāyu, Upastha; (five) Shrotra, Tvak, Nayana, Jihvā, Ghrāna; (four) Manas, Buddhi, Chitta, Ahangkāra.

[5] Or Mahāmāyā. The union of Chit (Shiva) and (Shakti), that is, "May I be like unto the universal Chaitanya united with Hrīng.

[6] Virajā, that is free Rajoguna which is the impulse to action.

[7] Vipāpmā, the "Sin" being Avidyā. This should be repeated at the end of each of the seven groups and an oblation made into Fire. The seven groups include that of the vital airs. This rite resembles Tattva-shuddhi. See p. 155, note 4. *Cf.* A. Avalon's "Serpent Power," v. 40.

Considering his body as dead and devoid of all function, and calling to mind the Supreme Brahman, let him take off his sacred thread (256). He, the knower of the Tattva, should take it from his shoulder, uttering the

MANTRA

Aing Klīng Hangsa*h*

Holding it in his hand while he recites the three Vyāh*ri*tis,[1] ending with Svāha, let him throw it steeped in ghee into the fire (257). Having thus offered the sacred thread as an oblation to the fire, he should, whilst uttering the Kāma Bīja,[2] cut off his crown-lock[3] and take and place it in the ghee[4] (258) [with the]

MANTRA

O Crown Lock! Daughter of Brahman! thou art an ascetic[5] in the form of hair. I am now giving there a place in the Purifying One.[6] Depart, O Devī! I make obeisance to thee (259).

He should then, whilst uttering the Kāma,[7] Māyā,[8] Kūrcha,[9] and Astra[10] Bījas, ending with the Mantra Svāhā,

---

[1] The seven Lokas, which are the seven limbs of Pra*n*ava, are collectively called Mahā-vyāh*ri*ti. Homa, with the first three, is called Vyāh*ri*ti Homa. The seven Lokas are: Bhū*h*, Bhuva*h*, Sva*h*, Maha*h*, Iana, Tapas, Satya. They have their places in the human body. See A. Avalon's "Serpent Power."

[2] Klīng.

[3] See pp. 165, note 4, 205, note 8.

[4] Clarified butter.

[5] Tapasvinī—feminine of Tapas-vin, one who has performed penances.

[6] Pāvaka = the purifier, *i.e.*, Fire.

[7] Klīng.

[8] Hrīng.

[9] Hūng.

[10] Pha*t*.

make the Homa[1] sacrifice of that lock of hair in the sanctified fire (260). The Pit*ri*s, Devas, and Devar*sh*is,[2] as also all acts performed in the worldly stage of life,[3] reside in that lock and have it as their support (261). Therefore the man who renounces the crown-lock and sacred thread after the performance of the oblation becomes one with Brahman (262). The twice-born enter the stage of an ascetic by renunciation of the crown-lock and sacred thread, and the Shūdras and Sāmānyas by the renunciation of the crown-lock[4] only (263). Then he whose crown-lock and sacred thread have been thus removed should make obeisance to the Guru, laying himself full length upon the ground. The Guru should then raise his disciple and say into his right ear: "O wise one! Thou art That.[5] Think within thyself 'I am He'[6] and 'He is I'.[7] Free from all attachments[8] and sense of Self,[9] do thou go as thou pleasest as moved thereto by thy nature"[10] (264-265). The Guru, knower of the Brahman, should then, after removal of the jar and the fire, bend his head in obeisance to the disciple, recognizing in him, his own very Self[11] (266), and say:

---

[1] Shikhā-Homa.

[2] See p. 246, n. 8.

[3] Āshramas. Or "previous stage," if, as according to the Āgama, there are, now, but two stages.

[4] These classes have no thread, which is worn by the "twice-born" only.

[5] Tat tvam asi, the Mahā vākya or Great Word of the Upani*sh*ads.

[6] Hangsa*h* Ahang+Sa*h*, the A being deleted.

[7] So'hang is Hangsa*h* reversed.

[8] Nir-mama—literally, devoid of the sense of mineness.

[9] Nir-ahaṁkāra.

[10] Sva-bhāva, which is now divine.

[11] Atma-svarūpa, which may also mean Brahman, which is the same thing.

"O Thou whose form is this Universe![1] I bow to Thee and to Myself. To Thee and Me I bow again and again. Thou art 'That' and 'That' is Thou. Again I bow to Thee." (267).

The worshippers of the Brahma-Mantra, who know the Tattva and have conquered themselves, attain the stage of an ascetic by cutting off the crown-lock with their own Mantra[2] (268). What need is there of sacrificial[3] or funeral[4] rites or ritual worship[4] for those purified by divine knowledge.[5] For those, who act as they please, there is no fault[6] (269). The disciple, devoid of all contraries,[7] of tranquil mind because desireless, may, as he pleases, roam the earth, the visible image of Brahman (270). He will think of everything, from Brahmā to a blade of grass, as the form of the Brahman,[8] and, meditating upon the Supreme in himself, will forget all name and form (271). Homeless, merciful, fearless, devoid of attachment, claiming nothing as his own, devoid of egoism, the ascetic will move about the earth (272). He is free of all injunctions and prohibitions. He shall not strive to attain what he has not, nor to protect what he has. He knows himself. He is equally unaffected by either joy or sorrow. He is calm, the conqueror of himself, and free from all desires (273). His soul is untroubled even in sorrow, desireless even in prosperity. He is ever joyful,

[1] Vishva-rūpa.

[2] That is, the Brahma-Mantra. See p. 242, note 18.

[3] Yajna.

[4] Shrāddha. Pūjana. On the contrary, disjunctive knowledge is inherent in ceremonial ordinances.

[5] Brahma-jnāna-vishuddhānām: that is, for those whose nature is purified by the knowledge of Brahma tattva.

[6] Pratyavāya, from prati+ava+i=to go downwards; hence detriment, decrease, omission, fault, etc. Such an one acts prompted by the divine light in him.

[7] *i.e.*, devoid of the sense of happiness and misery, etc.

[8] Sat=Truth, Being=Brahman.

pure, calm, independent and unperturbed. He will hurt no living thing, but will be ever devoted to the good of all being. He is free from anger and fear, with his senses under control and without desire. He strives not for the preservation of his body. He is not obsessed by any longing (274-275). He will be free from grief and resentment, equal to friend and foe, patient in the endurance of cold and heat, and to him both honour and disgrace are one and the same (276). He is the same in good or evil fortune, pleased with whatsoever, without effort, he may obtain.[1] He is beyond the three attributes,[2] and ignorance,[3] free of covetousness, and (wealth) he will hoard not[4] (277). He will be happy in the knowledge that, as the unreal universe, which is not Sat, has its support in Sat or the Truth,[5] so the body has the Spirit as its support (278). He attains Liberation by the realization that the Spirit is completely detached from the organs of sense which function each its own way, and is the witness of that which is done[6] (279).

[1] That is, whatever comes to him.

[2] Nis-traiguṇya. Tri-guṇa, the three qualities of manifested being, are Sattva, Rajas, Tamas. The state of possession of the three qualities is Traiguṇya, which is Sakāma and that of freedom from them Nis-traiguṇya.

[3] Nir-vikalpa, which, Bhāratī says, means here devoid of imaginings (Kalpanā). Vikalpa, according to Yoga-Sūtra (i, 9), is a notion conveyed by mere words, but of which there is no corresponding real object.

[4] Asanchayī. A Sanshayī is a person who makes provision for the uncertainty of the future not necessarily in a bad sense. An Asanchayī who leaves the future to take care of itself. So Jesus said "Take no heed for the morrow" which is Yoga practice.

[5] Satya—that is, the Supreme spirit = Paramātmā. Ātmā = Self or Spirit. "Supported" (Upāshritya) for the Self is the support of all (Āshraya). In it which is the eternally enduring Sat are the changing passing forms which are Asat. The term unreal leads to misconception. Asat is the contrary of Sat, and Sat is that which endures. As to "Reality" see "World as Power: Reality" (Ganesh & Co, Madras) by the author.

[6] The intelligent man becomes aware that his spirit is distinct from the body, and in no way dependent on it (see Chapter VIII, Part XII,

The ascetic should not touch any metal, and should avoid calumny, untruth, jealousy, all dallying with woman, and all discharge of seed (280). He should regard with an equal eye worms, men, and Devas. The ascetic wanderer should know that Brahman is in everything that is done (281). He should eat without making any distinction as to the fitness of place, time, or person, food whether it comes from a Vipra[1] or Cha*nd*āla,[2] or from any other source or person whatsoever (282). The ascetic, though passing his time as he pleases, should study the Scriptures relating to the Self[3] and in meditation upon the nature of That[4] (283). The corpse of an ascetic should on no account be cremated. It should be worshipped with scents and flowers, and then either buried or sunk into water (284). O Devī! the inclination of those men who have not attained union with the Supreme Spirit,[5] and who ever seek after enjoyment, is by nature turned towards the path of action[6] (285).

They remain attached to the practice of meditation, ritual worship, and recitation. Let them who are strong in their faith therein know that to be the best for them (286). It is on account of them[7] that I have spoken of various rites for the purification of the heart, and have with the same object devised many names and

of the Chhāndogya Upanis*h*ad). And so, according to the Vedānta—Ātmā sāks*h*ī cheta*h* kevalo nirgu*n*ashcha—"the Spirit is the one, intelligent, attributeless witness," and to its permanency is due, to use Kantian phraseology, the cause of "the synthetic unity of apperception".

[1] *Vide* p. 256, note 6. [2] *Vide* p. 52, note 1.

[3] Adhyātma-shāstra, such as the Vedānta and the like.

[4] Tattva—that is, Brahma-tattva.

[5] Aprāpta-yoga—that is, those who have not got Yoga, that is, Brahma-jnāna.

[6] Karma—that is, Karma-kā*nd*a; in worship, ritualism.

[7] That is, in the case of the Aprāpta-yoga.

forms[1] (287). O Devī! without knowledge of the Brahman and the abandonment of all action, man cannot attain Liberation, even though he performed countless such acts of worship[2] (288). The householder should consider the Kula ascetic, possessed of divine knowledge, to be the visible Nārāyana[3] in the form of man, and should worship Him as such (289). By the mere sight of one who has subdued his passions[4] a man is freed of all his sins, and earns that merit which he obtains by journeying to places of pilgrimage, the giving of alms, and the performance of all vows, penances, and sacrifices (290).

End of the Eighth Chapter entitled "The Dharma and Customs of the Castes and Àshramas."

---

[1] As Shāmkarāchārya, in the Commentary on the Chhāndogya Upanishad, says: "Rites are enjoined on one who is conscious of the nature of actor and recipient, and is subject to the defects of envy, anger, and the rest. Forms of knowledge contribute to the knowledge to the non-dual, and are easy of accomplishment. They are primarily propounded, and first of all adoration with ceremony, inasmuch as, mankind being habituated to ceremony, adoration without it is difficult. In the case, however, of him who has overcome disjunctive knowledge, there is no necessity for religious restraint, observances, or for penance (Tapas)."

[2] Because, as stated, only non-dual knowledge liberates, and duality is inherent in ceremonial worship.

[3] Vishnu as collective humanity.

[4] Yati.

CHAPTER IX

THE TEN SACRAMENTS

THE Adorable Sadâshiva said:

O Virtuous One![1] I have spoken to Thee of the custom and religious duties appropriate to the different castes[2] and stages of life.[3] Do thou now listen whilst I tell Thee of the purificatory rites[4] of the different castes (1). Without such rites, O Devī! the body is not purified, and he who is not purified may not perform the ceremonies relating to the Devas and the Pi*tr*is[5] (2). Therefore it is that men of every caste, commencing with the Vipras,[6] who desire their welfare in this life and hereafter, should, in all things and with care, perform the purificatory rites[7] which have been ordained for their respective castes (3).

The ten purificatory ceremonies[7] are those relating to conception,[8] pregnancy,[9] and birth[10] of the child; the giving

---

[1] Su-vrate—*i.e.*, Thou all of Whose Vratas are good.

[2] Var*n*a.

[3] Āshrama.

[4] Saṁskāra or Sacraments. See "Shakti and Shākta".

[5] The manes of deified ancestors.

[6] Brāhma*n*as is, in ordinary language, the equivalent. Strictly Vipra is one who has learnt the Vedas and Brāhma*n*a is he who knows the Brahman.

[7] Saṁgskāra (described in this Chapter).

[8] Jīva-seka, or Garbhādhāna.

[9] These are Pungsavana and Sīmantonnayana.

[10] Jāta-karma.

of its name,[1] its first view of the sun,[2] its first eating of rice,[3] tonsure,[4] investiture,[5] and marriage[6] (4).

The Shūdras and mixed[7] castes have no sacred thread, and but nine purificatory ceremonies; for the twice-born classes there are ten (5). O Beautiful Lady;[8] all observances, whether they be daily,[9] occasional,[10] or voluntary,[11] should be performed according to the injunctions of Shambhu[12] (6). O Dear One! I have already, in My form as Brahmā, spoken of the rules appropriate to the purificatory and other observances (7), and of the Mantras appropriate to the various purificatory and other observances, according to the differences in caste (8).

In the Satya, Tretā, and Dvāpara Ages,[13] the Mantras, O Kālikā! were in their application preceded by the Pranava[14] (9); but in the Kali Age, O Supreme Devī! the decree of Shaṁkara is that man do perform all rites with the aid of the same Mantras, but preceded by the Māyā Bīja[15] (10). All Mantras in the Nigamas,[16] Āgamas,[16] Tantras,[16] Saṁhitās[16] and Vedas, have been spoken by Me.

[1] Nāma-karana.

[2] Nishkrāmana.

[3] Anna-prāshana or Annāshana.

[4] Chūdā-karana.

[5] Upanayana.

[6] Udvāha.

[7] Sāmānya, or Varṇa-saṁkāra (Bhāratī).

[8] Varārohā—also a high-born woman.

[9] Nitya.

[10] Naimittika.

[11] Kāmya, rites performed with a specific object (Kāma). That is to give something particularly desired.

[12] Shiva.

[13] See p. 88, n. 5.

[14] Ongkāra (see *ibid.*).

[15] Hrīng.

[16] See "Principles of Tantra."

Their employment,[1] however, varies according to the Ages (11). For the benefit of men of the Kali Age, men bereft of energy and dependent for existence on the food they eat, the Kula doctrine, O Auspicious One! is given (12).

I will now speak to Thee in brief of the purificatory and other rites, suitable for the weak men of the Kali Age, whose minds are incapable of continued effort (13). Kusha*n*dikā[2] precedes all auspicious ceremonies. I shall, therefore, O Adored of the Devas! speak firstly of it. Do Thou listen (14). In a clean and pleasant spot, free from husks and charcoal,[3] let the wise one make a Square,[4] the sides of which are of one cubit's length (15). Then draw in it three lines from the West to East (of the Square). Let him then sprinkle water over them, uttering meanwhile the Kūrcha[5] Bīja. Then Fire should be brought to the accompaniment of the Vahni Bīja[6] (16). The Fire, when so brought, should be placed by the side of the Square the Sādhaka mentally saying the Vāgbhava Bīja[7] (17). Then, taking up a piece of burning wood with the right hand from the Fire, he should put it aside as the share of the Rāks*h*asas,[8] saying:

MANTRA

Hrīng: Salutation to the Raw-meat eaters:[9] Svāhā (18).

---

[1] Prayoga, or application.

[2] From Kusha + ka*n*dikā. The rite by which the Fire is purified for all the different kinds of Homa.

[3] So that the ground be smooth for the making of the sthandila.

[4] Stha*n*dila is a Vedī or low altar square in shape.

[5] Hūng.

[6] Rang.

[7] Aing.

[8] The share of the Rāks*h*asas (Demonic beings) should be put away on the South of the Stha*n*dila (Bhāratī).

[9] Hrīng Kravyādebhyo Nama*h*: Svāhā.

The worshipper, lifting up the consecrated Fire with both hands, should place it in front of him on the three lines (above mentioned), inwardly reciting the while the Māyā Bīja[1] before the Vyāhritis (19). Grass and wood should then be thrown upon the Fire to make it blaze, and two pieces of wood should be smeared with ghee and offered as an oblation to it. Thereafter Fire[2] should be named according to the object of the rite,[3] and then meditated upon as follows (20):

Dhyāna

Ruddily effulgent like the young Sun, with seven tongues and two crowned heads of matted hair, seated on a goat, and holding, in his hand his weapon Shakti[4] (21).

Having so meditated upon the Carrier of oblations,[5] He should be thus invoked with joined palms (22).

Mantra[6]

Hrīṁ: Come, O Carrier of Oblations to all the Immortals! Come with the Munis and Thy followers,

---

[1] That is, Hrīng Bhūh Bhuvah Svah: Hrīng to the terrestrial, atmospheric, and celestial worlds. As the Vaidika Sādhaka says, "Oṁ Bhūh Bhuvah Svah," the Tāntrika here substitutes for Oṁ the Bīja of Mahāmāyā, or Hrīng, and contemplates Her as the manifested Active Brahman pervading the three worlds which are Its revealed form.

[2] Dhananjaya.

[3] The *Shat*-karma-dīpikā says that, in Pūrnāhuti, Fire is called Mrida; in Shānti-kriyā, Vara-da; in Pushti-kriyā, Bala-da; in Abhichāra, Krodha; in Vashī-karana, Kāma-da; in Vara-dāna, Chūdaka: in Laksha-homa, Vahni; in Koti-homa, Hutāshana.

[4] The Shakti is the name of the weapon of Agni, as Pāsha is that of Varuna.

[5] Havya-vāhana, or Havya-vaha—Fire. Carries the oblation to the Devas.

[6] Hrīng ehi ehi sarvāmara-havya-vāha munibhih sva-ganaih saha adhvarang raksha raksha: Namah; Svāhā.

and protect the sacrifice. I make obeisance to Thee: Svahā (23).

Having thus invoked Him, the worshipper should say, "O Fire! this is Thy place,"[1] and then worship Him, with appropriate offerings. He should then worship the seven licking Tongues[2] of Fire: Kālī,[3] Karālī,[4] Manojavā,[5] Sulohita,[6] Sudhūmra-var*n*ā,[7] Sphuliṁginī,[8] and Vishvanirūpi*n*ī,[9] (24-25). Then, O Great Devī! the sides of the Fire should be thrice sprinkled with water from the hand, beginning from the East and ending at the North (26). Then the sides of the Fire, from the South to the North, should be thrice sprinkled with water, and following that the articles of sacrifice should be thrice sprinkled (27). Then spread Kusha grass on the sides of the square, beginning with the East and ending with the North. The ends of the blades of grass on the North should be turned towards the North, and the rest of the grass should be placed with its ends towards the East (28). The worshipper should then proceed to the seat placed for the Brahmā,[10] keeping the Fire on his right, and, picking up with his left thumb and little

---

[1] Vahno ayang te yoni*h*.

[2] Sapta-jihva = seven-tongued—a name of Fire.

[3] "The Black One," which brings about the end at the destined time (Mārka*n*deya Purā*n*a, chap. xcix, Hymn to Agni).

[4] "The Dreadful One." The cause of the great Dissolution of the world (*ibid.*).

[5] "Swift as thought," because of its quality of lightness (*ibid.*).

[6] "The Ruddy One" (very red), which accomplishes the desires of created things (*ibid.*).

[7] "Who is of a smoky colour," which destroys sickness amongst breathing things (*ibid.*).

[8] "Having sparks of Fire." It is altogether shapeless. The flame which grants prosperity (*ibid.*).

[9] "That which makes manifest the Universe, bestows blessings on all breathing things" (*ibid.*). The Purā*n*a reads Vishvā or Vishva-s*r*ij.

[10] A Brāhma*n*a who is the Brahmā or chief priest at the ceremony.

finger a blade of Kusha grass from the seat prepared for Brahmā, he should throw it along with the remaining blades of Kusha grass on the South side of the Fire, after uttering the

MANTRA

Hrīm : Parāvasu be expelled ![1] (29-30).

(The performer of the sacrifice should then say to the Brahmā):

O Brahman![2] Lord of Sacrifices! be thou seated here. This seat is made for thee.

The Brahmā, saying "I sit," should then sit down, with his face turned towards the North (31).

After worshipping the Brahmā with scent, flowers, and the other articles of worship, let him be supplicated thus (32):

MANTRA

O Lord of Sacrifices! protect the sacrifice. O Brihaspati![3] protect this sacrifice. Protect me also, the performer of this sacrifice. O Witness of all acts![4] I bow to thee (33).[4]

---

[1] Nirastah Parāvasuh. Parāvasu is the Hotā or Sacrificial priest of the Asuras. His presence is an obstruction. See Shatapatha Br., 1.5.1-23. The Bhāshya-kāra Guna-vishnu says that this is the place near the sacrificial Fire where preside the Rākshasas, enemies of the sacrificial rite.

[2] The Priests, or Ritviks, were in Vedic times divided into four classes—Adhvaryu, Hotā, Udgātā, and Brahmā. The first and second performed the rites, the third sang the hymns, and the fourth (who was a Master of the Shāstras) superintended and rectified any errors, and averted any ill-effects. He was known as Brahmā.

[3] Guru of the Devas said in praise of Brahmā.

[4] Karmasākshin. This is a request to the Brahmā to see that the ritual be correctly performed.

Brahmā should then say, "I protect," and if there is no Brahmā present, then the performer of the sacrifice should, for the success of the sacrifice, make an image with Darbha grass of the Vipra,[1] and himself say this (34). The worshipper should then invoke the Brahmā, saying, "O Brahman, come here, come here!" and, after doing honour to him by offering water for washing his feet and the like,[2] let him supplicate him, saying, "So long as this sacrifice be not concluded, do Thou deign to remain here," and then make obeisance to him (35). He should then sprinkle the space between the North-East corner[3] of the fire and the seat of Brahmā three times with water taken in his hand, and should thereafter sprinkle the fire also three times, and then, returning the way he went, take his own seat. Let him then spread on the North side of the Square some Darbha grass with the ends of the blades towards the North (36-37). He should then place thereon the articles necessary for the sacrifice, such as the vessel[4] (filled with water) for sprinkling, and the vessel[5] containing ghee, sacrificial fuel,[6] and Kusha grass. He should also place the sacrificial ladle[7] and spoon[8] on the Darbha grass, and purify them

---

[1] Or Brāhma*n*a. The Darbha or Kusha grass is used for making images on other occasions also thus if a man is lost and not heard of for 12 years his nearest kinsmen make an image of him with this grass and then cremate it when he is taken to be dead for all purposes.

[2] Pādya—the first offering to the guest, water to wash his feet, arghya, etc.

[3] Īshāna.

[4] Proksha*n*ī-pātra.

[5] Ājya-sthālī.

[6] Samidh, or samit-wood.

[7] Sruk.

[8] Sruva.

by sprinkling water over them, and then, regarding them with a celestial gaze,[1] uttering the

MANTRA

Hrāng Hrīng Hrūng (38-39).

Then, with his right knee touching the ground, let him put ghee into the spoon with the ladle, and, thinking of the object of his desire let him offer three oblations saying the

MANTRA

Hrīm: To Vishnu: Svāhā[2] (40).

Taking again ghee in the same way, and meditating upon Prajāpati, oblations should be offered with ghee streaked across the fire from the corner of Agni[3] to that of Vāyu[4] (41). Taking ghee again and meditating on India,[5] let him offer oblations from the corner of Nairṛita[6] to that of Īshāna[7] (42). O Devī! oblations should thereafter be offered to the North, the South, and to the middle of the fire, to Agni,[8] to Soma,[9] and to Agni and Soma together (43). Upon that three oblations should be offered, uttering the

---

[1] That is, without winking or moving the eyelids. Divya-*drishti* = Celestial gaze, for the Deva's eyes are steadfast in regard, and winkless.

[2] Hrīng Vi*shn*ave Svāhā.

[3] South-East.

[4] North-West.

[5] Purandara—a name of Indra.

[6] South-West.

[7] North-East.

[8] Fire.

[9] Moon. As to Agni and Soma who share the same Havi*h* see note 8, next page. Nārāyaṇa in his Comm. on Hangsa Up. says Agni = Haṁ = Pumān and Soma = Sa*h* = Prak*r*iti.

MANTRAS

Hrīṁ Salutation to Agni,[1]
Hrīṁ Salutation to Soma,[2]
Hrīṁ Salutation to both Agni and Soma,[3]

respectively. Having performed these (preliminary) rites,[4] the wise one should proceed to that prescribed for the Homa sacrifice which is to be performed (44). The offering of oblations (as above described, commencing with the three offerings made to Vi*sh*nu and ending with the offering to Agni and Soma), is called Dhārā Homa (45).

When making any offering, both the Deva, to whom the same is being made, and the thing offered should be mentioned, and upon the conclusion of the principal rite the priest should perform the Svi*sh*t*i-k*ri*t[5] Homa (46). O Beautiful One! in the Kali Age there is no Prāyashchitta Homa.[6] The object thereof is attained by Svi*sh*t*i-k*ri*t and Vyāh*ri*ti[7] Homas (47). O Devī! (for Svi*sh*t*i-k*ri*t Homa) ghee should be taken in manner[8] above mentioned, and, whilst mentally reciting[9] the name of Brahmā, oblation should be offered with the following:

---

[1] Hrīng Agnaye Nama*h*.

[2] Hrīng Somāya Nama*h*.

[3] Hrīng Agnī-*sh*omābhyāng Nama*h*. These are two Vedik divinities who jointly eat one oblation. Shruti says: "Agnī*sh*omīyaṁ pashum ālabheta."

[4] That is, offering of Āhuti.

[5] Su-i*sh*t*i-k*ri*t=good-sacrifice-making, or that which makes the sacrifice good or faultless. This Homa is done to make the sacrifice Samīchīna that is free from defect. The following is an example of the Mantra: Hrīng Vi*sn*nave Svāhā: havir idam Vi*sh*nave (Hrīng to Vi*sh*nu Svāhā: this offering is to Vi*sh*nu). The principal rite is called Prak*ri*takarma.

[6] Prāyashchitta Homa is an expiatory oblation.

[7] Vyāh*ri*ti—Bhūh, Bhuva*h*, and Sva*h* (see p. 179, note 9).

[8] That is, with the Sruv and Sruk (Bhāratī).

[9] Literally, remembering.

MANTRA

Hrīṁ: O Deva of the Devas! do Thou make faultless any shortcomings that there may be in this rite, and anything done needlessly, whether by negligence or mistake: Svāhā (48-49).

Then oblation should be offered to Fire, thus:

MANTRA

Hrīṁ: O Fire! Thou art the Purificator[1] of all things. Thou makest all sacrifices propitious,[2] and art the Lord of all. Thou art the Witness of all sacrificial rites, and the Insurer of their success. Do Thou fulfil all my desires: Svāhā (50).

The sacrificing priest, having thus concluded the Svi*sh*ti-k*r*it Homa, should thus (pray to the Supreme Brahman):

MANTRA

O Supreme Brahman! O Omnipresent One! for the removal of the effects of whatsoever has been improperly done in this sacrifice, and for the success of the sacrifice, I am making this Vyāh*r*iti Homa.

Saying this, he should offer three oblations with the three

MANTRAS

Hrīṁ: Bhū*h* Svāhā,
Hrīṁ: Bhuva*h* Svāhā,

---

[1] Pāvana.

[2] Svi*sh*ti-k*r*it.

Hrīṁ: Svah Svāhā,[1]

Thereafter offering one more oblation with the

MANTRA

Hrīṁ: Bhūh, Bhuvah: Svah Svāhā,[2]

the wise priest should, jointly with the giver of the sacrifice, offer the Complete Oblation[3] (51-53). If the latter has performed the sacrifice without a priest, he should offer the oblation himself. This is the rule in Abhisheka[4] and other observances (54). The Mantra for the Complete Oblation[5] is—

MANTRA

Hrīṁ: O Lord of Sacrifice! may this sacrifice of mine be complete. May all the Devatās of sacrifices be pleased and grant that which is desired:[6] Svāhā (55).

The wise one[7] should then, with the giver of the sacrifice, stand up, and, with a well-controlled mind, offer oblations with fruit and *pān* leaves, uttering the while the aforesaid Mantra (56).

---

[1] Salutation is made to the Terrestrial, atmospheric, and Celestial planes.

[2] This is to all three planes.

[3] Pūrnāhuti. The last offering (āhuti) which completes the sacrifice (Yagna).

[4] Abhisheka—primarily means bathing, then sprinkling and initiating: here initiatory ceremonies.

[5] Pūrnāhuti.

[6] After having uttered Māyā Bīja, say: "Yajna-pate! may my yajna be complete, may the Devatās be pleased, may they grant adequate fruits!" The Mantra ends with the Shakti of Vahni (Svāhā).

[7] Matimān: by this the Yajna-sādhaka is meant (Bhāratī): the same meaning is given for learned one (Vidvān) in next verse.

The learned one should, after offering the Complete Oblation, perform Shānti-karma.[1] Taking water from the sprinkling vessel, he should with Kusha grass sprinkle it over the heads of the persons present (57), reciting the

MANTRA

May the water be every friendly to me, may Water be like a medicament to me, may Water preserve me always; Water is Nārāya*n*a[2] Himself (58). O Waters! as you grant happiness so do you make sure our food.[3]

Having sprinkled water over the heads of those present with these two Mantras, a few drops of this water should be sprinkled on the ground (59).

MANTRA

To those who are ever hostile to me, and to those to whom we are ever hostile, may Water be their enemy and engulf them (60).

Sprinkling a few drops of water in the North-East[4] corner the while repeating the above-mentioned Mantra, the Kusha grass should be put away, and with joined palms supplication should be made to the Carrier of Oblations[5] as follows (61):

---

[1] Shānti-karma is that which is done at the end of the rite: the sprinkling of the assembly, the Mantras, the saying of "peace," "peace," "peace" (Shānti), etc. He who recites the Shānti Mantra does so for the benefit of the persons present, over whose heads he sprinkles the water (asperges).

[2] Vish*n*u.

[3] This last portion is Vedic, and the first line of the Mantra cited in full in verse 150: Āpo hi *shth*ā mayobhuva stā na ūrje dadhātana.

[4] Īshāna.

[5] Fire.

MANTRA

O Carrier of Oblations! do Thou grant unto me understanding,[1] knowledge,[2] strength, intelligence,[3] wisdom,[4] faith, fame, fortune, health, energy, and long life[5] (62).

Having thus prayed to Fire,[6] he should, O Shivā! be bidden to depart with the following (63):

MANTRA

Sacrifice! do thou depart to the Lord of Sacrifice.[7]
Eater of Oblations! do thou depart to the Sacrifice itself
Lord of Sacriffce! do Thou depart to Thine own place and fulfil my desires (64).
Oh Agni, forgive me: Svāhā.

After saying this Mantra an oblation of curds should be made and the fire should be moved to the South[8] (65).

Give a present[9] to the Brahmā,[10] and, after bowing to him respectfully, bid him go, and, with the ashes adhering to the ladle, the officiating priest should then make a mark[11] on his own forehead and on that of the giver of the

---

[1] Buddhi=Shāstrādi-tattvajnāna—capacity to understand the essence of the Shāstras (Bhāratī).

[2] Vidyā—Ātma-jnāna, Self-knowledge.

[3] Medhā=Dhāraṇāvatī dhi—retentiveness of the mind.

[4] Prajnā=Sārāsāra-viveka-naipuṇya—the power of discriminating the essential, spiritual wisdom.

[5] Tejas—vigour.

[6] Vīti-hotra—a name of Fire. The Eater of oblations, or the Carrier of oblations.

[7] Lord of Sacrifice—*i.e.*, Vishṇu. Do thou reach the place of Vishṇu

[8] The fire is moved by pouring curd on the North of the fire thus extinguishing the Fire on the North when there is fire on the South.

[9] Dakshiṇā.

[10] That is, the Brāhmaṇa who looked after the ritual.

[11] Tilaka.

sacrifice, uttering the Mantra "Hrīng, Klīng Be propitious in every way"[1] (66-67). Then a flower should be placed on the head with the

MANTRA

By the grace of Indra, of Agni, of the Maruts, Brahmā, the Vasus, the Rudras and Prajāpati, may there be peace, may there be prosperity.[2]

Thereafter the giver of the sacrifice should, as his means allow, offer a gift[3] for the success of the sacrifice[4] and for the Kushaṇḍikā rite (68-69).

I have spoken to Thee, O Devī! of Kushaṇḍikā, which is the groundwork of all auspicious ceremonies, and which all Kula worshippers should with care perform at the commencement thereof (70).

O Auspicious One! I will now speak to Thee of Charukarma, in order to insure that rites done in those families, in which the cooking of Charu[5] is a traditional practice in the performance of all rites, may be attended with success[6] (71). The pot for cooking Charu should be made of either copper or mud (72). In the first place, the articles should be consecrated according to the rules prescribed in Kushaṇḍikā, and then the pot of Charu should be placed in front of the worshipper (73). After careful examination to see that it is without holes and of a good surface, a blade of

---

[1] Hrīng Klīng Sarva-shānti-karo bhava. This is addressed to the Tilaka.

[2] To be recited when placing the flower on the head (*vide* next verse).

[3] Dakshina, given to the officiating priest.

[4] That is, of the Homa and of the object (Prakṛita-karma) for which the preliminary Kushaṇḍikā is done.

[5] Charu (see *post*). Charu = Devatārthang paramānnam (Bhārati).

[6] Hariharānanda Bhāratī says that this refers to Ṛitusaṁskāra and other purificatory rites. Charu is made with milk and rice.

Kusha grass[1] of the length of a Prādesha[2] should be put in the pot (74). The rice should be placed near the Square,[3] and then, O Adored of the Devas! the names of such of the Devatās as are to be worshipped in each particular ceremony should be uttered in the dative case, followed by the words "to please Thee,"[4] and then "I take," "I place in the pot," and "I put water in,"[5] and then put four handfuls of rice in the name of each Devatā in the pot, and pour water over it (75-77). O Virtuous One![6] milk and sugar should be added thereto, as is done in cooking. The whole should then be well and carefully cooked over the consecrated fire (78). And when he is satisfied that it is well cooked and soft, the sacrificial ladle, filled with ghee, should be let intoit (79). Thereafter, placing the pot on Kusha grass on the northern side of the Fire, and adding ghee to the Charu three times, the pot should be covered with blades of Kusha grass (80). Then, putting a little ghee into the sacrificial spoon, a little Charu should be taken from the pot. With it Jānu Homa[7] is done (81). Then after doing Dhārā Homa,[8] oblations should be made with

---

[1] Pavitra, or the pure thing. Kusha is so called because Garu*d*a placed the celestial nectar (Am*r*ita) on blades of Kusha grass.

[2] Prādesha is the distance between the top of the thumb and the fourth finger outstretched.

[3] Stha*nd*ila.

[4] Tvājus*ht*am.

[5] The meaning of this Mantra is: I take this handful of rice in the name of (the Deva); I put it in a pot in the name of (the same Deva), etc. After the name of the Devatā in dative say it is for him or his pleasure and then say the rest.

[6] Su-vrate. This word is by some translated "Virtuous".

[7] The Homa is so called because it is performed with the right knee (Jānu) touching the ground.

[8] The ghee is poured from one corner of the Stha*nd*ila (the altar on which Homa is done) to the next but one—thus, from N.E. to S.W., from N.W. to S.E., from S.W. to N.E., and from S.E. to N.W.

the Mantras of the Devas, who are directed to be worshipped in the principal rite (82). Completing the principal Homa after performance of Svi*sh*ti-k*ri*t Homa,[1] expiatory Homa[2] should be performed, and the rite thus completed (83). In the sacramental[3] and consecratory[4] ritual this is the method to be observed. In all auspicious ceremonies it should be followed for the complete success thereof (84).

Now, O Mahāmāyā![5] I will speak of Garbhādhāna[6] and other rites. I will speak of them in their order, beginning with *Ri*tusaṁskāra.[7] Do Thou listen (85).

After performing his daily duties and purifying himself, (the priest) should worship the five Deities—Brahmā, Durgā, Ga*n*esha, the Grahas,[8] and the Dikpālas[9] (86). They should be worshipped in the jars[10] on the East side of the square, and then the sixteen Māt*ri*kās[11]—namely, Gourī and others—should be worshipped in their order (87). The sixteen Māt*ri*kās are Gaurī, Padmā, Shachī, Medha, Sāvitrī, Vijayā, Jayā, Deva-senā, Svadhā, Svāhā, Shānti, Pu*sh*ti,

[1] See p. 199, verse 45.

[2] Prāyashchittātmaka—that is, the Vyāh*ri*ti Homa, which, according to this Tantra, is the equivalent of Prāyashchitta.

[3] Saṁskāra.

[4] Prati*sh*th*ā*.

[5] The Devī as the Great Māyā.

[6] See next note.

[7] The rite (purification of the menses) precedes the Garbhādhāna or Puberty rite, which takes place on the fifth day after their appear, ance. Garbhādhāna is, literally, the placing of the seed in the womb, which is preceded by the rite of that name.

[8] The nine Planets. As to the Tattva of these see Tantrarāja (Tantrik Texts, Vol. 12) Chs. 85 and 86.

[9] See p. 178, note 2. According to the Dharmma-Saṁgraha ("Anecdota Oxoniensia," Vol. i, part v, verses 8, 9)—a collection of Buddhist technical terms—there are four, eight, ten, or fourteen Dikpālas, or Loka-pālas, or Regents of the Quarters.

[10] That is, five jars placed there for these Devas (Bhāratī).

[11] Some read us Pu*sh*ti and Dh*ri*ti for Shānti and K*sh*amā.

Dh*ri*ti, Ks*h*amā, the worshipper's own tutelary Devatā,[1] and the family Devatā[2] (88).

MANTRA

May the Mothers that cause the joy of the Devas come and bring all success to weddings, Vratas,[3] and Yajnas.[4] May they come upon their respective carriers,[5] and in all the fulness of their power,[6] in their benign aspect, and add to the glory of this festival (89-90).

Having thus invoked the Mothers and worshipped them to the best of his powers, the priest should make five or seven marks with vermilion and sandal paste on the wall, at the height of his navel, and within the space of a Prādesha[7] (91).

The wise one should then, whilst breathing the three Bījas—Klīṁ, Hrīṁ, and Shrīṁ—pour an unbroken stream of ghee from each of the said marks, and there worship the Deva Vasu[8] (92). The wise man, having thus made the Vasu-dhāra[9] according to the directions which I have given, and having made the Square[10] and placed the Fire thereupon, and consecrated the articles requisite for Homa,

---

[1] Ātma-devatā

[2] Kula-devatā.

[3] Devotions.

[4] Sacrifices.

[5] The Vāhana, or vehicle, of the Deva, as Garuda of Vis*h*nu, etc.

[6] Yāna-shakti-samārū*dh*ā: This compound word may also mean "seated on their respective vehicles and attended by their respective Shaktis".

[7] See p. 170, note 2.

[8] There are eight Vasus. Chedi-rāja, or Indra, is here referred to (see Bhakta, 399).

[9] That is, the mark like the lower half of an ellipse, within which the five or seven marks are placed across it in a straight line, and from which the ghee is poured (see verse 92).

[10] Stha*n*dila.

should then cook the excellent Charu (93). Charu which is cooked in this (*Ri*tu-saṁskāra) is called Prājāpatya, and the name of this Fire is Vāyu. After concluding Dhārā Homa,[1] the rite of *Ri*tu-saṁskāra should be begun (94). Three oblations of Charu should be offered with the

MANTRA

Hrīṁ : To Prajāpati : Svāhā.[2]

Then one oblation should be offered with the following (95):

MANTRA

May Vi*shn*u grant thee power to conceive. May Tva*sht*ā give the form or limbs (of the child). May Prajāpati sprinkle[3] it, and may Dhātā give thee power to bear[4] (96).

This oblation should be made with either ghee or Charu, or with ghee and Charu, and should be offered meditating upon the Sun, Vi*shn*u, and Prajāpati (97).

[1] See p. 270, note 8.

[2] Hrīng Prajā-pataye Svāhā.

[3] *i.e.*, with my seed.

[4] Vi*shn*ur yoning kalpayatu, Tva*sht*ā rūpā*n*i pingshatu,
Āsinchatu Prajāpatir Dhātā garbhang dadhātu te.

"May Vi*shn*u make thy Yoni capable of offspring, may Tva*sht*ā give the visible shapes, may Prajāpati sprinkle, may Dhātā support thy uterus." This Mantra is in B*ri*hadāra*n*yaka Upani*sh*ad, Adhyāya VI, Brāhma*n*a IV, verse 21, and the Mantra in verse 98 follows this—the two, in fact, make one Mantra. Garbhādhāna is ordinarily performed by the husband after *Ri*tusnāna. The Bhavadeva Paddhati gives the meaning of the first Mantra as follows: O wife! may Vāsudeva make thy Yoni capable of bearing (Prasava-samarthāng karotu) may Tva*sht*ā make the forms (Rūpā*n*i) manifest (Pingshatu = Prakāshayatu). May Prajāpati sprinkle into the Yoni as much seed as will lead to conception. May Dhātā (Āditya) hold (Dadhātu = dhārayatu) thy womb (Garbham).

MANTRA

May Sinībālī[1] give support to thy womb, may Sarasvatī[2] give support to thy womb, may the two Ashvins,[3] who wear garlands of lotuses, give support to thy womb[4] (98).

Meditating upon the Devīs Sinībalī and Sarasvatī and the two Ashvins, excellent oblations should be offered with the above Mantra, followed by Svāhā (99). Then oblation should be offered to the sanctified Fire, meditating upon Sūrya[5] and Vishnu with the

MANTRA

Klīng, Strīng, Hrīng, Shrīng Hūm : Grant conception to her,[6] who desires a son : Svāhā (100).

Then, meditating upon Vishnu, oblations should be offered with the following:

MANTRA

As this widely extended Earth[7] ever carries a full womb, do thou likewise carry for ten months until delivery. Svāhā (101).

---

[1] The Vedic Devatā of conception. Garbham dhehi, *i.e*, hold the womb. Sinībālī is the Tithi preceding Amāvasyā (new moon day) or the digit of the moon seen on the Chaturdashī day as it enters the new moon period.

[2] Brāhmī, Shakti of Brahmā.

[3] Celestial Physicians.

[4] In the *Bri*hadāra*n*yaka Upani*sh*ad, from which these Mantras are taken, they are said by the husband desirous of offspring when he places his mouth on hers. The Bhavadeva Paddati gives the meaning as follows : Oh Sinībālī ! hold the womb of this wife of mine (that is remove her barrenness) Oh Sarasvatī ! hold the womb. O wife ! may the two lotus-garlanded Devas the Ashvins impregnate thee.

[5] The Sun.

[6] Here the name of the wife is given in the dative case.

[7] P*ri*thivī. She is the mother of all and always giving forth Her offspring. Be like Her.

Meditating upon the Supreme Vi*sh*nu, let a little more ghee be thrown into the Fire with the following:

MANTRA

Vi*shn*u! do Thou in Thy excellent form put into this woman an excellent son: Svāha (102).

And, uttering the following:

MANTRA

Klīng, Hrīng, Klīng, Hrīng, Strīng, Hrīng, Klīng, Hrīm let the husband touch his wife's head[1] (103). Then the husband, surrounded by a few married women having sons,[2] should place both hands on the head of his wife, and, after meditating on Vi*shn*u, Durga, Vidhi,[3] and Surya,[4] place three fruits on (the cloth of) her lap. Thereupon he should bring the ceremony to a close by making Svi*sht*i-k*ri*t oblations and expiatory rites[5] (104-105). Or the wife and husband may be purified by worshipping Gaurī and Shangkara in the evening, and by giving oblations to Sun (106).

I have now spoken of *R*itu-saṁskāra. Now listen to that relating to Garbhādhāna (107). On the same night,[6] or on some night having a date of an even number,[7] after

---

[1] Literally, let him, after reciting Māyā Vīja, preceded and followed by Kāma, and Badhū preceded and followed by Māyā, and then Kāma and Māyā, touch her head.

[2] Pati-putra-vatī—a woman whose husband and children are living.

[3] Brahmā.

[4] The Sun.

[5] To remedy mistake or error during the ceremony.

[6] The night of the day the Ritu-sangskāra has been done.

[7] Yugma—that is, a "coupled night," or a night on a date with an even number, such as the second or fourth of a month, as distinguished from uneven dates, such as the first or third. It is believed that union on an even date is productive of a son, and on an uneven date of a

the ceremony, the husband should enter the room with his wife, and, meditating on Prajāpati, should touch his wife and say:

MANTRA

Hrīṁ: O Bed! be thou propitious for the begetting of a good offspring of us two (108-109).

He should then with the wife get on the bed, and there sit with his face towards the East or the North. Then, looking at his wife, let him embrace her with his left arm, and, placing his right hand over her head, let him make Japa of the Mantra on the different parts of her body (as follows) (110): Let him make Japa over the head of the Kāma Bīja[1] a hundred times; over her chin of the Vāgbhava Bīja[2] a hundred times; over the throat of the Ramā Bija[3] twenty times; and the same Bīja a hundred times over each of her two breasts (111). He should then recite the Māyā Bīja[4] ten times over her heart, and twenty-five times over her navel. Next let him place his hand on her member,[5] and recite jointly the Kāma[6] and Vāgbhava Bījas[7] a hundred and eight times, and let him similarly recite the same Bījas over his own member[8] a hundred and eight times; and then, saying the Bīja "Hrīṁ," let him open

daughter. Here the even number is as counted from the day of the *Ritu-sangskārā*; the second, fourth, or sixth day, and so on, counted from that day.

[1] Klīng.

[2] Aing.

[3] Shrīng.

[4] Hrīng.

[5] Yoni.

[6] Klīng.

[7] Aing.

[8] Liṁga.

her member,[1] and let him go into her with the object of begetting a child (112-113). The husband should, at the time of the spending of his seed, meditate on Brahmā, and, discharging it below the navel into the Raktikā-nā*d*i in the Chitku*nd*a,[2] he should at the same time recite the following (114-115):

MANTRA

As the Earth is pregnant of Fire, as the Heaven is pregnant of Indra, as Space is pregnant of the Air it contains, so do thou also become pregnant[3] (by this my seed). (116).

If the wife then, or at a subsequent perid, conceived, the householder, O Maheshvarī! should perform in the third month after conception the Puṁsavana rite (117). After the performance of his daily duties, the husband should worship the five Devas[4] and the heavenly Mothers, Gaurī and others,[5] and should make the Vasudhārā[6] (118).

The wise one should then perform B*ri*ddhi Shrāddha,[7] and, as aforementioned, the ceremonies up to Dhārā-Homa,[8] and then proceed to the Puṁsavana rites (119). The Charu

[1] Vikāshya māyayā yoniṁ.

[2] The Chitku*nd*a is described to be that part of the uterus "which is below the navel". (Bhāratī.) The Vaidyaka-ratna-mālā speaks of the Raktikā-nā*d*i as the one which is of the colour of blood.

[3] Yathāgninā sagarbhā bhūr, dyaur, yathā Vajra-dhāri*n*ā,
Vāyunā dig garbha-vatī, tathā garbha-vatī bhava.

[4] Brahmā and the others (H. Bhāratī), that is Vi*sh*nu, Rudra, Īshāna, Sadāshiva.

[5] The Māt*ri*kās: see p. 271.

[6] *Vide ante*, p. 272, note 9.

[7] Performed on all auspicious occasions, the same as Ābhyudayika Shrāddha.

[8] See p. 270, note 28.

prepared for Puṁsavana[1] is called "Prājāpatya," and the fire is called Chandra[2] (120). One grain of barley and two Māsha[3] beans should be put into curd made from cow's milk, and this should be given to the wife to drink, and, whilst she is drinking it, she should be asked three times: "What is that thou art drinking, O gentle one?" (121). The wife should thrice make answer: "Hrīng: I am drinking that which will cause me to bear a son." In this manner the wife should drink three mouthfuls of the curd (122). The wife should then be led by women whose husbands and children are living[4] to the place of sacrifice, and the husband should there seat her on his left and proceed to perform Charu-Homa (123).

Taking a little Charu as aftermentioned,[5] and uttering the Māyā Bīja[6] and the Kūrcha Bīja,[7] he should offer it as oblation, with the following:

MANTRA

Do Thou destroy, do Thou destroy all those Bhūtas,[8] Pretas,[9] Pishāchas,[10] and Vetālas,[11] who are inimical to

---

[1] See p. 256, note 9.

[2] Moon.

[3] A kind of dhal.

[4] A woman none of whose children have died is Jīvatsutā. A blessing to a woman's Jīvat-vatsā bhava—may you never lose a child; a Mritavatsā or woman who has lost a child cannot join in the rite.

[5] *i.e.*, in a sacrificial spoon (Bhāratī).

[6] Hrīng.

[7] Hūng.

[8] "Those who have been," the departed ghosts.

[9] "Those who have gone before," technically applied to those disembodied souls whose obsequial rites have not been performed.

[10] Filthy and malignant spirits.

[11] Spirits occupying the corpses of the dead.

conception and destroyers of the child in the womb, and of the young. Do Thou protect (the child in) the womb: Svāhā (124-125).

Whilst reciting the above Mantra, meditate upon Fire, as Rakshoghna,[1] and meditating on Rudra and Prajāpati,[2] offer twelve oblations (126).

He should then offer five oblations with the

MANTRA

Hrīṁ: To Chandra:[3] Svāhā.

And then, touching his wife's heart, let him say inwardly the Bījas Hrīng and Shrīng one hundred times (127). He should then perform Svishti-krit Homa[4] and Prāyashchitta,[5] and complete the ceremony. Panchāmrita[6] should be given in the fifth month of pregnancy (128). Sugar, honey, milk, ghee, and curd in equal quantities make Panchāmrita. It is needful for the purification of the body (129). Doing Japa of the Bījas Aing, Klīng, Shrīng, Hrīng, Hūng, and Lang, five times over each of the five ingredients, the husband, after mixing them together, should cause his wife to drink it[7] (130).

Then, in the sixth or eighth month, the Sīmantonnayana[8] rite should be performed. It may, however, be performed any time before the child is born (131). The wise one should, after performing the rites as aforementioned,

---

[1] Destroyer of Rākshasas.

[2] Brahmā.

[3] The Moon—a name of Fire.

[4] See p. 264, n. 5.

[5] See p. 264, n. 6. That is, by Vyāhriti Homa.

[6] Five nectars, described in the next Shloka.

[7] In the fifth month.

[8] See p. 256, note 9,

do Dhārā-Homa,[1] and sit with his wife on a seat, and offer three oblations to Vishnu, Sūrya, and Brahmā, saying :

MANTRA

To Vishnu : Svāhā, to the Effulgent One :[2] Svāhā, to Brahmā :[3] Svāhā (132).

Then, meditating on Chandra,[4] let him offer seven oblations to Soma[4] into Fire under his name of Shiva (133). Then, O Shivā ! he should meditate upon the two Ashvins, Vāsava,[5] Vishnu, Shiva, Durgā, Prajāpati,[6] and offer five oblations to each of them (134). The husband should after that take a gold comb, and comb back the hair on each side of the head and tie it up with the chignon[7] (135). He should, whilst so combing the hair, meditate upon Shiva, Vishnu, and Brahmā, and pronounce the the Māyā Bīja[8] (136) and the

MANTRA

O Wife ! thou auspicious and fortunate one, thou of auspicious vows ! do thou in the tenth month, by the grace

---

[1] See p. 270, verse 8.

[2] Bhāsvat, or the Sun.

[3] Dhātri.

[4] Moon.

[5] Indra.

[6] Brahmā.

[7] In the old days the women used to dress the hair so as to divide it and let it hang on each side. The hair on each side was called Chūrna-kuntala. The portion tied up at the back was called Baddhakesha. During pregnancy the side hair used to be tied up with the Baddhakesha (ed. Bhakta, p. 411).

[8] Hrīng.

of Vishva-karma,[1] be safely delivered of a good child. May thou live long and happy. This comb, may it give thee strength and prosperity!

Saying this Mantra, the ceremony should be completed with Svish*t*i-k*ri*t Homa[2] and other rites (137-138). Immediately after the birth of the son the wise one should look upon his face and present him with a piece of gold, and then in another room perform Dhārā Homa[3] in the manner already described (139). He should then offer five oblations to Agni, Indra, Prajāpati,[4] the Vishvadevas,[5] and Brahmā (140).

The father should thereafter mix equal quantities of honey and ghee in a bell-metal[6] cup, and, doing Japa of the Vāgbhava Bīja[7] over it a hundred times, made the child swallow it (141). It should be put into the child's mouth with the fourth finger of the right hand, with the following:

---

[1] The divine Architect, son of Brahmā.

[2] See p. 264, n. 5.

[3] See p. 264, n. 6.

[4] Prajāpati is usually an epithet of Brahmā. It is also an epithet of Vishva-karmā, the divine Architect, also of Vish*n*u. Here Prajāpati is used for Vish*n*u.

[5] Vishva-devas. According to the Mahābhārata, they are the following: (1) Vasu, (2) Satya, (3) Kratu, (4) Daksha, (5) Kāla, (6) Kāma, (7) Dh*ri*ti, (8) Kuru, (9) Puru-ravas, and (10) Mādrava. The Sm*ri*ti says in Ish*t*i-shrāddha, Kratu and Daksha; in Nāndī-mukha, Satya and Vasu; in Naimittika, Kāla and Kāma; in Kāmaja, Dhuri and Lochana; and in Pārva*n*a, Puru-ravas and Mādrava are mentioned. From the above it will be seen that Dhuri and Lochana of the Sm*ri*ti do not occur in the first list, which mentions Dh*ri*ti and Kuru. Some say they are tweleve, thus avoiding the difficulty. The Amarakosha says that the Vishva-devas are a class of Ga*n*a-devatās, and the Shabda-Kalpa-Druma under this head quotes Ja*t*ā-dhara, who gives the Ādityas (12 in number), the Vishva-devas (10), the Vasus (8), the Tush*i*tas (36), the Bhāsvaras (64), the Vāyus (49), the Mahārājikas (220), the Sādhyas (12), and the Rudras (11).

[6] Kāṁsya, from Kaṁsa.

[7] Aiṁ.

MANTRA

Child, may thy life, vitality,[1] strength, and intelligence ever increase (142).

After performing this rite for the longevity of the child, the father should give him a secret name, by which at the time of the investiture with the sacred thread he should be called (143). The father should then finish the Jāta-karma[2] by the performance of the usual expiatory and other rites, and then the midwife should with firmness cut the umbilical cord (144). The period of uncleanliness[3] commences only after the cord is cut; therefore all rites relating to the Devas and the Pitṛis[4] should be performed before the cord is cut (145). If a daughter is born, all the acts as above indicated are to be performed, but the Mantras are not to be said. In the sixth or eighth month the boy should be given the name by which he is usually known (146). At the time of naming of the child the mother should, after bathing him and dressing him in two pieces of fine cloth, come to and place him by the side of her husband, with his face towards the East (147). The father should thereupon sprinkle the head of the child with water taken up upon blades of Kusha grass and gold, saying at the time the following:

MANTRA

May Jāhnavī, Yamunā, Revā, the holy Sarasvatī, Narmadā, Varadā, Kuntī,[5] the Oceans and Lakes—all

---

[1] Varchas = Vigour, Vitality, Energy, Firmness.

[2] Birth-rite (see p. 256, note 10).

[3] Ashaucha. The period of uncleanliness after the birth of a child, which begins after the cutting of the umbilical cord, is called Shubha Āshaucha (auspicious ashaucha), as opposed to the inauspicious uncleanliness after a death.

[4] Ancestors.

[5] Sacred Indian Rivers. Jāhnavī is a name of Gaṁgā.

these bathe thee for the attainment of Dharma, Kāma, and Artha [1] (149).

Oṁ: O Waters! inasmuch as you are the grantors of happiness therefore do you make sure our food and do you enable us to see the Beautiful (150) [2].

Oṁ, O Waters! you are most beneficent do you make us participators therein like unto a loving Mother (151) [3].

Oṁ, O Waters! we go to enjoy of that essence [4] fully. Do you produce enjoyment for us therein whereby all are pleased (152) [5].

The wise one should sprinkle water over the child, with the three preceding Mantras, and then, as aforesaid consecrate the fire and perform the rites leading up to Dhārā Homa in the manner already described, and then should offer five oblations (153). He should make the oblation to Agni, then to Vāsava,[6] then to Prajāpati,[7] then to the Vishva-Devas,[8] and then to Brahmā, into Vahni under his name of Pārthiva (154).

---

[1] Spiritual Merit, Fulfilment of Desire and Wealth—that is, May thou be pious and wealthy, and may all your desires be gratified.

[2] Ra*n*āya = Rama*n*īyāya = Parabrahma*n*e. The meaning of the Mantra is—"O waters! inasmuch as you lead to happiness, do you therefore unite us with (give us) the means of sustenance in this world, and unite us with the most excellent Brahman in the next" (Bhāratī).

[3] The meaning is—"O waters! as mothers, prompted by their affection, give enjoyment of good things to their children, equally so do thou grant us enjoyment of your beneficent Rasa" (Bhāratī).

[4] Rasa is the essence of the water which brings satisfaction. This may be physical but it is more than that. The feeling of pleasure produced by the water is itself a form of the Supreme Bliss of which water is a form.

[5] The meaning of the Mantra is—"O waters! give us our enjoyment in that Rasa whereby you please the whole Universe, that we may get Satisfaction therein" (Bhāratī).

[6] Indra.

[7] Here, Vi*sh*nu.

[8] See Agni Purā*n*a, Ga*n*abheda Adhyāya; also p. 281, note 5.

Then, taking the son in his lap, the wise father should speak into his right ear an auspicious name[1]—one that is short, and that can easily be pronounced (155). After whispering the name three times into the son's ear, he should inform the Brāhmaṇas who are present, of it, and then conclude the ceremony with Svishṭikrit Homa and the other concluding rites (156)[2].

For a daughter there is no Nishkramaṇa, nor is Briddhi Shrāddha necessary. The wise man performs the naming, the giving of the first rice, and tonsure of a daughter without any Mantra (157).

In the fourth or sixth month after birth, the Nishkramaṇa Saṁskāra ceremony of the son should be performed (158).

After performing his daily duties, the father should, after bathing, worship Gaṇesha, and then bathe and adorn his son with clothes and jewels, and, placing him in front of himself, pronounce the following (159).

MANTRA

Brahmā, Vishṇu, Shiva, Durgā, Gaṇesha, Bhāskara[3] Indra, Vāyu, Kuvera, Varuṇa, Agni, and Brihaspati:[4] May They always be propitious to this child, and may They always protect him when he goes forth (from the house) (160).

Having said this, he should take the child in his arms, and, preceded by vocal and instrumental music, and surrounded by his rejoicing kinsmen, take the son out of

[1] The names given to Indian children are names of or words denoting attributes of Deity or such names as raise in the mind of the worshipper a pious thought. Similarly amongst Catholics a saint's name is always given.

[2] Taking the child outside the home to see the Sun.

[3] *i.e.*, Sūrya, the Sun.

[4] Guru of the Devas.

the house (161). Going a little distance, he should show the Sun to the child, with the following (162):

MANTRA

Oṁ: Yonder is the Eye (of Heaven) who excels even Shukra[1] in his effulgence, who is beneficent even to the Devas. May we see him a hundred years. May we live a hundred years[2] (163).

Having shown the Sun to his child, the father should return to his own house, and, after making offering[3] to the Sun, feast his kinsmen (164).

O Shivā! in the sixth or eighth month either the father's brother or the father himself should give the first rice to the child[4] (165). After worshipping the Devas and purifying fire as aforementioned, and duly performing the ceremonies leading to Dhārā Homa, the father should make five oblations into Fire, under his name of Shuchi, to each of the following Devas: He should make the oblations first to Agni, next to Vāsava, after him to Prajāpati,[5] then to the Vishva-devas, and then the fifth Āhuti to Brahmā (166-168). He should then meditate upon the Devī Annadā,[6] and, after giving Her five oblations in Fire, place the son, adorned with clothes and jewels, in his lap, and give him

---

[1] The planet Venus.

[2] This should be the average age of man in the Kali Age, though, owing to the common violation of natural laws, it is the exception rather than the rule. The text says 'one hundred autumns' (Sharada*h* shataṁ). The reference seems to be to the autumnal festivities held all over India.

[3] Arghya.

[4] *Vide ante*, p. 257, note 3.

[5] Here, Vi*sh*nu. See *ante* pape 283, Verse 154.

[6] A form of the Devī, as the Giver of food.

Pāyasa,[1] either in the same or in another room (169). The Pāyasa should be put into the child's mouth five times, uttering the Mantras for making oblations to the five vital airs[2]; and after that a little rice and curry should be put into the child's mouth (170). The ceremony should be brought to a close by the blowing of conches and horns[3] and other music, and by performing the concluding expiatory rite.[4]

I have done speaking of the rice-eating ceremony. I shall now speak of the tonsure ceremony.[5] Do Thou listen (171).

In the third or fifth year, according to the custom in the family, the tonsure of the boy should be performed for the success of the future sacramental rites[6] of the boy (172). The wise father should, after concluding the preliminary rites beginning with the worship of the Devas and leading up to Dārā Homa, place on the north side of the Fire, called Satya, a mud platter filled with cow-dung, tila-seeds, and wheat, also a little lukewarm water and a keen-edged razor (173-174).

The father should place the son on his mother's lap, the mother sitting on her husband's left, and, after saying the Varuṇa Bīja[7] ten times over the water, rub the hair of the boy's head with lukewarm water. He should then tie the hair with two blades of Kusha grass

---

[1] Rice boiled in milk, with sugar and a little ghee.

[2] To Prāṇa, Svāhā, to Apāna, Svāhā, to Samāna, Svāhā, to Udāna, Svāhā, to Vyāna, Svāhā—that is, Salutation to the five Airs or functions of vital force as to which see author's "Serpent Power" and "World as Power:—Life".

[3] Tūrya.

[4] *i.e.*, Vyāhṛiti Homa.

[5] Chūḍākaraṇa.

[6] Saṁskāra.

[7] Vang.

into a knot, uttering meanwhile the Māyā Bīja[1] (175-176). Then, saying the Māyā and Lakshmī Bījas[2] three times, he should cut off the knot with the steel razor and place it in the hands of the child's mother (177). The boy's mother should then take it with both hands and place it in the platter containing the cow-dung, and the father should then say to the barber: "Barber, do thou at thine ease proceed with the shaving of the boy's hair, Svāhā." Then, looking at the barber, he should make three oblations, into Vahni[3] who is named Satya, to Prajāpati[4] (178-179). After the boy has been shaved by the barber he should be bathed and adorned with clothes and jewels, and placed near the fire on the left of his mother, and the father should, after performance of Svi*shti*-k*ri*t Homa and the expiatory rites,[5] offer the Complete Oblation[6] (180-181). Then, uttering the following:

MANTRA

Hrīṁ: O Child! may the Omnipresent Creator of the Universe grant thee well-being,

he should pierce the ears of the boy with gold or silver needles (182). He should then sprinkle the child with water, uttering the

MANTRA

O Waters! As You grant, (as aforementioned)[7];

[1] Hrīng.

[2] Hrīng and Shrīng.

[3] Fire.

[4] See p. 281, note 4. After the worship of Fire oblation is offered into it to Prajāpati.

[5] Prāyashchitta by means of Vyāh*ri*ti Homa.

[6] Pūr*n*āhuti followed by Shānti, Tilaka (made of ashes mixed with ghee) and Dak*shi*nā.

[7] The Mantra as in verse 59.

and, after performing Shānti Karma[1] and other rites, and making presents,[2] bring the ceremony to a close (183).

The sacramental rites from Garbhādhāna to Chūdākarana are common to all castes. But for Shūdras and Sāmānyas[3] they must be performed without Mantras (184).

In the case of the birth of a daughter, all castes are to perform the rites without Mantras. In the case of a daugher there is no Nishkramana (185).

I will now speak of the Sacred Thread Ceremony[4] of the twice-born classes, by which the twice-born become qualified for performing rites relating to the Devas and Pitris (186).

In the eighth year from conception, or the eighth year after birth, the boy should be invested with the sacred thread. After the sixteenth year the son should not be invested, and one so invested is disqualified for all rites (187).

The father versed in Shāstra should, after finishing his daily duties, worship the five Devas, as also the Mātris, Gaurī, and others, and make the Vasudhārā[5] (188). He should thereafter perform Briddhi Shrāddha[6] for the satisfaction of the Devas and Pitris,[7] and perform the rites, ending with Dhārā Homa,[8] as directed in the performance of Kushandikā[9] (189).

The boy should early in the morning be given a little to eat; then his head, with the exception of the crown lock,

[1] Rite that produces tranquillity and averts evil.

[2] Dakshinā.

[3] *i.e.*, mixed castes (see Chapter VIII, verses 4-6).

[4] Upavīta-kriyā, Upanayana.

[5] See *ante*, p. 272, note 9.

[6] *Vide ante*, p. 277, note 7. Also called Ābhyudayika Shraddhā.

[7] The manas.

[8] *Vide ante*, p. 264, verse 45.

[9] *Vide ante*, p. 269, verse 70.

should be shaved, and after that he should be well bathed and decked with jewels and silken clothes (190).

The boy should then be taken to the Chhāyā-ma*nd*apa [1] near Fire under his name of Samudbhava, and there made to sit on a clean seat to the left (of his father or Guru) (191). The Guru should say: "My son, do thou adopt Brahmachārya." [2] The disciple should say respectfully: "I do adopt it" (192). The Preceptor should then with a cheerful mind give two pieces of Kā*sh*āya [3] cloth for the long life and strength of mind of the gentle boy (193). Then when the boy has put on the Kā*sh*āya cloth, he should, without speaking, give him a knotted girdle [4] made of three strings of Munja or Kusha grass (194). On that the boy should say, "Hrīng, may this auspicious girdle prove propitious"; and, saying this, and putting it round his waist, let him sit in silence before the Guru (195).

Mantra

This sacrificial thread is very sacred; B*ri*haspati of old first wore it. Do thou wear this excellent white sacrificial thread which contributes to prolong life. May it be for thee strength and courage (196).

With this Mantra the boy should be given a sacrificial thread made of the skin of the black buck,[5] as also a staff [6]

[1] *i.e.*, a clean space with an awning over it.

[2] Literally, Brahman-path. Here the Āshrama so called which is that of the chaste student life. To be the Dīk*sh*ā Guru is the privilege of the father who may depute the office to another Brāhma*n*a.

[3] A cotton cloth of brick-red colour, as worn by Sannyāsīs. One piece is for Dhoti or loin cloth and the other is Chādar or cloth for upper body.

[4] Mekhalā. Munja grass is used to make ropes.

[5] Worn by Sannyāsis until as Avadhūtas they burn the sacred thread.

[6] Da*nd*a.

made of bamboo, or a branch of Khadira, Palāsha, or Ks*h*īra tree (197). When the boy has put the sacred thread round his neck and holds the staff in his hand, the Guru should three times recite the

MANTRA

"O Waters! you are," (rest as aforementioned),[1]

preceded and followed by Hrīng, and should sprinkle the boy with water taken with Kusha grass, and fill the joined palms of the latter with water (198). After the boy has offered the water to Sūrya, the Guru should show the boy the Sun, and recite the

MANTRA

"Yonder is the Sun," (as aforementioned)[2] (199)

After the boy has viewed the Sun, the Guru should address him as follows: "My Son! place thy mind on my observances. I bestow upon thee my disposition.[3] Do thou my child follow the observances with an undivided mind. May my word contribute to thy well-being" (200). After saying this, the Guru, touching the boy's heart, should ask, "My Son! what is thy name?" and the boy should make reply: ". . . Sharmā,[4] I bow to thee" (201). And to the question of the Guru, "Whose Brahma-chārī[5] art thou?" the disciple will reverently answer: "I am thy Brahma-chārī" (202). The Guru should

[1] The Mantra is at verse 59.

[2] The Mantra is at verse 168.

[3] Chitta.

[4] *i.e.*, I am (so-and-so) Sharmā. Whenever an orthodox Brāhma*n*a is asked his name, he should give his first name, followed by Sharmā. A Ks*h*atriya should say Varmā, a Vaishya, Bhūti, and a Shūdra, Dāsa.

[5] Student disciple of the second Āshrama.

thereupon say: "Thou art the Brahma-chārī of Indra, and Fire is thy Āchārya."[1] Saying this, the good Guru should consign him to the protection of the Devas (203). "My Son! I give thee to Prajāpati, to Savitri, to Varuna, to Prithivī, to the Vishva-devas,[2] and to all the Devas. May they all ever protect thee" (204).

The boy should thereafter go round the sacrificial fire and the preceptor, keeping both upon his right, and then resume his own seat (205). The Guru, O Beloved! should then, with his disciple touching him, offer five oblations into Fire named Samudbhava to Five Devas (206)—namely, Prajāpati,[3] Shakra,[4] Vishnu, Brahmā, and Shiva (207). When the oblations are offered into Fire, under his name of Samudbhava, the names of each of the Devas should be pronounced in the dative, preceded by Hrīng and followed by Svāhā. Where there is no Mantra mentioned, this method is to be followed in all cases (208). After this, oblation should be offered to Durgā, Mahālakshmī, Sundarī, Bhuvaneshvarī, and to Indra and the other nine regents of the quarters,[5] and Bhāskara[6] and the eight planets (209). The name of each of these should be mentioned whilst the

[1] Āchārya is instructor. Fire is that because by doing Homa into Fire the boy makes progress in spiritual knowledge.

[2] *Vide ante*, p. 281, note 5.

[3] Prajāpati—Lord of Creatures—an epithet in the Veda originally applied to Savitri, Soma, Tvashtri, Hiranya-garbha, Indra, and Agni; afterwards the name of a separate Deva presiding over procreation (Manu, xii, 121), and the bestower of progeny and cattle. Prajāpati is sometimes invoked as the Creator, and sometimes as one of the thirty-three *Rishis*. It is also an epithet of the mental sons of Brahmā, who, according to Manu (i, 34), are Marīchi, Atri, Angiras, Pulastya, Pulaha, Kratu, Vashishtha, Prachetas or Daksha, Bhrigu, and Nārada. Some say that there are seven Prajāpatis (the first seven), and others three Prajāpatis (the last three).

[4] Indra.

[5] Dikpālas (see p. 178, note 2; p. 271, note 9).

[6] Sūrya, the Sun. There are nine "Planets" (Nava-graha), including the Sun.

offering of oblations is made. The wise Guru should then cover the boy with cloth, and ask him, who is desirous of attaining Brahma-chārya: "What is the Āshrama[1] thou desirest, my son! and what is thy heart's desire?" (210). The disciple should thereupon hold the feet of the Preceptor, and, with a reverent mind, say: "First instruct me in Brahmavidyā,[2] and then in that of the householder" (211).

O Shivā! when the disciple in this manner has beseeched his Guru, the latter should three times whisper into his disciple's right ear the Pra*n*ava,[3] which contains all the Mantras in itself, and should also utter the three Vyāh*ri*tis,[4] as also the Sāvitrī[5] (212). Sadhāshiva is its *Rishi*, the metre is Tris*ht*up,[6] the presiding Deva is Sāvitrī, and its object is the attainment of final Liberation (213). The Gāyatrī Mantra is:

MANTRA

Oṁ: Let us contemplate the wonderful Spirit of the Divine Creator. May He direct our understanding.[7] Oṁ.

[1] State of life.

[2] That is, the Gāyatrī Mantra.

[3] Oṁ.

[4] Bhū*h*, Bhuva*h*, Sva*h*.

[5] The Gāyatrī Mantra (see *post*). The word Gāyatrī means that which saves the Gāyat (singer, reciter). It is called Sāvitrī, because the world is produced from It. Sū=bring forth. See Author's "Garland of letters".

[6] A form of metre.

[7] Oṁ : Tat savitur vare*n*yam bhargo devasya dhīmahi

Dhiyo yo na*h* prachodayāt : Oṁ.

' Bhāratī says that before doing Japa of the Gāyatrī, *Rishi*-nyasa should be done: on the head, to Sadāshiva the *Rishi*, obeisance; on the mouth, to the Metre Tris*ht*up, obeisance; on the head, to Sāvitrī the presiding Devatā thereof, obeisance. The employment (Viniyoga) is for the attainment of Liberation.

The Guru should then explain the meaning of the Gāyatrī (214-215). By the Tāra,[1] which contains three letters—*i.e.*, A, U, and M—the Paresha[2] is meant. He is the Protector, Destroyer, and Creator. He is the Deva[3] Who is beyond (the manifestation of) Prak*ri*ti[4] (216).

This Deva is the Spirit of the three worlds,[5] containing in Himself the three qualities.[6] By the three Vyāh*ri*tis,[7] therefore, the all-pervading Brahman[8] is expressed (217). He Who is indicated by the Pra*n*ava[9] and the Vyāh*ri*tis is also known by the Sāvitrī[10]. Let us meditate upon the great inner Light,[11] of Savitā,[12] the Creator

---

[1] Oṁ.

[2] *i.e.*, the Paramātma considered as Parama Puru*sh*a in relation to Prak*ri*ti (Bhāratī).

[3] Deva here means He in whom are the functions of illumination (Dīpti) and the like, Who functions as Creator, Destroyer and Maintainer. Destroyer = Hartā = Saṁhāraka (derived from root Hri = to take). God does not destroy in our sense but He takes back the world which he has created (*ibid.*).

[4] Prak*ri*te*h* para*h* : Bhāratī says that Para = Dūra (distant from) = Uttama, highest. That is, though Prakriti-svarūpa is Himself, He is beyond Her manifestation. Or as Shiva-Shakti are One and equal (in their Svarūpa) Para may mean "other aspect of or counterpart" of Shiva. The latter is one aspect and Prak*ri*ti or Shakti another aspect of the one Brahman.

[5] Trilokātmā. Or regions—Bhū*h*, Bhuva*h*, Sva*h*.

[6] The Gu*n*as—Sattva, Rajas, and Tamas.

[7] Bhū*h*, Bhuva*h*, Sva*h*.

[8] Vishvamaya.

[9] The Deva Who is indicated by the Pra*n*ava is—He Who is Trilokasvarūpa, the Reality which is beyond and in the form of the three worlds, Who contains the three Gu*n*as. Therefore, the three Vyāh*ri*tis or three Lokas indicate Him.

[10] That is, the Gāyatrī Mantra. The Paramātmā who is designated by Tāra and the Vyāh*ri*tis is also designated by the Sāvitrī (Bhāratī).

[11] Antar-gatang mahad-varchcha*h*, which is the Bharga (Spirit of the Sun). Omnipresence and Radiance are qualities of Deva (*ibid.*).

[12] Though Savitā and Bharga might appear to be distinct, They are in reality one (*ibid.*) when rightly considered (Paramārtha-chintāyām).

of and in the form of the world[1], the Supreme, eternal[2], all pervading Truth, adored by the self-controlled. May the Bharga[3] Who witnesseth all, and is the Lord of all,[4] direct, and keep engaged our mind, intelligence, and senses towards and in those acts, which lead to the attainment of Dharma, Ārtha, Kāma and Moksha[5] (218-220).

O Devī! the excellent Guru, having thus instructed the disciple, and explained to him the Divine Wisdom,[6] should direct him in the duties of a householder (221). "My Son! do thou now discard the garments of a Brahmachārī,[7] and honour the Devas and Pitris[8] according to the way revealed by Shambhu"[9] (222). Thy body is sanctified by the instructions thou hast received in Divine Wisdom. Do thou, now that thou hast reached the stage of a householder, engage thyself in thy duties appropriate

---

[1] Jāgad-rūpa, which is His form as effect.

[2] Sanātana or that which has neither beginning nor end.

[3] Bharga is the Āditya Deva in the solar circle possessed of various forms of greatness (Māhātyam).

[4] Sarvasākshīsha: that is, who sees and directs all Karma both good and evil (Bhāratī).

[5] Piety or right conduct, Wealth, Fulfilment of Desire, and Liberation.

> Tāra-vyāhriti-vāchyo yah Sāvitryā jneya eva sah
> Jagadrūpasya savituh sangsrashtur divyato vibhoh
> Antargatam mahadvarchcho varanīyang yatātmabhih
> Dhyāyema tat parang satyang sarvavyāpi sanātanam
> Yo bhargah sarvasākshisho mano-buddhīndriyāni nah
> Dharmārtha-kāma-mokshheshu prerayed viniyojayet.

[6] Brama-vidyā contained in the Gāyatrī.

[7] Student. A Brahmachārī is a student who lives a celibate life with his preceptor after his initiation until he qualifies to enter upon the life of a householder.

[8] Forefathers.

[9] Shiva.

to that mode of life[1] (223). Put on two sacred threads,[2] two good pieces of cloth, jewels, shoes, umbrella, fragrant garland and paste" (224). The disciple should then take off his Kāshāya cloth and his sacred thread of black-buck skin and his girdle, and give them and his staff, begging-bowl, and also what has been received by him in the shape of customary[3] alms, to his Guru.

He should then put on two sacred threads and two fine cloths,[4] and wear a garland of fragrant flowers, and perfume himself, and thereafter sit in silence near the Guru, who should address him as follows (225-227).

"Conquer the senses, be truthful and devoted to the acquisition of Divine Knowledge and the study of the Vedas, and discharge the duties of a householder according to the rules prescribed in the Dharma Shāstras"[5] (228).

Having thus instructed the disciple, the Guru should make him offer three oblations into Fire in the name of Samudbhava with the

MANTRA

Hrīm : Earth, Firmament, Heaven : Om.[6]

---

[1] Āshrama.

[2] *i.e.*, two white cotton-threads. At the first part of the ceremony a thread of black-buck skin is put round the Brahma-chārī, which is afterwards removed. The cotton-thread has three strands. One is called Kāya-da*n*da, another Vāg-da*n*da, and the third Mano-da*n*da—that is, controller of body, speech, and mind. They are also emblematic to the three Gu*n*as—Sattva, Rajas, and Tamas.

[3] The custom is that immediately after the investiture the friends and relatives should give him money as alms.

[4] *i.e.*, he puts on a fine dhoti, or loin-cloth, and wraps an equally fine chuddur, or sheet, round the upper part of his body.

[5] The moral and legal Scriptures.

[6] Literally, with the three Bhū*h*, Bhuva*h*, Sva*h*, preceded by Māyā, and followed by Pra*n*ava—that is, Hrīng, Bhūr Bhuva*h* Sva*h*, Oṁ, or the three planes—terrestrial, atmospheric, and celestial.

He should then himself perform Svish*t*i-k*r*it Homa,[1] and then, O Gentle One! he should bring the investiture ceremony to a close by offering the Complete Oblation[2] (229-230).

Beloved! all nine ceremonies, from the Jīvaseka[3] to Upanayana[4] are performed by the father alone.

The ceremony relating to marriage may be performed either by the father or by the bridegroom himself (231). The pious man should on the day of marriage perform his ablutions and finish his daily duties, and should then worship the five Devas and the Divine Mothers, Gaurī and others, and making the Vasu-dhārā,[5] do B*r*iddhi Shrāddha[6] (232). At night the betrothed bridegroom, preceded by vocal and instrumental music, should be brought to the Chhāyā-ma*n*dapa[7] and seated on an excellent seat (223). The bridegroom should sit[8] facing the East,[9] and the giver of the bride should face the west, and the latter, after rinsing his mouth, should, with the assisting Brāhma*n*as, ask for the words "Svasti" and "*R*iddhi"[10] (234).

---

[1] See p. 264, verses 48 *et seq.*

[2] Pūr*n*āhuti.

[3] *Vide* v. 4.

[4] *Ibid.*

[5] *Vide* p. 272, note 9.

[6] *Vide* p. 308, n. 2.

[7] *i.e.*, the pandal (see *ante*).

[8] At the time of the actual ceremony.

[9] Ordinarily a giver sits with face to East, and the person to whom the gift is given sits with his face to the North. But in the case of the gift of the bride in marriage the rule is as in the text.

[10] *i.e.*, one party says, Svasti-vachana ("Be it well"), to which the others reply *R*idhyatām ("May it be well done"): words of benediction and prosperity. The giver of the bride first asks for Punyāha-vachana —that is, he calls upon those present to declare that the time is auspicious. Upon their so declaring, the giver then asks for *R*iddhi-vachana —that is, he calls upon them to express their wish that the marriage

The giver of the bride should ask after the bridegroom's welfare, and ask also his permission to honour him, and upon receiving his answer should honour him by the offer of water for his feet and the like [1] (235), and saying, "I give this to you," [2] let him give the bridegroom the gifts. The water [3] should be given at the feet and the oblation [4] at the head (236). Articles for the rinsing of the mouth should be offered at the mouth, and then scents, garlands, two pieces of good cloth, beautiful ornaments and gems, and a sacred thread should be given to the bridegroom (237). The giver should make Madhuparka by mixing together curd, ghee, and honey in a bell-metal cup, and place it in the hand of the bridegroom with the words, "I give you" (238). The bridegroom, after taking it, should place the cup in his left hand, and, dipping the thumb and ring fingers of his right hand into the Madhuparka, should smell it five times, reciting meanwhile the Prā*n*āhuti Mantra,[5] and then place the cup on his north. Having offered the Madhu-parka, the bridegroom should be made to rinse his mouth (239-240).

The giver of the daughter should then, holding Dūrvā- and Ak*sh*ata,[6] touch the right knee of the bridegroom with his hand, and then, first meditating on Vi*shn*u and saying

---

may prove prosperous. On their saying, "May it be prosperous," the giver lastly asks them to say the word of benediction (Svasti-vachana, "Be it well"). The following Mantra is then recited: "May Indra who listens to the wise, bless us. May Pu*sh*ā the all-knowing bless us. May Tārk*sh*ya (Aru*n*a), the felloe of whose chariot-wheel is ever unbroken, bless us. May B*ri*haspati bless us; Ong Svasti, Ong Svasti, Ong Svasti."

[1] Pādya, etc.

[2] This is said with each gift.

[3] Pādhya.

[4] Arghya.

[5] *i.e.*, Prā*n*āya Svāhā, Apānāya Svāhā, Samānāya Svāhā, Udānāya Svāhā, Vyānāya Svāhā (see p. 164, note 7).

[6] Dūrvā Grass and sun-dried rice.

"Tat Sat,"[1] he should mention the name of the month, the Paksha,[2] and Tithi,[3] motive[4] and then the Gotra[5] and Pravara[6] of the bridegroom and the names of his ancestors in the possessive case one by one, from the great-grandfather, beginning with the last, and ending with the father.[7] The bridegroom's name should be said in the objective case along with his Gotra and Pravara. Then he says the bride's name and the names of her ancestors, their Gotra, and so forth; and he should then say: "I honour thee with the object of giving her to thee in Brāhma marriage" (241-244).[8]

---

[1] See p. 28, note 2.

[2] The lunar month is divided into two Pakshas (which literally means turn or wing)—the Shukla (=white or light) and the *Krishna* (=black or dark).

[3] Each half of a lunar month is divided into fifteen Tithis, or lunar days.

[4] Nimittāni; *i.e.*, the motive or object with which the gift is made. The giving away of a girl in marriage is an act of merit and usually the girl of the bride say "For the attainment of imperishable heaven" or like pious wish.

[5] and [6] Gotra means lineage, descent, family. The Gotra of each family is derived from its founder (Ādi-purusha). Manu speaks of eight Gotras, and the Dharma-pradīpa of forty-two Gotras. Castes other than Brāhmanas derive their Gotra and Pravara from their Gurus. Pravara means well-known, excellent, illustrious. Thus, in Jamadagni Gotra, the Pravaras are Jamadagni, Aurva, and Vashishtha. In Bhāradvāja Gotra they are Bhāradvāja, Angiras, and Bārhaspatya. In each Gotra there are usually three or five Pravara Purushas (illustrious men). Pravara is, therefore, the branch of a Gotra named after a distinguished member of it. A person, therefore, has both a Gotra and a Pravara from which he is descended.

[7] As follows: The great-grandson of A, the grandson of B, the son of C, D, him I honour. The Gotra and Pravara should be mentioned.

[8] Thus: I, A (the giver), give to thee, B (the bridegroom), the great-grandson of C of W Gotra and X Pravara, the grandson of D of W Gotra and X Pravara, the son of E of W gotra and X Pravara, F. I give to thee, (name of bride) of Y Gotra and Z Pravara, the great-granddaughter of G of Y Gotra and Z Pravara, the granddaughter of N of Y Gotra and Z Pravara, the daughter of I of Y Gotra and Z Pravara in Brāhma marriage.

The bridegroom should then say: "I am honoured." The giver upon this should say, "Perform the ordained marriage rites," and the bridegroom should then say: "I will do it to the best of my knowledge" (245). The bride, adorned with beautiful clothes and jewels, and covered with another piece of cloth, should then be brought and placed in front of the bridegroom (246). The giver of the bride should once again show his respect to the bridegroom by the present of clothes and ornaments, and join the right hand of the bridegroom with that of the bride (247). He should place in their joined hands five gems or a fruit and a pan-leaf, and having saluted the bride, should consign her to his hands (248). At the time of giving the bride the giver should, as before, mention his name in the nominative case, and should state his wish,[1] and should also mention the names of the three ancestors of the bridegroom, with their Gotras, all in the possessive case, as before.

He should then mention the name of the bridegroom in the dative singular, and then the names of the three ancestors of the bride, with their Gotras, etc., in the possessive case. At the time of mentioning the bride's name in the objective singular he should say after that, "The honoured, adorned, clothed, and Prajāpati-devatāka,"[2] and saying, "to thee I give," he should give away the bride. The bridegroom should, by saying "Svasti,"[3] agree to take her as his wife (249-251). Let the giver then say, "In Dharma,[4] in Artha,[5] in Kāma,[6] thou should be with

---

[1] Kāma, *viz.*, that this is done for the attainment of the three Purushārthas—Dharma, Kāma, Artha.

[2] As adjective of her name, meaning She who is dedicated or belongs to Prajāpati (the Lord of Procreation).

[3] Su + asti = it is well. See p. 296, note 10.

[4] Religious observances.

[5] Worldly affairs.

[6] Enjoyment.

thy wife"; and the bridegroom should reply, saying, "So I shall," and then recite the praise of Kāma[1] (252).

MANTRA

It is Kāma who gives and Kāma who accepts. It is Kāma who has taken the Kāminī[2] for the satisfaction of Kāma. Prompted by Kāma, I take thee. May both our Kāma[3] be fulfilled[4] (253).

The giver should then, addressing the son-in-law and the daughter, say: "May, by the grace of Prajāpati, the desire of you both be accomplished. May you two fare well. Do you two together perform the religious observances"[5] (254). Then both the bride and bridegroom, to the accompaniment of music and blowing of conch-shells, should be covered with the cloth, so that they may have their first auspicious glance at one another (255). Then gold and jewels, according to the giver's means, should be offered to the son-in-law as presents. The giver should then think to himself that the ceremony has been faultlessly done[6] (256). The bridegroom either, on the same night or the day following, should establish fire, according to the rules of Kusha*nd*ikā[7] (257).

[1] The God of Love. Kāma means also desire.

[2] Woman.

[3] Desire of Bride and Bridegroom.

[4] That is, the giver has expressed his desire or wish (Kāma). The bridegroom desires and, prompted by desire for Dharma Artha, takes the Kāminī, which literally means a passionate, and then any, woman. It is the Kāma or wish of the father to give and the Kāma of the bridegroom is to accept.

[5] Literally, "Protect the Dharma," by which is meant "Perform pious and religious acts".

[6] As should be done in every ceremony for the T*r*ipti (satisfaction) of the Parama-puru*sh*a; for, if the worshipper is satisfied, the Brahman in him is satisfied.

[7] *Vide* p. 269, verse 70.

The fire that is made in this Kusha*nd*ikā is called Yojaka,[1] and the Charu[2] which is cooked is called Prājāpatya.[3] After performing Dhārā Homa[4] in the fire, the bridegroom should offer five oblations (258). The oblation should, after meditation upon Shiva, Durgā, Brahmā, Vi*shn*u, and the Carrier of Thunder,[5] be made to them one after the other, singly, in the sanctified fire (259). Taking both his wife's hands, the husband should say: "I take thy hands O fortunate one![6] Do thou be devoted to the Guru and the Devatās, and duly perform thy household duties according to the religious precepts" (260). The wife should then, with ghee given by the husband, and fried paddy[7] given by her brother, make four oblations in the name of Prajāpati (261). The husband should then rise from his seat with his wife and go round the Fire with her and offer oblation to Durgā and Shiva, Ramā and Vi*shn*u, Brahmī and Brahmā, three times to each couple (262).

Then, without reciting any Mantra, the bride should step on a stone,[8] and, standing thereon, the bride should take seven steps. If the Kusha*nd*ikā[9] ceremony is performed at night, the bride and bridegroom, surrounded by the ladies

[1] The Uniter.

[2] See p. 269, verse 71.

[3] Relating to, or dedicated to, Prajāpati (the Lord of Procreation).

[4] See p. 264, verse 45.

[5] Vajradhārī, that is, Indra.

[6] She is so addressed not because She is fortunate in having him as a husband but because her good fortune will make him fortunate. The wife is called G*ri*halak*sh*mī or Devī of prosperity in the husband's house (G*ri*ha). *Cf.* Gribeshvari in v. 266, *post*.

[7] Lāja.

[8] This is called the Ashmāroha*n*a or Shilāroha*n*a and Saptama*n*dala-gamana or Sapta-padī-gamana. Until these seven steps the marriage is not complete. At each step a Mantra is uttered.

[9] See p. 269, verse 70.

present, should gaze upon the stars Dhruva and Arundhatī[1] (263). Returning to their seats and seated thereon, the bridegroom should bring the ceremony to a close by performing Svi*sh*t*i*-k*r*it Homa and offering Complete Oblation[2] (264). The Brāhma marriage, according to Kula-dharma, in order to be faultless, should take place with a girl of the same caste as the husband, but she should not be of the same Gotra,[3] nor should she be a Sapi*nd*ā[4] (265). The wife married according to Brāhma rites is the Queen of the house, and without her permission another wife should not be married according to those rites (266). O Kuleshvari! if the children of the Brāhma wife are living or any of her descendants be living, then the children of the Shaiva[5] wife shall not inherit (267).

O Parameshvari! the Shaiva wife and her children are entitled to food and clothing from the heir of her Shaiva husband in proportion to the property of the latter (268). Shaiva marriage[6] celebrated in the Chakra[7] is of two kinds. One kind is terminated with the Chakra and the other is lifelong (269). At the time of the formation of the Chakra the Vira,[8] surrounded by his friends, relatives,

[1] Dhruva was a son of King Uttānapāda. The King having slighted him to please a favourite wife—Dhruva though a mere child went into the forest vowing that he would get what his father never got and by his devotion and austerities became by the grace of Vi*sh*n*u* the fixed star named after him and which is the Polar Star, emblem of fixity (or devotion). Arundhatī was the wife, celebrated for her devotion to her husband, of Vashi*sh*t*h*a. The morning star or according to some one of the Pleiades personifies her.

[2] Pūr*n*āhuti, and as to the Homa see p. 264, verse 48.

[3] As the husband's father and mother.

[4] See *post*.

[5] See *post* (see Chapter VIII, verse 178).

[6] Shaiva Marriage is referred to in verse 178, Chapter vii. The following verses give the Rules of Shaiva Marriage.

[7] The Circle of Worship (see "Shakti and Shākta").

[8] Hero (see *ibid.*).

and fellow-worshippers, should, with a well-controlled mind, by mutual consent, perform the marriage ceremony (270). He should first of all submit their wishes, saying to the Bhairavīs[1] and Vīras[1] there assembled, "Approve our marriage according to Shaiva form" (271). The Vīra should, after obtaining their permission, bow to the Supreme Kālikā, repeating the Mantra of seven letters (Kālikā Mantra)[2] one hundred and eight times (272).

O Shivā! he should then say to the woman: "O Devi! accept me as thy husband with a guileless heart." (273).

O Queen of the Devas! the Kaula bride should then honour her beloved with scents, flowers, and sundried rice,[3] and with trust place her own hands on his (274). The Lord of the Chakra should then sprinkle them with the following Mantra, and the Kaulas, seated in the Chakra, should approve and say: "It is well"[4] (275)

Mantra

May Rāja-rājesvarī, Kalī, Tārinī, Bhuvaneshvarī, Bagalā, Kamalā, Nityā, Bhairavī,[5] ever protect ye both (276).

The Lord of the Chakra should sprinkle them twelve times with wine or water of oblation,[6] reciting the above Mantra. The two should then bow to him, and he should upon that repeat to them the Bījas of Vāgbhavā and Ramā[7] (277). O Kuleshvari! the Kulīna husband and wife, who are

[1] The Shaktis or Women worshippers of the circle.

[2] Parameshvari Svāhā.

[3] Akshata. Ordinarily paddy is half boiled, and then husked. Akshata is husked without boiling.

[4] Svasti.

[5] That is, Eight of the Dasha (ten) Mahāvidyās.

[6] Arghya.

[7] Aing, Shrīng. Ramā is Lakshmī.

married according to the injunctions of Shambhu, should very carefully carry out whatever they have promised (278). There is no restriction of caste or age in Shaiva marriage. By the command of Shambhu, any woman who is not a Sapi*n*da,[1] and has not already a husband, may be married [2] (279).

If a woman is married according to Shaiva Dharma and the rules of Chakra to a man who desires to have a son by her, then such a man may leave her if, after the Chakra is over, she has her flowers (280).[3] The offspring of the Shaiva marriage is of the same caste as the mother if it be an Anuloma marriage, and a Sāmānya if the marriage is Viloma [4] (281). These mixed castes should, at the time of their fathers' Shrāddha and other ceremonies give presents of edibles to, and feast the Kaulas [5] only (282).

Eating and sexual union, O Devi! are desired by, and natural to, men, and their use is regulated for their benefit in the ordinances of Shiva [6] (283). Therefore, O Maheshāni! he who follows the ordinances of Shiva undoubtedly acquires, Dharma, Artha, Kāmā and Mok*sh*a [7] (284).

End of the Ninth Chapter, entitled "The Ten Kinds of Purificatory Rites (Saṁskāra)".

[1] Blood relation within six degrees, together with the wives of the males. Among them are Sapi*n*da relations to each other.

[2] There are some additional rules observed by the Vi*sh**n*u-krāntā School of Tāntrikas (*vide* Bhakta ed., p. 457).

[3] That is, as the begetting of a child is the object of the union it no longer exists, when the purpose for which it was entered into is not achieved.

[4] Anuloma is where the man is of the same or a higher caste than the woman, and Viloma is where the man is of a lower caste than the woman.

[5] Tāntrikas who know and observe injunctions of Kuladharma.

[6] N*ri**n*āng svabhāva-jang devi priyang bhojana-maithunam.
Sangk*sh*epāya hitārthāya shaiva-dharme nirūpitam.

[7] Religious Merit, Piety, Wealth, Fulfilment of Desire, and Liberation.

CHAPTER X

RITES AND INITIATION

SHRĪ DEVĪ said:

I have now learned from Thee, O Lord! of the ordinances relating to Kusha*nd*ikā[1] and the ten Saṁskāras.[2] Do Thou now, O Deva! reveal to Me the ordinances relating to B*ri*ddhi Shrāddha[3] (1). O Shaṁkara! tell Me in detail, both for My pleasure and the benefit of all beings, in which of the sacramental[4] and dedicatory[5] ceremonies Kusha*nd*ikā and B*ri*ddhi Shrāddha[6] should be, or be not, performed. Say this, O Maheshāna (2-3).

Shrī Sadāshiva said:

O Gentle One! I have already in detail spoken of all that should be done in the ten Saṁskāras[7] commencing from Jīva-seka and ending in marriage (4), and of all that which should be performed by wise men who desire their own weal.[8] O Beauteous One! I will now speak of what should be done in other rites. Do Thou listen to it (5).

---

[1] *Vide* p. 269, verse 70.

[2] The ten "Sacraments" or purificatory ceremonies of the Hindus (see "Shakti and Shākta").

[3] See verses 11 *et seq.* to verse 63, *post.*

[4] Saṁskāra.

[5] Commemorative offering to the Pit*ri*s done on all auspicious occasions.

[6] Pratish*th*ā.

[7] *Vide ante*, Chapter VII.

[8] May also mean "The well-being of all".

My Beloved! in consecrating tanks, wells, and ponds, images of Devatās, houses, gardens and in Vrata,[1] the five Devas[2] and the celestial Mothers[3] should be worshipped, and the Vasu-dhārā[4] should be made and B*ri*ddhi Shrāddha[5] and Kusha*nd*ikā[6] should be performed (6-7). In ceremonies which may be, and are, performed by women alone there is no B*ri*ddhi Shrāddha, but (in lieu thereof) a present of edibles[7] should be made for the satisfaction of the Devatās and the Pit*ri*s (8).

O Lotus-faced One! in such ceremonies the worship of the Deva, Vasu-dhārā, and Kusha*nd*ika should be devoutly performed by the women through the aid of priests (9). If a man cannot perform a rite himself, then his son, the son's son, the daughter's son, agnate relatives, sister's son and son-in-law and the priest, are, O Shivā! good substitutes (10). I will, O Kālikā! now in detail speak of B*ri*ddhi Shrāddha. Do Thou listen to it (11).

After performing the daily duties, a man should, with mind intent, worship Gaṅgā, Vis*h*nu—the Lord of Sacrifice,[8] the Divinity[9] of the homestead, and the King[10] (12); and inwardly reciting the Pra*n*ava, he should make nine, seven, five, or three Brāhma*n*as of Darbha grass[11] (13).

---

[1] See "Shakti and Shākta."

[2] Brahmā and others up to Sadāshiva.

[3] The Māt*ri*s—Gaurī and others.

[4] *Vide* p. 272, note 9.

[5] *Vide* p. 277, note 7.

[6] *Vide* p. 269, verse 70.

[7] Bhojya.

[8] Bhūpati as Lord of the soil.

[9] Vis*h*nu Yajneshvara.

[10] Vāstvīsha, or Vāstu-devatā.

[11] Little bundles of Kusha Grass are tied up in a particular way to represent Brāhma*n*as.

The Brāhma*n*as should be made with ends of the grass which have no knots in them,[1] by twisting the upper ends of the blades from right to left two and a half times (14).

In B*ri*ddhi Shrāddha and Pārva*n*a Shrāddha[2] there should be six Brāhma*n*as, but, O Shivā! in Ekoddi*sh*ta[3] Shrāddha there should be only one (15). The wise one should place the Brāhma*n*as made of Kusha grass all in one receptacle, with their faces to the north, and bathe them with the following (16)

MANTRA

Hrīṁ:[4] May the Divinity of water, be propitious for the attainment of our desire. May She be propitious in that which we drink. May She be propitious for our good[5] (17).

Then with scents and flowers the Brāhma*n*as[6] made with Kusha grass should be worshipped (18). The wise one should then place on the west and the south six vessels in pairs with Kusha, sesamum-seed, and Tulasī[7] (19). On the two vessels placed on the west two of the Brāhma*n*as should be seated facing east, and on the four seats on the south the four Brahma*n*as should be seated facing north (20).

---

[1] Nirgarbha.

[2] The Shrāddha performed on the new moon day, called Mahālayā, preceding the Durgā Pūjā. Water and sesamum-seed (Til seed) are daily offered to the Pit*r*is during the half month preceding Mahālayā; on the last day the Shrāddha is performed.

[3] Shrāddha in name of one person only, and performed only once. The first Shrāddha (see verses 70, 71, and 73, *post*).

[4] Māyā bīja—the Svarūpa of the Jaladevatā (Tarkālaṁkāra).

[5] The Mantra is Vaidika, and the Bīja in it Tāntrika. The meaning is that the Devatā of Water is identical with the Devī Māyā. The Ādyā is invoked as such that She may be beneficent.

[6] Bhū-sura=Devas on earth, or Brāhma*n*as.

[7] The Tulasī plant (*Ocymum sanctum*), which is sacred to Vi*sh*nu.

The Divinities should be imagined to be in the two seated on the west and the paternal Ancestors in the two seated on the left of those on the south and the maternal ancestors on the right. Know this, O Pārvatī (21).

In Ābhyudayika[1] Shrāddha the Nāndīmukha fathers and the Nāndīmukhī[2] mothers, as also the maternal Ancestors in the male line and in the female line, should be mentioned by name. Before this, however, one should turn to his right and face the north, and after the performance of the requisite ceremonies for the worship of the Devas he should turn to his left and face the south and perform the rites necessary for the offering of the Pi*nd*as[3] (22-23).

In this Ābhyudayika Shrāddha, O Shivā! all the rites should be performed in their order, beginning with the rites relating to the Devas, and if there be any deviation the Shrāddha fails in its object[4] (24).

The word of supplication addressed to the Devas should be said whilst facing the north, and when the same is addressed to the paternal or maternal Ancestors it should be said whilst facing south. And now, O Thou of pure Smile! I will first state the words of entreaty[5] which should be addressed to the Devas (25).

---

[1] Also called Nāndīmukha Shrāddha.

[2] See below, note 4.

[3] Funeral cakes.

[4] This Shrāddha is performed on all joyful occasions, such as marriage. The world Ābhyudayika is derived from Abhyudaya, which means prosperity, happiness, festival. It is also called Nāndīmukha Shrāddha. The word Nāndīmukha means the prelude (Mukha=face) of any auspicious rite (Nāndī being derived from Nand=to please). In this rite the name of each of the Ancestors is preceded by the word Nāndīmukha in the case of a male, and Nāndīmukhī if a female. It is a Shrāddha or commemorative offering to the Pit*r*is preliminary to any joyous occasion, initiation, marriage, etc., to the father, grandfather, great-grandfather, maternal grandfather, etc.

[5] Anujnā=Assent, Permission, Command, Entreaty (see *post*, verses 26-29).

After mentioning the name of the month and Paksha,[1] the Tithi[2] and the occasion, the excellent worshipper should say "for the prosperous result of the ceremony."[3] Then he should repeat the names and Gotras[4] of the three fathers[5] and of the three mothers,[6] and of the three maternal grandfathers[7] and of the three maternal grandmothers,[8] in the possessive case, and he should thereafter say: "I am performing the Shrāddha of the Vishva-Devas[9] represented by the image of the two Brāhmanas made of Kusha grass." These, O Great Devī! are the words of entreaty[10] (26-29).

---

[1] Divisions of the lunar month, of which there are two—the light and dark half.

[2] A lunar day, which may be less than twenty-four hours.

[3] Karmābhyudayārtham.

[4] Lineage.

[5] Father, Grandfather, Great-grandfather.

[6] Mother, Grandmother, Great-grandmother.

[7] Maternal Male Ancestors.

[8] Maternal Female Ancestors.

[9] That is, Vasu, Satya, Kratu, Daksha, Kāla, Kāma, Dhriti, Kuru.

[10] The words of the ritual are as follows: Vishnur Ong Tat Sat: to-day ——, in the month of ——, when the Sun is in Rāshi ——, in Paksha ——, the Tithi ——, I, —— Deva Sharmā, —— for the prosperity of this —— ceremony, of my father, Nāndīmukha, whose Gotra is ——, and name is ——; of my grandfather, the Nāndīmukha, whose Gotra is —— and name is ——; of my great-grandfather, the Nāndīmukha, whose Gotra is —— and name is ——; of my mother, the Nāndīmukhī, whose Gotra is ——and name is ——; of my paternal grandmother, the Nāndīmukhī, whose Gotra is —— and name is ——; of my paternal great-grandmother, the Nāndīmukhī, whose Gotra is —— and name is ——; of my maternal grandfather, the Nāndīmukha, whose Gotra is —— and name is ——; of my maternal great-grandfather, the Nāndīmukha, whose Gotra is —— and name is ——; of my maternal great-great-grandfather, the Nāndīmukha, whose Gotra is —— and name is ——; of my maternal grandmother, the Nāndīmukhī, whose Gotra is ——and name is ——; of my maternal great-grandmother, the Nāndīmukhī, whose Gotra is —— and name is ——; of my maternal great-great-grandmother, the Nāndīmukhī, whose Gotra is —— and name is ——; and of the Vishva-Devas ——, beg leave to perform the Ābhyudayika Shrāddha with the Brāhmanas made of Kusha grass. The

O Pārvatī! when the Anujnā-vākya[1] is either for paternal or maternal Ancestors, the same words should, with the necessary alterations, be said for the paternal and maternal Ancestors,[2] and the Vishva-Devas left out (30). Then, O Shivā! the worshipper should recite the Brahma-Vidyā Gāyatrī[3] ten times (31). He should next say the following

MANTRA

I salute the Divinities, the Fathers—*i.e.*, the Fathers and Mothers—the great Yogīs; I salute Pu*sh*t*i*[4] and Svāhā[5]; may we have such auspicious occasions over and over again (32).

The excellent worshipper, having repeated the above Mantra three times, and taking water in his hand, should wash the Shrāddha articles with the

MANTRA

Vang, Hūng, Pha*t* (33).

Shrāddha is performed of—(1) On Father's side: Father, Mother, Grandfather, Grandmother, Great-grandfather, Grand-grandmother; (2) on mother's side: Grandfather, Grandmother, Great-grandfather, Great-grandmother, Great great-grandfather, Great-great-grandmother; and (3) the Vishva-devas. It may be noted that the Gotra of the father and his Ancestors and the mother in the same, and the Gotra of the maternal Ancestors is the same. A woman's Gotra changes, some say, after marriage, others after her death and Sapi*nd*īkara*n*a Shrāddha ceremony, and becomes that of her husband.

[1] See p. 308, n. 5.

[2] If any of the Ancestors be living, he or she should be presented with food, drink, etc.

[3] See p. 56, vv. 109-111.

[4] Vedic Devī—also called Pu*sh*an, who nourishes living beings—wife of Ga*n*apati. She is also a Māt*r*ikā (Mārka*nd*eya Purā*n*a, xxii, 18). Pu*sh*t*i* is also a title of the Devī (see Lalitā-Sahasra-Nāma, verse 94).

[5] The consort of Agni (Fire).

O Mistress of the Kula! a vessel should next be placed in the corner of Agni.[1] Then utter the

MANTRA

O Water! Thou art the nectar which killest the Rākshasas, protect this sacrifice of mine.

Water with Tulasī-leaves and barley should next be put into it; and the wise one should, after first offering handfuls of water to the Devas and then to the Vipras,[2] give them seats of Kusha grass (34-35).

The learned man, O Shivā! should then invoke the Vishva-Devas,[3] the fathers, the mothers, the maternal grandfathers, and the maternal grandmothers (36). Having so invoked them, the Vishva-Devas should first be worshipped; and then the three fathers, the three mothers, the three maternal grandfathers, and the three maternal grandmothers should be worshipped, with offers of Pādya, Arghya, Āchamanīya,[4] incense, lights, cloths. Then, O Beauteous One! permission should be asked in the first place of the Devas for the spreading of the leaves[5] (37-38).

Then a four-sided figure[6] should be drawn uttering the Māyā Bīja[7] and then in a similar way for the paternal and maternal sides two figures each should be drawn (39). After these have been sprinkled with the Vāruna Bīja,[8] leaves should be spread over the figures. These leaves should be sprinkled with the Vāruna Bīja,[8] and then

[1] South-East.

[2] Brāhmanas made of Kusha grass.

[3] *Vide ante*, p. 281, note 5.

[4] Water for the feet, offering, sipping water, etc.

[5] Plantain leaves are spread to place the Pindas thereon.

[6] Mandala.

[7] Hrīng.

[8] Vang.

drinking-water and different kinds of edibles should be distributed in their order[1] (40).

After giving honey and grains of barley and sprinkling the offerings with water, accompanied by the

MANTRA

Hrāng, Hrūng, Phat,

the worshipper should dedicate the edibles uttering the names of the Vishva-Devas,[2] the fathers, the mothers, the maternal grandfathers and the maternal grandmothers, and thereafter repeat the Gāyatrī ten[3] times and thrice repeat the

MANTRA

"I salute the Divinities," as aforesaid.[4]

After this, O Ādyā![5] he should take the directions (of the officiating Brāhmana) relating to the disposal of the remnants of edibles[6] and of the Pindas[6] (41-43).

Upon receiving the directions of the Brāhmana, he should, O Beloved! make twelve Pindas of the size of bael fruits with the remnants of the Akshata[7] and other

---

[1] That is, beginning with the Devas.

[2] See p. 281, note 5.

[3] Bhāratī says this. The text contains no direction as to how often it has to be repeated.

[4] *i.e.*, the Mantra "Devatābhyah," etc., verse 82.

[5] Primordial One.

[6] Thus:

Question: "Oṁ. There is some edible left over; to whom should it be given?"

Answer: "Oṁ. Give it to the honoured ones."

Question: "Oṁ. I wish to give Pindas."

Answer: "Oṁ. Do so."

[7] See p. 308, note 8.

things (44). He should make one more Pi*nd*a equal in size with the others, and then, O Ambika![1] he should spread some Kusha grass and barley on the Nair*ri*ta corner[2] of the Ma*nd*ala[3] (45).

MANTRA

Such of my family as have none to offer Pi*nd*as to them whom neither son nor wife survive, who were burnt to death or were killed by tigers or other beasts of prey, such kinsmen[4] of mine as themselves are without kinsmen,[5] all such as were my kinsmen in previous births, may they all obtain imperishable satisfaction by the Pi*nd*a and water hereby given by me (46-47).

O Adored of the Devas! having with the above Mantra offered the Pi*nd*a to those who have no one to offer them Pi*nd*as, he should wash his hands and inwardly recite the Gāyatrī,[6] and repeat the

MANTRA

"I salute the Divinities,"[7] and so forth,

three times, and then make some Ma*nd*alas[8] (48).

O Devī! the wise man should in front of the vessels containing the remnants of the offerings make such squares

---

[1] A title of the Devī. Ambikā = Mother.

[2] That is, the South-West corner.

[3] See verse 39, *ante*.

[4] Bāndhavas.

[5] Without anyone to offer Pi*nd*as to them.

[6] See "Garland of Letters".

[7] *i.e.*, the Mantra "Devatābhya*h*," etc. (in verse 32).

[8] Ma*nd*alas which in this case are to be square in shape.

in twos (for his Ancestors), beginning with the paternal Ancestors (49).

O Shivā! he should then sprinkle the squares with water with the Mantra already prescribed,[1] and then spread Kusha grass over them and sprinkle them with the Vāyu Bīja[2], beginning with the Kusha spread on the square for the paternal (male) Ancestors, and then offer three Pi*nd*as, one at the top, another at the bottom, and one in the middle, in each of the squares[3] (50).

O Maheshvarī! the names of each of the Ancestors should be mentioned, inviting him or her, and then the Pi*nd*a should be given with honey and barley,[4] concluding with Svadhā (51). After the Pi*nd*as are given (in manner aforesaid) the Lepa-bhojī[5] Ancestors should be satisfied by the offer to them of the remnants which remain on the hand. These should be scattered on all sides with the

MANTRA

Oṁ: May the Lepa-bhojī Ancestors be pleased.

---

[1] *i.e.*, the Varu*n*a Bīja, Vang.

[2] Yang.

[3] The Ma*nd*ala is drawn with water, and four Ma*nd*alas are so drawn. The first Ma*nd*ala is for the paternal male Ancestors—father, father's father, and father's father's father. The second Ma*nd*ala is for the female Ancestors—mother, father's mother, father's father's mother. These two Ma*nd*alas are for the paternal side. The third Ma*nd*ala is for the maternal male Ancestors—mother's father, mother's father's mother, and the father of the last. The fourth Ma*nd*ala is for the maternal female Ancestors—mother's mother mother's father's mother, mother's father's father's mother. The last two Ma*nd*alas are for the female Ancestry.

[4] The Pi*nd*as are offered as follows: I offer thee (of such and such Gotra), highly praiseworthy (Nāndīmukha) and well known (Pravara, see p. 298, note 5), this Pi*nd*a with honey and barley. It is thine: Svadhā.

[5] Lepa-bhojī Ancestors are the fourth, fifth, and sixth Ancestors. From the seventh upwards there are no Pi*nd*as to be offered.

In Ekoddish*t*a Shrāddha[1] the offering to the Lepa-bhojī Ancestors is not made (52).

Then for the satisfaction of the Devas and Pit*r*is the Gāyatrī[2] should be inwardly recited ten times, and the Mantra, "I salute the Divinities,"[3] as aforesaid should be similarly recited three times, and then the Pi*n*d*as should be worshipped[4] (53). Lighting an incense-stick and a light, the wise one should, with closed eyes, think of the Pit*r*is in their celestial forms partaking of their allotted Pi*n*d*as, each his own, and should then bow to them, uttering the following (54)

MANTRA

My father is my highest Dharma.[5] My father is my highest Tapas.[6] My father is my Heaven. On my father being satisfied, the whole Universe is satisfied (55).

Taking up some flowers[7] from the remnants, the Pit*r*is should be asked for their blessings, with the following (56)

MANTRA

Give me your blessings, O Merciful Pit*r*is. May my knowledge, progeny, and Kinsmen always increase. May my benefactors prosper. May I have food in profusion. May many always beg of me, and may I not have to beg of any (57-58).

---

[1] Shrāddha for one particular Ancestor only.

[2] *Vide* "Garland of Letters".

[3] "Devatābhya*h*," etc. (verse 82).

[4] The commentator adds: "With scents and flowers."

[5] Pitā. Here collectively used for all the Pit*r*is. My duty to him and them is my highest duty.

[6] Here = object of devotion.

[7] Nirmālya—Flowers left over after the Shrāddha. Bhāratī says 'flowers and the like' (Pus*h*pādi).

Then he should remove the Devas and Brāhma*n*as made of Kusha grass, as also the Pi*nd*as, commencing with the Devas. The wise one should then make presents for all three[1] (59).

He should then make Japa of the Gāyatrī ten times, and the Mantra, "I salute the Divinities,"[2] five times, and, after looking at the fire and the Sun, should, with folded palms, ask the Vipra[3] the following question (60):

"Is the Shrāddha complete?"[4]

and the Brāhma*n*a should make reply:

"It has been completed according to the injunctions"[5] (61).

Then, for the removal of the effects of any error or omission, the Pra*n*ava[6] should be inwardly recited ten times, and the ceremony should be brought to a close uttering the following

MANTRA

"May the Shrāddha rite be faultless[7]";

and then the food and drink in the vessels as also the Pi*nd*as should be offered to the officiating Brāhma*n*a (62).

In the absence of a Vipra, it should be given to cows and goats, or should be thrown into water. This is called "B*r*iddhi Shrāddha," enjoined for all obligatory

---

[1] *i.e.*, the Devas and the paternal and maternal Ancestors. The present is made with the prescribed Mantra to be Brāhma*n*a.

[2] The Mantra "Devatābhya*h*," etc. (verse 82).

[3] The Brāhma*n*a who is always present to assist at these ceremonies.

[4] *i.e.*, faultlessly done.

[5] Vidhāna.

[6] Ongkāra.

[7] This is called Achhidrābhividhāna.

sacramental[1] rites (63). Shrāddha performed on the occasion of any Parvan[2] is called "Pārvana Shrāddha"[3] (64).

In ceremonies relating to the consecration of emblems or images of Devas, or while starting for, or returning from, pilgrimage, the Shrāddha should be according to the injunctions laid down for Pārvana Shrāddha (65). On the occasion of Pārvana Shrāddha the Pitris should not be addressed with the prefix "Nāndīmukha," and for the words "Salutation to Pushti"[4] should be substituted the words "Salutation to Svadhā"[5] (66).

O Beautiful One! if any of the three Ancestors be alive, then the wise one should make the offerings to another Ancestor of higher degree (67). If the father, grandfather, and great-grandfather[6] be alive, then, O Queen of the Devas! no Shrāddha need be performed. If they are pleased, then the object of the funeral rite and sacrifice[7] is attained (68).

If his father be living, then a man may perform his mother's Shrāddha, his wife's Shrāddha, and Nāndīmukha Shrāddha; but he is not entitled to perform the Shrāddha of anyone else (69). O Queen of Kula![8] at the time of Ekoddishta Shrāddha[9] the Vishva-Devas[10] are not to be

---

[1] Saṁskāra.

[2] Name given to certain days of the lunar month, such as Amāvasyā (New Moon), Pūrnimā (Full Moon), Ashtamī (Eighth Day). A festival.

[3] Pārvana-Shrāddha is Shrāddha performed on the occasions last mentioned—not only on Mahālayā Day—the New Moon preceding the Durgā Pūjā.

[4] Namo'stu Pushtyai. See v. 32 *ante*.

[5] Namo'stu Svadhāyai, (*ibid.*).

[6] Literally, three Ancestors, beginning with father.

[7] Shrāddha and Yajna. If all the three Ancestors are alive, they are feasted instead of Pindas being offered to them.

[8] Kuleshvarī.

[9] See p. 315, note 1.

[10] See p. 281, note 5.

worshipped. The word of entreaty[1] should be addressed to one Ancestor only[2] (70).

At the time of Ekoddi*shta* Shrāddha[3] cooked rice and Pi*nd*a should be given whilst facing south. The rest of the ceremony is the same as that which has been already described, with the exception that sesamum should be substituted for barley (71).

The peculiarity in Preta Shrāddha[4] is that the worship[5] of Gaṁgā[6] and others is omitted, and in the framing of the Mantra the deceased should be spoken of as Preta[7] whilst rice and Pi*nd*as are offered to him (72).

The Shrāddha performed for one particular dead ancestor is called "Ekoddi*shta*". In offering Pi*nd*a to the Preta, fish and meat should be added (73). O Mistress of the Kula![8] know this, that the Shrāddha which is performed on the day following the end of the period of uncleanliness[9] is Preta Shrāddha (74). If there is a miscarriage, or if the child dies immediately on birth, or if a child is born or dies, then the period of uncleanliness is to be reckoned according to the custom of the family (75).

The period of uncleanliness in the case of the twice-born is ten days (for Brāhma*n*as), twelve (for Ks*h*atriyas), and a fortnight (for Vaishyas); for Shūdras and Sāmānyas the period is one month (thirty days) (76).

---

[1] Anujnā-vākya.

[2] *i.e.*, the person whose Ekoddi*shta* Shrāddha is being performed.

[3] *i.e.*, the first of Ekoddi*shta* Shrāddha.

[4] See note 7.

[5] Archchana.

[6] The Devī of the Ganges.

[7] *i.e.*, the spirit before obsequial rites.

[8] Kaula Tāntrikas.

[9] Ashaucha: Erroneously called period of mourning.

On the death of an Agnate[1] who is not a Sapi*nd*a,[2] the period of uncleanliness is three days, and on the death of a Sapi*nd*a,[3] should information of it arrive after the period prescribed, one becomes unclean for three days (77).

The unclean man, O Primordial One! is not entitled to perform any rite relating to the Devas and the Pit*ri*s, excepting Kula worship[3] and that which has been already commenced (78).

Persons over five years of age should be burnt in the burning-ground, but, O Kuleshāni! a wife should not be burnt with her dead husband[4] (79). Every woman is Thy image—Thou residest concealed in the forms of all women in this world.[5] That woman, who in her delusion[6] ascends the funeral pyre of her lord, shall go to hell (80).

Kālikā! the corpses of worshippers of the Brahma Mantra should be either buried, thrown into running water, or burnt, according as they may direct (81).

Ambikā![7] death in a holy place or a place of pilgrimage, or near the Devī, or near the Kaulikas,[8] is a happy one (82).

He who at the time of his death meditates on the one Truth, forgetful of the three worlds becomes one with the Paramātmā[9] (83).

---

[1] Jnāti.

[2] *i.e.*, having the same Pi*nd*a, or funeral rice-ball offering. A kinsman connected by the offering of the Pi*nd*a.

[3] Kula-Pūjā.

[4] This passage condemns the practice of Satī.

[5] Tava svarūpā rama*n*ī, jagatyāchchhanna-vigrahā.

[6] Moha is ignorance of right and wrong due to excess of grief, desire and the like.

[7] See p. 318, note 1.

[8] Followers of Kulāchāra.

[9] Svarūpe pratis*ht*hati—literally, "stays in his own Essential Being." Sva-rūpa is here the equivalent of Paramātmā (Bhāratī).

After death the corpse should be taken to the burning-ground, and when it has been washed it should be smeared with ghee and placed on the pyre, with the face to the north[1] (84).

The deceased should be addressed by his name, and Gotra and as Preta.[2] Giving the Pi*nd*a to the mouth of the corpse, the pyre should be lighted by applying the torch to the mouth of the corpse, the while inwardly reciting the Vahni Bīja[3] (85).

Beloved! the Pi*nd*a should be made of boiled or unboiled rice, or crushed barley, or wheat, and should be of the size of an emblic myrobalam[4] (86). To the eldest son of the Preta is given the privilege of performing the Shrāddha; in his absence to the other sons, according to the order of their seniority (87).

The day after the day upon which the period of uncleanliness expires, the mourner should bathe and purify himself, and give away gold and sesamum for the Liberation of the Preta[5] (88).

The son of the Preta should give away cattle, lands, clothes, carriages, vessels made of metals, and various kinds of edibles, in order that the Preta may attain Heaven (89).

He should also give away scents, garlands, fruits, water, a beautiful bed, and everything which the Preta himself liked to insure his passage to Heaven (90).

---

[1] Uttarābhimukha.

[2] See p. 318, note 7.

[3] Rang—the Bīja of Fire.

[4] Harītakī.

[5] The Mantra said whilst giving away is: "Ong: to-day (here mention month, Paksha, Tithi, etc.), for the Liberation of my father, whose Gotra is —— and whose name is ——, I give away gold, etc., to the Brāhma*n*a, whose name is —— and whose Gotra is ——."

Then a bull should be branded with the mark of a trident, and decorated with gold and ornaments, and then let loose, with the object that the deceased may attain Heaven (91).

He should then with a devout spirit perform the Shrāddha, according to the injunctions laid down for the performance of Preta Shrāddha,[1] and then feed Brāhma*n*as and Kaula knowers of the Brahman[2] and the hungry (92).

The man who is unable to make gifts should perform the Shrāddha to the best of his ability, and feed the hungry, and thus liberate his father from the state of existence of a Preta[3] (93).

This Preta Shrāddha is known as Ādya Ekoddi*sh*ta Shrāddha,[4] and it liberates the deceased from the state of Preta. After this every year on the Tithi[5] of his death edibles[6] should be given to the deceased (94).

There is no necessity for a multitude of injunctions nor for a multitude of rituals. Man may attain all Siddhi[7] by honouring a Kaulika. The object of all Saṁskāras[8] is completely attained if, in lieu of the prescribed Homa,

---

[1] See p. 318, verse 74.

[2] Brahmajna.

[3] The impure earth-bound state after Sapi*nd*īkara*n*a he joins the other Pit*r*is and then reaps the result of his karma.

[4] This is the first (Ādya) Shrāddha done immediately after (verse 88) the expiry of the period of uncleanliness for the liberation from the State of a Preta of the person who is dead. Ekoddi*sh*ta means directed (Uddi*sh*ta) towards one (Eka).

[5] A lunar day, which may be less than twenty-four hours.

[6] The offering of Pi*nd*as on the anniversary of his death is called Vātsarika (annual) Shrāddha.

[7] Sarva-siddhi—Success in all things.

[8] "Sacraments" described in Ch. IX.

Japa, and Shrāddha,[1] even a single Kaulika[2] is (at the time of the rite) duly honoured (96).

The injunction of Shiva is that all auspicious ceremonies should be performed between the period beginning with the fourth day of the light half of the lunar half-month, and ending on the fifth of the dark half-month (97).

He, however, who is desirous of performing any rite which must be performed may perform it even on an inauspicious day,[3] provided he be so directed by his Guru, by a *Ritvik*,[4] or a Kaulika (98).

A Kaulika should commence the building of a house, should first enter a house, start on a journey, wear new jewels, and the like, only after worshipping the Primordial One with the five Elements[5] (99).

Or the excellent worshipper may shorten the rite. He may, after meditating on the Devī, and inwardly reciting the Mantra and bowing to the Devī, go wherever he may desire (100).

In the worship of all Devatās, such as the Autumnal Festival[6] and others, Dhyāna and Pūjā[7] should be performed according to the ordinances laid down in the Shāstras relating to such worship (101).

---

[1] That is, the burnt sacrifice, recitation of Mantra, or obsequial rites.

[2] Follower of Kulāchāra who has realised the ONE underlying the diversity of the world.

[3] Viruddhe'hni.

[4] Priest.

[5] Pancha-tattva—Wine, meat, etc. (see "Shakti and Shākta").

[6] Shāradīyotsava. The Durgā Pūjā is so called because it is celebrated in Autumn. Durgā Pūjā is also celebrated in Spring, and is then called Vāsantī, or Vernal Festival.

[7] Meditation and worship.

According to the ordinances relating to the worship of the Primordial Kālī, animal sacrifice[1] and Homa[2] should be performed, and the rite should be brought to an end by the honouring of Kaulikas[3] and making of presents[4] (102).

The general rule is that Gaṁgā, Vishnu, Shiva, Sūrya, and Brahmā should first be worshipped, and then the Deva the special object of worship (103).

The Kaulika is the most excellent Dharma,[5] the Kaulika is the most excellent Deva, the Kaulika is the most excellent pilgrimage,[6] therefore should the Kaula be always worshipped[7] (104).

The three and a half Kotis[8] of Places of Pilgrimage, all the Devas beginning with Brahmā Himself, reside in the body of the Kaula. What, therefore, is there which is not attained by worshipping him? The land in which the good and Fully initiated[9] Kaula resides is blessed and deserving of honour. It is most holy, and is coveted even by the Devas (105-106). Who can, in this world, understand the majesty of the "Fully initiated" Sādhaka,[10] who is Shiva[11] Himself, and to whom there is nothing either holy or sinful? (107).

---

[1] Vali.

[2] Sacrifice in fire.

[3] Followers of Kulāchāra, who see the Brahman in all and all in the Brahman. *Vide ante.*

[4] Dakshinā.

[5] *i.e.*, embodiment of righteousness.

[6] *i.e.*, he is the embodiment of all the Holy Places. A visit to him is the equivalent of the visit to all Holy Shrines.

[7] Archchayet.

[8] A Koti is a crore or ten million—*i.e.*, all the multitude.

[9] Pūrnābhishikta=*lit.* Fully sprinkled. Pūrnābhisheka follows initiation.

[10] One who is intently striving to attain Siddhi.

[11] Shivātmā that is, he is the embodiment of goodness and beneficence.

Such a Kaula, possessing merely the form of man, moves about this earth for the salvation of the entire world and the instruction of men in the conduct of life (108).

Shrī Devī said:

Thou hast, O Lord! spoken of the Greatness[1] of the fully initiated Kaula. Do Thou in Thy mercy speak to Me of the ordinances relating to such initiation[2] (109).

Shrī Sadāshiva said:

In the three Ages[3] this rite was a great secret; men then used to perform it in all secrecy, and thus attain Liberation (110).

When the Kali Age prevails, the followers of Kula rite should declare themselves as such, and, whether in the night or the day, should openly be initiated[4] (111).

By the mere drinking of wine,[5] without initiation,[6] a man does not become a Kaula. The Kula worshipper becomes the Lord of the Kula Chakra only after "full initiation"[2] (112).

The Guru should, the day before the initiation, worship the Deva of Obstacles[7] with offerings, according to his ability for the removal of all obstacles (113).

If the Guru is not qualified to officiate at a "Full initiation"[2] ceremony, then it should, O Beloved! be performed by a duly initiated Kaula[8] (114). Gang is the Bīja of

---

[1] Māhātmya = Prabhāva = Power, goodness, sanctity.

[2] Pūrnābhisheka.

[3] Yuga—that is, Satya, Tretā, and Dvāpara, the three past Ages.

[4] See Ch. IV, verse 78.

[5] Kevalang madya-sevanāt.

[6] Abhisheka.

[7] Ganesha.

[8] *Vide* p. 328, note 3. Changing one's Guru is not allowed unless the latter is not qualified when the services of a qualified preceptor

Ga*n*apati (Ga*n*esha) (115). Ga*n*aka is the *Rishi*, the Chhanda is Nīv*rit*,[1] the Lord of Obstacles[2] is the Devatā, and the Mantra is applicable for the removal of obstacles to the performance of the rite[3] (116).

Adding successively six long vowels to the Mūla Mantra,[4] *Shada*ṁga-nyāsa[5] should be performed, and O Shivā! after doing Prā*n*āyāma[6] let Ga*n*apati be meditated upon (117).

---

may be sought. It is however said "the disciple thirsting for knowledge may go from one Guru to another in the same way that a bee longing for honey goes from flower to flower."

Tarkālangkāra says: At the time of Mantragraha*n*a (reception of Mantra) the person imparting it becomes Guru; at time of Abhi*sh*eka the quality of Guru is transferred to him who performs it. Tantrasāra says that by renouncing the Guru man incurs death, by giving up Mantra poverty comes, and by giving up both, goes to Raurava hell. The sense of this is that there is no fault in giving up the Guru if the disciple desires to be initiated in the Saṁskāra in which the person who gave him Mantra is not initiated and disqualified. If however the Guru is initiated and qualified the disciple cannot leave him. The intention of Shiva is that the disciple who wishes to be initiated in Shāktābhi*sh*eka, Pūr*n*ābhi*sh*eka, Kramadīk*sh*ā and the like, may leave the Guru who gave the Mantra and go to another who can fill his desires.

[1] A form of metre.

[2] Vighna—that is, Ga*n*esha.

[3] *i.e.*, initiatory rite.

[4] Gang.

[5] *Shada*ṁga-nyāsa proper is also called Hridayādi-*shada*ṁga-nyāsa—*i.e.*, of the six parts of the body, beginning with the Heart: (1) Heart, (2) the Head, (3) the Crown-lock, (4) the Thorax, (5) the three Eyes, (6) the palm and back of the Hand. Kara-nyāsa is called Aṁgu*sh*-*th*ādi-*Shada*ṁga-nyāsa—*i.e.*, Nyāsa of six parts, beginning with the Aṁgu*shtha*, or thumb: (1) Thumb, (2) Index finger, (3) Middle finger, (4) Ring finger, (5) Little finger, and (6) the palm and back of the Hand.

[6] For the details of this practice, see ed. Bhakta, p. 497. Commence inhalation with the left nostril, making Japa of the Bīja Gang sixteen times; retain the breath, making Japa sixty-four times; lastly, exhale through right nostril, making Japa thirty-two times. Then the order is reversed by commencing with right nostril, and lastly with the left nostril. These three actions make one Prā*n*āyāma. This Tantra speaks of two ways of Prā*n*āyāma—the Ghera*nd*a Saṁhitā of seven and the Ha*th*a-yoga-pradīpikā of three.

DHYĀNA

Meditate on Gaṇa-pati as of the colour of vermilion, having three eyes, a large belly, holding in His lotus-hands the conch,[1] the noose,[2] the elephant-goad,[3] and the sign of blessing.[4] His great trunk is adorned with the jar of wine which it holds. On His forehead shines the young Moon.[5] He has the head of the King of elephants; His cheeks are constantly bathed in wine. His body is adorned with the coils of the King of servants. He is dressed in red raiment,[6] and His body is smeared with scented ointments (118).

Having thus meditated upon Gaṇapati, he should be worshipped with mental offerings,[7] and then the protecting powers of the seat[8] should be worshipped.[9] These are Tībrā, Jvālinī, Nandā, Bhoga-dā, Kāma-rūpiṇī, Ugrā, Tejasvatī, Satyā, and Vighna-vināshinī.[10] The (first eight) should be worshipped in their order, beginning from the east, and the last should be worshipped in the middle of the Maṇḍala. Having thus worshipped

---

[1] Shaṁkha.

[2] Pāsha.

[3] Aṁkusha—the hook for driving elephants.

[4] The text has Ishṭa. Vara Mudrā = Sign of Blessing. This is done by merely turning in the thumb, its end touching the palm below the ring finger, all the fingers being held straight out.

[5] Bhāratī explains this passage to mean—"His diadem shining with the young Moon." For another Dhyāna of Gaṇesha see Ch. XIII. 144.

[6] Bhāratī interprets this passage to mean—"His body aglow with His red raiment." His is of the colour of vermilion.

[7] See Ch. V, verses 142 *et seq.*

[8] Pīṭha-shakti (see Ādhāra-shakti, *ante*).

[9] Bhāratī adds—"With Mantras made up of the Praṇava, the name of the Devatā and Namaḥ."

[10] The first eight are to be worshipped on the eight sides, and the last—the "Destructress of Obstacles"—in the middle.

them all, the Lotus-seat itself should be worshipped (119-120).

Meditating on Ganesha once again, He should be worshipped with offerings of the five elements.[1] On each of His four sides the excellent Kaulika should worship Ganesha, Gana-nāyaka, Gana-nātha, Gana-krīda, Ekadanta, Rakta-tunda, Lambodara, Gajānana, Mahodara, Vikata, Dhūmrābha, and Vighna-nāshana[2] (121-123).

Then the eight Shaktis, Brāhmī,[3] and others, and the ten Dikpālas[4] and their weapons, should be worshipped, and after that Vighna-rāja[5] should be bidden to depart[6] (124).

Having thus worshipped the King of Obstacles, the worshipper should perform the preliminary[7] ceremony, and then entertain the Kaulas versed in divine knowledge with the five elements[8] (125).

The next day, having bathed[9] and performed his ordinary daily duties as already enjoined, he should, O Beloved! give away sesamum-seed and gold for the destruction of all sins from his birth, and a Bhojya[10] for the satisfaction of the Kaulas (126). Then, giving

---

[1] Pancha-tattva—*i.e.*, wine, meat, fish, parched food, and woman.

[2] These are called the surrounding (Āvarana) Deities. They are forms of Gana-pati, Who is called by these names Himself.

[3] Brāhmī, Nārāyanī, Maheshvarī, Chāmundā, Kumārī, Aparājitā, Vārāhī, Nārasimhī (*cf.* Chapter V, verse 134; and Chapter VI, verse 100).

[4] Indra, etc. (see Chapter VI, verse 103).

[5] King of Obstacles--Ganesha.

[6] "Lord of Obstacles! Pardon me," is the Mantra of dismissal.

[7] Adhivāsana. The worshipper here is the Guru.

[8] Pancha-tattva.

[9] Bhakta adds—"With Sarvaushadhi or Āmalakī (a kind of Myrabolam) water."

[10] *i.e.*, uncooked rice, vegetables, ghee, sugar, salt—what, in short, is given uncooked for the purpose of making a meal.

Arghya [1] to Sūrya, and having worshipped Brahmā, Vishnu, Shiva, and the nine Planets, as also the sixteen divine Mothers, he should make a Vasu-dhārā [2] (127).

He should then perform Vriddhi Shrāddha for the good result of the rite, and, going up to the Guru, bow to him, and pray to him as follows (128):

(PRAYER TO THE GURU)

Save me, O Lord! Thou that art the Sun of the Kaulas. Protect my head, O Ocean of Mercy! with the shade of thy lotus-foot (129). Grant us leave, O Exalted One! in this auspicious Pūrnābhisheka that by thy grace I may attain the success of my undertaking without any hindrance (130).

(The Guru should then reply :)

My son! be thou, by the permission of Shiva-Shakti,[3] initiated with the "full initiation". May thou attain the object of thy desire by the command of Shiva (131).

Having thus obtained the permission of the spiritual Preceptor, he should make the Saṁkalpa [4] for the removal of all obstacles and for the attainment of long life, prosperity, strength, and good health (132).

The Sādhaka, having solemnly formed his resolve, should do honour to the Guru, by presenting him with clothes and jewels, and Kārana [5] with Shuddhi,[6] and invite him to perform the rite (133).

---

[1] Offering.

[2] See p. 272, note 9.

[3] Shiva and Shakti—the Two in One,

[4] "Solemnly declare his purpose." See ed. Bhakta, p. 508, for details.

[5] A symbolic name for wine. See Ch. VII, vv. 22, 23.

[6] See Ch. VI, verse 11. The invitation is done with a Mantra. See ed. Bhakta, p. 504.

The Guru should then make with earth an altar four fingers in height and measuring one and a half cubit either way in a beautiful room painted with red earth, etc., decorated with pictures, flags, fruits, and leaves, and strings of small bells.

The room should have a beautiful ceiling-cloth,[1] lighted with lines of lamps fed with ghee to dispel all traces of darkness, and should be scented with burning camphor, incense-sticks, and incense, and ornamented with fans,[2] fly-whisks,[3] the tail feathers of the peacock, and mirrors, etc., and then he should with rice, powdered and coloured yellow, red, black, white, and dark blue draw the Ma*nd*ala[4] called Sarvato-bhadra,[5] beautiful and auspicious in every way (134-138).

Then each person should perform the rite preparatory to mental worship, according to his own Kalpa,[6] and then, having made mental worship, should purify the five elements with the Mantra previously mentioned (139). After the Pancha-tattvas[7] have been purified, the jar, which must be either of gold or silver or copper or earth, should be placed with the Brahma Bīja[8] on the Ma*nd*ala.[9] It should be washed with the Weapon Mantra[10] and smeared with curd, Aksh*a*ta,[11] and then a vermilion mark should be placed on it with the Mantra "Shrīng" (140-141).

---

[1] Chandrātapa is an awning with various designs thereon.

[2] Vyajana.

[3] Made of the tuft of the tail of yak.

[4] Diagram.

[5] Name of a Yantra—Sarvato-bhadra Ma*nd*ala.

[6] Sva-sva-kalpokta-vidhinā. Kalpa = Body of Ritualistic rules. Different Sampradāyas have different Kalpas.

[7] *i.e.*, the wine, meat, fish, Mudrā, and woman.

[8] Ong.

[9] Square—the Sarvato-bhadra Ma*nd*ala.

[10] Pha*t*.

[11] See p. 808, note 8.

He should then recite three times the letters of the alphabet, with the Bindu superposed from K*sh*a to A,[1] and recite inwardly the Mūla Mantra, and fill the jar with wine[2] or water from some holy place, or with ordinary pure water, and then throw into the jar nine gems or a piece of gold[3] (142-143).

The merciful Guru should then place over the mouth of the jar a leafy branch of a Jack-tree, a Fig-tree,[4] an Ashvattha-tree,[5] and of a Vakula and Mango-tree, with the Vāgbhava Bīja[6] (144).

He should then place on the leafy branches a gold, silver, copper, or earthen platter with fruits and sundried rice, uttering the Ramā Bīja[7] and Māyā Bīja[8] (145). Then, O Beauteous One! two pieces of cloth should be tied to the neck of the jar. When worshipping Shakti the cloth should be of a red colour, and in the worship of Shiva and Vi*sh*nu it should be white (146).

Inwardly reciting the

MANTRA

Sthāng, Sthīng, Hrīng, Shrīng,

the jar should be put in its place, and after putting into it the Pancha-tattvas[9] the nine cups should be placed in

---

[1] *i.e.*, the Māt*r*ikā Bīja in the reversed (Viloma) form.

[2] Kāra*n*a.

[3] Diamond, sapphire, emerald, coral, pearl, moonstone, gomeda, topaz, ruby. A piece of gold is used weighing one tola, or a gold mohur.

[4] *Ficus glomuiata rox.* Kaulikārchana-dīpikā substitutes Vata, or *Ficus indica*.

[5] *Ficus religiosa.*

[6] Aing. [7] Shrīng. [8] Krīng.

[9] Wine, meat, etc., not actually but by saying the Mantra "I here place meat" and so forth.

their order (147). The Shakti Pātra should be of silver, the Guru Pātra of gold, the Shrī Pātra[1] should be made of the human skull,[2] the rest of copper (148). Cups made of stone, wood, and iron should be rejected; the material of the cups in the worship of the Mahā-devī should be according to the means of the worshipper (149).

After placing the cups, libations should be offered to the four Gurus[3] and the Devī, and the wise one should then worship the jar filled with nectar (150). Lights and incense should then be waved[4] and sacrifices made to all beings,[5] and after worshipping the divinities of the Pī*th*as[6] he should perform S*h*a*d*aṁganyāsa[7] (151). He should then do Prā*n*āyāma, and, meditating on the Great Devī, invoke Her, and thereafter worship Her, the Object of his worship, to the best of his ability and without niggardliness (152). The excellent Guru, O Shivā! should perform all the rites ending with Homa, and then honour the Kumārīs[8] and worshippers of Shakti by presenting them with flowers, sandal-paste, and clothes (153).

The Guru should then ask the permission of those present with the following words:

O you Kaulas! who are vowed to Kula-worship, be kind to my disciple. Do you give your permission to his Saṁskāra of Pūr*n*ābhis*h*eka (154).

The Lord of the Chakra having thus asked, those present should respectfully say: "By the grace of

---

[1] Shrī-pātra is the cup from which liquid is taken for sprinkling, etc., and which is not used for drinking. In some schools the drinking-cup is made of a skull.

[2] Mahā-shaṁkha (the great Conch-shell)—that is, human skull.

[3] See Chapter VI, verse 50.

[4] *i.e.*, Ārati.

[5] Sarva-bhūta-vali.

[6] Or seat (see p. 120, note 1).

[7] See *ante* under verse 117.

[8] Unmarried girls.

Mahāmāyā[1] and the glory of the Supreme Spirit,[2] may thy disciple be perfect and devoted to the Supreme Tattva"[3] (155).

The Guru should then make the disciple worship the Devī in the jar, which has been worshipped by himself, and then, mentally repeating the

MANTRA

Klīng, Hrīng, Shrīng[4]

over it, move the pure jar, with the following

MANTRA

Rise, O Brahma-kalasha,[5] thou art the Devatā[6] and grantest all success. May my disciple, being bathed with thy water and leaves, be devoted to Brahman (156-157).

Having moved[7] the jar in this manner, the Guru should mercifully sprinkle the disciple seated with his face to the North with the Mantras about to be spoken (158).

The *Rishi* of the Mantra of this auspicious Pūrṇābhisheka rite is Sadāshiva, the metre is Anushtup, the presiding Devatā is the Adyā Kālī, the Bīja is "Oṁ," and its applicability is for the auspicious sprinkling[8] on the occasion of the Pūrṇābhisheka ceremony (159).

---

[1] The Devī.

[2] Paramātmā.

[3] Para-tattva-parāyaṇa, that is, a seeker of the Brahman.

[4] That is, the Vījas of Kāma, Māyā, and Ramā, or Lakshmī.

[5] Jar—which is the Brahman.

[6] Devatātmaka, that is, in which are all the Devatās.

[7] That is, by the Mantra.

[8] That is, Consecration.

MANTRA

May the Gurus sprinkle[1] thee. May Brahmā, Vi*sh*nu, and Maheshvara[2] sprinkle thee; may the Mothers Durgā, Lak*sh*mī, Bhavānī, sprinkle thee[3]; may *Shod*ashī, Tāri*n*ī,[4] Nityā,[5] Svāhā,[6] Mahi*sh*a-mardinī,[7] all These sprinkle thee with the water that has been sanctified by the Mantra; may Jaya-durgā, Vishālāk*sh*ī, Brahmā*n*ī, Sarasvatī,[8] may all These sprinkle thee; may Bagalā, Varadā, and Shivā[9] sprinkle thee; may the Shaktis, Nārasiṁhī, Vārāhī, Vai*sh*navī,[10] Vana-mālinī, Indrā*n*ī, Vāru*n*ī, Raudrī,[11] sprinkle thee; may Bhairavī,[12] Bhadra-kālī,[13] Tu*sh*ti, Pu*sh*ti, Umā, K*sh*amā, Shraddhā, Kānti, Dayā, Shānti,[14] always sprinkle thee; may Mahā-kālī, Mahā-lak*sh*mī, Mahānīla-sarasvatī,[15]

---

[1] Or Consecrate (Abhi*sh*inchantu).

[2] Shiva.

[3] Pārvatī, Shakti of Vi*sh*nu, Shakti of Shiva as Bhava. These and the other Devatās are aspects of the one Ādyā.

[4] Two of the ten Mahavidyās.

[5] A name of Tripurasundarī as Aṁgīnityā and of the fifteen Aṁga-devatās of Hers.

[6] Shakti of Agni.

[7] A name of the Devī as destructress of the demon of Anger in buffalo form. See Introduction to Kulachū*d*āma*n*i Tantra and Karpūrādi-stotra, Vols. IV, and IX Tantrik Texts, Ed. A. Avalon.

[8] Durgā, Vāsalī, and Shaktis of Brahmā.

[9] One of the Mahāvidyās, Devī as giver of boons, Shakti of Shiva.

[10] Three of the eight Mātrikās.

[11] Shaktis of Vi*sh*nu, Indra, Varu*n*a and Rudra.

[12] Shakti of Bhairava. Bhairava = Udyama (effort), the inner Parispanda which is the sense of complete I-ness (Pūr*n*āhambhāva); with him all Shaktis are in Sāmarasa. (Bhāskararāya Comm. on v. 2, ch. 6, Nityā*shod*ashikā). Popularly a Raudrī Mūrti.

[13] An aspect of Durgā.

[14] The eight names beginning wish Tu*sh*ti are different Kalās of the Devī personifying different qualities.

[15] Kālī, Lak*sh*mī and Tārā. Mahālak*sh*mī is also a name of one of the Mātrikas.

Ugra-Chandā, Prachandā,[1] constantly sprinkle thee; may Matsya, Kūrma, Varāha, Nrisimha, Vāmana, Rāma, Bhrigu-Rāma,[2] sprinkle thee with water; may Asitāmga, Ruru, Chanda, Krodhonmatta, Bhayamkara, Kapālī, Bhīshana,[3] sprinkle thee; may Kālī, Kapālinī, Kullā, Kurukullā, Virodhinī, Viprachittā, Mahogrā,[4] ever sprinkle thee; may Indra, Agni, Shamana,[5] Rakshah, Varuna, Pavana, Dhana-da, Maheshāna,[6] who are the eight Dikpālas,[7] sprinkle thee; may Ravi, Soma, Mamgala,[8] Budha, Jīva,[9] Sita,[10] Shani,[11] Rāhu, Ketu,[12] with all their Satellites, sprinkle thee; may the Nakshatras, the Karanas,[13] the Yogas,[14] the Days of the Week, and the two Divisions of the Month,[15] the Days, Seasons, Months, and the Year

---

[1] Raudrī Mūrtis of the Devī.

[2] Avatāras of Vishnu.

[3] Bhairavas. See p. 120.

[4] Bhairavīs. As to Kurukullā mātri-rūpā, see Introduction, Tantrarāja, vol. 8, Tantrik Texts, Ed. A. Avalon.

[5] Lord of the celestials, Lord of fire, an epithet of Yama.

[6] Nirrit protector of S. E. Corner, the direction of Yama, Lord of Ocean, Lord of Air, Kuvera, Lord of Wealth, another Dikpāla.

[7] Protectors of the Quarters.

[8] Sun, Moon and Mars.

[9] Mercury, Brihaspati or Jupiter.

[10] Shukra, the planet Venus.

[11] Saturn.

[12] Ketu is the descending node, considered as the ninth planet, and the body or trunk of the demon Samhikeya. Rāhu is the ascending node—a demon with head and without body, swallowing the Sun and Moon in eclipse. The name of Rāhu means Bhu-chhāyā or earth-shadow.

[13] These are also divisions of time and are eleven in number: Vava, Vālava, Kaulava, Taitila, Vanija, Vishti, Shakuni, Chatushpada, Kintughna, and Nāga-Gara. The Nakshatras are the constellations. Time is divided according to their respective positions day after day.

[14] Astrological divisions of time numbering twenty seven according to conjunctions of Planets or Stars.

[15] The Pakshas, which are Shukla and Krishna—light and dark.

anoint thee always; may the Salt Ocean, the Sweet Ocean, the Ocean of Wine,[1] the Ocean of Ghee, the Ocean of Curd, the Ocean of Milk, the Ocean of Sweet Water sprinkle thee with their consecrated waters; may Gaṁgā, Yamunā, Revā, Chandra-bhāgā, Sarasvatī, Sarayū, Ga*nd*akī, Kuntī, Shveta-gaṁgā, Kaushikī,[2] may all These sprinkle thee with their consecrated waters; may the great Nāgas[3] beginning with Ananta, the birds beginning with Garu*d*a,[4] the trees beginning with the Kalpa tree,[5] and the great Mountains sprinkle thee! may the beneficent Beings[6] residing in Pātāla,[7] on the earth, and in the air, pleased at this hour of thy Pūr*n*ābhis*h*eka, sprinkle thee with water (160-175). May thy ill-luck, bad name, illness, melancholy and sorrows be destroyed by the Pūr*n*ābhis*h*eka, and by the glory of the Supreme Brahman (176). May Alaks*h*mī,[8] Kālakar*n*ī,[9] the *D*ākinīs, and the Yoginīs,[10] being driven away by the Kālī Bīja, be destroyed by the Abhis*h*eka (177). May the Bhūtas,[11] Pretas,[12] Pishāchas,[13] and the maleficent Planets be driven

---

[1] Surā.

[2] Names of sacred Rivers.

[3] Serpent-divinities, with human head and tail of serpent, said to inhabit the Nether Worlds (Pātāla).

[4] The Vāhana of Vis*hn*u.

[5] Tree in Indra's heaven that yields all that is desired.

[6] Ks*h*emakāri*n*a*h*.

[7] The Nether World.

[8] Devī of Adversity as regards loss of wealth.

[9] Devī of Misfortune.

[10] Here Bad Female Spirits. Yoginī is a name given to the Supreme Devī Herself and Yoginīs are Her various powers. Some of which are great and beneficent. The *D*ākinīs and Yoginīs here are evil spirits. *D*ākinī is also the name of Devī in the Mūlādhāra.

[11] Spirits, Ghosts primarily means the Elements.

[12] Spirits before performance of Shrāddha.

[13] Bad and filthy disembodied souls, who are invoked by those who are Pishācha-siddha.

out, put to flight, and destroyed by the Ramā Bīja;[1] may all misfortune caused thee by magic and by the incantations of thy enemies, may all thy transgressions of mind, word, and body be destroyed as the result of this initiation; may all thy adversities be destroyed, may thy prosperity be undisturbed, may all thy desires be fulfilled as the result of this Pūrnābhisheka (178-180).

With these twenty-one Mantras the disciple should be sprinkled with water; and if he has obtained already the Mantra from the mouth of a Pashu,[2] the Guru should make him hear it again[3] (181).

The Kaulika Guru should, having informed the worshippers of Shakti, call his disciple by his name and give him a name ending with Ānandanātha (182).

Being thus initiated in the Mantra by the Guru, the disciple should worship his Ishta-devatā[4] in the Yantra[5] and then honour the Guru by offering him the Panchatattva[6] (183).

The disciple should also give as Dakshinā[7] cows, land, gold, clothes, drinks, and jewels to the Guru, and then honour the Kaulas,[8] who are the very embodiments of Shiva[9] (184).

The self-possessed, purified, and humble disciple, having honoured the Kaulas, should touch the sacred feet of the Guru with veneration, and, bowing to him, pray to him as follows (185):

---

[1] Shrīng.

[2] See Shakti and Shākta.

[3] From his own mouth.

[4] The Divinity of his worship.

[5] Diagram.

[6] Wine, meat, etc.

[7] Presents.

[8] Who are present.

[9] Shivātmaka.

Prayer to Guru

Holy Lord! Thou art the Lord of the world. Lord! Thou art my Lord. O Ocean of Mercy! do Thou gratify my heart's desire by the gift of the excellent nectar (186).

The Guru should then say:

"Give me leave, O Kaulas! you who are the visible images of Shiva Himself, that I may give to my good and humble disciple the excellent nectar" (187).

The Kaulas will then say:

"Lord of the Chakra! Thou art the Supreme Lord Himself, Thou art the Sun of the Kaula lotus. Do Thou gratify this good disciple, and give him the Kula nectar" (188).

The Guru, having obtained the leave of the Kaulas, should place in the hand of the disciple the drinking-cup filled with the excellent nectar, as also the Shuddhi (189).

The Guru should then, devoutly meditating on the Devī in his heart, place the Tilaka[1] on the forehead of the disciple, as also of the Kaulas, with the ashes adhering to the sacrificial spoon (190).

Let the Guru then distribute the Tattvas offered[2] to the Devī, and partake of the food and drink as directed in the injunctions relating to the formation of Chakra[3] (191).

O Devī! I have spoken to Thee of the auspicious rites relating to Pūr*n*ābhis*h*eka. By this one attains divine knowledge and becomes Shiva Himself (192).

The Pūr*n*ābhis*h*eka should be performed for nine or seven or five or three or one night (193).

---

[1] Sectarian mark.

[2] Prasāda-tattva = Prasāda is food offered to a Deva or Guru, and is deemed holy food.

[3] See Chapter VI, verse 189 *et seq.*

There are, O Kuleshānī! five different forms[1] in this purificatory rite. In the rite which lasts nine nights the Mandala[2] known as Sarvato-bhadra[3] should be made (194).

Beloved! in the rite which lasts seven nights the Mandala Nava-nābha, in the rite which lasts five nights the Mandala Panchābja, in the rite which lasts three nights and in the rite which lasts one night the Mandala of eight-petalled lotus should be respectively made (195).

O Devī! the injunction is that on the Sarvato-bhadra and Nava-nābha Mandalas nine jars[4] should be placed on Panchābja Mandala five, and on Ashta-dalābja Mandala one jar, and the Aṁga-Devatās[5] and the Āvarana-Devatās[6] should be worshipped in the filaments and other parts of the lotuses (196-197).

The Kaulas who have been Fully Initiated are pure of soul. All things are purified by their look, touch, and when smelt by them (198). All men, whether they are Shāktas, Shaivas, Vaishnavas, Gānapatas, or Sauras,[7] should worship the Kaula Sādhu[8] with devotion (199).

It is good for a Shākta to have a Guru who is a Shākta, for a Shaiva a Shaiva Guru is commendable, and for a Vaishnava a Vaishnava, for a Saura a Saura as Guru is advised, and a Gānapata is the proper Guru for a Gānapata, but a Kaula is excellent as Guru in the case of all; therefore the wise one should with all his soul be initiated

---

[1] Kalpa which varies according to the Devatā, the Sampradāya and competency (Adhikāra).

[2] Yantra. For these Mandalas, see Tantra-sāra, pp. 124-129, and p. 168.

[3] All-propitious.

[4] Ghatas.

[5] The limbs or parts of the chief Devatā which are considered as Devatās.

[6] The attendant Devatās.

[7] These are the five classes of worshippers—(Panchopāsaka).

[8] Holy man, or Sage.

by a Kaula (200-201). Those who with devotion worship the Kaulas with Pancha-tattva,[1] cause the salvation[2] of their Ancestors, and themselves attain the highest end (202).

The man who has obtained the Mantra from the mouth of a Pashu[3] is of a certainty a Pashu, and he who has obtained the Mantra from a Vīra[3] is a Vīra, and he who obtains it from a Kaula knows the Brahman (203). One who has been initiated according to Shākta rites[4] is a Vīra; he may purify the Pancha-tattvas only in the worship of his own I*sh*t*a*-devatā,[5] he may never be the Chakreshvara[6] (204).

He who kills a Vīra, he who drinks wine which has not been consecrated,[7] he who seduces the wife of or steals the property of a Vīra, these four are great sinners, and the man who associates with any of these is the fifth sinner (205). Those evil-natured men who disparage the Kula Way,[8] Kula articles, and the Kula worshipper go down the low and vile path (206).

The Rudra-*d*ākinīs and Rudra-bhairavīs[9] dance in joy (at the thought of) chewing the bones and flesh of men who disparage wine and the Kaulas (207). They (the Kaulas) are merciful and truthful, and ever desire the good of others. For such as insult them there is no escape from Hell (208).

---

[1] Wine, etc.

[2] Uddh*r*itya = lifting up, rescuing, etc.

[3] As to the meaning of these classes of men, see "Shakti and Shākta".

[4] *i.e.*, Shāktābhi*sh*eka as distinct from the higher initiation called Pūr*n*ābhi*sh*eka.

[5] Special tutelary Devatā.

[6] Lord of the Chakra, who alone can pour out wine from the jar, and drink and distribute as he thinks right. The others are prohibited from doing so.

[7] V*r*ithā-pāyī = Vain-drinker. These are Mahāpātakīs.

[8] Kula Worship, etc.

[9] Fierce Spirits of that name, attendant on Shiva and Kālī.

I have (in various Tantras) spoken of many and various methods and rites[1]; but in the case of a Kaula who is devoted to the Brahman alone, the performance or non-performance of such rites is one and the same[2] (209).

There is one Supreme Brahman Who is spread throughout the Universe. He is worshipped by the worship of the Universe,[3] because everything exists in Him (210).

Beloved! even those who look to the fruit of action and are governed by their desires and by the worship of different Devas, and addicted to various rituals worshipping the Devatās as other than themselves[4] go to and enter That (211). He who sees everything in Brahman, and who sees Brahman everywhere, is undoubtedly known as a true Kaula, who has attained Liberation while yet living[5] (212).

End of the Tenth Chapter, entitled "Rites relating to B*ri*ddhi Shrāddha, Funeral Rites, and Pūr*n*ābhis*h*eka."

---

[1] Prayoga and Karma: the former including the meanings, application, method, object. The latter is ritual action.

[2] Because he is free from Rāga and Dves*h*a in whatever he does (Tarkālaṁkāra).

[3] Vishvārchayā: that is, worship of anything in the universe. Everything is the form of the Brahman and provided what is worshipped is so worshipped with this knowledge it is worship of Brahman.

[4] P*ri*thăktvena yajanta*h*. The reference is to dualists who think God is wholly separate from themselves and not, as the Advaitins hold, their own essential self. By 'That' the Nis*h*kala Brahman is meant.

[5] Jīvanmukta.

CHAPTER XI

EXPIATORY ACTS

LISTENING to the Rules [1] of Shambhu relating to the different Castes and Stages of Life, Aparṇā [2] was greatly pleased, and questioned Shaṁkara thus (1):

Shrī Devī said:

Thou hast, O Lord! out of Thy kindness for Me and in Thy omniscience, spoken of the customs and the rules of religious conduct and sacraments [3] for the well-being of the world (2). But the men of the Kali Age, being wicked, and blinded by anger and lust, atheists,[4] of wavering minds and addicted to the gratification of their senses, will not in their ignorance and folly, follow the way laid down by Thee; it behoves Thee, O Īshāna! to say what will be the means of their Liberation (3-4).

Shrī Sadāshiva said:

Thou hast asked well, O Devī! Thou who art the Benefactress of the world, the Mother of the world, Thou art Durgā,[5] Thou dost liberate people from the bonds of birth and the toils of this world (5). Thou art the Primordial One, Thou fosterest and guardest this world, Thou art beyond the most excellent; Thou, O Devī! dost support the moving and the motionless Universe (6). Thou art

---

[1] Dharma.

[2] Devī—so called because during the time She was doing penance She would not so much as eat a leaf to appease Her hunger.

[3] Saṁskāras,

[4] Nāstika—Unbeliever in the Vedas and in a Future Life.

[5] "Mother" (Jananī), which Bhāratī interprets as equivalent of *Janayitri*. Durgā = "Difficult to understand and attain."

Earth,[1] Thou art Water, Thou art Fire, Thou art Air, Thou art the Ether,[2] Thou art Ahaṁkāra,[3] Thou art Mahat-tattva[4] (7). Thou art Life in this world; Thou art the Knowledge[5] of Self, and Thou art the Supreme Divinity. Thou art the Senses; Thou art Manas, Thou art Buddhi; Thou art the motion and existence of the Universe[6] (8).

Thou art the Vedas, Thou art the Pra*n*ava,[7] Thou art the Sm*r*itis, the Saṁhitās, the Nigamas, the Āgamas, and the Tantras,[8] Thou pervadest all the Shāstras, and art the Abode of all that is good (9). Thou art Mahākāli,[9] Mahālaks*h*mī,[10] Mahā-nīla-sarasvatī,[11] Mahodarī,[12] Mahāmāyā,[13] Mahāraudri,[14] and Maheshvarī[15]; Thou art Omniscient[16] and Knowledge itself,[17] there is nothing which Thou

---

[1] P*r*ithivī. [2] Void = Viyat = Ākāsha = Ether of Space.

[3] As to Ahaṁkāra, the I-making faculty of mind, see Woodroffe's "World as Power: Mind."

[4] The Sankhya category of that name: the cosmic Buddhi. See *ibid.*

[5] Knowledge = Vidyā—here Atma-jnāna.

[6] By the senses are meant the eyes, ears, etc. Manas is the faculty of attention and Buddhi the faculty of determination. Bhāratī says that mind (Manas) means heart (H*r*idaya), and understanding (Buddhi) means Shāstrādi-tattva-jnāna (knowledge of the essence of the Shāstras, etc.).

[7] Ongkāra.

[8] Sm*r*itis are the Dharma-Shāstras of Manu and others and the Saṁhitās refer to the Mahābhārata and other similar writings (Bhāratī).

[9] As the devourer of Time and who is therefore Destructress of the Universe, which is Brahman in time and space.

[10] As the Cause of all prosperity and intelligence.

[11] As the Source of all learning.

[12] For She holds the Universe in Her womb.

[13] She Who is one with Brahman, Who holds the Universe under Her spell.

[14] She Who is the great Destructress withdrawing all to Herself.

[15] As She dominates and is the Lord of all.

[16] Sarvajnā.

[17] Jnānamayī = Moks*h*avis*h*aya-prajnā-svarūpā = illumining and liberating knowledge (Bhāratī).

knowest not; yet, O Wise One! since Thou askest Me, I will speak of it for Thy pleasure (10-11).

Thou hast truly spoken, O Devī! of the evil ways of men, who, knowing what is for their welfare, yet, maddened by sinful desire for things which bring immediate enjoyment, are devoid of the sense of right and wrong, and desert the True Path. I speak now of that which will contribute to their Liberation (12-13).

In the doing of what is forbidden and in the omitting of what is enjoined men sin, and sins lead to pain, sorrow, and disease (14).

O Kula-nāyikā![1] know that there are two kinds of sin—that which contributes merely to the injury of one's own Self, and that which causes injury to others (15). Man is released of the sin of injuring others by the punishment inflicted by the King, and from other sins by expiatory rites[2] with self-restraint[3] (16).

Those sinful men who are not purified by either punishment or expiation cannot but go to hell, and are despised both in this world and the next (17).

O Ādyā! I shall first of all speak of the Rules relating to punishment by the King. O Maheshānī! The King who deviates from these, himself goes upon the downward path (18).

In the administration of justice, servants, sons, strangers,[4] friends and foes should all be treated alike (19).

If the King is guilty of any sin himself, or if he should have punished one who is not guilty, then he shall purify

[1] The Devī as sovereign mistress of the Kaulas.

[2] Prāyashchitta.

[3] Samādhi—Chitta-vritti-nirodha, or Yoga. But here it means ordinary restraint of the inclinations of the Chitta; that is, practising acts of self-restraint or doing Prāyashchitta with self-restraint (Bhāratī).

[4] Udāsīna—Detached Persons who are neither friends nor foes (Bhāratī).

himself by fasting and by placating those he has wronged by gifts (20). If the King should consider that he is guilty of any sin which is punishable by death, he should then abdicate his kingdom and go to a forest, and there labour for his purification by penances (21). The King should not, without sufficient reason, inflict heavy punishment on persons guilty of a light offence, nor should he inflict light punishment on persons guilty of a great offence (22). But the punishment by which many offenders may be deterred from ill-doing, and (punishment) in the case of an offender who is fearless[1] of crimes, should be heavy, although the offence be a light one (23).

In the case of one who has committed the offence but once only and is ashamed of his ill-deed, or of one who fears crime and is a respectable man, a light punishment should be inflicted, even if the offence be a grave one (24).

If a Kaula or a Brāhmaṇa is guilty of a slight offence, they should even, though otherwise worthy of respect, be punished by the King by a rebuke (25).

The King who does not bestow adequate rewards and punishments after consultation with his ministers is a great sinner (26).

A son should not leave his mother and father, the subjects should not leave their King, nor the wife her husband, if they are in trouble or in disgrace, unless they are greatly guilty[2] (27).

The subjects should actively protect the kingdom, property, and life of the just King; otherwise they will go upon the downward path (28).

Shivā! those who knowingly go with their mother,[3] daughter,[3] or sister,[3] those who have killed their

---

[1] *i.e.*, in the cause of hardened criminals.

[2] The text is read according to Ram Mohun Roy.

[3] Each of these terms is suggestive of a class. Thus, *Mother* would include her sister, her sister-in-law, etc.

Mahāgurus,[1] those who have, after having taken refuge in the Kula Faith, abandoned it, and those who have broken the trust placed in them, are very great sinners (29-30).

Shivā! the punishment of those that go with their mother, sister, and daughter is death, and if the latter are wilful participants the same punishment should be inflicted upon them (31).

The sinful man, who with a lustful mind goes to the bed of his mother's or father's sister, or to his daughter-in-law, or mother-in-law (wife's mother), the wife of his preceptor, the wife of his maternal or paternal grandfather, the daughter or wife of his mother's or father's brother, the wife or daughter of his brother, the sister's daughter, the master's wife or daughter, or with an unmarried girl, should be punished by castration,[2] and these women also if they are wilful participants in the offence should be punished by the cutting of their noses and turning them out of the house that they may be released from sin (32-34).

The punishment of the man who goes with the wife or daughter of a Sapi*nd*a,[3] or with the wife of a man who has trusted him, is to be deprived of all his property and to have his head shaved (35).

If through mistake (by ignorance) one should happen to marry any of these,[4] either in Brāhma or Shaiva form, then she should be left at once (36).

A man who goes with the wife of another man of the same caste as himself, or of a caste inferior to his own, should be punished by the imposition of a fine and by being kept on a diet of grains[5] for one month (37).

[1] *i.e.*, Father and Mother, and Husband in the case of married women. Here are Atipātakīs named.

[2] Liṁga-chchheda = Cutting off the genitals.

[3] Kinsman. [4] *i.e.*, one of the prohibited degree.

[5] Ka*n*a = grains, broken rice, etc.

If a Ks*h*atriya, Vaishya, Shūdra, or Sāmānya, O Thou of Beauteous Face! goes with a Brāhma*n*a woman knowing her to be such, then his punishment is castration, and the Brāhma*n*a woman should be disfigured and banished from his kingdom by the King. For such as go with the wives of Vīras, and, for such wives, the punishment should be the same (38-39).

The wicked man who enjoys the wife of one of a higher caste should be heavily fined, and kept on a diet of grains for three months (40).

And if the woman is a wilful party, she should be similarly punished. If the wife is the victim of a rape, then she should be separated from, but maintained by, her husband (41).

A wife, whether married according to Brāhma or Shaiva form, should in all cases be renounced if she has gone with another man even if it be only once, and then whether of her own desire or against it (42).

Those who have intercourse with public women, or with cows or other animals, should, O Deveshi! be purified by being kept on a diet of grains for three nights (43).

The punishment of those wicked men who have unnatural intercourse[1] with a woman is death; this is the injunction of Shambhu (44).

A man who ravishes a woman, even if she be the wife of a Cha*nd*āla should be punished by death, and should never be pardoned (45).

A man should consider as wife only that woman who has been married to him according to Brāhma or Shaiva form. All other women are the wives of others[2] (46).

A man who with lust looks at another man's wife should fast for a day to purify himself. He who has converse

---

[1] Pāyung gachchhatām.

[2] Para-strī.

with[1] her in a secret place should fast for two days. He who touches her should fast for four days; and he who embraces[2] her should fast for eight days to purify himself (47).

And the woman who with a lustful mind behaves in the same manner should purify herself by following the same rules of fasting (48).

The man who uses offensive language towards a woman, who sees the private parts of a woman who is the wife of another[3] and laughs mockingly at her, should fast for two days to purify himself (49).

A man who shows his naked body to another, or who makes another person naked, should cease eating for three days to purify himself (50).

If the husband proves that his wife has had intercourse with another, then the King should punish her and her paramour according to the injunction laid down (51).

If the husband (has good cause to believe and yet) is unable to prove the faithlessness of his wife, then he should separate from her, but he should maintain her if she remains under his control (52).

If the husband, on seeing his wife enjoying with her paramour, kills her with her paramour, then the King should not punish him with death (53).

If the husband prohibits the wife to go to any place or to talk with anyone, then the wife should neither go to that place nor talk with that person (54).

If, on the death of the husband, the widow lives with the relatives of the husband under their control, following the customs[4] of a widow's life, or in their absence she lives with the relatives of her father, then she is entitled to inherit her husband's property (55).

---

[1] Sambhāshya, lewd talk, etc.

[2] Parishvajya.

[3] Para-strī.

[4] See *post*.

The widow should not eat twice a day, nor should she eat food cooked by one who is not her husband's Agnate; she should renounce sexual enjoyment, animal food, jewels, sleeping on soft beds,[1] and coloured clothes[2] (56).

The widow faithful to her Dharma should not anoint herself with fragrant ointment, she should avoid village gossip,[3] and should spend her time in the worship of the Devatās and in the performance of Vratas[4] (57).

In the case of the boy who has neither father, mother, nor paternal grandfather, the mother's relatives[5] are the best guardians (58). The mother's mother, mother's father, mother's brother, mother's brother's son, mothers's father's brother, these are the relatives[5] on the mother's side (59).

Father's mother, father, brother, father's brother's and sister's sons, father's father's brother, are known as paternal relatives[6] (60).

The husband's mother, father, brother, the husband's brother's and sister's sons, and the husband's father's brothers, all these are known as the relatives of the husband[7] (61).

Ambikā! the King should compel a man, according to his means, to give food and clothes to his father, mother, father's father, father's mother, the wife whose son cannot support her, and to the maternal grandfather and grandmother, who are poor and have no son (62-63).

If a man speaks rudely[8] to his wife he must fast for a day, if he beats her he must go without food for three days,

[1] Paryaṁka—that is, with mattresses (gadi) and the like.
[2] Rakta—literally, red. The widow should dress in white.
[3] Grāmyālāpa, *i.e.*, vulgar and obscene talk.
[4] Vows.
[5] Mātṛi-bāndhavas.
[6] Pitṛi-bāndhavas.
[7] Pati-bāndhavas.
[8] Durvāchyang kathayan.

and if he causes her bloodshed then he must fast for seven days (64).

If a man in his anger or folly calls[1] his wife his mother, his sister, or daughter, then he should purify himself by fasting seven days (65).

If a girl be married to an impotent man, then the King should cause her to be married again, even if the fact is discovered after the lapse of some time. This is Shiva's injunction (66).

If a girl becomes a widow before consummation of marriage, she also ought to be remarried by her father. This also is the command of Shiva (67).

The woman who is delivered of a child within six months of her marriage, or after the lapse of a year following her husband's death, is not a wife, nor is the child legitimate (68).

The woman who causes a miscarriage before the completion of the fifth month, as well as the person who helps her thereto, should be heavily punished (69).

The woman who after the fifth month destroys the child in her womb, and the person who helps her thereto, are guilty of killing a human being (70).

The cruel man who wilfully kills another man should always be sentenced to death by the King (71).

The King should correct the man who kills another man through negligence,[2] or mistake,[3] or by ignorance, either by taking his property[4] from him or by giving him a severe beating[5] (72).

[1] *i.e.*, if a man says to his wife, "You are my mother," meaning that she was not his wife.

[2] Pramāda.

[3] Bhrama.

[4] Dravi*nādāna*ta*h*, *i.e.*, by imposing a fine on the offender.

[5] Tībra tā*dana*.

The man who tries to compass his own death, whether by himself or by the aid of another, should be awarded the same punishment as the man who kills another through ignorance (73).

The man who kills another in a duel, or kills an enemy who attempts to kill him, is not guilty of any offence (74).

The King should punish the man who has maimed another by maiming him, and the man who has beaten another by having him beaten (75).

The wicked man who flings any missile, or lifts his hand to strike a Vipra,[1] or one who should be honoured, or who strikes either of them, should be punished by a pecuniary fine for the first offence, and by the burning of his hand for a second offence (76).

If a man dies consequent upon a wound inflicted by any weapon or otherwise after six months, then the offender should be punished for the assault, and shall not be punished with death by the King (77).

If the King kills subverters of his government, men who plot to usurp his kingdom, servants secretly befriending the King's enemies, men creating dissatisfaction against the King among the troops, subjects who wish to wage war against the King, or armed highway robbers, he shall not be guilty of any sin (78-79).

The man who kills another, compelled by his master's order,[2] is not himself guilty of the killing, for it is the master's killing. This is the command of Shiva (80).

If a man's death is caused by a beast belonging to, or weapons in the hand of, a careless man, then the latter should be corrected by a pecuniary or bodily punishment (81).

Those wicked men who disobey the King's command, who are arrogant in their speech in the King's

---

[1] Brāhmaṇa.

[2] Aparihāryayā ājnayā, *i.e.*, by order he is unable to disobey.

presence, or who decry the Kula faith, should be punished by the King (82).

He who misappropriates property entrusted to him, the malicious man, the cheat, he who creates ill-feeling between men, or who makes people quarrel with one another, should be banished from the kingdom by the King (83).

The King should banish from his kingdom those abandoned[1] and wicked-minded men who give away their sons and daughters in marriage for money, and who give their daughters (in marriage) to impotent husbands (84).

Persons who attempt to harm others by the spreading of baseless calumnies should be punished by the just King in accordance with their offence[2] (85).

The King should compel the calumniator to pay the sufferer money commensurate with the harm done (86).

For such persons as steal gems, pearls, gold and other metals, the punishment should be either the cutting off of the hand or the entire arm, according to the value of the stolen property (87).

Those who steal buffaloes, horses, cattle, jewels, etc., and children, should be punished by the King as thieves (88).

Thieves who steal food and articles of small value should be corrected by being kept on a diet of grains for a week or a fortnight (89).

O Adored of the Devas! the faithless and the ingrate can never attain Liberation by sacrifices, votive observances, penances, acts of charity, and other expiatory rites (90).

The King should, after severely punishing them, exile from his dominion men who give false evidence, or who are partial as arbitrators (91).

[1] Patita = Fallen. This verse literally means who gives away for money his son or daughter to a sexless person etc.

[2] "According to the gravity of the calumny:" according to a variation in the Text.

The testimony of six, four, or even three witnesses is sufficient to prove a fact; but, O Shivā! the testimony of two witnesses of well-known piety is enough (92).

Beloved! if witnesses contradict one another on questions of place, time, and other details of fact, then their testimony should be rejected (93).

O Beloved! the word of the blind and the deaf should be accepted as evidence, and the signs and writing of a dumb man and of one who is both deaf and dumb should also be accepted (94).

Of all evidence and in all cases, and particularly in litigation, documentary evidence is the best, as it does not perish and always endures (95).

The man who fabricates a writing for his own use or for the use of another should be punished with double the punishment of a false witness (96).

The statement on oath, on his own behalf, of a careful and reliable man is of a higher probative value than the word of many witnesses (97).

O Pārvatī! as all virtues find their support in Truth, so do all vices find their support in untruth (98).[1]

Therefore, the King shall incur no blame by chastizing those who are devoid of Truth and are the receptacle of all vices. This is the command of Shiva (99).

Devī! if a man says, "I tell the truth," at the same time touching any of the following—a Kaula, the Guru, a Brāhma*n*a, water of Gaṁgā, an image of a Devatā, a Kula religious Book, Kulām*ri*ta,[2] or the offerings made to a Devatā, he has taken an oath. If after that he speaks an untruth, then he will go to hell for one Kalpa[3] (100-101).

---

[1] Yathā tis*hth*anti pu*n*yāni satyam āshritya Pārvati.
Tathā, n*ri*tang samāstritya pātakānyakhilānyapi.

[2] *i.e.*, Consecrated Wine.

[3] 4,320,000 years of mortals—till the end of creation.

An oath that an act which is not sinful will be or will not be done, should always be kept by men (102).

The man who has broken his oath should purify himself by a fortnight's fast; and one who has broken it by mistake should live on grains for twelve days (103).

Even the Kula-dharma, if not followed according to Truth and the injunctions, not only fails to secure final Liberation and Beatitude, but leads to sin (104).

Wine is Târâ Herself in liquid form,[1] Who is the Saviour of beings, the Mother of Enjoyment and Liberation, Who destroys danger and diseases, burns up the heaps of sins, and purifies the worlds. O Beloved! She grants all success, and increases knowledge, intellect, and learning, and, O Âdyâ! She (wine) is ever taken by those who have attained final Liberation and those who are desirous of attaining final Liberation, by those that have become and those striving to be adepts,[2] and by Kings and Devas for the attainment of their desires (105-107).

Mortals who drink wine with their minds well under control[3] and according to the injunctions (of Shiva) are, verily, Immortals[4] on Earth (108).

By partaking, in accordance to the injunctions, of any of the Tattvas,[5] man becomes like unto Shiva. What, then, is the result of partaking of all the five Tattvas[5]? (109).

---

[1] Surâ drava-mayî Târâ jîva-nistâra-kârinî
Jananî bhoga-mokshânâng nâshinî vipadâng rujâm (105).
Dâhinî pâpa-samghânâng pâvinî jagatâng, Priye!
Sarva-siddhi-pradâ jnâna-buddhi-vidyâ vibardhinî (106).
Muktair mumukshubhih siddhaih sâdhakaih kshiti-pâlakaih
Sevyate sarvadâ devair, Âdye! svâbhîshta-siddhaye (107).

[2] Siddhas.

[3] Susamâhitachetasâ.

[4] Amartya, Amara—*i.e.*, the Devas who do not die.

[5] Wine, meat, etc.

But the drinking of this Devī Vāruṇī[1] in disregard of the injunctions destroys the intellect, life, fame, and wealth of men (110).

By the excessive drinking of wine the drunkard destroys the understanding,[2] which is the means for the attainment of the Fourfold End[3] of human existence (111).

Only harm at every step, both to himself and to others, results for a man whose mind is distracted and who knows not what should and what should not be done (112).

Therefore, the King or the Lord of the Chakra should correct by bodily and pecuniary punishments those who are over-addicted to wine and intoxicating drugs (113).[4]

The understanding of men is clouded by the drinking of wine, whether in small or large quantities, according to the difference in the quality of the wine, to the temperament of the individual, to the place where and the time when it is taken (114).

Therefore, excessive drinking is to be judged, not from the quantity drunk, but from the result as shown in difficulty of speech and from the unsteadiness of hands, feet, and sight (115).

The King should burn the tongues and confiscate the money of, and inflict corporal punishments on, men who

---

[1] Wine here spoken of as a manifestation of the Devī.

[2] Buddhi.

[3] Dharma, Artha, Kāma, Moksha.

[4] Iyang ched vāruṇī devī nipītā vidhibarjitā
Nṛināng vināshayet sarvang buddhim āyur yasho dhanam (110).
Atyantapānān madyasya chaturvarga-prasādhanī
Buddhir vinashyati prāyo lokānāng mattachetasām (111).
Vibhrāntabuddher manujāt karyākāryam ajānataḥ
Svānishṭhang cha parānishṭhang jāyate 'smāt pade pade (112).
Ato nripo vā chakresho madye mādakavastushu
Atyāsaktajanān kāyadhanadaṇḍena shodhayet (113).

Bhāratī says the excessive drinking of wine leads to the destruction of one's intellect and to evil both for the self and others. The King should therefore punish such men as stated in v. 113.

hold not their senses under control, whose minds are distracted by drink, who deviate from the duty they owe to Devas and Gurus, who are fearful to behold, who are the source of all folly, who are sinful, and transgressors of the injunctions of Shiva, and bring ruin on themselves (116-117).

The King should severely chastise and fine the man who is unsteady in hands, feet, or in speech, who is bewildered, maddened, and beyond himself with drink (118).

The King, who labours for the happiness of his subjects, should inflict pecuniary punishment on the drunkard who is guilty of evil language and is devoid of fear and shame[1] (119).

O Kuleshvarī! a Kaula, even if he has been initiated[2] a hundred times, should be regarded as a Pashu, for he has fallen from the Kula Dharma[3], if he drinks to excess (120).

The Kaula who drinks excessively of wine, be it consecrated or not, should be renounced by all Kaulas and punished by the King (121).

The drunken twice-born man who makes his Brāhmī wife[4] drink wine should purify both himself and his wife by living on a diet of grains[5] for five days (122).

The man, who has drunk wine which has not been sanctified, should purify himself by fasting for three days, and who has eaten meat which has not been sanctified should fast for two days (123).

If a man partakes of fish and parched food[6] which have not been sanctified, he should fast for a day, but he

---

[1] *i.e.*, a confirmed and shameless drunkard.

[2] *i.e.*, let him be ever so initiated.

[3] Duty of a Kaula.

[4] Wife married in Brāhma form.

[5] Ka*n*a—that is, the broken grain left on husking; or the text may mean—a spare diet.

[6] Mudrā.

who participates in the fifth Tattva[1] without conforming to the rites should be corrected by the King's punishment (124).[2]

He who knowingly eats human flesh or beef should purify himself by a fortnight's[3] fast. This is the expiation for this sin (125).

Beloved! a man who has eaten the flesh of animals of human shape, or of carnivorous animals, should purify himself by a three day's fast (126).

The man who partakes of food cooked by Mlechchhas, Cha*nd*ālas, and Pashus, and enemies of Kula, is purified by a fortnight's[3] fast (127).

And, O Kuleshvarī! if anyone knowingly partakes of the leavings[4] of these,[5] then he should fast for a month to purify himself, and if he has done so unknowingly he should fast for a fortnight[3] (128).

My injunction is that if a man partakes of food cooked by a man of a caste inferior to his own, he should, to purify himself, fast for three days (129).

By the partaking of food of a Pashu, Cha*nd*āla, and Mlechchha, which has been placed in the Chakra or in the hands of a Vīra, no sin is incurred (130).

One who partakes of forbidden food at a time when food is scarce, in times of famine and danger, or when life is at stake, is guiltless of any transgression (131).

If food is eaten on the back of an elephant, or on a large block of stone, or on a piece of wood, which can be carried only by several men, or in places where nothing

[1] Coition (Surata or Maithuna).

[2] Avaidhang panchamang kurvan rājno da*nd*ena shuddhyati.

[3] Paks*h*a.

[4] Uchchhis*ht*a.

[5] Mlechchhas, etc.

objectionable is actually perceived, there is no fault[1] (132).

Animals the flesh of which is forbidden, as also diseased animals, should not be killed even for the purpose of sacrifice to the Devas. By killing such animals sin is incurred (133).

If anyone knowingly kills a bull, then he shall do penance (as described below), and if he does so unknowingly he shall do half of such penance. This is the command of Shaṁkara (134).

So long as the penance is not performed he shall not shave or pare his nails nor wear clean[2] raiments (135).

Shivā! he should fast for a month, and should live on grains for another month, and should live eating food which he has begged during the third month. This is called K*ri*chchhra-Vrata[3] (136).

At the end of the penance,[4] he should shave his head and free himself from the sin of wilful killing of the bull by feasting Kaulas, relatives (Agnates), and Bāndhavas[5] (137).

If the death of a cow or bull is caused by want of care, the expiation is an eight days' fast for a Brāhma*n*a, and for a Ks*h*atriya and the (two other) inferior castes fasting for six, four, and two days respectively (138).

---

[1] Bhaks*h*ya-dos*h*a. Bhaks*h*ya=Food, Dos*h*a=Fault, Defect. The term is used, not as regards the quality of food so much as the place where it is eaten, with whom it is eaten, and in whose presence it is eaten. Some consider that their food is polluted if another looks at it (D*ri*s*h*ti-dos*h*a); others deem their food to be polluted by being taken out of the *chauka*, or enclosed space, where it is cooked, and so forth. In the cases given there is no such Dos*h*a. Thus a Brāhma*n*a and Cha*nd*āla going by the same boat may eat in it.

[2] *i.e.*, washed by any alkaline preparation (Ks*h*āra).

[3] *i.e.*, expiatory rite, penance. K*ri*chchhra=attended with pain, painful and humiliating.

[4] V*ra*ta.

[5] Cognates and connections.

O Kaulini! the sin of wilfully slaughtering an elephant or a camel, or a buffalo, or a horse is expiated by a three days' fast (139).

Expiation for killing a deer, sheep, goat, or a cat, is a fast for one whole day and a night, and one who has killed a peacock, a parrot, or a gander should abstain from food till sunset of the day on which the sin is committed (140).

If anyone kills any other inferior animal which possesses bones, he should live on vegetable food for a night. The killing of a boneless animal is expiated by repentance (141).

There is no blame upon Kings who kill beasts, fish, and oviparous creatures when hunting; for hunting, O Devī! is an immemorial practice[1] among Kings (142).

Killing should always be avoided, O Gentle One! except if it be for the purpose of sacrifice to a Deva. The man who kills according to the injunctions sins not[2] (143).

Should a man be unable to complete a religious devotion[3] which he has undertaken, if he walks across the remnants after the worship of any Devatā, or if he touches an image of a Deva when he is unclean, then in all such cases he should recite the Gāyatrī (144).

The father, the mother, and the giver[4] of the Brahma-mantra are the Mahā-gurus. He who speaks ill of, or towards, them, should, in order to purify himself, fast for five days (145).

Similarly, O Beloved! if anyone speaks ill of other persons entitled to respect, Kaulas and Vipras, then he should purify himself by fasting two days and a half (146).

---

[1] Sanātana-dharma.

[2] That is, killing for the purpose of sacrifice is not sinful killing.

[3] Vrata.

[4] *i.e.*, the Preceptor who initiates one in the Brahma-Mantra.

A man may for the acquisition of wealth go to any country, but he should avoid such countries and Shāstras as prohibit Kaulika rites (147).

The man who of his own free-will goes to a country where the Kaula-dharma is prohibited falls from his status, and should be purified by Pūrṇābhishheka[1] (148).

In expiatory penance, that which is recognized as a fast is going without food for eight Yāmas[2] from sunrise (149).

The fast is, however, not broken should one drink a handful of water or enjoy the air[3] for the preservation of his life (150).

If one is unable, by reason of old age or disease, to fast, then, in lieu of each day of fast, he should feast twelve Brāhmaṇas (151).

The sins of speaking ill of others, self-laudation, evil habits,[4] impropriety in speech or action, should be expiated by repentance[5] (152).

All other sins, whether committed knowingly or unknowingly, are destroyed by repeating the Gāyatrī of the Devī and feeding the Kaulas (153).

These general rules are applicable to men, women, and the sexless; the only difference is that in the case of the women the husband is their Mahā-guru (154).

Men who are suffering from very great disease and those who are always ailing become purified and entitled to perform rites relating to the Devas and the Pitṛis by giving away gold (155).

---

[1] Initiatory rite of a higher degree than Dīkshā. The word literally means 'complete ablution'.

[2] Yāma—eighth part of a day.

[3] *i.e.*, enjoy fresh air. During the fast, the person fasting should not leave the house.

[4] Vyasana.

[5] Manu says that this repentance should be accompanied by determination not to repeat the sin.

A house which has been defiled by unnatural death, or which has been struck by lightning, should be purified by one hundred Vyāh*ri*ti[1] Homas (156).

If the dead body of an animal possessing bones be found in a lake, tank, or well, then it should be at once taken out, and the same should be purified (157).

The method of purifying such places is as follows: Twenty-one jars of pure water should, after being consecrated with Pūr*n*ābhis*h*eka Mantra, be poured into it (158).

If such places contain but a small quantity of water, and this has been polluted by the stench of the dead body, then they should be dewatered and the loose mud removed therefrom, and when this has been done, water should be poured in the manner described (159).

If they contain water of sufficient quantity to drown an elephant, then a hundred jars of water should be removed, and then consecrated water should be poured into them (160).

If not so purified, then the waters of the reservoirs polluted by the touch of the dead body become undrinkable, and the reservoir cannot be consecrated (161).

Bathing in these reservoirs is useless,[2] and any rite performed with their waters becomes fruitless, and any person using the water for any purpose whatever should remain without food for a day and take Panchām*ri*ta[3] to purify himself (162).

Should anyone perchance see a wealthy man who begs, a warrior averse to battle, a detractor of the Kuladharma, a lady[4] of the family who drinks wine, a faithless friend,

---

[1] Vyāh*ri*ti = Bhū*h*, Bhuva*h*, Sva*h* (see p. 292, note 4).

[2] *i.e.*, does not purify.

[3] The five nectars (see p. 279, note 7).

[4] Kula-strī = the Brāhmī wives and their daughters.

or a learned man addicted to sin,[1] then in any of these cases he should view the Sun, utter the name of Vi*sh*nu, and bathe in the clothes which he is wearing at the time (163-164).

Men of the twice-born classes should, if they sell donkeys, fowls, or swine, or if they engage in any low pursuits, purify themselves by observing the three days' Vrata [2] (165).

The Tri-dina-vrata, O Ambikā! is thus performed: the first day is to be spent in fasting, the second day is to be spent in eating grain meals only, and the third in drinking water only (166).

The man who, without being asked, enters a room the door of which is closed, and one who speaks of things which he has been asked to keep secret, should go without food for five days (167).

The man who from pride fails to rise when he sees anyone worthy of veneration coming towards him,[3] or when he sees the Kula Scriptures being brought in, should go without food for a day in order to purify himself (168).

In this Shāstra spoken by Shiva the meanings of the words used are plain; those who put far-fetched meanings upon them go the downward path (169).

I have spoken to Thee, O Devī! of that which is the Essence of essences,[4] of that which is above the most excellent, of that which conduces to the well-being (of men), in this world and the next, as also of that which is both purifying and beneficent and according to Dharma (170).

End of the Eleventh Chapter, entitled "The Account of Expiatory Rites".

---

[1] Pāpa-rata. [2] Tri-dina-vrata.

[3] Such as the father and the like.

[4] Which as Bhārati says is "more reasonable than what is reasonable" that is very reasonable or the essence of all reason.

CHAPTER XII

THE ETERNAL DHARMA

SHRĪ SADĀSHIVA said:

O Primordial One! I am speaking to Thee again of the everlasting laws, the which if a wise King follows he may easily rule his subjects (1).

If Kings did not establish rules,[1] men in their covetousness would quarrel among themselves, even with their friends, relatives, and their superiors (2).

These self-seeking men, O Devī! would for the sake of wealth kill one another, and be full of sin by reason of their maliciousness and desire to thieve (3).

It is therefore for their good that I am laying down the rules in accordance with Dharma,[2] by following which men will not swerve from the right (path) (4).

As the King should punish the wicked for the removal of their sins, so should he also divide the inheritance according to the relationship (5).

Relationship is of two kinds—by marriage and by birth; of these, relationship by birth is stronger than relationship by marriage (6).

In inheritance, O Shivā! descendants have a stronger claim than ascendants, and in this order of descendants and ascendants the males are better qualified for inheritance than females (7).

But among these, again, the proximate relation is entitled to the inheritance; the wise ones should divide the property according to this rule and in this order (8).

---

[1] Niyama.

[2] Dharma-sammata—in accordance with righteousness.

If the deceased leaves son, son's son, daughters, father and wife, then the son is entitled to the whole of the inheritance, and not any of the others (9).

If there are several sons, they are all entitled to equal shares. (In the case of a King) the kingdom goes to the eldest son, but that is in accordance to the custom of the family[1] (10).

If there be any paternal debt which should be paid out of the paternal property, such property should not be divided[2] (11).

If men should divide and take paternal property, then the King should take it from them, and discharge the paternal debt (12).

As men go to hell by reason of their own sins, so they are bound by their individually incurred debts, and others are not (13).

Whatever general property there may be, either immovable or of other kinds, sharers shall get the same according to their respective shares (14).

The division is complete on the co-partners agreeing to it. If they do not agree, then the King should divide it impartially (15).

The King should divide the value or profits of property which is incapable of division, whether the same be immovable or movable (16).

If a man proves his right to a share after the property is divided, then the King should divide the property over again, and give the person entitled his share (17).

O Shivā! the King should punish the man who, after property is once divided by the consent of the co-partners, quarrels again with respect to it (18).

[1] Primogeniture is a family custom. (Bhāratī.)

[2] *i.e.*, until the debt is paid.

If the deceased dies leaving behind him son's son, wife, and father, then the son's son is entitled to the property by reason of his being a descendant[1] (19).

If the childless man leaves (surviving him) father, brother, and father's father, then the father inherits the property by reason of the closeness of consanguinity (20).

Beloved! if the deceased leaves daughters (surviving him), although they are closer to him, yet the grandsons (sons' sons) are entitled to his property, because the rights of the male are prior[2] (21).

From the grandfather the property goes to the grandson by the deceased son, and thus it is that men proclaim that the father's self is in the image of the son (22).

In marital relationship, the Brāhmī wife is the superior, and the sonless man's property should go to the wife, who is half his body[3] (23).

The sonless widow, however, is not competent to sell or give away property inherited from her husband, except what is her own[4] by her own right (24).

Anything given by the fathers and fathers-in-law approved by Dharma, whatever is earned by her personal efforts, is to be recognized as Woman's Property[5] (25).

On her death it goes to the husband, and to his heirs according to the grades of descendants and ancestors (26).

If the woman remains faithful to her Dharma, and lives under the control of the relations of her husband, and in their absence under the control of her father's relations, then only is she entitled to inherit (27).

---

[1] Adhastāt janma-gauravāt. Adha*h* = lower, Janma-gaurava = gravity, weight, or pride of birth. Literally, by the weight of his posterior birth—that is, property primarily descends.

[2] Mukhya-tara.

[3] Dehārddha-dhāri*n*ī, Ardhāṁginī.

[4] Sva-dhana.

[5] Stri-dhana: Earned by artistic skill and the like.

If a woman be even suspected of irregular conduct[1] she is not entitled to inherit the husband's property. She is merely entitled to a living allowance from the heirs of her husband (28).

If the man who has died[2] has many wives, all of whom are pious, then, O Thou of pure Smiles! they are entitled to the husband's property in equal shares (29).

If the woman who inherits her husband's property dies leaving daughters, then the property is taken to have gone back to the husband[3] and from him to the daughter (30).

In this way, if there is a daughter and the property goes to the son's widow, then, on the death of the latter, it will go back to the husband, and from the father-in-law descend to the daughter of the latter (31).

Similarly, O Shivā! if property goes to the mother in the lifetime of the paternal grandfather, then, on her death, it goes to her father-in-law through her son and husband (32).

As the property of the deceased ascends to the father, so it also ascends to the mother if she is a widow (33).

But the stepmother shall not inherit if the mother is living, but on the death of the mother it goes to the stepmother through the father (34).

Where, in the absence of descendants, the inheritance cannot descend, it will ascend the same way by which it descends (35).

Therefore, even when the father's brother is alive, the sister inherits the property, and if she dies childless then such property goes to the father's brother (36).

---

[1] Apparently refers to the case of a woman who has a bad general reputation though wrong conduct may not in any particular case be proved against her.

[2] Literally, who has gone to heaven.

[3] Literally, "goes back to the husband"—*i.e.*, the daughters take as heirs of their father, and not of their mother.

As inheritance descends in the male line, the stepbrother inherits even when there is a uterine sister (37).

And when there is a uterine sister and sons of stepbrother, it is the latter who inherit the property (38).

If the deceased leaves (surviving him) both uterine and stepbrother, then, by reason of the property descending through the father, they are entitled to inherit in equal shares (39).

In the lifetime of the daughters their sons are not entitled to inherit until the obstruction is removed by the death of the daughters (40).

In the absence of sons, the daughters divide among themselves the paternal property, after deducting the marriage expenses of an unmarried daughter (if any) out of the general estate[1] (41).

On the death of a childless woman the Strī-dhana[2] goes to her husband, and the property which she inherited from anyone else goes back to the line of the person from whom she inherited (42).

The woman may spend property inherited by her on her own maintenance, and she may spend profits of it on acts of religious merit, but she is not entitled to sell or make gifts of it (43).

Where the daughter-in-law of the grandfather (father's father) is living, and the stepmother of the father is living, the inheritance goes to the grandfather, and through his son to the (grandfather's) daughter-in-law (44).

Where the grandfather, the father's brother, and the brother are living, the brother succeeds by reason of the priority in claim of the descendant (45).

---

[1] That is, the unmarried daughter is entitled to these expenses in addition to a share equal to her sisters.

[2] See p. 364, vv. 24 and 25, *ante*,

If a man dies leaving (surviving him) his grandfather, brother, and uncle, both of the former are nearer in degree than the last, and the property descends through the father to the deceased's brother (46).

If the deceased leaves a daughter's son and father (surviving him), then the daughter's son inherits, because property (in the first place) descends (47).

If both the father and the mother of the deceased be living (at his death), then, O Kālikā! by reason of the superior claim of the male, the father takes his property (48).

If the mother's brother is living, the Sapi*nd*as of the father take the property of the deceased by reason of the superior claim of the paternal relationship (49).

Property failing to go downwards has (here) gone upwards, but, O Shivā! by reason of the superior claim of the male line it has gone to the father's family. The mother's brother, in spite of the nearness of his relationship, does not inherit (50).

The grandson by a deceased son inherits from his grandfather's estate the share which his father would have inherited along with his (the father's) brothers (51).

Similarly, the son's daughter who has no brother and whose parents are dead, inherits, if she be well conducted, her grandfather's (father's father) property with her father's brothers (52).

On the death of the grandfather leaving (surviving him) his wife, his daughter, and granddaughter,[1] the last, O Devī! is the heiress of the property, since she takes it through her father (53).

In property which descends, the male among the descendants, and in property which ascends, the male among the ascendants, are pre-eminently qualified (to inherit) (54).

---

[1] Son's daughter.

Therefore, O Beloved! if the deceased has daughter-in-law, granddaughter,[1] and daughter surviving him, then his father cannot take the property (55).

If there is no one in the family of the father of the deceased entitled to inherit his property, then in manner above indicated it goes to the family of his mother's father (56).

Property which has gone to the maternal grandfather shall ascend and descend, and go both to males and females in the same way as in the father's family through the maternal uncle and his sons and others (57).

If the line of Brāhmī marriage or if the Sap*ind*as of the father or of the mother, be in existence, then the issue of the Shaiva marriage[2] are not entitled to inherit the father's property (58).[3]

The wife and children of the Shaiva marriage, O Gentle One, are entitled to receive, from the person who inherits the property of the deceased, their food and clothes in proportion to the property left (59).

Beloved! the Shaiva wife, if well conducted, is entitled to be maintained by the Shaiva husband alone. She has no claim to the property of her father and others (60).

Therefore, the father who marries his well-born daughter according to Shaiva rites by reason of anger or covetousness will be despised of men (61).

In the absence of issue of the Shaiva marriage, the Sodaka,[4] the Guru, and the King shall, by the injunctions of Shiva, take the property of the deceased (62).

---

[1] Pautrī—son's daughter.

[2] See p. 302, Ch. ix, v. 267 *et seq*.

[3] Bhāratī says that in their absence they are entitled to inherit.

[4] Samānodaka (see verse 63). The Sodaka has preference over the Guru and the latter over the King.

Beloved! ancestors within the seventh degree are Sapi*n*das, and beyond them to the tenth degree are Sodakas, and beyond them are Gotra-jas merely (63).

Where property which has been divided is again wilfully mixed together, it should be divided again as if it had not been divided (64).

The heirs of a deceased are on his death entitled to such share of property, whether partitioned or not partitioned, as the deceased himself was entitled to (65).

Those who inherit the property of another should offer him Pi*n*das as long as they live; it is otherwise in the case of a son by Shaiva marriage[1] (66).

Just as the rules relating to Uncleanliness should, in this world, be observed by reason of birth-connection, so they should be observed for three nights by reason of connection by heirship (67).

The twice-born and other classes shall purify themselves by observing the rules as to Uncleanliness from the day they hear (the cause) of it until the end of the period prescribed; this is so both in the case of Pūr*n*āshaucha[2] and of Kha*n*ḍāshaucha[3] (68).

If the period has expired when one hears (the cause) of it, then there is no Kha*n*ḍāshaucha. And as regards Pūr*n*āshaucha, it should be observed for only three days, but if one hears of the cause of the uncleanliness after the lapse of a year there is no period of Uncleanliness to be observed (69).

---

[1] Bhāratī reads this as meaning that the Shaiva son is not competent to give Pi*n*da (Tatpi*n*da-dāne adhikāro nāsti). But is this so? The general rule is that inheritance cannot be taken without giving Pi*n*da and under certain circumstances the Shaiva son may inherit (see v. 58). The verse may therefore mean that the Shaiva son is to offer Pi*n*da to his father whether he inherits or not as a pious duty.

[2] The period of Ashaucha or Uncleanliness to be observed by Agnates within the seventh degree.

[3] The period of Ashaucha observed by Agnates not within the seventh degree.

If a son hears of his father's or mother's death, or if the faithful wife hears of her husband's death after one year, then the son or the widow shall observe the period of Uncleanliness for three nights (70).

If during the continuance of a period of Uncleanliness another new period begins, then the period comes to an end with the end of the Garu-ashaucha[1] (71).

The degree[2] of different kinds of Uncleanliness depends on the greater or lesser length of the period which should be observed. Of the various kinds of Uncleanliness, that which is extensive in point of time is greater than that which is less extensive (72).

If on the last day of a period of Uncleanliness another period commences, then the Uncleanliness is removed on the last day of the first period of Uncleanliness; but if the cause of Uncleanliness be such as to necessitate the observance of the full period, then the pre-existing period should be extended by two days[3] (73).

The unmarried female shall observe the period of Uncleanliness of the father's family, but after she is married she is to observe impurity for three days on the death of her parents (74).

After her marriage the wife becomes of the same Gotra[4] as her husband; the adopted son similarly becomes of the same Gotra as the person who adopts him (75).

A son should be adopted with consent of his father and mother, and at the time of adoption the adopter should,

[1] *i.e.*, the Pūr*n*āshaucha.

[2] Gurutva=weight.

[3] *i.e.*, if a Kha*nd*āshaucha commences on the last day of a Pūr*n*āshaucha, then both expire at the same time on expiration of the Pūr*n*āshaucha; but if another Pūr*n*āshaucha occurs on the last day, then the period of the first Pūr*n*āshaucha is extended two days, and both expire on the same day.

[4] Family, line of descent.

with his kinsmen, perform the sacramental rites,[1] mentioning his own Gotra and name (76).

The adopted son shall have the same right to the property of his adoptive mother and father, and the same rights to offer Pi*nd*as to them as the natural-born son has, since they are his mother and father (77).

A boy of less than five years of age and of one's own caste should be adopted and brought up; a boy of over five years of age is not eligible (78).

O Kālikā! if a brother adopts his brother's son, then the brother adopting becomes the father, and the natural father becomes the uncle of the boy so adopted (79).

He who inherits the property of another should observe the Dharma of the person he inherits;[2] he should also follow his family custom and please his kinsmen (80).

In the case of the death of Kānīnas,[3] Golakas,[4] Ku*nd*as,[5] and persons guilty of very great sins,[6] there is no Uncleanliness to be observed, and they are not qualified to inherit (81).

In the case of the death of a man who has been punished by castration, or of a woman who has been punished by the cutting of her nose, or of persons guilty of great sins,[7] there is no period of Uncleanliness to be observed (82).

The King should for twelve years protect the family and property of those of whom no news is known, and

---

[1] Sangskāra.

[2] By this is meant—Should carry out religious worship of the deceased, as where a Shākteya inherits property of a Vai*sh*n*a*va, he need not change his own mode of worship, but should simply maintain the service of the Devatā in the way the deceased used to.

[3] Child of unmarried woman.

[4] Son of a widow.

[5] Bastard born in the lifetime of husband.

[6] Ati-pātakī. Such as incest. See *ante*, XI, 29, 30.

[7] Mahā-pātakī. Such as drinking unconsecrated wine, killing a Vīra and others as in Ch. X, 205, *ante*.

who have disappeared without any trace of their whereabouts (83).

On the expiration of twelve years the image of such a person should be made with Kusha grass and cremated. His children and others should observe a period of uncleanliness for three days, and liberate him from the condition of a Preta[1] (84).

The King should then divide his property among the members of his family in their order, beginning with the son; otherwise he (the King) incurs sin (85).

The King should protect the man who has no protector, who is powerless, who is in the midst of adversity, because the King is the Lord of his subjects (86).

Kālikā! if the man who has disappeared returns after the lapse of twelve years, then he shall recover his wife, children, and property; there is no doubt of that (87).

Even a man is not competent to give away ancestral, immovable property, either to his own people or to strangers, without the consent of his heirs (88).

A man may, at his pleasure, give away self-acquired property, be it movable or immovable, and may also give away ancestral movable property (89).

If there be a son or wife living, or daughter or daughter's son, or father or mother, or brother or sister, even then one may give away self-acquired property, both movable and immovable, and inherited movable property (90-91).

If a man gives away or dedicates such property to any religious object, then his sons and others cannot annul such gift or dedication (92).

Property dedicated to any religious object should be looked after by the giver. The latter is, however, not

[1] See p. 318, note 7, *ante*.

competent to take it back, because the ownership of such property is in Dharma[1] (93).

Ambikā![2] the property or the profits thereof should be employed by the dedicator himself, or his agent, for the religious object[3] to which it was dedicated (94).

If the proprietor out of affection gives away half his self-acquired property to any of his heirs, then his other heirs shall not be able to annul the gift[4] (95).

If the proprietor gives half his self-acquired wealth to any of his heirs, in such a case the other heirs shall not be able to avoid such gift (96).

If one of several brothers earns money with the help of the paternal property, then, while the other brothers are entitled to proportionate shares of the paternal property, no one but the acquirer is entitled to the profits (97).

If one brother acquires ancestral property which was lost, then he shall receive two shares, and the other brothers shall each receive one share (98).

Religious merit, wealth, and learning are all dependent on the body, and inasmuch as this body comes from the father, then (in such sense) what is there which is not paternal property? (99).

If whatever men earn, even when separate in mess and separate in property, is to be considered paternal property then what is there that is self-acquired? (100).

Therefore, O Great Devī![5] whatever money is earned by one's own individual labour shall be self-acquired; the

---

[1] *i.e.*, the property belongs to the purpose for which it has been dedicated.

[2] Mother. An epithet of the Devī—as the Universe is from Her.

[3] Dharmārtham.

[4] Bhāratī says that this applies to cases where one of several heirs is preferentially treated.

[5] Maheshī.

person acquiring it shall be the owner thereof, and no one else (101).

O Devī! the man who even lifts his hand against his mother, father, Guru, paternal and maternal grandfathers,[1] shall not inherit (102).

The man who kills another shall not inherit his property; but the other heirs of the person killed shall inherit his property (103).

Ambikā! eunuchs and persons who are crippled are entitled to food and clothes so long as they live, but they are not entitled to inherit property (104).

If a man finds property which belongs to another, on the road or anywhere else, then the King shall, after due deliberation, make the finder restore it to the owner (105).

If a man finds property, or a beast of which there is no owner, then the finder becomes the owner of the same, but should give the King a tenth share of such property or beast (or of the value thereof) (106).

If there be a competent buyer for immovable property, who is a near neighbour,[2] then it is not competent for the owner of the immovable property to sell the same to another[3] (107).

Among buyers who are near, the agnate[4] and one of the same caste[5] are specially qualified, and in their absence friends, but the desire of the seller should prevail[6] (108).

---

[1] By this other ancestors are also meant.

[2] Sānnidhyavartī. Tarkālangkāra renders "relation".

[3] This and the following verses deal with the right of pre-emption.

[4] Jnāti—*i.e.*, a person within the same Gotra.

[5] Savar*n*a.

[6] Bhāratī adds—If there be several buyers belonging to any of these classes, the person to whom the seller wishes to sell the property will have a predominant claim.

If immovable property is about to be sold at a price fixed, and a neighbour pays the same price, then the latter is entitled to purchase it and no other (109).

If the neighbour is unable to pay the price and consents to the sale (to another), then only may the house-holder sell the property to another (110).

O Devī! if immovable property be brought without the knowledge of the neighbour, the latter is entitled to have it upon the condition of his paying the price immediately he hears of such sale (111).

Should, however, the buyer, after purchasing it, have converted the place into a garden, or built a house thereon, or if he has pulled down any building, the neighbour is not entitled in such a case to obtain the immovable property by the payment of its price (112).

A man may, without permission, without payment, and without obstruction, bring under cultivation any land which rises from the water,[1] which is in the middle of a forest, or otherwise difficult of access (113).

Where land has been brought under cultivation by considerable labour, the King, since he is the Lord of the soil, should be given a tenth of the profits of the land, and the rest should be enjoyed by him who has reclaimed it (114).

One should not excavate tanks, reservoirs, or wells, nor plant trees, nor build houses in places where they are likely to injure other people (115).

All have the right to drink the water of tanks and wells dedicated to Devas, as also the water of rivers, but the neighbours alone have the right to bale[2] it out (116).

The water should not be baled out of tanks and so forth, even by neighbours, if to do so would cause a water famine (117).

---

[1] *Chur*, or alluvial land.

[2] Sechana—for irrigation purposes.

The mortgage[1] and sale of property which is undivided without the consent of the co-sharers, as also when the right of the parties therein is not determined, is invalid (118).

If property mortgaged or deposited with another is destroyed wilfully or by negligence, then the King should make the mortgagee or depositee restore the value thereof to the owner (119).

If any animal or any other thing is used with the consent of the depositor by the person with whom they are placed, then the depositee should bear the expense of food and keep (120).

Where immovable or movable property is made over to another for profit, such transaction will be invalid if it be not for a definite time, or if the amount of profits is indeterminate (121).

Common (joint) property should not, on the father's death, be employed for profit without the consent of all the co-sharers (122).

If articles are sold at improper prices,[2] then the King may set aside such sale (123).

As a body is born and dies only once, and property can be given away only once, so there can be but one Brāhma marriage of the daughter[3] (124).

The man, devoted to his ancestors, who has an only son, should not give him away (in adoption), and, similarly, he should not give away an only wife or an only daughter in Shaiva marriage (125).

In rites relating to the Devas and the Pit*ri*s, in mercantile transactions, and in Courts of Law,[4] whatever

---

[1] Nyāsa.

[2] Krama-vyatyaya-mūlya—*i.e.*, articles of less value at a higher price or of greater value at a less price.

[3] This verse is against remarriage in Brāhma form, but as regards Shaiva Wife, see next verse.

[4] Rājadvāra = (*lit.*) King's door.

the Substitute (Agent) does is the act of the employer (126).

The immutable rule is that the Agent[1] should not be punished for the guilt of the employer (127).

In monetary dealings, in agriculture, in mercantile transactions, as also in all other dealings, whatever is undertaken, the same should be performed if in agreement with Dharma[2] (128).

The Lord protects this universe. Whoever wish to destroy it will be themselves destroyed, and whosoever protect it, then the Lord of the Universe Himself protects. Therefore should one act for the good of the world (129).

End of Twelfth Chapter, entitled, "An Account of the Eternal and Immutable Vyavahāra."

---

[1] Dūta—Emissary.

[2] Dharma-sammata.

CHAPTER XIII

INSTALLATION OF THE DEVATA

PĀRVATĪ, the Mother of the three worlds, Her mind engrossed with thoughts for the purification of men polluted with the impurities of the Kali Age, humbly questioned Mahesha, the Deva of Devas, who had thus spoken of the essence of all the Nigamas, which is the Seed of heaven[1] and final Liberation[2] (as follows) (1).

Shrī Devī said:

How can Mahākālī be endowed of form, She who is the Great Cause,[3] the Primordial Power,[4] the Great Light, more subtle than the subtlest Elements? (2).

It is only that which is the Effect of Prakriti which has form.[5] How should She have form? She is above the most high. It behoves Thee, O Deva! to completely remove this doubt of Mine (3).

Shrī Sadāshiva said:

Beloved! I have already said that to meet the needs[6] of the worshippers the image of the Devī is formed according to Her qualities and actions (4).

---

[1] Svarga.

[2] Moksha.

[3] Mahad-yoni or Great Womb. Bhāratī says the reference is to Mahat Tattva. From the Devī originated Mahat.

[4] Ādī-Shakti.

[5] Rūpang prakriteh kāryānām, that is, Vikriti.

[6] So it has been said—Upāsakānāng kāryārtham Brahmano rūpakalpanā. The Supreme Brahman takes on various forms for the benefit of the worshipper. See Shāktānanda-taramginī, Ch. III, where the necessity of an image is dealt with.

As white, yellow, and other colours all disappear in black, in the same way, O Shailajā![1] all beings enter Kālī (5).

Therefore it is, that by those who have attained the Knowledge[2] of the means of final Liberation, the attributeless, formless, and beneficent Kālashakti[3] is endowed with the colour of blackness (6).

As the eternal and changeless and beneficent One in the form of Kāla[4] is nectar itself, therefore the sign of the Moon is placed on Her forehead[5] (7). As She surveys the entire universe, which is the product of Time,[6] with Her three eyes—the Moon, Sun and Fire[7]—therefore She is endowed with three eyes (8).

As (at the final Dissolution) She devours[8] all existence,[9] as She chews all things existing with Her fierce[10] teeth, therefore a mass of blood[11] is said to be the apparel of the Queen of the Devas (9).

As time after time She protects all beings from danger, and O Shivā, as She directs them in the paths of duty, Her hands are lifted up to dispel fear[12] and grant blessings[13] (10)

---

[1] Shailajā—Born of the Mountain. So She is also called Girijā.

[2] Yoga = Jnāna here means Brahmajnāna.

[3] *i.e.*, Kālī.

[4] Kāla-rūpa. Kāla is Time (see p. 192, notes 3 and 4). By Kālashakti in v. 6, Kālī is meant without Her Time ceases to be.

[5] From the Moon flows nectar. On Her forehead is the seventeenth digit (Saptadashī Kalā) known as Amākalā.

[6] The Universe is Brahman seen under the forms of Time and Space that is Māyā.

[7] That is the white, red and mixed Bindus which form the Kāmakalā. See "Garland of Letters" and Kāmakalāvilāsa, Vol. IX, Tāntrik Texts, Ed. A. Avalon.

[8] Grasana. See *ante*, Ch. V, 141.

[9] Sarva-sattva.

[10] Kāla-danta or teeth which is Time (Kāla).

[11] Bhāratī adds—of all beings.

[12] Abhaya.

[13] Vara.

As She encompasses the worlds, which are the product of Rajoguna,[1] She is spoken of, O Gentle One! as the Devī who is seated on a red lotus. The Devī, Who as Consciousness itself[2] witnesseth all things[3] is gazing at Kāla elated with the wine of ignorance and playing[4] with the universe[5] (11-12).

It is for the benefit of such worshippers as are of little understanding that the different forms[6] are imagined[7] according to the attributes (of the Divinity) (13).

Shrī Devī said:

What merit does the worshipper gain who makes an image of the Great Devī of mud, stone, wood, or metal, in accordance with the representation[8] described by Thee for the salvation of humanity, and who decks the same with clothes and jewels, and who, in a beautifully decorated house, consecrates it? (14-15).

---

[1] *i.e.*, the active quality.

[2] Chinmayī=Jnānasvarūpā, for She is one with the Supreme Brahman who is Chit.

[3] Sarva-sākshi-sva-rūpini. "Sva-rūpinī," because, though it is the Purusha who is the witness, She is Herself the Brahman, and therefore also a witness, just as She, too, is also Chinmayī.

[4] *i.e.*, the restless play of Time with the universe is seen in the never-ceasing changes it effects.

[5] Universe—Kālika (because it is originated from Kāla, or Time). In the Dhyāna in verse 141, Chapter V, Kāla is described as dancing before the Devī. The "wine" is Moha or Avidyā, ignorance. Pītvā mohamayīm surām.

[6] Rūpa.

[7] Kalpita—that is, imagined by the Devī who assumes such forms to meet the needs of the ordinary man, who in such matters is generally weak of intelligence.

Evaṁ gunānusārena rūpāni vividhāni cha
Kalpitāni hitārthāya bhaktānām alpa-medhasām

(See as to this "Principles of Tantra," by Sir John Woodroffe).

[8] Dhyāna, or representation which is the subject of it.

O Lord! out of Thy kindness for Me, reveal this also, with all the particular rules according to which the image of the Devī should be consecrated (16).

Thou hast already spoken of the consecration of Tanks, Wells, Houses, Gardens, and the images of Devas, but Thou didst not speak in detail (17).

I wish to hear the injunctions relating to them from Thy lotus-mouth. Out of Thy kindness, speak, O Parameshāna! if it pleases Thee (18).

Shrī Sadāshiva said:

O Parameshvarī! this is a very secret and weighty Question[1] which Thou hast asked. Do thou, therefore, listen attentively (19).

There are two classes of men—those who act with,[2] and without,[3] a view to the fruits of action. The latter attain final Liberation. I am now speaking of the former (20).

Beloved! the man who consecrates the image of a Deva goes to the region of such Deva, and enjoys that which[4] is there attainable (21).

He who consecrates an image of mud stays in such region for ten thousand Kalpas. He who consecrates an image of wood stays there ten times that period. In the case of the consecration of a stone image the length of stay is ten times the latter period, and in the case of the consecration of a metal image, it is ten times the last-mentioned period (22).

Listen to the merit[5] which is acquired by the man who, in the name of any Deva, or for the attainment of

---

[1] Tattva.

[2] Sakāma, or Kāmī.

[3] Nishkāma, or Akāma.

[4] Bhogān tadudbhavān, *i.e.*, the pleasures produced there.

[5] Punya.

any desire, builds and consecrates and gives away a temple made of timber and thatch and other materials, or renovates such a temple, decorated with flags and images of the carriers[1] of the Deva (23).

He who gives away a thatched temple shall live in the region of the Devas for one thousand *Koti*[2] years (24).

He who gives away a brick-built temple shall live a hundred times that period, and he who gives away a stone-built temple, ten thousand times the last-mentioned period (25).

Ādyā![3] the man who builds and dedicates a bridge or causeway shall not see the region of Yama, but will happily reach the abode of the Suras,[4] and will there have enjoyment in their company (26).

He who dedicates trees and gardens goes to the region of the Devas,[5] and lives in celestial houses surrounded by Kalpa[6] trees in the enjoyment of all desired and agreeable enjoyments (27).

Those who give away tanks[7] and so forth for the comfort of all beings are washed of all sins, and, having attained the blissful region of Brahmā, reside there a hundred years for each drop of water which they contain (28).

Devī! the man who dedicates the image of a Vāhana[8] for the pleasure of any Deva shall live continually in the region of such Deva, protected by Him (29).

---

[1] *i.e.*, the Vāhanas or carriers of the Devas—*e.g.*, the peacock of Kārtikeya (see *post*).

[2] Koti = Crore = 100 lacs—*i.e.*, 10,000,000.

[3] Primordial One.

[4] *i.e.*, Devas whose abode is heaven.

[5] Tridasha-mandira.

[6] Trees which grant all desires.

[7] Jalāshaya—places where water can be had.

[8] Each Deva has got his separate Vāhana, or carrier, usually an animal. Thus, Vi*sh*nu has Garu*d*a, Shiva the Bull, Yama the Bison, etc.

Ten times the merit which is acquired on earth by the gift of a Vāhana made of mud is acquired by the gift of one made of wood, and ten times the latter is acquired by the gift of one made of stone. Should one made of brass or bell-metal or copper, or any other metal, be given, then the merit is multiplied in each case tenfold (30-31).

The excellent worshipper should present a great lion[1] to the temple of Devī, a bull[2] to the temple of Shaṁkara,[3] and a Garuḍa[4] to the temple of Keshava[5] (32).

The great lion has sharp teeth, a ferocious mouth, and mane on his neck and shoulder. The claws of his four feet are as hard as the thunderbolt (33).

The bull is horned, is white of body, and has four black hoofs, a large hump, black hair at the end of his tail, and black shoulders (34).

The Garuḍa is winged, has thighs like a bird, and a face like a man's, with a long nose. He is seated on his hunches, with folded palms (35).

By the present of flags and flag-staffs the Devas remain pleased for a hundred years. The flag-staffs should be thirty-two cubits long (36), and should be strong, without defects, straight, and pleasant to look at. It should be wrapped round with a red cloth, with a Chakra[6] at its top (37).

The flag should be attached to the top of the staff, and should be marked with the image of the carrier[7] of the particular Devatā. It should be broad at the part nearest

---

[1] Mahā-siṁha.

[2] Vṛishabha.

[3] Shiva.

[4] Garuḍa is the Bird King Vāhana of Vishṇu.

[5] Vishṇu.

[6] The discus carried by Vishṇu.

[7] Vāhana.

the staff and narrow at the other end. It should be made of fine cloth. In short, whatever ornaments the top of the flag-staff is a flag (38).

Whatever a man presents with faith and devotion in the name of a Deva, be it clothes, jewels, beds, carriages, vessels for drinking and eating, Pān plates,[1] spittoon, precious stones, pearl, coral, gems, or anything else with which he is pleased, such a man will reach the region of such Deva and receive in turn a Ko*t*i,[2] times the presents he made (39-40).

Those who worship with the object of attaining[3] a particular reward gain such reward which (however) is as perishable as a kingdom enjoyed in a dream. Those, however, who rightly act without[4] hope of reward attain Nirvā*n*a,[5] and are released from rebirth (41).

In ceremonies relating to the dedication[5] of a reservoir of water, a house, a garden, a bridge, a causeway, a Devatā, or a tree, the Vāstu Daitya[6] should be carefully worshipped (42).

The man who performs any of these ceremonies without worshipping the Vāstu-Daitya is troubled by the Vāstu-Daitya and his followers (43).

---

[1] Pān plates—Plates for serving made-up betel-leaves (Pān, or Tāmbula).

[2] Ten millions.

[3] Kāmī.

[4] *i.e.*, for the sake of right itself, and without regard to the fruits thereof.

[5] Pratish*th*ā—which is derived from Prati and Sthā=to stay, means the act of making anything, stand firmly, establishing firmly.

[6] Vāstu signifies homestead land. All Vāstu lands—in fact all lands—are controlled by the Vāstu Spirit—called Vāstu Purus*h*a—and the Vāstu Purus*h*a also called Vāstu Daitya should be propitiated by Vāstu-yajna. The Tantrarāja (Tantrik Texts, XII) treats this differently.

The twelve followers of the Vāstu-Daitya are Kapilāsya,[1] Piṁgakesha,[2] Bhīshana,[3] Raktalochana,[4] Kotarāksha,[5] Lambakarna,[6] Dīrghajaṁgha,[7] Mahodara,[8] Ashvatunda,[9] Kākakantha,[10] Vajrabāhu,[11] and Vratāntaka,[12] and these followers of Vāstu should be propitiated with great care (44-45).

Now, listen! I am speaking of the Mandala where the Vāstu-Purusha should be worshipped (46)

On an altar[13] or on a level space, which has been well washed with pure water, a straight line should be drawn, one cubit in length, from the Vāyu[14] to the Īshāna[15] corner. In the same manner another line should be drawn from the Īshāna[15] to the Agni[16] corner, and another from the Agni[16] to the Nairrita[17] corner, and then from the Nairrita[17] to the Vāyu[14] corner (47-48).

By these straight lines a square Mandala should be drawn (49). Then two lines should be drawn from corner to corner (diagonally) to divide the Mandala into four parts, like four fish-tails (50).

---

[1] Of a tawny face.

[2] Of tawny hair.

[3] The ferocious one.

[4] With red eyes.

[5] Having deep-sunk eyes.

[6] Having long ears.

[7] Having long shins.

[8] Having a large belly.

[9] Horse-faced.

[10] Having the voice of a crow.

[11] Having arms like the thunder-bolt, *i.e.*, strong arms.

[12] Destroyer of Vratas as were the Anāryas.

[13] Vedī.

[14] N. W. corner.

[15] N. E. corner.

[16] S. E. corner.

[17] S. W. corner.

The worshipper versed in ritual should then draw two lines, one from the West to the East, and other from the North to the South, through the point where the diagonal lines cut one another, so as to pass through the tip of the fish-tails (51).

Then four diagonal lines should be drawn connecting the corners of the four inner squares so formed by the lines at each of the corners (52).

According to these rules, sixteen spaces should be drawn with five different colours, and an excellent Yantra thus made (53).

In the four middle rooms draw a beautiful lotus with four petals, the pericarp of yellow and red colour, and the filaments of red (54).

The petals may be white or yellow, and the interstices may be coloured with any colour chosen (55).

Beginning with the corner of Shambhu,[1] the twelve spaces should be filled up with the four colours—*viz.*, white, black, yellow, and red (56).[2]

In filling up the spaces one should go towards one's left, and in the worship of the Devas therein one should go to the right (57).

The Vāstu Spirit should be worshipped in the lotus, and the twelve Daityas,[3] Kapilāsya and others, should be worshipped in the twelve rooms, beginning with the Īshāna[4] corner (58).

Fire should be consecrated according to the injunctions laid down for Kusha*nd*ikā,[5] and after offer of oblations to

---

[1] *i.e.*, Īshāna corner=N. E.

[2] These are the colours of water, air, earth and fire. In doing worship one should follow the direction the hands of a clock move.

[3] Demonic Spirits—that is, the Vāstu Daityas.

[4] N. E. Corner.

[5] See Chapter IX, vv. 14-89, *ante*.

the best of one's ability, the Vāstu-yajna should be concluded (59).

I have thus described, O Devī! the auspicious Vāstu worship, by the performance of which a man never suffers dangers from Vāstu (and his followers) (60).

Shrī Devī said:

Thou hast described the Ma*nd*ala of, and the injunctions relating to, the worship of Vāstu, but, My Husband, Thou hast not spoken of the Dhyāna; do Thou now reveal it (61).

Shrī Sadāshiva said:

I am speaking of Dhyāna of the Vāstu-Rāk*sh*asa,[1] by constant and devoted repetition of which all dangers are destroyed. O Maheshānī! do Thou listen (62).

The Deva Vāstu-pati[2] should be meditated upon as four-armed, of great body, his head covered with matted hair, three-eyed, of ferocious aspect, decked with garlands and earrings, with big belly and long ears and hairy body, wearing yellow garments, holding in his hand the mace, the trident, the axe, and the Kha*t*vāṁga.[3] Let him be pictured as (red) like the rising Sun and like the Deva of Death to the enemies, seated in the Padmāsana[4] posture on the back of a tortoise, surrounded by Kapilāsya and other powerful followers, carrying swords and shields (63-66).

Whenever there is panic caused by pestilence or epidemics, an apprehension of any public calamity, danger due to evil influences to one's children, or fear arising from ferocious beasts or Rāk*sh*asas,[5] then Vāstu with his followers

---

[1] Another name of Vāstudaitya.

[2] Lord of Vāstu. Vāstu means a site or locality,

[3] Kha*t*vāṁga is a staff with a skull at the top of it, considered to be a weapon of Shiva carried by yogins.

[4] The ordinary posture in worship.

[5] Demonic Spirits.

should be meditated upon as above, and then worshipped, and thus all manner of peace may be obtained by the offer of oblations of sesamum-seeds, ghee, and Pāyasa[1] (67-68).

O Suvratā![2] in these rites the Grahas[3] and the ten Dikpālas[4] should be worshipped in the same way as Vāstu is worshipped (69).

Brahmā, Vis*h*nu, Rudra,[5] Vā*n*ī, Laks*h*mī, Shaṁkarī the celestial mothers, Ga*n*esha, and the Vasus,[6] should also be worshipped (70).

O Kālika! if in these rites the Pit*ri*s[7] are not satisfied, then all which is done becomes fruitless, and there is danger in every stage (71).

Therefore, O Maheshī! in all these rites Ābhyudayika Shrāddha[8] should be performed for the satisfaction of the Pit*ri*s (72).

I shall now speak of the Graha-yantra,[9] which is the cause of all kinds of peace. If the Dikpālas Indra and others and all the planets are worshipped therein they grant every desire (73).

In order to draw the Yantra three triangles[10] should be drawn with a circle outside them, and outside, but touching the circle, eight petals should be drawn (74).

---

[1] Pāyasa is a kind of custard made with milk, sugar, ghee, and rice usually (no eggs). For rice, other grains, or soojee (coarse wheat flour), are sometimes substituted.

[2] Virtuous One.

[3] The nine Planets.

[4] Guardian regents of the quarters.

[5] Shiva. Vā*n*ī is Sarasvatī. Shaṁkarī is the consort of Shaṁkara or Shiva. As to Celestial Māt*ri*kās, see p. 37, note 8 and p. 119, note 10.

[6] They are eight in number.

[7] The forefathers—Manes.

[8] See p. 308, note 4.

[9] Diagram of the nine Planets.

[10] Of these two are downward turned, and the three intersect one another so that nine triangles are formed.

Then should a beautiful Bhūpura[1] be drawn (outside the petals of the Yantra) with four entrances, and (outside the Bhūpura) between the East and North-East corners a circle should be drawn with its diameter the length of a Prādesha,[2] and between the West and the South-West-corners another similar circle should be drawn (75-76).

Then the nine triangles[3] should be filled up with the colours of the nine planets, and the left and right sides of the middle triangle should be made white and yellow, and the base should be black. The eight petals should be filled up with the colours of the eight regents of the quarters[4] (77-78).

The walls of the Bhūpura should be decorated with white, red, and black powders, and, O Devī! the two circles each of which measure a Prādesha outside the Bhūpura should be coloured the upper one red and the lower white, and the intervening spaces of the Yantra may be coloured in any manner the wise may choose (79-80).

Listen now to the order in which each planet should be worshipped in the particular houses, and in which each Dikpati[5] should be worshipped in the particular petals, and to the names of the Devas who are present at each particular entrance (81).

In the inner triangle the Sun should be worshipped, and in the angles on the two sides Aruṇa[6] and Shikhā.[7]

---

[1] The part with four doors which surrounds and is common to every Yantra.

[2] See Ch. VI, verse 150 at p. 178.

[3] Formed by the intersection of the three triangles.

[4] Dikpālas. Their colours are—Yellow (Indra), Red (Agni), Black (Yama), Shyāmala or Dark blue or Dark green (Nirṛiti), White (Varuṇa), Black (Vāyu), Golden (Kuvera), and colour of the Full Moon (Īshāna). Also see v. 99 *post* for Brahmā and Ananta.

[5] Or Dikpāla.

[6] The charioteer of the Sun.

[7] The rays of the Sun.

Behind Him with the garland of rays [1], the two standards of the two fierce ones (Shikhā and Aruṇa) should be worshipped (82).

Worship the Maker of nights [2] in the triangle above the Sun on the East, in the Agni [3] corner Maṁgala,[4] on the South side Budha,[5] in the Nirṛita [6] corner Vṛihaspati,[7] on the West Shukra,[8] in the Vāyu [9] corner Shani,[10] in the corner on the North Rāhu,[11] and in the Īshāna [12] corner Ketu,[13] and, lastly, round about the Moon the multitude of stars (83-84). Sun is red, Moon is white,[14] Maṁgala is tawny, Budha is pale [15] or yellowish-white, Vṛihaspati is yellow,[16] Shukra is white,[17] Shani is black,[18] and Rāhu and Ketu are of variegated colour; thus I have spoken of the different colours of the Grahas (83-85).

The Sun should be meditated upon as having four hands, in two of which he is holding lotuses; and of the other two, one hand is lifted up to dispel fear,[19] and the

---

[1] Aṁshumālī, *i.e.*, the Sun.

[2] Rajanīkara—the Moon.

[3] South-East.

[4] Mars.

[5] Mercury.

[6] South-West.

[7] Jupiter.

[8] Venus.

[9] North-West.

[10] Saturn.

[11] Rāhu. Ascending node of the Moon or point where the Moon intersects the ecliptic in passing northward.

[12] North-East.

[13] Ketu the descending node. See n. 15.

[14] Shukla

[15] Pāṇḍu.

[16] Pīta.

[17] Shveta.

[18] Asita.

[19] Abhayakara.

other makes the sign of blessing.[1] The Moon should be meditated upon as having nectar in one hand, and the other hand in the attitude of giving.[2] Maṁgala should be meditated upon as slightly bent and holding a staff in his hands. The son of Moon, Budha, should be meditated upon as a boy, the locks of whose hair play about upon his forehead. Guru[3] should be meditated upon with a sacred thread, and holding a book in one hand and a string of Rudrāk*sh*a beads in the other; and the Guru of the Daityas[4] should be meditated upon as blind of one eye, and Shani as lame, and Rāhu as a trunkless head, and Ketu as a headless trunk, both deformed and wicked (86-88).

Having worshipped each of the planets in this manner, the eight Dikpālas, Indra and others, beginning from the East, should be worshipped (89).

He of a thousand eyes,[5] of a yellow colour, should first be worshipped. He is dressed in yellow silk garments, and, holding the thunderbolt in his hand, is seated on Airāvata[6] (90).

The body of Agni is of red hue. He is seated on a goat; in his hand is the Shakti.[7] Yama is black, and, holding a staff[8] in his hand, is seated on a bison. Nir*ri*ti is of dark green colour,[9] and, holding a sword in his hand,

---

[1] Vara.

[2] *i.e.*, making the Dāna-mudrā (Gesture of bestowing).

[3] B*ri*haspati—the Guru of the Devas.

[4] Shukra (Venus), the Guru of the Daityas (Demonic Spirits). The Daityas are the offspring of Kashyapa by Diti one of his consorts. Kashyapa is another form of Pashyaka=the Seer, *i.e.*, the Supreme. From Him all creatures originated. See the first chapter of Harivaṁsha.

[5] Indra.

[6] Airāvata is the name of the Indra's elephant, so called because he was churned out of the Ocean (Irāvat).

[7] The name of Agni's weapon shaped like an axe.

[8] Da*nd*a.

[9] Shyāmala.

is seated on a horse. Varu*n*a is white, and, seated on a Makara,[1] holds a noose[2] in his hand. Vāyu should be meditated on as possessed of a black radiance, seated on a deer and holding a goad.[3] Kuvera is of the colour of gold, and seated on a jewelled lion-seat,[4] holding the noose[5] and hook[6] in his hands. He is surrounded by Yaks*h*as,[7] who are singing his praises. Īshāna is seated on the bull; he holds the trident in one hand, and with the other bestows blessings. He is dressed in raiments of tiger-skin, and his effulgence is like that of the full moon (91-95).

Having thus meditated upon and worshipped them in their order, Brahmā should be worshipped in the upper circle, which is outside the Ma*nd*ala, and Vis*h*n*u in the lower one. Then the Devatās at the entrances should be worshipped (96).

Ugra,[8] Bhīma, Pracha*nd*a, and Īsha, are at the eastern entrance; Jayanta, Ks*h*etra-pāla, Nakulesha, and V*ri*hat-shirā*h*, are at the southern entrance; at the door on the west are V*ri*ka, Ashva, Ānanda, and Durjaya; and Tri-shirā*h*, Purajit, Bhīmanāda, and Mahodara are at the northern entrance. As protectors of the entrances, they are all armed with weapons, offensive and defensive (97-98).

Suvratā! listen to the Dhyāna[9] of Brahmā and Ananta. Brahmā is of the colour of the red lotus, and has four hands and four faces. He is seated on a swan.

---

[1] Makara is a mythological animal a cross between a fish and an alligator. It is the Vāhana of Devī Gaṁgā.

[2] Pásha.

[3] Aṁkusha.

[4] Siṁhāsana—Throne.

[5] Pāsha.

[6] Aṁkusha.

[7] Devayoni (see p. 2, note 7, *ante*) of that name.

[8] This and the others are the Dvāra-devatās.

[9] Dhyāna, mental image.

With two of his hands he makes the signs which dispel fear and grant boons, and in the others he holds a garland and a book. Ananta is white as the snow, the Kunda flower, and the Moon. He has thousands of eyes and feet, thousands of hands and faces, and he should be meditated upon by Suras and Asuras[1] (99-101).

Beloved! I have now spoken of the meditation,[2] the mode of worship, and the Yantra.[3] Now, my beloved, listen to their Mantras in their order, beginning with the Vāstu Mantra (102).

Mantras

When K*sh*a-kāra[4] is placed on the Carrier[5] of Oblations, and the six long vowels are then added to it, and adorned with the Nāda-Bindu,[6] the six-lettered Vāstu Mantra is formed (103).

The Sūrya Mantra is thus formed: first the Tāra[7] should be said; then the Māyā[8]; then the word Tīgma-rashme[9]; then the word Ārogya-da[10] in the dative singular; and, last of all, the Shakti[11] of Fire (104).

---

[1] Devas and Daityas. Thousands of eyes, etc., in the sense of countless eyes and so on. *Cf.* Puru*sh*a-sūkta.

[2] Dhyāna, mental image.

[3] Diagram.

[4] *i.e.*, the letter K*sh*a.

[5] Agni (Fire)—*i.e.*, the Bīja of Fire, Ra.

[6] The sound point (Chandra-bindu)=Ng or M. The Vāstu Mantra is—K*sh*rāng, K*sh*rīng, K*sh*rūng, K*sh*raing, K*sh*raung, K*sh*rnga*h*.

[7] *i.e.*, Ong-kāra = Oṁ.

[8] *i.e.*, Māyā-bīja = Hrīng.

[9] O Thou with burning rays!

[10] To the giver of good health.

[11] Svāhā. The Mantra is—Ong Hrīng Tīgma-rashme ārogyadāya Svāhā.

The approved Mantra of Soma is formed by saying the Bījas[1] of Kāma, Māyā and Vāṇī, then Amṛita-kara, amṛitam plāvaya plāvaya Svāhā (105).

The Mantra of Maṁgala is Aing Hrāng Hrīng Sarva-dushṭān nāshaya nāshaya Svāhā[2] (106).

The Mantra of the son of Soma[3] is Hrāng, Shrīng, Saumya sarvān kāmān pūraya Svāhā[4] (107).

The Mantra of the Sura-Guru[5] is formed thus: Let the Tāra[6] precede and follow the Bīja of Vāṇi, and then say, Abhīshṭam yachchha yachchha, and lastly Svāhā[6] (108).

The Mantra of Shukra is Shāng, Shīng, Shūng, Shaing, Shaung, Shngaḥ (109).

The Mantra of the Slowly Moving One[7] is Hrāng Hrāng Hrīng Hrīng Sarva-shatrūn vidrāvaya vidrāvaya Mārtaṇḍasūnave Namaḥ—Destroy, destroy all enemies—I bow to the son of Mārtaṇḍa[8] (110).

The Mantra of Rāhu is Rāng, Hraung, Bhraung,[9] Hrīng—Soma-shatro shatrūn vidhvaṁsaya vidhvaṁsaya Rāhave Namaḥ—O Enemy of Soma (Moon)! destroy, destroy all enemies. I bow to Rāhu (111).

Krūng, Hrūng, Kraing Ketave Svāhā is the Mantra of Ketu[10] (112).

---

[1] Bījas of Kāma, etc., are—Klīng, Hrīng, Aing. The Mantra is—Klīng, Hrīng, Aing Amṛitam plāvaya plāvaya Svāhā (O Thou with nectar rays! do thou pour nectar, do thou pour nectar).

[2] Destroy all the wicked, destroy all the wicked.

[3] Budha.

[4] O Son of Soma! gratify all desires.

[5] Bṛihaspati.

[6] The Mantra is: Ong Aing Ong Suraguro abhīshṭam yachchha yachchha Svāhā—O, Guru of the Suras (Devas)! grant the wished-for thing (Abhīshṭa—Abhi-ishṭa, from root Ish, to wish for).

[7] Shani, who is lame.

[8] *i.e.*, the Sun.

[9] A variation is Bhraing.

[10] See p. 384, note 12.

Lang, Rang, M*ri*ng, Strūng, Vang, Yang, K*sh*ang, Haung, Brīng, and Ang are in their order[1] the ten Mantras of the ten Dikpālas, beginning with Indra and ending with Ananta (113).

The names of the other attendant Devas are their Mantras; in all instances where there is no Mantra mentioned this is the rule as enjoined by Shiva (114).

Sovereign Mistress of the Devas[2]! the wise man should not add Nama*h* to Mantras that end with the word Nama*h*, nor should he put the Shakti[3] of Vahni to a Mantra that ends with Svāhā (115).

To the Planets and others should be given flowers, clothes, and jewels, but the colour of the gifts should be the same as that of the respective Planets; otherwise they are not pleased (116).

The wise man should place Fire in the manner prescribed for Kusha*nd*ikā,[4] and perform Homa either with flowers of variegated colours or with sacred fuel[5] (117).

In rites for the attainment of peace[6] or good fortune, or nourishment[7] or prosperity, the Carrier of Oblations[8] is called Varada[9]; in rites relating to consecration[10] he

---

[1] Lang, Indra; Rang, Agni; M*ri*ng, Yama; Strūng, Nir*ri*ti; Vang, Varu*n*a; Yang, Vāyu; K*sh*ang, Kuvera; Haung, Īshāna; Brīng, Brahmā and Ang, Ananta or Vi*sh*nu. The last two are above and below and the others at the eight corners of the Yantra.

[2] Deveshi.

[3] Svāhā.

[4] See pp. 258, note 2: 269, v. 70.

[5] Samidh—certain kinds of wood used as fuel for sacrificial purposes.

[6] Shānti. Rite to avert evil.

[7] Pu*sh*ti. Rite for the attainment of worldly prosperity.

[8] Havya-vāhana = Fire.

[9] One who grants boons.

[10] Prati*sh*thā.

is called Lohitāksha[1]; in destructive rites[2] he is called Shatruhā[3] (118).

Maheshānī! in Shānti,[4] Pushti,[4] and Krūra[4] rites the man who worships the Planets will obtain the desired end (119).

As in the rites relating to the consecration[5] the Devas should be worshipped and libations offered to the Pitris,[6] so also should there be the same sacrifices to Vāstu and the Planets (120).

Should one have to perform two or three consecratory and sacrificial rites on the same day, then the worship of the Devas, the Shrāddha of the Pitris, and Consecration of Fire are required once only (121).

One who desires the fruit of his observances should not give to any Deva reservoirs of water, houses, gardens, bridges, causeways, carriers,[7] conveyances,[8] clothes, jewels, drinking-cups, and eating-plates, or whatever else he may desire to give, without first purifying[9] and consecrating the same (122-123).

In all rites performed with an ultimate object the wise one should in all cases perform a Saṁkalpa,[10] in accordance with directions, for the full attainment of the good object (124).

---

[1] The Red-eyed one.

[2] Krūra-karmani—that is, in rites to avenge a wrong or injure an enemy, etc.

[3] Destroyer of enemies.

[4] See previous Shloka (118).

[5] Pratishthā.

[6] The forefathers—Manes.

[7] Vāhana.

[8] Yāna.

[9] Saṁskritya.

[10] Preliminary rite expressive of determination. Saṁkalpa means determination.

Complete merit is earned when the thing about to be given is first purified, worshipped, and mentioned by name, and then the name of him to whom it is given is pronounced (125).

I will now tell you the Mantras for the consecration of reservoirs of water, houses, gardens, bridges, causeways and trees. The Mantras should always be preceded by the Brahma-Vidyā [1] (126).

Mantras

Reservoir of Water! thou that givest life to all beings! thou that art presided over by Varu*n*a! may this consecration of thee (by me) give satisfaction to all beings that live and move in water, on land, and in air (127).

House, thou art made of timber and grass, thou art the favourite of Brahmā; I am consecrating thee with water; do thou be always the cause of pleasure (128).

When consecrating a house made of bricks and other materials, one should say: "House made of bricks," and so forth (129).

Mantras

Garden! thou art pleasant by reason of thy fruits, leaves, and branches, and by thy shadows. I am sprinkling thee with sacred water [2]; grant me all my wishes (130).

Bridge! thou art like the bridge across the Ocean of Existence, thou art welcome to the wayfarer; do thou, being consecrated by me, grant me the fitting reward thereof (131).

---

[1] *i.e.*, Brahma-gāyatrī (see p. 55, vv. 109-111).

[2] Tīrtha-vāri: Consecrated water.

Causeway! I am consecrating thee, as thou helpest people in going from one place to another: do thou likewise help me on my way to Heaven (132).

The wise should use the same Mantra is consecrating a tree as is prescribed for the sprinkling of a garden (133).

In consecrating all other things, the Pranava,[1] Vāruna,[2] and Astra[3] should be used (134).

Those Vāhanas that can (or ought to) be bathed should be bathed with the Brahma-gāyatrī[4]; others should be purified by sprinkling with Arghya-water taken up with the ends of Kusha grass (135).

After performing Prāna-pratishthā,[5] calling it by its name, the Vāhana called by its name should be duly worshipped, and decked out and then be given to the Devatā (136).

Whilst consecrating a reservoir, Varuna, the Lord of aquatic animals, should be worshipped. In the case of a house, Brahmā, the Lord of all things born,[6] should there be worshipped. Whilst consecrating a garden, a bridge, a causeway, Vishnu, Who is the Protector of the universe,[7] the Spirit of all,[8] Who witnesseth all and is omnipresent, should be worshipped (137).

Shrī Devī said:

Thou hast spoken of the different injunctions relating to the different rites, but Thou hast not yet shown the order in which man should practise them (138).

---

[1] Oṁ.

[2] Vāruna Bīja, Vang.

[3] Phat.

[4] See p. 55. vv. 109-11.

[5] The life-giving rite.

[6] Prajāpati.

[7] Jagatpātā.

[8] Sarvātmā.

Rites not properly performed according to the order enjoined do not, even though performed with labour, yield the full benefit to men who follow the life of Karma[1] (139).

Shrī Sadāshiva said:

O Parameshānī! Thou art beneficient like a mother. What Thou hast said is indeed the best for men whose minds are occupied with the results (or their efforts) (140).

The practices relating to the aforementioned rites are different. Devī! I am relating them in their order, beginning with the Vāstu-yāga. Do Thou listen attentively (141).

He (who wishes to perform the Vāstu-yāga) should the day previous thereto live on regulated food.[2] After bathing in the early auspicious hour of morning, and performing the ordinary daily religious duties, he should worship the Guru and Nārāyana[3] (142).

The worshipper should then, after making Saṁkalpa,[4] worship Ganesha and others for the attainment of his own object, according to the rules shown in the ordinances (143).

Dhyāna

Worship Ganapati,[5] Who is of the colour of the Bandhūka[6] flower, and has three eyes; Whose head is that of the best of elephants; Whose sacred thread is made of the King of Snakes; Who is holding in his four lotus hands the Conch, the Discus, the Sword, and a spotless Lotus; on

---

[1] Karmānujīvī: a man who does pious acts in the hope of reward.

[2] Such as Havishyānna.

[3] Vishnu as collective humanity.

[4] See p. 396, n. 10.

[5] Ganesha. He is also called Siddhidātā—the Giver of Success—and therefore is first worshipped (*cf.* Chapter X, verse 118, *ante*). Ganesha has fifty-one names and aspects.

[6] A red flower.

Whose forehead is the rising young moon; the shining effulgence of Whose body and raiments is like that of the Sun; Who is decked with various jewels, and is seated on a red lotus (144).

Having thus meditated upon and worshipped Ga*n*esha to the best of his ability, he should worship Brahmā, Vā*n*ī,[1] Vi*sh*nu, and Lak*sh*mī (145).

Then, after worshipping Shiva, Durgā, the Grahas,[2] the sixteen Mothers, and the Vasus in the Vasudhārā,[3] he should perform the B*ri*ddhishrāddha[4] (146).

Then the Ma*nd*ala[5] of the Vāstu-daitya should be drawn, and there the Vāstu-daitya with his followers should be worshipped (147).

Then make there a Stha*nd*ila[6] and purifying fire as before; first perform Dhārā-homa,[7] and then commence Vāstu-homa[8] (148).

Oblations should be offered to the Vāstu-puru*sh*a and all his followers according to the best of one's ability. The sacrifice should be brought to a close by the offering of oblations to the Devas worshipped[9] (149).

When Vāstu-yajna is separately performed, this is the order which is prescribed, and in this order also the sacrifice to the planets should be performed (150).

Moreover, the Planets being here the principal objects of worship, they should not be subordinately worshipped.

---

[1] Sarasvatī.

[2] Planets.

[3] See p. 272, note 9.

[4] See p. 305, n. 5 which has changed place with n. 6.

[5] Diagram.

[6] A square.

[7] See p. 270, verse 82.

[8] Fire sacrifice to the Vāstu spirit.

[9] That is when it is the principal rite. In a case like this the order prescribed for any other rite is to be followed.

The Vāstu should be worshipped immediately after the Saṁkalpa[1] (151).

Ganesha and the other Devas should be worshipped as in Vāstu-yāga. I have already spoken to Thee of the Yantra[2] and Mantra and Dhyāna[3] of the Planets (152).

I have, O Gentle One! during My discourse with Thee, spoken of the order to be observed in the Yajnas of the planets and of Vāstu. I shall now speak to Thee of the various praiseworthy acts, beginning with the consecration of wells (153).

After making Saṁkalpa[1] in the proper manner, Vāstu should be worshipped either in a Mandala, or a jar,[4] or a Shālagrāma,[5] according to inclination (154).

Then Ganapati[6] should be worshipped, as also Brahmā and Vānī,[7] Hari[8] and Ramā,[9] Shiva and Durgā, the Planets and the Dikpatis[10] (155).

Then the Mātrikās[11] and the eight Vasus[12] having been worshipped, Pitrikriyā[13] should be performed. Since Varuna is principal Deva (for the purposes of this ceremony), He should be worshipped with particular care (156).

---

[1] See p. 396, n. 10. In all other worships the Navagraha-pūjā (worship of the nine Planets) is done, and the Planets are objects of subordinate worship (Anga-pūjā). Here the Planets are worshipped as the chief (Mukhya) objects.

[2] Diagram.

[3] Meditation.

[4] Kalasa.

[5] Sacred stone emblematic of Nārāyana, or Vishnu.

[6] Ganesha.

[7] Sārasvatī.

[8] Vishnu.

[9] Lakshmī.

[10] Dikpālas (see p. 389, n. 4).

[11] See p. 39, note 3.

[12] See Bhava, Dhruva, Soma, Vishnu, Anala, Anila, Prabhūsha and Prabhava who originated from Gamgā.

[13] Ābhyudayika-shrāddha (see p. 309, note 10).

Having worshipped Varu*n*a with various presents to the best of his ability, Vāru*n*a Homa[1] should then be performed in Fire duly consecrated (157). And after offering oblations to each of the Devas worshipped, he should bring the Homa rite to an end by giving the Pūr*n*āhuti[2] (158).

Then he should sprinkle the excellent well, decorated with flagstaffs and flags, garlands, scents, and vermilion, with the Proks*h*a*n*a Mantra,[3] spoken of before (159).

Then he should, in the name of the Deva,[4] or for the attainment of the object of his desire, give away the well or tank for the benefit of all beings (160).

Then the most excellent worshipper should make supplication with folded palms as follows:

"Be well pleased, all beings, whether living in the air or on earth or in water; I have given this excellent water to all beings; may all beings be satisfied by bathing in, drinking from, or plunging into this water; I have given this common water to all beings. Should anyone by his own misfortune be endangered in this, may I not be guilty of that sin,[5] may my (good) work bear fruit!" (161-163).

Then presents should be made, and Shānti[6] and other rites performed, and thereafter Brāhma*n*as, Kaulas, and the hungry poor should be fed. Shivā! this is the order to be observed in the consecration of all kinds of reservoirs of water (164-165).

---

[1] *i.e.*, he should offer oblations to Varu*n*a in the Fire.

[2] Complete or Final Oblation.

[3] The Mantra said when sprinkling. See Shloka 127, *ante*.

[4] The dedication is made merely to the Is*ht*adevatā by a Nis*h*kāma dedicator and the Sakāma man mentions the object of his desire (Kāma).

[5] The sin of such man's death.

[6] An auspicious rite to secure peace, happiness, and wealth.

In the consecration of a Tadāga[1] and other kinds of reservoirs of water there should be a Nāgastambha[2] and some aquatic animals[3] (166).

Aquatic animals, such as fish, frogs, alligators, and tortoises, should be made of metal, according to the means of the person consecrating (167).

There should be made two fish and two frogs of gold, two alligators of silver, and two tortoises, one of copper and another of brass (168).

After giving away the Tadāga or Dīrghikā or Sāgara with these aquatic animals, Nāga[4] should, after having been supplicated, be worshipped (169).

Ananta, Vāsuki, Padma, Mahāpadma, Takshaka, Kulīra, Karkata, and Shaṁkha[5]—all these are the protectors of water (170).

These eight names of the Nāgas should be written on Ashvattha[6] leaves, and, after making Japa of the Pranava[7] and the Gāyatrī, the leaves should be thrown into a jar (171).

Calling upon Sun and Moon to witness, the leaves should be mixed up together, and one should be drawn

---

[1] Tadāga is a reservoir over 2,000 square cubits in area, and not less than 45 cubits in width. Other kinds are—(1) Drona, 40 by 40 cubits and over; (2) Vāpī, 130 by 130 cubits and over; (3) Sarovara is a large tank where the lotus grows; (4) a Dīrghikā should be 85 cubits wide, with a superficial area of not less than 1,200 square cubits; (5) Pushkarinī is not less than 20 by 20 cubits; (6) Kūpa is a well; (7) Sāgara is one that is larger than any of the above. These reservoirs should be long in shape from North to South; even those which are of a square form should be slightly longer from North to South.

[2] When a tank is first dug out, a thick column or piece of wood is driven into its centre. It is also called Yūpa.

[3] See next Shloka. Artificial fish or frogs, etc., made of brass, etc., are placed in the tank.

[4] The serpent protector, of water (see *ante*). As to Tadāga, etc., see note 1 above.

[5] All names of Nāgas or Serpent-Divinities.

[6] *Ficus religiosa*.

[7] Oṁ.

therefrom, and the Nāga whose name is drawn should be made the protector of water (172).

Then a wooden post, auspicious and straight, should be brought and smeared with oil and turmeric, and bathed in consecrated water, to the accompaniment of the Vyāh*r*īti [1] and the Pra*n*ava,[2] and then the Nāga who has been made the protector of the water should be worshipped with the Shaktis Hrī, Shrī, Ks*h*amā, and Shānti (173-174).

MANTRA

O Nāga! Thou art the couch of Vis*hn*u, thou art the adornment of Shiva; do thou inhabit this post [3] and protect my water (175).

Having thus made supplication to Nāga, the pillar should be set in the middle of the reservoir, and the dedicator should then go round the Ta*d*āga,[4] keeping it on his right (176).

If the post has been already fixed, then the Nāga should be worshipped in a jar, and, throwing the water of the jar into the reservoir, the remainder of the rites should be performed (177).

Similarly, the wise man who has taken a vow to consecrate a house should perform the rites, beginning with the worship of Vāstu, and ending with that of the Vasus, and perform the rites relating to the Pit*r*is as prescribed for the consecration of a well, and the excellent devotee should worship Prajāpati and do Prājāpatya [5] Homa (178-179).

---

[1] Bhū*h*, Bhuva*h*, Sva*h*.

[2] Oṁ.

[3] Stambha.

[4] See note 1, p. 403.

[5] Prājāpatya is an adjective derived from Prajāpati.

The house should be sprinkled with the Mantra already mentioned, and then worshipped with incense, etc.; after that, with his face to the Īshāna[1] corner, he should pray as follows (180):

MANTRA

"O House! Prajāpati is thy Lord; decked with flowers and garlands and other decorations, be thou always pleasant for our happy residence" (181).

He should then offer presents,[2] and, performing Shānti rites,[3] accept blessings.[4] Thereafter he should feed Vipras,[5] Kulīnas, and the poor to the best of his ability (182).

O Daughter of the Mountain! if the house is being consecrated for someone else, then such person should be mentioned by name and in the place "our residence" should be said "his residence". Now listen to the ordinances relating to the consecration of a house or temple for a Deva (183).

After consecrating the house in the above manner, the Deva should be approached with the blowing of conchshells

---

[1] North-East.

[2] Dakshinā.

[3] See p. 402, note 6, *ante*.

[4] The blessings referred to are the blessing of Kaulas, Brāhmanas, Veshyās, and other honoured persons (Bhakta, ed. 679). By Veshyā is not to be understood a prostitute, which the word also means but a Shakti who has received her Pūrnābhisheka. The root Vish=to surround.

The Veshyās are divided into seven classes, namely, Guptaveshyā, Mahāveshyā, Kulaveshyā, Rājaveshyā, Devaveshyā, Brahmaveshyā, Sarvaveshyā. Their Lakshanas are described in Guptasādhana Tantra and Prānatoshinī. They are Āvarana Devatās of the Mahāvidyā. The Mahāvidyās themselves are sometimes called Veshyā.

[5] Brāhmanas.

and the sound of other musical instruments, and He should be supplicated thus (184):

MANTRA

Rise, O Lord of the Deva among Devas! Thou that grantest the desires of Thy votaries! come and make my life blessed,[1] O Ocean of Mercy! (185).

Having thus invited (the Deva) into the room, he should be placed at the door, and the Vâhana[2] should be placed in front of Him (186).

Then on the top of the house a trident[3] or a discus[4] should be placed, and in the Ishāna[5] corner a staff should be set with a flag flying from it (187).

Let the good worshipper then decorate the room with awnings,[6] small bells, garlands of flowers, and mango leaves, and then cover the house up with celestial cloth[7] (188).

The Deva should be placed with His face to the North, and in the manner to be described He should be bathed with the things prescribed. I now am speaking of their order; do Thou listen (189).

After saying Aing, Hring, Shring, the Mūla Mantra[8] should be repeated, and then let the worshipper say:

---

[1] Janmasāphalya—Fulfil the object of my life.

[2] Carrier of the Deity.

[3] The Trident (Trishūla) is placed if the divinity is Shiva or any connected Deva.

[4] The Discus (Chakra) is placed if the Deva be Vi*shn*u or connected with Him.

[5] North-East.

[6] Chandrâtapa.

[7] Divyavâsa—*i.e.*, cloth of fine texture.

[8] The principal Mantra of the Devata.

MANTRA

I am bathing Thee with milk; do Thou cherish me like a mother[1] (190).

Repeating the three Bījas aforesaid and the Mūla Mantra[1], let him then say:

MANTRA

I am bathing Thee to-day with curds; do Thou remove the tribulations[2] of this mundane existence (191).

Repeating again the three Bījas and the Mūla Mantra, let him say:

MANTRA

O Giver of Joy to all! being bathed in honey,[3] do Thou make me joyful (192).

Repeating the Mūla Mantra as before, and inwardly reciting the Pra*n*ava and the Sāvitri, he should say:

MANTRA

I am bathing Thee in ghee, which is dear to the Devas, which is longevity, seed, and courage[4]; do Thou, O Lord! keep me free from disease (193).

Again repeating the Mūla Mantra, as also the Vyāh*r*iti and the Gāyatrī, let him say:

---

[1] Because it is the mother who suckles.

[2] Literally "heat" (Tāpa), *i.e.*, the trials and tribulations. Curd is cooling and is offered to cool the feet.

[3] Madhu also means consecrated wine.

[4] Ghee is heat-producing. Longevity etc. *i.e.*, which prolongs life, increases semen (Shukra) and courage.

MANTRA

O Devesha! bathed by me in sugar water, do Thou grant me (the object of) my desire (194).

Repeating the Mūla Mantra, the Gāyatrī, and the Vāruṇa Mantra,[1] he should say:

MANTRA

I am bathing Thee with cocoanut-water, which is the creation of Vidhi,[2] which is divine, which is welcome to Devas, and is cooling, and which is not of the world[3]; I bow to Thee (195).

Then, with the Gāyatrī and the Mūla Mantra, the Deva should be bathed with the juice of sugar-cane (196).

Repeating the Kāma Bīja[4] and the Tāra,[5] the Sāvitrī,[6] and the Mūla Mantra, he should, whilst bathing the Deva, say:

MANTRA

Be Thou well bathed in water scented with camphor, Aguru[7], saffron, musk, and sandal; be Thou pleased to grant me Enjoyment[8] and Liberation[8] (197).

After bathing the Lord of the World in this manner with eight jarfuls (of water, etc.), He should be brought inside the room and placed on His seat (198).

---

[1] Vang.

[2] Brahmā, that is, it is the best of created things (Stuti).

[3] Alaukika. The idea is that it is uncommon.

[4] Klīng.

[5] Oṁ.

[6] Gāyatrī. (See "Garland of Letters".)

[7] A kind of tree native in the Garo hills. The wood of this yields a strong sweet scent.

[8] Bhukti and Mukti.

If the image be one which cannot be bathed,[1] then the Yantra,[2] or Mantra, or the Shālagrāma-shilā,[3] should be bathed and worshipped (199).

If one be not able to bathe (the Deva) in manner above, then he should bathe (Him) with eight, seven, or five jars of pure water (200).

The size and proportions of the jar[4] have been already given whilst speaking of Chakra worship. In all rites prescribed in the Āgamas that is the jar which is appropriate (201).

Then the Great Deva[5] should be worshipped according to the injunctions to be followed in His worship. I shall speak of the offerings. Do Thou, O Supreme Devī! listen (202).

A seat,[6] welcome,[7] water[8] to wash the feet, offerings,[9] water[10] for rinsing the mouth, Madhuparka,[11] water[10] for sipping, bathing water,[12] clothes and jewels, scents and flowers, lights, and incense-sticks, edibles and words of

---

[1] *e.g.*, a mud image.

[2] Diagram.

[3] See p. 401, note 5, *ante*.

[4] Ghaṭa. See *ante*, ch v. 182.

[5] The word in the text is Mahādeva, by which Shiva is generally meant. As the principal object of worship is for the time being raised above the rest, the particular Deva whose temple is being consecrated is called here Mahādeva.

[6] Āsana.

[7] Svāgata.

[8] Pādya.

[9] Arghya—respectful oblations of rice, Dūrvā grass, flowers, etc., and water.

[10] Āchamanīya.

[11] Mixture of curd, ghee, and honey offered to an honoured guest (see ch. x).

[12] Snānīya.

praise,[1] are the sixteen[2] offerings requisite in the worship of the Devas (203-204).

Pādya,[3] Arghya,[3] Āchamana,[3] Madhuparka,[3] Āchamana,[3] Gandha,[4] Pus*h*pa,[5] Dhūpa,[6] Dīpa,[7] Naivedya[8]—these are known as Dashopachāra (ten requisite offerings) (205).

Gandha,[4] Pus*h*pa,[5] Dhūpa,[6] Dīpa,[7] and Naivedya,[8] are spoken of as the Panchopachāra (five offering) in the worship of a Deva (206).

The articles should be sprinkled with water taken from the Offering[9] with the Weapon Mantra,[10] and be worshipped with scents and flowers, the names of separate articles being mentioned (207).

Mentally repeating the Mantra that is to be said, as also the Mūla Mantra,[11] and the name of the Deva in the dative case, the words of gift should be repeated (208).

I have told Thee of the way in which the things to be given to the Devas should be dedicated. He who is versed in the ritual should in this manner give away an article to a Deva (209).

I have shown (whilst describing) the mode of worship of the Ādyā[12] Devī how Pādya, Arghya, etc., should

---

[1] Vandana.

[2] These are called the *Shod*ashopachāra. *Cf.* this list with that given in Chapter vi, and mark the order in which they are given there. The Pūjā there described is Rahasya-pūjā, or Secret worship.

[3] See previous Shloka and Notes.

[4] Scent.

[5] Flowers.

[6] Incense-Stick.

[7] Light.

[8] Edibles.

[9] Arghya.

[10] Pha*t*.

[11] See p. 406, note 8.

[12] The Primeval Shakti.

be offered, and how Kāra*n*a and the like[1] should be given (210).

To such of the Mantras as were not spoken then, do Thou, O Beloved! listen to them here; these should be said when Āsana[2] and other requisites are offered (211).

MANTRA

(O Deva!) Thou who residest within all beings! who art the innermost Ātmā of all beings! I am offering this seat[3] for Thee to sit. I bow to Thee again and again (212).

O Deveshī! after giving the excellent Āsana in this way, the giver of the Āsana should with folded palms bid Him welcome as follows (213):

MANTRA

(O Deva!) Thou art He whom even the Devas seek for the accomplishment of their objects, yet for me Thy auspicious visit has easily been obtained. I bow to Thee, O Supreme Lord! (214).

My life's aim is accomplished to-day; all my efforts are crowned with success; I have obtained the fruits of my devotion[4]—all this by Thy auspicious coming (215).

Ambikā[5]! the Deva should thus be invited, prayed to, and questioned as to His auspicious coming,[6] and then,

---

[1] *i.e.*, Wine, meat, etc.

[2] The seat offered to the Devas.

[3] Āsana.

[4] Tapas.

[5] Mother.

[6] *i.e.*, whether he has had a good journey, etc.

taking Pādya,[1] the following Mantra should be repeated (216):

MANTRA

By the mere touch of the washings of Thy feet the three worlds are purified; I am offering Thee Pādya for washing Thy lotus feet (217). He by Whose grace is attained supreme Bliss, to Him Who is the Spirit[2] in all beings I offer this Ānandārghya[3] (218).

Then pure water or water which has been scented with nutmeg, cloves, and Kakkola,[4] should be consecrated, and taken and offered with the following (219):

MANTRA

(O Lord!) by the mere touch of that which Thou hast touched[5] the whole of this impure world is purified; for washing that lotus mouth I offer Thee this Āchamanīya[6] (220).

Then, taking Madhuparka,[7] offer it with devotion and with the following (221):

MANTRA

For the destruction of the Three Afflictions,[8] for the attainment of uninterrupted Bliss, I give Thee to-day,

---

[1] Water to wash the feet.

[2] Sarvātma bhūta.

[3] The Arghya, or Offering of Bliss.

[4] *Cocculus indicus.*

[5] Uchchhi*sh*ta = Leavings; for what has been touched by another—*e.g.*, food—is impure. And so the saying is—Nochchhi*sh*tam kasyachid dadyāt ("Offer leavings to none").

[6] Water for rinsing the mouth.

[7] Honey, curds, etc. (*vide ante*).

[8] *i.e.*, Ādhyātmika, Ādhidaivika, Ādhibhautika.

O Parameshvara! this Madhuparka; be Thou propitious (222).

By the mere touch of anything which has touched Thy mouth things impure become pure: this Punarāchamanīyam[1] is for the lotus mouth of Thine (223).

Taking water for the bath, and pouring it and consecrating it as before, it should be placed before the Deva, and the following Mantra should be repeated (224):

MANTRA

To Thee Whose splendour envelopes the world, from Whom the world was born, Who is the support of the world, I offer this water for Thy bath (225).

When offering bathing water, clothes, and edibles, Āchamanīya should be given as each is offered, and, after offering other articles, water should be given once after each offering is made[2] (226).

Bringing the cloth consecrated[3] as aforementioned, holding it up with both hands, the Sādhaka should repeat the following (227):

MANTRA

Raimentless though Thou art, Thou hast kept Thy glory[4] concealed by Thy Māyā.[5] To Thee I offer these two pieces of cloth. I bow to Thee (228).

---

[1] *i.e.*, Second Āchamanīya offered to rinse the mouth after the Deva takes the Madhuparka.

[2] For Āchamana.

[3] Shodhita = Purified, sanctified.

[4] Tejas.

[5] Māyā. By absence of raiment is shown the all-pervasiveness of the deity. The offer made by the Sādhaka is for his own satisfaction overpowered as he is by the Māyā of the Devatā.

Taking different kinds of ornaments made of gold and silver and other materials, and sprinkling and consecrating them, he should offer them to the Deva, uttering the following (229):

MANTRA

To Thee Who art the ornament of the Universe, Who art the one cause of the beauty of the universe, I offer these jewels for the adornment of Thy image[1] which Thou hast shown by Thy Māyā (230).

MANTRA[2]

To Thee Who through the subtle Element of Smell[3] hast created the Earth whose property is Smell, to Thee, the Supreme Spirit, I offer this excellent scent (231).

MANTRA[4]

By me have been dedicated with devotion beautiful flowers, and charming and sweet scents prepared by Devas: do Thou accept this flower (232).

MANTRA[5]

This incense-stick is the sap of the incense-bearing trees; it is divine, and possesses a delicious scent, and is charming, and pleasing to all beings. I give it to Thee to smell (233).

---

[1] Māyā-vigraha. The image is Māyā, and exists through the Devatā, power of Māyā.

[2] Mantra for offering scents.

[3] Gandha-tanmātra from which comes the gross Prithivī-tattva.

[4] Mantra for offering flowers.

[5] Mantra for offering incense-stick,

MANTRA[1]

Do Thou accept this light which illumines and is very bright, which removes all darkness, and which is both the inner and outer light[2] (234).

MANTRA[3]

This offering of food is of delicious taste, and consists of various kinds of edibles. I offer it to Thee in a devout spirit; do Thou partake of it (235).

MANTRA[4]

O Deva! this clear drinking-water, perfumed with camphor and other scents which satisfies all, I offer to Thee—Salutation to Thee (236).

The worshipper should then offer Pān[5] made with camphor, catechu, cloves, cardamums, and, after again offering Āchamanīya, bow to Him[6] (237).

If the offerings are presented along with the vessels in which they are contained, then the names and description of the offerings may jointly be repeated when making the present, or the names (or description) of the vessels may separately be said and the same given[7] (238).

Having worshipped the Deva in this manner, three double handfuls of flowers should be given to the Deva.

---

[1] For offering light.

[2] That is, as I give Thee this light which illumines the outer darkness may my very inner being be illumined by Thy Light.

[3] For offering edibles (Naivedya).

[4] For offering water.

[5] Betel-leaves.

[6] This is the second Āchamanīya, called Punarāchamanīya in the original.

[7] *i.e.*, it may be said: "I give you——in this vessel," or "I give you——and this vessel."

Then, sprinkling the temple and its awnings with water, the following Mantra should be said with folded palms (239):

MANTRA

Temple! thou art adorable for all men; thou grantest virtue[1] and fame. In affording a resting-place to this Deva, do thou be like unto Sumeru[2] (240). Thou art Kailâsa,[3] thou art Vaiku*ntha*,[4] thou art the abode of Brahmā. Since thou art holding within thee the Deva,[5] Thou art the adorned of the Devas (241).

Since thou holdest within thyself the image of Him Who has assumed form by His Māyā, and within Whose belly exists this universe, with all that is movable and immovable therein (242), thou art the equal of the Mother of the Devas: all the holy places are in thee. Do thou grant all my desires, and do thou bring me peace. I bow to thee (243).

Having thus praised the temple decorated with the discus, flag, and so forth and worshipped it three times, the worshipper should give it to the Deva, mentioning the object of his desire (244).

MANTRA

To Thee, whose abode is the universe, for Thy residence[6] I dedicate this temple. O Maheshāna! do Thou accept it and in Thy mercy abide here (245).

---

[1] Pu*n*ya. The merit earned by pious acts.

[2] *i.e.*, Be as great and as strong as the Himālaya Mountain.

[3] Shiva's Heaven.

[4] Vi*sh*n*u's Heaven.

[5] That is, the Deva whose image is consecrated and installed in the Temple.

[6] The word used is Vāsāya = for a residence, Ram Mohan Roy reads Vishvāya as such an adjective qualifying "Thee" and meaning "Who art the Universe".

Having said this and having made presents, the Deva to whom the temple has been dedicated should be placed on the altar to the accompaniment of the music of conches, horns, and other instruments (246).

He should then touch the two feet of the Deva and utter the Mūla Mantra, and say, "Sthāng! Sthīng! do Thou remain here; this temple is made by me for Thee," and, having placed[1] the Deva there, he should pray again to the temple thus (247):

MANTRA

Temple! be thou always in every way pleasant for the residence of the Deva; thou hast been dedicated by me; may the Lokas[2] be assured to me without encountering danger (248).

Help my fourteen generations of ancestors, my fourteen generations of successors, and me and the rest of my family to reside in the abode of the Devas (249).

May I, by Thy grace, gain the fruits attainable by performing all forms of Yajnas, and by visiting all the places of pilgrimage (250).

May my line continue so long as this world, so long as these mountains, so long as the Sun and Moon endure (251).

The pious man, after having thus addressed the temple should again worship the Deva, and dedicate mirrors and other articles and the flag to Him (252).

Then the Vāhana appropriate to the Devatā should be given. To Shiva should be given a Bull. Then prayer to him should be made thus (253):

---

[1] Sthirīkṛitya, when repeating the Mantra the dedicator touches the feet of the image.

[2] That is, the higher regions. Some interpret "Lokas" in this verse to mean Svar-loka, or Heaven, and say that the plural is "Gauravārthe" *i.e.*, honorific.

MANTRA

O Bull! thou art large of body, thy horns are sharp, thou killest all enemies, thou art worshipped even by the Tridashas,[1] as thou carriest on thy back the Lord of the Devas[2] (254).

In thy hoofs are all the holy shrines, in thy hair are the eternal Vedas,[3] in the tip of thy teeth are all the Nigamas, Āgamas, and Tantras (255).

May the husband of Pārvatī,[4] pleased with this gift of thee, give me a place in Kailāsa,[5] and do thou protect me always (256).

O Maheshānī! do Thou listen to the manner of prayer upon giving a Lion to Mahādevī[6] or a Garuda[7] to Vishnu (257).

MANTRA

Thou didst display thy great strength in the wars between the Suras[8] and the Asuras[9]; thou didst give victory to the Devas, and didst destroy the Dānavas. Thou formidable one, thou art the favourite of the Devī, thou art the favourite of Brahmā, Vishnu, and Shiva; with devotion I have dedicated thee to the Devī. Do thou destroy my enemies. I bow to thee (258-259).

---

[1] Devas, Brahmā and others.

[2] Devesha.

[3] Which according to Tarkālaṁgkāra are the Vedic Mantras.

[4] *i.e.*, Shiva.

[5] Shiva's Heaven.

[6] The Great Devī in Her aspect as Durgā. See p. 383, n. 1.

[7] See *ante*, p. 382, note 4.

[8] Devas.

[9] Daityas, or Demons. See Durgāsaptashatī or Chandī.

O Garu*d*a! most excellent bird! thou art the favoured one of the Husband of Laksh*m*ī[1]; thy beak is hard like adamant[2]; thy talons are sharp, and golden are thy wings. Obeisance to thee, most excellent among birds! I bow to thee, O King of birds! (260).

As thou abidest near Vish*n*u with folded palms, do thou, O Destroyer of the pride of enemies! help me to be there as thou art there (261). When thou art pleased, the Lord of the Universe is pleased, and grants success[3] (262).

When a gift is made to any Deva, present[4] should be made to the Deva and the merit acquired by such gift and rites[5] should also be given to Him in a spirit of devotion (263).

He should then, with dancing, singing, and music, go round the temple, accompanied by his friends and kinsmen, keeping the temple on his right, and, having bowed to the Deva, feed the twice-born![6] (264).

This is the way in which a temple to a Deva should be dedicated, and the same rule is to be observed in the dedication of a garden, a bridge, a causeway, or a tree (265).

It is imperative that in these rites the ever-existing Vish*n*u should be worshipped; but Pūjā,[7] Homa,[8] and

---

[1] Shrīpati: Vish*n*u.

[2] Vajra-chanchu.

[3] Siddhi.

[4] Daksh*in*ā in addition to the gift.

[5] Karma-phala—the fruit of the work.

[6] Dvija, which, though including the first three castes, probably here refers to the Brāhma*n*as only.

[7] Honour, worship.

[8] Fire sacrifice.

other rites, are the same as in the case of the dedication of a house (266).

No temple or other thing should be dedicated to a Deva whose image has not been consecrated. The rules laid down above are for the worship of and dedication to a Deva who has been consecrated and worshipped (267).

I shall now speak of the manner in which the auspicious Ādyā[1] should be installed, and by which the Devī grants quickly all desires (268).

On the morning of the day (of Prati*shth*ā) the worshipper should, after, bathing and purifying himself, sit facing the North, and, having in manner enjoined made Saṁkalpa,[2] worship the Vāstu-devatā (269).

After performing the worship of the Planets,[3] the Protectors of the Quarters,[4] Ga*n*esha and others, and having performed the Shrāddha of his Pit*ris*,[5] he should approach the image with a number of devout Vipras[6] (270).

The excellent worshipper should then bring the image to the temple which has been dedicated, or to some other place decorated for the reception, and there duly bathe it (271).

It should first be bathed with water, then with mud from an ant-hill, then with mud thrown up by the tusk of a boar and an elephant, then with mud taken from the

---

[1] *i.e.*, Kālī.

[2] See p. 396, n. 10.

[3] Grahas. See *ante*, vv. 82-85.

[4] Dikpālas. See p. 389, n. 5.

[5] Forefathers. This is the Ābhyudayika Shrāddha.

[6] Brāhma*n*as who are Sādhakas of the Devī. The true Vipra is one versed in the Vedas. Every twice born is not entitled to the name of Vipra or Brāhma*n*a.

door of a Veshyā,[1] and then with mud[2] from the lake of Pradyumna[3] (272).

The wise man should then bathe the image with Panchakashāya[4] and Pancha-pushpa,[5] and three leaves,[6] and then with scented oil (273).

The infusion of Vātyāla,[7] Vadarī,[7] Jambu,[7] Vakula,[7] and Shālmalī,[7] are called the five Kashāyas[8] for bathing the Devī (274).

Karavīra, Jātī, Champaka, Lotus, and Pātalī, are the five flowers (275).

By three leaves are meant the leaves of Barvara,[9] Tulasī,[9] and Vilva[9] (276).

With the above-mentioned articles water should be mixed, but no water should be put into scented oil and the five nectars[10] (277).

He should, after repeating the Vyāhriti,[11] the Pranava,[12] the Gāyatrī, and the Mūla Mantra, say, "I bathe Thee with the water of these articles" (278).

---

[1] See p. 405, n. 4, *ante*. Literally means a Kept Woman, or Prostitute. When a man visits the house of a prostitute, it is said that he leaves all the merits of his good acts at the door, with the result that the mud thereat is holy. This is the current explanation of the use of mud in general practice—an explanation which has the air of a modern attempt to explain that, the origin and significance of which has been forgotten. As Tarkālangkāra points out (Bhakta, edn. 676), a Veshyā is a Shakti who is Pūrnābhishiktā, and is Āvarana (attendant) Devī of one or other of the ten Mahāvidyās, and it is such a Veshyā who is here referred to, and not a common prostitute.

[2] Mrit.

[3] Pradyumna-hrada. Pradyumna = God of Desire. The "mud" is the excreta of the Nābhi-mūla.

[4] See Verse 274. [5] See Verse 275. [6] See Verse 276.

[7] These are names of certain trees.

[8] Astringent.

[9] Names of Sacred trees—the leaves of which are used in worship.

[10] Panchāmrita.

[11] Bhūh, Bhuvah, Svah.

[12] Om̐.

The good Sādhaka should then bathe the image with the eight jars filled with milk and other ingredients in manner aforementioned (279).

The image should then be rubbed with powdered white wheat or sesamum cakes,[1] or powdered Shāli rice,[2] and thus cleansed (280).

After bathing the image with eight jars of holy[3] water, and rubbing it with cloth of fine texture, it should be brought to the place of worship (281).

Should one be unable to perform all these rites, then he should in a devout spirit bathe the image with twenty-five jars of pure water (282).

On each occasion that the Great Devī is bathed, She should, to the best of one's ability,[4] be worshipped (283).

Then, placing the Image on a well-cleaned seat,[5] She should be worshipped by offering Pādya,[6] Arghya,[7] and so forth and then with joined palms prayed to (as follows) (284):

MANTRA

O Image! thou that art the handicraft of Vishvakarmā,[8] I bow to thee; thou art the abode of the Devī, I bow to thee; thou fulfillest the desire of the votary, I bow to thee (285).

In thee I worship the most excellent[9] primordial[10] Supreme Lady[11]; if there be any defect in thee by reason

---

[1] Oil-cakes. [2] Rice that ripens in Winter.

[3] Tīrtha.

[4] That is, with such articles as one can afford.

[5] The altar.

[6] Water to wash the feet.

[7] Offerings (see *ante*).

[8] The Architect of the Devas.

[9] Parātparā. [10] Ādyā. [11] Parameshī.

of the want of skill of him who has fashioned thee, do thou make it good; I bow to thee (286).

He should then placing his hand over the head of the Image, inwardly do Japa of the Mūla Mantra[1] one hundred and eight times, and thereafter touch the different parts of the image (287).

He should then perform *Shad*aṁga-nyāsa[2] and Māt*ri*kā-nyāsa[2] on the Image, and, when performing *Shad*aṁga-nyāsa, add one after the other the six long vowels[3] to the Mūla Mantra (288).[4]

The eight groups[5] of the letters of the alphabet preceded by the Tāra,[6] Māyā,[7] and Ramā,[8] with the Bindu,[9] added to them, and followed by Nama*h*, should be placed in different parts of the body of the Deva (289).

The pious worshipper should place the Vowels in the mouth; Kavarga[10] in the throat; Chavarga[11] on the belly; *T*avarga[12] on the right and Tavarga[13] on the left arm;

---

[1] See *ante*.

[2] This is called Sakalīkara*n*a. See *ante* pp. 160-161.

[3] *i.e.*, Ā, Ī, Ū, Ai, Au, A*h*.

[4] The Mūla Mantra is here Hrīm to the base (Hr) of which is added the other vowels. The Mantra of the *Shad*aṁga-nyāsa—Oṁ Hrāng H*ri*dayāya (Heart) Nama*h*; Oṁ Hrīng Shirase (Head) Svāhā; Oṁ Hrūng Shikhāyai (Crown-lock) Va*shat*; Oṁ Hraing Kavachāya (Upper part of the body) Hung; Oṁ Hraung Netratrayāya (three Eyes) Vau*shat* Oṁ Hrnga*h* karatala-p*rishth*ābhyāṁ (the two sides of Palm) Pha*t*.

[5] Varga.

[6] Oṁ.

[7] Hrīm.

[8] Shrīm.

[9] The nasal point.

[10] Ka to Nga.

[11] Cha to Nya.

[12] *T*a to *N*a (the first of the two Ta groups).

[13] Ta to Na (the second Ta group).

Pavarga[1] on the right thigh, and Yavarga[2] on the left thigh, and Shavarga[3] on the head[4] (290-291).

Having placed these groups of the letters of the alphabet on different parts of the Image (the worshipper) should perform Tattva-nyāsa[5] (as follows): (292).

Place on the two feet, Pṛithivī-tattva; on the Liṁga,[6] Toya-tattva; on the region of the navel, Tejas-tattva; on the lotus of the heart, Vāyu-tattva; on the mouth, Gagana-tattva; on the two eyes, Rūpa-tattva; on the two nostrils, Gandha-tattva; on the two ears, Shabda-tattva; on the tongue, Rasa-tattva; on the skin, Sparsha-tattva.[7] The foremost of worshippers should place Manas-tattva[8] between the eyebrows, Shiva-tattva, Jnāna-tattva, and Para-tattva on the Lotus[9] of a thousand petals; on the heart Jīva-tattva and Prakṛiti-tattva. Lastly, he should place Mahat-tattva and Ahaṁkāra-tattva all over the body. The Tattvas should, whilst being placed, be preceded by Tāra, Māyā, and Ramā, and should be uttered in the dative singular, followed by Namaḥ (293-297).

---

[1] Pa to Ma.

[2] Ya to Va.

[3] Sha to Ha.

[4] In some of the Tantras in worship of the Devas, particularly in worship of Ādyā Kālikā, Panchāṁga-nyāsa is performed—*i.e.*, on heart, two hands, and two feet.

[5] Described in the following verses (293-297).

[6] Here meaning Yoni.

[7] The Tattvas are constituent principles of the universe Pṛithivī (Earth), Toya (Water), Tejas (Fire), Vāyu (Air), Ākāsha or Gagana (the void or Ether), Rūpa (Form, visibility), Gandha (Smell), Shabda (Sound), Rasa (Taste), Sparsha (Touch). The "Serpent Power" by A. Avalon particularly v. 40 and notes thereunder.

[8] The names of these Tattvas, or principles mean Mind, Shiva, Knowledge, the Supreme, Embodied Spirit, Prakṛiti, and Principle of Intelligence and Egoism. See Ch. V, verse, 89.

[9] Sahasrāra-padma (see "Serpent Power" and "Shakti and Shākta").

Repeating the Mūla Mantra, preceded and followed by each of the Mātrikā-varnas,[1] with Bindu[2] added to them, and followed by the word Namah, Mantra-nyāsa should be performed at the Mātrikā-sthānas[3] (298).

(The worshipper should then say):

MANTRA

The Body is the glory which is all sacrifices and all beings.[4] In this Image here which has been made of Thee, I place Thee (299).

Thereafter the Devī should be meditated upon and invoked, according to the rules of worship,[5] and after Prāna-pratishthā[6] the Supreme Devatā (Devī) should be worshipped (300).

The Mantras which are ordained for the dedication of a temple to a Deva should be used in this ceremony,[7] the necessary changes in Mantra and gender being made (301).

The Devī should then be invoked into the fire, which has in due form been consecrated by the offer of oblations to the Devatās who are to be worshipped; and thereafter the Devī should be worshipped, and Jāta-karma,[8] and so forth should be performed (302).

---

[1] Letters of the alphabet.

[2] Nāda-bindu.

[3] The places where the letters of the alphabet should, in doing Mātrikā-nyāsa, be placed (see Chapter V, verse 118 *ff.*).

[4] Tejas which is Sarvayajnamayam Sarvabhūtamayam.

[5] Pūjā-vidhāna.

[6] "Life-giving" ceremony (see "Shakti and Shākta").

[7] *i.e.*, the Pratishthā of the image.

[8] Birth-rite.

The Saṁskāras[1] are six in number—*viz.*, Jātakarma. Nāmakaraṇa, Nishkramaṇa, Annaprāshana, Chūḍākaraṇa, and Upanayana—this has been said by Shiva[2] (303).

Repeating the Praṇava,[3] the Vyāhṛitis[3] the Gāyatrī,[3] the Mūla Mantra,[3] the worshipper versed in the injunctions should addressing the Devatā say, "Thine," and then the name of (the Saṁskāra) Jātakarma, and others, and uttering, "I perform, Svāhā," offer five oblations at the end of each Saṁskāra[4] (304-305).

Thereafter repeating the Mūla Mantra and the name given (to the Devī), one hundred oblations should be offered to Her, and the remnants of each oblation should be thrown over the head of the image (306).

The wise man, after having brought the ceremony to a close by Prāyaschitta[5] and other rites, should feed and thus please Sādhakas[6] and Vipras[7] and the poor and the helpless (307).

Should anyone be unable to perform all these rites, he should bathe (the image) with seven jars of water, and, having worshipped to the best of his ability, repeat the name of the Devatā (308).

Beloved! I have now spoken to Thee of the Pratishṭhā[8] of the adorable Ādyā.[9] In a similar way should men versed in the ritual carefully perform the Pratishṭhā[8] of

---

[1] Purificatory or Sacramental rites (alluded to in the previous Shloka).

[2] See Chapter III, 109, 110; V, 68; and IX, 214, 225.

[3] The Beneficent source of all good.

[4] "I perform Thy (addressing the image) Jāta-karma" and so on in other Saṁskāras (sacramental rites).

[5] Expiatory rite.

[6] Worshippers who are on the path of Spiritual advancement.

[7] Brāhmaṇas.

[8] Installation.

[9] Kālī.

Durgā[1] and other Vidyās,[2] Mahesha,[3] and other Devas, and of the Shiva-limgas that may be moved[4] (309-310).

End of the Thirteenth Chapter entitled "Installation of Devatās".

---

[1] A form of the Supreme Shakti usually worshipped in autumn.

[2] Different manifestations of the Supreme Shakti.

[3] Shiva.

[4] Shiva-limgas, or phallic emblems of Shiva, ordinarily should not be moved from where they are fixed (*cf.* Chālayet sarva-limgāni Shiva-limgam na chālayet). The Bāna-limgas, however, are never fixed. Those which are fixed should not be moved.

CHAPTER XIV

CONSECRATION AND AVADHUTAS

SHRĪ DEVĪ said:

I am grateful to Thee, O Lord of Mercy! in that Thou hast in Thy discourse upon the Worship of the Ādyā Shakti, spoken, in Thy mercy, of various modes of Worship (1).

Thou hast spoken of the Installation of a Movable Shiva-liṁga, but what is the object of installing an immovable Shiva-liṁga, and what are the rites relating to the installation of such a Liṁga? (2).

Do Thou, O Lord of the Worlds! now tell Me all the particulars thereof; for say, who is there but Thee that I can honour by My questions anent this excellent subject? (3).

Who is there that is Omniscient, Merciful, All-knowing, Omnipresent, easily satisfied, Protector of the humble, like Thee? Who makes My joys increase like Thee? (4).

Shrī Sadāshiva said:

What shall I tell Thee of the merit[1] acquired by the installation[2] of a Shiva-liṁga? By it a man is purified of all great sins, and goes to the Supreme Abode (5).

There is no doubt that by the installation of a Shiva-liṁga a man acquires ten million times the merit which is acquired by giving the world and all its gold, by the performance of ten thousand horse-secrifices,[3] by the

---

[1] Māhātmya, *lit.* = greatness, here, great merit.

[2] Sthāpana.

[3] Ashva-medha.

digging of a tank[1] in a waterless country, or by making happy the poor and such as are enfeebled by disease (6-7).

O Kālikā! Brahmā, Vi*sh*nu, Indra, and the other Devas reside where Mahādeva is in His Liṁga form (8).

Thirty-five million known and unknown places of pilgrimage and all the holy places abide near Shiva. The land within a radius of a hundred cubits of the Liṁga is declared to be Shiva-k*sh*etra[2] (9-10).

This land of Īsha[3] is very sacred. It is more excellent than the most excellent of holy places,[4] because there always abide all the Immortals and there are all the holy places (11).

He who in a devout spirit lives there, be it even for but a little while, becomes purged of all sins, and goes to the heaven of Shaṁkara[5] after death (12).

Anything great or small (meritorious or otherwise) which is done in this holy land of Shiva becomes multiplied (in its effect) by the majesty of Shiva (13).

All sins committed elsewhere are removed (by going) near Shiva, but sins committed in Shiva-k*sh*etra[2] adhere to a man with the strength of thunderbolt (14).

The merit acquired by the performance, there, of Purashchara*n*a,[6] Japa,[6] acts of charity, Shrāddha,[7] Tarpa*n*a,[6] or any other pious acts is endless (15).

---

[1] Nistoye toyakara*n*am: *i.e.*, making it easy to get water in a waterless desert.

[2] The holy land of Shiva.

[3] The Beneficent one, an epithet of Shiva.

[4] Tīrthas.

[5] Shiva.

[6] See "Shakti and Shākta".

[7] Funeral rites.

The merit acquired by the performance of a hundred Purashcharana at times of lunar or solar eclipse is acquired by merely performing one Japa[1] near Shiva (16).

By the offering of Pinda[2] once only in the land of Shiva, a man obtains the same fruit as he who offers ten million Pindas at Gayā, the Gaṁgā, and Prayāga (17).

Even in the case of those who are Atipātakīs[3] and Mahāpātakīs attain the supreme abode if Shrāddha be performed in their names in the land of Shiva (18).

The fourteen worlds[4] abide there where abides the Lord of the Universe in His Liṁga form with the auspicious Devī Durgā (19).

I have spoken a little about the majesty[5] of the immovable Mahādeva[6] in His Liṁga form. The Sanctity and Majesty[7] of the Anādi[8]-liṁga is beyond the power of words to express (20).

O Suvratā[9]! even in Thy worship at the Mahāpīthas[10] the touch of an untouchable is unclean, but this is not so in the worship of Hara[11] in His Liṁga image (21).

---

[1] Recitation of Mantras. See *ante* Ch. III, 114; Ch. VI, 166, 167; Ch. VII, 80, 81.

[2] Funeral cakes.

[3] For Atipātakīs see Ch. XI, 29, 30, and Mahāpātakīs, Ch. X—205.

[4] The seven lower Atala and so on and the seven higher Bhūh and the rest.

[5] Māhātmya.

[6] Shiva.

[7] Mahimā.

[8] An-ādi—literally, without beginning—*i.e.*, those Liṁgas which spring from the ground, otherwise called Svayambhu, or self-generated, as distinguished from those which are fashioned and installed by men, such as the Liṁgas of Vaidyanātha, Tārakeshvara, the Chandrashekhara at Chittagong, and other places.

[9] Of good resolve, or Virtuous One.

[10] Holy places, where different parts of the body of Devī as Satī fell to earth.

[11] Shiva.

O Devī! as there are no prohibitions at the time of Chakra[1] worship, so know this, O Kālikā! that there are none in the holy shrine in Shiva's land (22).

What is the use of saying more? I am but telling Thee the very truth when I say that I am unable to describe the glory, majesty, and sanctity[2] of the Liṁga image of Shiva (23).

Whether the Liṁga is placed on a Gaurī-paṭṭa[3] or not, the worshipper should, for the successful attainment of his desires, worship it devoutly (24).

The excellent worshipper earns the merit of (performing) ten thosuand horse-sacrifices[4] if he performs the Adhivâsa[5] of the Deva in the evening previous to the day of installation (25).

The twenty articles to be used in the rite of Adhivāsa are: Earth, Scent, a Pebble,[6] Paddy, Dūrvā grass, Flower, Fruit, Curds, Ghee, Svastika,[7] Vermillion, Conchshell, Kajjala,[8] Rochanā,[9] White Mustard Seed, Gold, Silver, Copper, Lights, and a Mirror (26-27).

---

[1] The Tāntrika Circle. See *ante*, Chs. V, VI and VII.

[2] Prabhāva.

[3] Gaurī is a name of the Devī, and the Gaurī-paṭṭa is the emblem of the Yoni, or female organ, in which the male Liṁga is generally set. The latter is symbolical of static Feeling-Consciousness and the former of its active Power which in the form of its creations surround the Bindu or Point.

[4] Ashva-medha.

[5] Adhivāsa is the rite below described preliminary to all auspicious ceremonies.

[6] Shilā the pebble is warmed and applied to the face.

[7] Here a figure made of pounded rice.

[8] Lamp-black collyrium, applied to the eyelashes medicinally, or for beautifying the eyes.

[9] A yellow pigment obtained from the inside of the head of a cow, also called Go-rochanā. Tilaka is made with it by some sects.

Taking each of these articles, the Māyā Bīja [1] and the Brahma-Gáyatrī [2] should be repeated, and then should be said "Anena" (with this) and "Amushya" (of this one's or his)—"may the auspicious Adhivāsa be" [3] (28).

And then the forehead of the divinity to be installed should be touched with the earth and all other articles aforesaid. Then Adhivāsa should be performed with the Prashastipātra [4]—that is, the receptacle should be lifted up, and with it the forehead of the image should be touched three times (29).

The worshipper conversant with the ordinances, having thus performed the Adhivāsa of the Deva, should bathe the Devatā with milk and other liquids, as directed in the ceremony relating to the dedication of a temple (30).

Rubbing the Liṁga with a piece of cloth and placing it on its seat, Ganesha and other Deities should be worshipped according to the rules prescribed for their worship (31).

Having performed Kara-nyāsa [5] and Aṁga-nyāsa [5] and Prāṇāyāma [5] with the Praṇava,[6] the Sadāshiva should be meditated upon [7].

---

[1] Hrīng.

[2] See *ante*, p. 55, vv. 109-111.

[3] Adhivāsa is a preliminary rite in all auspicious ceremonies. Bṛiddhi-shrāddha is a part of it, *e.g.*, taking earth, say: "Hrīng! with this earth may the auspicious Adhivāsa of this Deva be made." Then the image is touched with the earth.

[4] *i.e.*, receptacle—usually a flat bamboo basket—in which all the above-mentioned articles are placed. The image is first touched with each of the articles mentioned singly, and then the Pātra in which the articles were brought and put back is lifted up and the forehead of the image touched as above.

[5] See Ch. III, 41-43; V, 125-127, *ante*.

[6] Oṁ.

[7] The Dhyāna given here is of the Sthūla aspect. The other aspects are Sūkshma or subtle and Para or Transcendent. The Sadhaka advances in the path of spirituality his Dhyāna changes till he realises his oneness with the Supreme.

DHYĀNA

Tranquil, possessed of the effulgence of ten million Moons; clothed in garment of tiger-skins; wearing a serpent as His sacred thread[1]; His whole body covered with ashes; wearing ornaments of serpents[1]; His five faces are of reddish-black,[2] yellow, Morning Sun red,[3] white, and red colours, with three eyes each; His head is covered with matted hair; He is Omnipresent; He holds Gaṁgā[4] on His head, and has ten arms, and in His forehead shines the (crescent) Moon; He holds in His left hand the skull, fire, the noose,[5] the Pināka,[6] and the axe,[7] and in His right the trident,[8] the thunderbolt,[9] the arrow,[10] and blessings[11]; He is being praised by all the Devas and great Sages; His eyes half-closed[12] in the excess of bliss; His body is white as the snow and the Kunda flower and the Moon; He is seated on the Bull; He is by day and night surrounded on every side by Siddhas, Gandharvas, and Apsarās[13] who are chanting hymns in His praise; He is the husband of Umā; the devoted Protector of His worshippers (32-38).

---

[1] Nāga.

[2] Dhūmra, or the colour of fire seen through smoke.

[3] Aru*n*a—the red colour of the rising Sun. The last red is Rakta.

[4] The River Ganges, which fell upon His matted hair on its descent from Heaven at the prayer of Bhagīratha. "Shaṁkara-mauli-vihāri*n*ī vimale!" as the Gaṁgā-stotrā of Shaṁkarāchārya says.

[5] Pāsha.

[6] Shiva's weapon in shape like a snake with seven heads.

[7] Parashu.

[8] Shūla.

[9] Vajra.

[10] Shara.

[11] Vara—*i.e.*, the hands make the Vara-Mudrā.

[12] The eyes are half-seen being turned upwards in a state of, or, leading to Samādhi.

[13] Beautiful and voluptuous Deva Yoni of Indra's Heaven.

Having thus meditated upon Mahādeva and worshipped Him with articles of mental worship, He should be invoked into the Liṁga, and worshipped to the best of one's powers, and as laid down in the ordinances relating to such worship (39).

I have already spoken of the Mantras for the giving of Āsana and other articles of worship.[1] I shall now speak of the Mūla Mantra[2] of the Great Mahesha (40).

Māyā,[3] Tāra,[4] and the Shabda Bīja,[5] with the vowel Au[6] and Ardhendu-Vindu[7] added to it, is the Shiva Bīja —that is, "Hrīng Ong Haung" (41).

Covering Shamkara[8] with clothes and garland of sweet-smelling flowers, and placing Him on a beautiful conch, the Vedī[9] should be consecrated in manner above-mentioned (42).

The Devī should be worshipped in the Vedī according to the following rites: with the Māyā Bīja,[10] Aṁga-nyāsa, Kara-nyāsa, and Prāṇāyāma should be performed (43);

The Great Devī should, to the best of the worshipper's ability, be worshipped after meditation upon Her as follows:

DHYĀNA

I meditate upon the stainless One, Whose splendour is that of a thousand rising Suns, Whose eyes are Fire,

---

[1] See p. 410, n. 2.

[2] Primary Mantra.

[3] Hrīng.

[4] Ong.

[5] Hauṁ.

[6] Sandhyarṇāntākshara: the last vowel letter formed by Sandhi which Au is.

[7] The half Moon and the Bindu, *i.e.*, Chandra-Bindu.

[8] Shiva—*i.e.*, the Liṁga as His emblem.

[9] That is, the Gaurīpaṭṭa personates Devī. See *ante*, p. 431, n. 8.

[10] Hrīng. In the case of Shiva the Praṇava is used. See *ante*, v. 32.

Moon and Sun,[1] and Whose lotus face in smiles is adorned with golden earrings[2] set with lines of pearls. With Her lotus hands She makes the gestures which grant blessings and dispel fear,[3] and holds the discus and lotus; Her breasts are large and rounded; She is the Dispeller of all fear, and She is clothed in saffron-coloured raiment.

Having thus meditated upon Her, the ten Dikpālas[4] and the Bull[5] should be worshipped to the best of one's powers (44-45).

I will now speak of the Mantra of the Bhagavatī,[6] by which the World-pervading One should be worshipped (46).

Repeating the Māyā,[7] and Lak*sh*mī[8] Bijas, and the letter which follows Sa[9] with the sixth vowel,[10] with the Bindu[11] added to it, and thereafter uttering the name of the Shakti of Fire,[12] the Mantra is formed (which is as follows):

MANTRA

Hrīng Shrīng Hūng Svāha (47).

Placing the Devī as aforementioned,[13] offerings[14] should be made to all the Devas with a mixture of boiled Mā*sh*a

---

[1] The white, red, and mixed Bindus of the Kāmakalā. See "Kāmakalāvilāsa" and "Garland of Letters".

[2] Ku*nd*ala.

[3] *i.e.*, She holds in her hands Vara and Abhaya Mudrās.

[4] See *ante*.

[5] Shiva's vāhana. To the ordinary man V*ri*s*h*abha is a Bull, but the higher Sādhaka sees the embodiment of Dharma in the white Bull.

[6] The Devī.

[7] Hrīng.

[8] Shrīng.

[9] *i.e.*, Ha.

[10] *i.e.*, Ū.

[11] Chandra-bindu—the nasal point, see *ante*.

[12] Svāhā.

[13] Clothed and garlanded like Shiva.

[14] Vali.

beans[1], and curd, with sugar, and so forth added to it (48).

These articles of worship should be placed in the Īshāna[2] corner, and purified with the Varuna Bīja,[3] and should be offered after purification with scents and flowers and the following (49):

MANTRA

O Devas, Siddhas,[4] Gandharvas,[6] Uragas,[5] Rākshasas, Pishāchas,[6] Mothers,[7] Yakshas, Bhūtas,[8] Pitris,[9] *Rishis*,[10] and other Devas! do you quietly take this offering, and do you stay surrounding Mahādeva and Girijā[11] (50-51).

Then Japa should be made of the Mantra of the Great Devī as often as one may, and then with excellent songs and instrumental music let the festival be celebrated (52).

Having completed the Adhivāsa[12] in manner above, the following day, after performance of the compulsory daily duties, and having taken the vow, the Five Devas[13] should be worshipped (53).

---

[1] A kind of kidney beans.

[2] North-East.

[3] Vang.

[4] See p. 2, notes 5 and 7.

[5] *i.e.*, one that goes on its breast—*i.e.*, Nāga, or Snake.

[6] See p. 37, note 2.

[7] See p. 37, note 3.

[8] Ghosts.

[9] See *ibid.*

[10] See *ibid.*

[11] A title of the Devī as Pārvatī (see p. 2, note 9).

[12] Preliminary rite.

[13] Brahmā and others.

After worshipping the Mātris[1] and making the Vasudhārā,[2] and performing Briddhi-Shrāddha,[3] the Door-keepers of Mahesha[4] should, in a calm and devout frame of mind, be worshipped (54).

The Door-keepers of Shiva are—Nandī, Mahābala, Kīshavadana, and Gana-nāyaka; they are all armed with missiles and other weapons (55).

Bringing the Limga[5] and Tārinī,[6] as represented by the Gaurī-patta,[7] they should be placed on a Sarvato-bhadra Mandala,[8] or on an auspicious seat (56).

Shambhu should then be bathed with eight jars of water with the Mantra[9] "Tryambaka," etc., and worshipped with the sixteen articles of worship[10] (57).

After bathing the Devī in a similar way with the Mūla Mantra, and worshipping Her, the good worshipper should pray to Shamkara with joined palms (58).

Mantra

Come, O Bhagavān! O Shambhu! O Thou before Whom all Devas bow! I bow to Thee, Who art armed with the Pināka,[11] Thee the Lord of all, O Great Deva (59).

---

[1] The sixteen Mātrikās, beginning with Gaurī, etc.

[2] See p. 272, note 9.

[3] See p. 305.

[4] Shiva.

[5] *i.e.*, Shiva-linga.

[6] A title of Devī—"She Who saves."

[7] Vedīrūpām tārinīm, *i.e.*, Tārinī in the form of a Vedī or Altar. The Gaurī-patta which symbolises the cosmic yoni and into which the Limga is fixed is like a Vedī to it. See p. 431, note 3.

[8] A form of Yantra.

[9] See ch. v, verse 210.

[10] See p. 410, n. 2.

[11] Shiva's weapon, see *ante*.

O Deva! Thou Who conferrest benefits on Thy votaries! do Thou in Thy mercy come to this temple with Bhagavatī:[1] I bow to Thee again and again (60).

O Mother! O Devī! O Mahāmāyā![2] O All-beneficent One! be Thou, along with Shambhu, pleased: I bow to Thee, O Beloved of Hara[3] (61).

Come to this house, O Devī! Thou Who grantest all boons, be Thou pleased, and do Thou grant me all prosperity (62).

Rise O Deva! Rise, O Queen of Devas! and Each with Thy followers abide happy in this place; may Both of You be pleased, You Who are kind to Your devotees (63).

Having thus prayed to Shiva and the Devī, They should first be carried three times round the Temple, keeping the latter on the right[4] to the accompaniment of joyful sounds,[5] and then taken inside (64).

Repeating the Mūla Mantra, one-third of the Limga should be set in a hollow made in a piece of stone or in a masonry hole (65), (with the following Mantra):

MANTRA

O Mahādeva! do Thou remain here so long as the Moon and the Sun endure, so long as the Earth and the Oceans endure: I bow to Thee (66).

Having firmly fixed Sadāshiva with this Mantra, the Gaurī-paṭṭa, with its tapering end to the North, should be

---

[1] The Devī.

[2] The Devī as the wielder of, and liberator from, Māyā.

[3] Shiva.

[4] Pradakshina.

[5] Such as Uludhvani.

placed over the Liṁga, that it may be pierced by the latter[1] (67).

MANTRA

Be Thou here, O Jagad-dhātrī[2]! Thou That art the Cause of creation, existence, and destruction of things; abide Thou here so long as the Sun and the Moon endure (68).

Having firmly fixed it, the Liṁga should be touched and the following (Mantra) should be repeated (69):

MANTRA

I invoke that Deva Who has three eyes, the imperishable Īshāna,[3] around whose lion-seat[4] are tigers, Bhūtas, Pishāchas,[5] Gandharvas,[6] Siddhas,[7] Chāraṇas,[8] Yakshas,[9] Nāgas,[10] Vetālas,[11] Loka-pālas,[12] Maharshis,[13] Mātṛis,[14] Gaṇa-nāthas,[15] Vishṇu, Brahmā, and Bṛihaspati,[16] and all beings

---

[1] The Liṁga is already fixed and erect, the head enters the aperture of the Gaurī-paṭṭa, which is then slipped over the Liṁga until it reaches its resting-place.

[2] The Devī as World-Creatrix.

[3] Lord, Ruler.

[4] Siṁhāsana, *i.e.*, throne.

[5] Ghosts, Ghouls and filthy spirits.

[6] See p. 2, note 7.

[7] See p. 2, note 5.

[8] See p. 2, note 6.

[9] Attendants of Kuvera the Deva of Wealth.

[10] Serpent divinities.

[11] See p. 24, note 1; 87, note 2.

[12] Guardians of the Quarters, p. 178, note 2.

[13] Great *Rishi*s, or Sages.

[14] Divine Mothers, Gaurī, etc.

[15] See p. 2, note 8.

[16] Guru of the Celestials.

which live on earth or in the air; come, O Bhagavān! to this Yantra, which is the handiwork of Brahmā, for the prosperity and happiness of all (70-72).

Beloved! Shiva should then be bathed according to the injunctions relating to the consecration of a Deva, and, having been meditated upon as before-mentioned, should be worshipped with mental offerings[1] (73).

After placing a special Arghya,[2] and having worshipped the Gaṇa-devatās,[3] and meditated upon Mahesha[4] again, flowers should be placed on the Liṁga (74).

Repeating the Shakti Bīja[5] between Pāsha[6] and Aṁkusha,[7] and the letters from Ya to Sa[8] with Nāda-bindu, and then "Haung Haṁsaḥ,"[9] the Prāṇas of Sadāshiva should be placed into the Liṁga[10] (75).

Then, smearing the Husband of the Daughter of the Mountain[11] with sandal, aguru, and saffron, He should be worshipped with the sixteen articles of worship according to the injunctions laid down after performing the Jāta, the Nāma,[12] and other rites (76).

After concluding everything according to the injunctions, and after worshipping the Devī in the Gaurī-paṭṭa,

---

[1] Articles of worship. See Ch. III, 52, *ante*.

[2] Offering. See Ch. V, 158.

[3] The surrounding Devas.

[4] Shiva.

[5] *i.e.*, Hrīng.

[6] Āng.

[7] Krong.

[8] Ya, Ra, La, Va, Sha, *Sha*, Sa.

[9] The Mantra so formed is—Āng Hrīng Krong Yang Rang Lang Vang Shang *Sh*ang Sang Haung Hangsa*h*.

[10] The Liṁga is vitalised by the Prā*n*a-prati*shth*ā or life-giving ceremony. As to Prā*n*a, see author's "World as Power: Life".

[11] Girijā-pati—the Husband (Lord=Pati) of the Daughter (-Jā) of the (Himālaya) Mountain (Giri), whose emblem the Liṁga is.

[12] See Ch. ix, 131-143, for Jāta (Birth), and Nāma (Naming) rites of children.

the eight images of the Deva should be carefully worshipped (77).

By the name Sharva[1] his relation to the Earth is shown; by Bhava, Water; by Rudra, Fire; by Ugra, Wind; by Bhīma, Ether;[2] by Pashu-pati the Employer of a priest for sacrifice,[3] by Mahādeva the Source of Nectar,[4] and by Īshāna, the Sun; these are declared to be the Eight forms (78-79).

Each of these should be invoked and worshipped in their order (in the corners), beginning with the East and ending with the North-East, uttering the Pra*n*ava[5] first and Nama*h* last[6] (80).

After having worshipped Indra and the other Dikpālas,[7] the eight Māt*r*is, Brāhmī, and others, the worshipper should give to Īsha the Bull, awning,[8] house, and the like (81).

---

[1] This and the following are the names of the eight forms of Shiva. As Sharva he is the presiding Deva of Earth, as Bhava of water and so on.

[2] Ākāsha.

[3] Yajamāna. By this name (Pashupati) Shiva is denoted as Lord of Men (see note 6 below).

[4] Sudhā-kara—*i.e.*, the Moon.

[5] Ong.

[6] The Mantras which are said are—Oṁ Sharvāya ksh*i*ti-mūrtaye Nama*h*; Oṁ Bhavāya jalamūrtaye Nama*h*; Oṁ Rudrāya agni-mūrtaye Nama*h*; Oṁ Ugrāya vāyumūrtaye Nama*h*; Oṁ Bhīmāya ākāsha-mūrtaye Nama*h*; Oṁ Pashu-pataye yajamāna-mūrtaye Nama*h*; Oṁ Mahādevāya somamūrtaye Nama*h*; Oṁ Īshānāya sūryamūrtaye Nama*h*. Bhava means existence—and water—the first of things. Rudra means fierce, and so is Agni (Fire). Ugra means strong beyond measure, and Pavana or Vāyu is that. Bhīma means terrific, and the great Void is terrific. The Yajamāna is like an animal (Pashu), which requires to be guided, and the Lord of Pashus (Pashu-pati) does that. Mahādeva is the great benignant Deva—the abode of all which is sweet and life-giving. Īshāna is the Lord of all.

[7] The Protectors of the Quarters Indra and others. See *ante*, under vv. 70-72.

[8] Placed on temple at time of consecration.

Then, with joined palms, he should with fervour pray to the Husband of Pārvatī (as follows) (82).

MANTRA

O Ocean of Mercy! O Lord! Thou hast been placed in this place by me; be Thou pleased (with me). O Shambhu! Thou Who art the Cause of all causes, do Thou abide in this room, O Supreme Deva! so long as the Earth with all its Oceans exist, so long as the Moon and the Sun endure. I bow to Thee. Should there occur in this temple, the death of any living being,[1] may I, O Dhūrjjati![2] by Thy grace, be kept from that sin (83-85).

The dedicator should go round the image, keeping it on his right, and, having bowed before the Deva, go home. Returning again in the morning, he should bathe Chandrashekhara[3] (86).

He should first be bathed with consecrated Panchāmrita and then with a hundred jars of scented water; and the worshipper, having worshipped Him to the best of his powers, should pray to Him (as follows) (87-88):

MANTRA

O Husband of Umā![4] if there has been any irregularity, omission, want of devotion in this worship, may they

---

[1] *i.e.*, in the Temple or its precincts.

[2] Dhūrjjatī—Shiva having the burden—dhūr—of the three worlds.

[3] Shiva, so called on account of the crescent Moon which He has on His forehead.

[4] Umā is a name of Devī. See Canto I of Kālidāsa's Kumārasambhava;

Umeti mātrā tapaso nis*h*iddhā,
Pashchād umākhyeyāng sumukhī jagāma.

("'Oh (u) do not (mā).' Thus was She restrained from Tapas by (Her) mother: thereafter She of beautiful face went by the name of Umā.")

all by Thy grace, be rectified, and may my fame remain incomparable in this world so long as the Moon, the Sun, the Earth, and its Oceans endure (89-90).

I bow to the three-eyed Rudra, Who wields the excellent Pināka, to Him Who is worshipped by Vishnu, Brahmā, Indra, Sūrya, and other Devas, I bow again and again (91).

The worshipper should then make presents,[1] and feast the Kaulika-dvijas,[2] and give pleasure to the poor by gifts of food, drink, and clothes (92).

The Deva should be worshipped every day according to one's means. The fixed[3] Shiva-limga should on no account be removed (93).

Parameshvarī! I have in brief spoken to Thee of the rites relating to the consecration of the immovable[4] Shiva-limga, gathering the same from all the Āgamas (94).

Shrī Devī said:

If, O Lord! there be an accidental omission in the worship of the Devas, then what should be done by their votaries—do Thou speak in detail about this (95).

Say, on account of what faults are images of Devas unfit for worship, and should thus be rejected,[5] and what should be done? (96).

Shrī Sadāshiva said:

If there be an omission to worship an image for a day, then (the next day) the worship should be twice performed; if for two days, then the worship should be four times

[1] Dakshinā.

[2] *i.e.*, a Kaula who has received his Pūrnābhisheka initiation, upon which he is born again. The passage may also be interpreted to mean Kaulikas and Dvijas (twice-born classes).

[3] Sthāvara. The image of any other Deva may be moved, but not a Shiva-limga. Where it has been fixed it must remain.

[4] Achala.

[5] *e.g.*, where the image is polluted or injured, and the like (*vide post*, verse 100).

performed; if for three days, then it should be celebrated eight times (97).

If the omission extends three days, but does not exceed six months, then the wise man should worship after bathing the Deva with eight jars of water (98).

If the period of omission exceeds six months, then the excellent worshipper should carefully consecrate the Deva according to the rules already laid down, and then worship Him (99).

The wise man should not worship the image of a Deva which is broken or is holed, or which has lost a limb, or has been touched by a leper, or has fallen on unholy ground (100).

The image of a Deva with missing limbs, or which is broken or has holes in it, should be consigned to water. If the image has been made impure by touch, it should be consecrated, and then worshipped (101).

The Mahāpīṭhas and Anādi-liṅgas[1] are free from all deficiencies, and these should always be worshipped for the attainment of happiness by each worshipper as he pleases (102).

Mahāmāyā! whatever Thou hast asked for the good of men who act with a view to the fruits of action, I have answered all this in detail (103).

Men cannot live without some actions even for half a moment. Even when men are unwilling, they are, in spite of themselves, drawn by the force of Action[2] (104).

By Action men enjoy happiness, and by Action again they suffer pain. They are born, they live, and they die the slaves of Action[3] (105).

[1] See *ante*, p. 430, note 8.

[2] Karmavāyu. Human activity is compared to Air (Vāyu) as its characteristic is Motion (Chalanapara).

[3] That is, Karma prompted by worldly motives (see verse 112, *post*).

It is for this that I have spoken of various kinds of action, such as Sādhana and the like, for the guidance of the intellectually weak in the paths of righteousness, and that they may be restrained from wicked acts (106).

There are two kinds of action—good and evil; the effect of evil action is that men suffer acute pain (107).

And, O Devī! those who do good acts with minds intent on the fruits thereof go to the next world, and come back again to this, chained by their action[1] (108).

Therefore men will not attain final Liberation even at the end of a hundred Kalpas[2] so long as action, whether good or evil, is not destroyed (109).

As a man is bound, be it by a gold or iron chain, so he is bound by his action, be it good or evil (110).

So long as a man has not Knowledge,[3] he does not attain final Liberation, even though he be in the constant practice of religious acts and a hundred austerities (111).

The Knowledge of the wise from whom the darkness of ignorance[4] is removed, and whose souls are pure,[5] arises from the performance of duty without expectation of fruit or reward,[6] and by constant meditation on the Brahman[7] (112).

He who knows that all which is in this universe from Brahmā to a blade of grass is but the creation of Māyā,[8]

---

[1] For action which involves the thirst for life leads to life in birth and rebirth.

[2] A Kalpa is 4,320,000,000 years.

[3] Jnāna: that is, Brahma-jnāna. A distinction is made between Jnāna, which leads to Liberation and Vijnāna which is proficiency in the Arts and Sciences.

[4] *Kshīnatamah*—from whose mind the Tamo-*guna* has disappeared.

[5] Nirmalātmā.

[6] Nis*h*kāma-karma.

[7] Tattva-vichāra—that is, meditation on the Tattvas and the Supreme Tattva, the Brahman.

[8] The Power of Shiva, whereby the worlds appear. See "Shakti and Shākta". *Cf.* Ch. ii, verses 34, 46.

and that the Brahman is the one and supreme Reality is happy (113).

That man is released from the bonds of action who, renouncing Name and Form, has attained to complete knowledge of the Reality[1] of the eternal and immutable Brahman (114).

Liberation[2] does not come from Japa,[3] Homa,[4] or a hundred fasts; man becomes liberated by the knowledge that he himself is Brahman[5] (115).

Final Liberation is attained by the knowledge that the Ātmā (Spirit) is the Witness,[6] is the Truth,[7] is omnipresent, is one,[8] free from all illuding distractions of self and not-self,[9] the supreme, and, though abiding in the body, is not in the body[10] (116).

All imagination of Name, Form and the like are but the play of a child. He who put away all this and is firmly attached to the Brahman, is, without doubt, liberated (117).

If the form imagined by the (human) mind were to lead to Liberation, then undoubtedly men would be Kings by virtue of such kingdoms as they gain in their dreams (118).

---

[1] Tattva. "Being, Manifestation and Bliss belong to the Brahman. Name and Form to the manifested world."

[2] Mukti.

[3] Recitation of Mantras.

[4] Sacrifice (see *ante*, Ch. VI, 119-164).

[5] Brahmaivāham—*i.e.*, Brahma eva aham="I verily am the Brahman"; or So'ham—*i.e.*, Sa*h* Aham="I am He."

[6] *i.e.*, independent witness of a man's actions—as it is said, Ātmā sāk*sh*ī cheta*h* kevalo nirgu*n*ashcha. (Svetāshvatara, 6, 11.)

[7] Satyam, that is the Real, that is the True.

[8] Pūr*n*a=Impartite, which Bhāratī renders by Akha*n*da.

[9] Advaita.

[10] The Spirit, being One, is not confined to the body. There is but one Spirit, in which all bodies inhere.

Those who (in their ignorance) believe that Īshvara is (only) in images made of clay, or stone, or metal, or wood, merely trouble themselves by their devotion.[1] They can never attain Liberation without Knowledge[2] (119).

Can men attain final Liberation[3] by restriction in food, be they ever so emaciated thereby, or by uncontrolled indulgence, be they ever so gross therefrom, unless they possess the knowledge of Brahman? (120).

If by observance of a vow[4] to live on air, leaves of trees, bits of grain, or water, final Liberation may be attained, then snakes, cattle, birds, and aquatic animals should all be able to attain final Liberation (121).

Brahma-sad-bhāva[5] is the highest; Dhyāna-bhāva[6] is middling; Stuti[7] and Japa[8] is the last; and external worship is the lowest of all (122).

---

[1] Tapas.

[2] For the explanation of these three verses see the "Tantra Tattva" edited by the Author.

> M*ri*chchhilā-dhātu-dārvādi-mūrtāvīshvara-buddhaya*h*
> Klishyantastapasā jnānang vinā moksha*ng* na yānti te.

They are not authority against the worship of images. This Tantra throughout deals with images, and image worship which it would not do if image worship was considered by its author to be wrong. But whilst image worship of the kind mentioned in v. 119 is legitimate and the only possible at that stage of development man must pass on much higher before he can attain Liberation.

[3] Nis*h*k*ri*ti.

[4] Vrata. *Cf.* Kulār*n*ava (Author's Tantrik Texts, Vol. V), Ch. I, 76 *et seq.*

[5] The state of mind in which it is realised that all is Brahman, and in which the identity of Self with Brahman is realized. Bhāratī says that it is the state in which Brahman alone is Sat and all else is Asat.

[6] The meditative state of mind in which there is constant meditation on the Brahman.

[7] Praise.

[8] Recitation of Mantra.

Yoga is the unity of the embodied spirit[1] and the Supreme Spirit;[2] Pūjā[3] is the union of the worshipper and the worshipped; but he who realizes that all things are Brahman for him there is neither Yoga nor Pūjā (123).

For him who possesses the knowledge of Brahman,[4] the supreme Knowledge, of what use are Japa,[5] Yajna,[6] Tapas,[7] Niyama,[8] and Vrata?[9] (124).

He who sees the Brahman, Who is Truth, Knowledge, Bliss, and the One, is by his very nature one with the Brahman.[10] Of what use to him are Pūjā, Dhyāna, and Dhāra*n*ā?[11] (125).

For him who knows that all is Brahman there is neither sin[12] nor virtue,[13] neither heaven nor future birth. There is none to meditate upon, nor one who meditates (126).

The Spirit which is detached from all things, is ever liberated; what can bind Him? From what do fools desire to be liberated? (127).

He abides in this Universe, the creation of His power of Māyā,[14] which is incomprehensible even to the Devas. He is seemingly in the Universe, but not in it (128).

---

[1] Jīva.

[2] Ātman.

[3] Worship.

[4] Brahma-jnāna.

[5] Recitation of Mantra.

[6] Sacrifice.

[7] Penance.

[8] Regulations of conduct.

[9] Voluntary vows.

[10] Brahma-bhūta.

[11] Worship, Meditation and Concentration. Bhāratī defines Dhāra*n*ā as Chittav*r*itti-nirodha.

[12] Pāpa.

[13] Suk*r*ita.

[14] Māyā is defined as She who can do what is impossible (Agha*t*ana-gha*t*ana-ga*t*īyasī).

The Spirit [1] is in its own nature, the Eternal Witness,[2] and like the Ether exists both outside and inside all things, and has neither birth nor childhood, nor youth nor old age, but is the mere Feeling Consciousness which is ever the same, knowing no change (129-130).

It is the body which is born, matures, and decays.[3] Men enthralled by illusion, seeing this, understand it not (131).

As the Sun (though one and the same) when reflected in different platters of water appears to be many, so by Māyā the one soul appears to be many in the different bodies in which it abides (132).

As when water is disturbed the Moon which is reflected in it appears to be disturbed, so when the intelligence [4] is disturbed ignorant men think that it is the Spirit which is disturbed (133).

As the void inside a jar remains the same even after the jar is broken, so the Spirit remains the same after the body is destroyed (134).

Self-knowledge,[5] O Devī! is the one means of attaining final Liberation; and he who possesses it, is verily—yea, verily—liberated in this world, even yet whilst living;[6] there is no doubt of that (135).

Neither by acts, nor by begetting offspring, nor by wealth is man liberated; it is by the Knowledge of

---

[1] Sadrūpa ātmā=Paramātmā=Supreme Spirit.

[2] Sadrūpah sākshī: that is, Being which ever endures and witnesses all and participates in nothing.

[3] Yauvana and Bārddhakya.

[4] Buddhi.

[5] Ātma-jnāna=Self-knowledge, reālization of the oneness of the individual with the universal Spirit.

[6] Jīvanmukta.

the Spirit,[1] by the Spirit[2] that man is liberated[3] (136).

It is the Spirit that is dear to all! there is nothing dearer than the Spirit; O Shivā! it is because the Spirit is One[4] that men become dear to one another (137).

Knowledge,[5] Known,[6] Knower[7] appear by Māyā[8] to be three different things; but if careful discrimination is made, one Spirit alone is (138).

Knowledge[5] is Consciousness;[9] the object of knowledge[6] is Consciousness;[10] the Knower[11] is Consciousness; He who knows this knows the Self[12] (139).

I have now spoken of Knowledge which is the true cause of final Liberation.[13] This is the most precious possession[14] of the four classes of Avadhūtas[15] (140).

---

[1] *i.e.*, the Supreme Spirit.

[2] *i.e.*, the Individual Spirit.

[3] This is Shruti (Kaivalya 2), which says: Na karma*n*ā, na prajayā, dhanena, tyāgena ekena am*ri*tatvam ānashu*h* ["It is not by meritorious acts and sacrifices, not by Pi*nd*a offered by children, not by the giving of wealth, but by renunciation (of the particular Self) have men attained Liberation"].

[4] Ātmā-sambandha.

[5] Jnāna.

[6] Jneya.

[7] Jnātā. Māt*ri*, Māna, Meya are the three Bindus, products of the Nirvā*n*a Bīja in which they potentially are in seed form. See Kāmakalāvilāsa, v. 13.

[8] Māyā. Māt*ri*, Māna, Meya is the gist (Saṁkalitīrtha) of manifested Shakti.

[9] Chid-rūpa.

[10] Chin-maya.

[11] Vijnātā.

[12] *i.e.*, knows himself, and thereby knows his identity with the Supreme Spirit.

[13] Nirvā*n*a.

[14] Dha*n*a (Wealth).

[15] See Chapter VIII, vv. 227 *et seq*, also, *post*.

Shrī Devī said:

Thou hast spoken of the two stages in the life of man —namely, that of householder[1] and mendicant;[2] what is this wonderful distinction of four classes of Avadhūtas[3] which I now hear? (141).

I wish to hear and clearly understand the distinctive features of the four classes of Avadhūtas. Do Thou, O Lord! speak (about them) truly (142).

Shrī Sadāshiva said:

Those Brāhma*n*as, Ks*h*atriyas, and other castes who are worshippers of the Brahma-mantra[4] should be known to be Yatis,[5] even though they be living the life of a householder (143).

O Worshipped of the Kulas! those men who are sanctified by the rites of Pūr*n*ābhīs*h*eka[6] should be known and honoured[7] as Shaivāvadhūtas (144).

Both the Brāhma and Shaiva Avadhūtas shall do all acts in their respective states of life according to the way directed by Me (145).

They should not partake of forbidden food or drink unless the same has been offered to the Brahman or offered in the Chakra[8] (146).

O Beauteous One! I have already spoken of the way and Dharma of the Kaulas,[9] who are Brāhma Avadhūtas,

---

[1] Gr*i*hastha.

[2] Bhiks*h*uka.

[3] See "Shakti and Shākta".

[4] See Chapters II and III.

[5] Yatis—Self-controlled men; men who have subdued their passions.

[6] See *ante*, Ch. X, 109-212.

[7] Pūjanīya—or worshipped.

[8] Circle of Worship. This shloka means—"Unless in the case of a Brāhma Avadhūta it has been offered to the Brahman, and in the case of a Shaiva Avadhūta it has been offered to the Chakra."

[9] Sādhakas of the Kaula Sampradāya. See Kulār*n*ava, II, 7 and 8.

and of the Kaulas who have been initiated.[1] For Brāhma and Shaiva Avadhūtas, bathing, eating evening meals, drinking, the giving of charities, and if married marital duties should be done according to the way prescribed by the Āgamas (147-148).

The above Avadhūtas are of two classes, according as they are perfect[2] or imperfect.[3] Beloved! the perfect one is called Parama-hangsa, and the other or imperfect one is called Parivrā*t* (149).

The man who has gone through the Saṁskāra[4] of an Avadhūta, but whose knowledge is yet imperfect,[5] should, by living the life of a householder,[6] purify his Self (150).

Retaining his caste-mark and practising the rites of a Kaula, he should, remaining constantly devoted to the Brahman, do Sādhanā for attainment of the highest Knowledge (151).

With his mind ever free from attachment, yet discharging all his duty,[7] he should constantly repeat "Oṁ Tat Sat," and constantly think upon and realize the saying, "Sa*h* aham"[8] (152).

Doing his duties, his mind as completely detached as the water on the lotus leaf, he should constantly strive to

[1] *i.e.*, who have received Abhis*h*eka, *i.e.*, Shaiva Avadhūtas.

[2] Pūr*n*a, or complete.

[3] Apūr*n*a, or incomplete.

[4] Purificatory rites, etc.

[5] Jnāna-durbala—one who has not realized the oneness of himself with the Supreme Self.

[6] Literally, living among men—a life in the world. The married Avadhūta looks on his wife as a form of his Self as he is a form of herself. "Marital duties" in vv. 147-8 is Dārarak*s*h*a*n*a.

[7] Duty = Ātmochita-karma which may mean acts which are fit for him or his position.

[8] So'ham = I am He—*i.e.*, I am one with the Supreme.

free his Self by the knowledge of Divine Truth[1] acquired through discrimination[2] (153).

The man, be he a householder[3] or an ascetic,[4] who commences any undertaking with the Mantra "Oṁ Tat Sat," is ever successful therein (154).

Japa,[5] Homa,[6] Pratishṭhā,[7] and all sacramental rites,[8] if performed with the Mantra "Oṁ Tat Sat," are faultless beyond all doubt (155).

What use is there of the various other Mantras? What use of the other multitudinous practices?[9] With this Brāhma Mantra alone may all rites be concluded (156).

Ambikā![10] this Mantra is easily practised, is not prolix, and gives complete success, and there is no other way besides this great Mantra (157).

If it be kept written in any part of the house or on the body, then such house becomes a holy place[11] and the body becomes sanctified[12] (158).

O Deveshi! I am telling the very truth when I say that the Mantra "Oṁ Tat Sat" is superior to the essence of essences of the Nigamas, the Āgamas, and the Tantras[13] (159).

[1] Tattva-jnāna.

[2] Viveka = Faculty of distinguishing things by their properties, and classing them according to their real, and not apparent, nature. In the Vedānta it is the power of distinguishing Truth from untruth, Reality from appearance.

[3] Gṛihastha.

[4] Udāsīna

[5] Recitation of Mantras. See "Shakti and Shākta".

[6] Sacrifice to Fire.

[7] Consecration.

[8] Saṁskāras (see *op. cit.*).

[9] Sādhana (see *op. cit.*).

[10] Mother (see *op. cit.*).

[11] Mahā-tīrtha.

[12] Puṇyamaya.

[13] See Tantra Tattva.

This most excellent of Mantras, "Oṁ Tat Sat," has pierced through the palate, the skull, and crownlock of Brahmā, Vi*sh*nu, and Shiva, and has thus manifested itself (160).[1]

If the four kinds of food and other articles are sanctified[2] by this Mantra, then it becomes useless to sanctify them by any other Mantras (161).

He is a King among Kaulas, who sees the Great Being[3] everywhere, and constantly makes Japa[4] of the great Mantra "Tat Sat" (*i.e.*, Oṁ Tat Sat), who acts as he so inclines,[5] and is pure of heart withal (162).

By Japa of this Mantra a man becomes a Siddha[6]; by thinking of its meaning he is liberated, and he who, when making Japa, thinks of its meaning, becomes like unto the Brahman in visible form (163).

This Great, Three-footed[7] Mantra is the cause of all causes; by its Sâdhana[8] one becomes the Conqueror of Death[9] himself (164).

O Maheshâni! the worshipper attains Siddhi[8] in whatsoever way he makes Japa of it[10] (165).

He who, renouncing all rites, has been cleansed by the Saṁskāra[11] of a Shaiva Avadhūta, is no longer competent

[1] They practised the Mantra and on becoming adept in it revealed it.

[2] Shodhita.

[3] *i.e.*, the Ever-Existent Brahman.

[4] Repetition (see Introduction).

[5] Svechhâchâra (see p. 58, note 6).

[6] *i.e.*, One possessed of the Siddhis, or one or some of them. Here, one who has mastered the Mantra and reached his goal.

[7] Tri-pada.

[8] See "Shakti and Shâkta".

[9] M*r*ityun-jaya, or Shiva.

[10] As thus—Whether he says Oṁ Tat Sat; Oṁ Sat; Tat Sat; Oṁ; Tat; Sat.

[11] *i.e.*, Pūr*n*âbhi*sh*eka, which qualifies one to be a Shaiva Avadhūta.

for the worship of Devas, the performance of the Shrâddha of the Pit*ri*s,[1] or the honouring of the *Rish*is[2] (166).

Of the four classes of Âvadhûtas, the fourth is called the Haṁsa (Parama-haṁsa). The other three both practise Yoga and have enjoyment.[3] They are all liberated and are like unto Shiva (167).

The Haṁsa should not have intercourse with women, and should not touch metals. Unfettered by restrictions, he moves about enjoying the fruits of his ripened Karma[4] (168).

---

[1] The forefathers.

[2] Seers, the meaning is that such an one is above such observance.

[3] Yogabhogâ*dh*yâ*h*.

Tarkâlaṁkâra says that to-day there are some Paramahaṁsas who are unable to state what authority governs their Âchâra. He collects from Bhairava*d*âmara and other Tantras some rules regarding the Laks*ha*n*a* of the Avadhûtas. Of the four classes, the Shaivâvadhûtas are of two kinds, *viz.*, Paribrâjaka and Paramahaṃsa. Yatis or Brâhmâvadhûtas are also of two kinds, *viz.*, Paribrâjaka and Paramahaṁsa or Haṁsa. Imperfect (Apûr*n*a) Shaivâvadhûta or Brâhmâvadhûta although he may be a householder is to be accounted a Paribrâjaka. If the householder Avadhûta be excluded then there are six classes of Avadhûta—of which the first is (1) Shaivâvadhûta (Apûr*n*a). He is a great Sannyâsî like Shiva although he lives in the family. On this account he is called Shaivâvadhûta. (2) Paribrâjaka is the second stage of Shaivâvadhûta. He gives up the Saṁsâra, wanders from Tîrtha to Tîrtha and does Pûjâ, Japa and the like. He does Sâdhanâ with the assistance of his Shakti. (3) Paramahaṁsa is the third stage of Shaivâvadhûta. He does no rite; wears a Kaupîna and is Sannyâsî. He may according to the rules of Yoga and Bhoga satisfy the desire of a woman who approaches him. (4) Brâhmâvadhûta. He is like the Shaivâvadhûta of the first kind but has no competency for Parâshakti in Shaiva marriage. He may have his own Shakti. (5) Brâhmâvadhûta Paribrâjaka. His duties are like those of the Shaivâvadhûtas of second class but may not unite with a woman who seeks intercourse. He is however competent under instuctions of the Guru to practise Yoga with the assistance of a Shakti. This applies to the fourth and fifth classes. (6) Haṁsâvadhûta. He is like Shaivâvadhûta of third degree. He may not however unite with a woman, receive gift of any kind of metal and is free from all duties (Karma).

Bhairava*d*âmara deals with Kulâvadhûta, Shaivâvadhûta, Brâhmâvadhûta and Haṁsâvadhûta. There is only a difference in name between these and those given in Mahânirvâ*n*a.

[4] Prârabdha—literally, that which has been commenced.

The fourth class,[1] discarding his caste and household duties, moves about in this world without desires or care for the preservation of his body[2] (169).

Always pleased in his own mind, he is free from sorrow and illusion, homeless and forgiving, fearless, and doing harm to none (170).

For him there is no offering of food and drink (to any Deva); for him there is no necessity for Dhyāna or Dhāraṇā;[3] the Yati[4] is liberated, is free from attachment, unaffected by all opposites,[5] and follows the ways of a Haṁsa[6] (171).

O Devī! I have now spoken to Thee in detail of the distinctive marks of the four classes of Kula-Yogīs, who are but forms of Myself[7] (172).

By seeing them, by touching them, conversing with them, or pleasing them, men earn the fruit of pilgrimage to all the holy places (173).

All the shrines and holy places which there are in this world, they all, O my Beloved! abide in the body of the Kula-Sannyāsī[8] (174).

Those men who have worshipped Kula Sādhus[9] with Kula-dravya[10] are indeed blessed and holy, have attained

[1] *i.e.*, the Parama-haṁsa.

[2] Niḥsaṁkalpa and Nirudyama. Bhāratī says the last term, which literally = Effortless, means as stated in the text for having given up all household and caste duties there is nothing to be cared for except the body which is no longer to be an object of solicitude.

[3] See Arthur Avalon's "Serpent Power".

[4] Self-controlled.

[5] Nir-dvandva—that is, heat and cold, love and hate, etc.

[6] Highest class of ascetic.

[7] Mat-svarūpī.

[8] Kaula ascetic, or Avadhūta.

[9] Holy men.

[10] Wine, etc.

their desired aim, and have earned the fruit of all sacrifices (175).

By the mere touch of these Sādhus the impure becomes pure, the untouchable becomes touchable, and food unfit to be eaten [1] becomes fit to be eaten. By their touch even the Kirātas,[2] the sinful, the wicked, the Pulindas,[3] the Yavanas,[4] and the wicked and malicious,[5] are made pure; who else but they should be honoured? (176-177).

Even those who but once worship the Kaulika Yogī with Kula-tattva [6] and Kula-dravya [6] become worthy of honour in this world (178).

O Thou with the lotus face! there is no Dharma superior to Kaula-Dharma,[7] by seeking refuge in which even a man of inferior caste becomes purified and attains the state of a Kaula (179).

As the footmarks of all animals disappear in the footmark of the elephant, so do all other Dharmas disappear in the Kula-Dharma (180).

My Beloved! how holy are the Kaulas! They are like the images of the holy places. They purify by their mere presence even the Cha*nd*ālas and the vilest of the vile (121).

As other waters falling into Gaṁgā become the water of Gaṁgā, so all men following Kulāchāra reach the stage of a Kaula (182).

[1] By reason of its having been cooked or touched by a low caste man, or for any other cause.

[2] Hunters—a low caste.

[3] Pulindas are a class of Cha*nd*ālas, one of the lowest castes.

[4] Foreigners, Barbarians.

[5] Krūra.

[6] Bhâratī says—the first is meat, etc., and the second wine.

[7] Of the Kaula-Tāntrika division of worshippers.

As water gone into the sea does not retain its separateness, so men sunk in the ocean of Kula lose theirs (183).

All beings in this world which have two feet,[1] from the Vipra[2] to the inferior castes, are competent for Kulāchāra (184).

Those that are averse to the acceptance of Kula-Dharma, even when called thereto, are divorced from all Dharma and go the downward path (185).

The Kulīna who deceives those men who seek for Kulāchāra shall go to the hell named Raurava (186).

That low Kaula who refuses to initiate a Cha*nd*āla[3] or a Yavana[4] into the Kula-Dharma, considering them to be low, or a woman out of disrespect for her is himself low and goes the downward way (187).[5]

The merit acquired by a hundred Abhis*h*eka,[6] by the performance of a hundred Purashcharana*n*a,[7] ten million times that merit is acquired by the initiation of one man into the Kula-Dharma (188).

All the different castes, all the followers of the different Dharmas in this world, are, by becoming Kaulas, freed from their bonds, and go to the Supreme Abode (189).

The Kaulas who follow that Shaiva-Dharma are like places of pilgrimage, and are themselves Shiva. They

---

[1] As opposed to the quadrupeds and the quadrumani. Here it means all men and women.

[2] A Brāhma*n*a.

[3] A very low caste.

[4] Here used generally for non-Aryan. The Greeks specifically were so-called.

[5] Chāndālang yavanang nīchang matvā striyam avajnayā.

Kaulang na kuryāt ya*h* kaula*h* so'dhamo yātyadhogatim.

The unsectarian and universal character of the Kauladharma is here markedly shown; the Vaidika ritual has no place for these.

[6] A higher form of Initiation. See Ch. X, 109 *et seq.*

[7] A ritual form of Japa accompanied by other ceremonies. See Ch. III, 114, 115, also Ch. VII, v. 77.

worship and honour one another with affection, respect, and love (190).

What is the use of saying more to Thee? I am speaking the very truth before Thee when I say that the only bridge for the crossing of this ocean of existence is the Kula-Dharma and none other (191).

By the following of Kula-Dharma all doubts are cut through, all the accumulation of sins is destroyed, and the multitude of acts is destroyed[1] (192).

Those Kaulikas are excellent who, truthful and faithful to the Brahman, in their mercy call men that they may purify them by Kulāchāra (193).

Devī! I have spoken to Thee the first portion[2] of the Mahā-nirvā*n*a Tantra for the purification of men. It contains the conclusions[3] of all Dharmas (194).

He who hears it daily or enables[4] other men to hear it becomes freed from all sins, and attains Nirvā*n*a at the end (195).

By knowing this King among Tantras, which contains the essence of essence of all the Tantras, and is the most excellent among the Tantras, a man becomes versed in all the Shāstras (196).

The man who knows this Mahā-tantra is freed from the bonds of actions. Of what use is it to him to go on pilgrimage, or to do Japa, Yajna, and Sādhana?[5] (197).

Kālikā! he who knows this Tantra is conversant with all the Shāstras, he is pre-eminent among the virtuous,[6] is wise, knows the Brahman, and is a Sage (198).

[1] Together with the Karma resulting from such acts.

[2] The second portion of the Tantra has been generally supposed to be lost, but see Preface.

[3] Nir*n*aya.

[4] *e.g.*, by engaging someone to read the Tantra to the public.

[5] See "Shakti and Shākta".

[6] Dharma-vid.

There is no use of the Vedas, the Purāṇas, the Smṛitis, the Saṁhitās, and the various other Tantras, as by knowing this Tantra one knows all (199).

All the most secret rites and practices and the most excellent knowledge[1] have been revealed by me in reply to Thy questions (200).

Suvratā![2] as Thou art My most excellent Brāhmī Shakti, and art to Me dearer than life itself, know Thou that the Mahānirvāṇa Tantra is likewise (201).

As the Himālaya is among the Mountains, as the Moon is among the Stars, as the Sun is among all lustrous bodies, so this Tantra is the King among Tantras (202).

All Dharmas are to be found in this Tantra. It is the only means for the acquirement of the knowledge of Brahman.[3] The man who repeats himself or causes others to repeat it will surely acquire such knowledge (203).

In the family of the man in whose house there is this most excellent of all Tantras there will never be a Pashu[4] (204).

The man blinded by the darkness of ignorance, the fool caught in the meshes[5] of his actions, and the illiterate man, by listening to this Great Tantra, are released from the bonds of Karma (205).

Parameshānī! reading, listening to, and worshipping this Tantra, and singing its praise, gives Liberation to men (206).

Of the other various Tantras each deals with one subject only. There is no other Tantra which contains all the Dharmas (207).

[1] Tattva-jnāna. [2] Virtuous one. [3] Brahma-jnāna.

[4] Here the term means one ignorant of divine knowledge.

[5] See Bhagavad-gītā, iv, *pari passu*; also Shiva-Saṁhitā, chap. i, verses 4-9.

The last part contains an account of the nether, earthly, and heavenly worlds.[1] He who knows it (along with the first) undoubtedly knows all (208).

The man who knows the second part with this book is able to speak of the past, present, and future, and knows the three worlds (209).

There are all manner of Tantras and various Shāstras, but they are not equal to a sixteenth part (in value) of this Mahānirvā*n*a Tantra (210).

What further shall I tell Thee of the greatness of the Mahānirvā*n*a Tantra? Through the knowledge of it one shall attain to Brahma-nirvā*n*a (211).

End of the Fourteenth Chapter of the First Part of the Mahānirvā*n*a, entitled, "The Consecration of Shiva-liṁga and Description of the Four Classes of Avadhūtas."

THE END

---

[1] Pātāla-chakra, Bhū-chakra, and Jyotish-chakra respectively.